Wars on Terrorism and Iraq

Wars on Terrorism and Iraq provides a timely and critical analysis of the impact on human rights, particularly internationally, of the wars on terrorism and Iraq as well as examining the related tensions between unilateralism and multilateralism in U.S. foreign policy.

The distinguished contributors examine the consequences for international relations and world order of the traditional standard-bearer for human rights and democracy, the United States, appearing not to be championing the rule of law and negotiated conflict resolution. The authors also suggest effective policies to promote greater fulfillment of human rights in order to achieve peaceful accord within nations and stability internationally.

Contributors include Mary Robinson, Tom J. Farer, Judith Lichtenberg, David P. Forsythe, Jack Donnelly, Kenneth Roth, Edward C. Luck, Mohammed Ayoob, Chantal de Jonge Oudraat, José E. Alvarez and Bruce D. Jones.

Thomas G. Weiss is Presidential Professor of Political Science at The CUNY Graduate Center and Director of the Ralph Bunche Institute for International Studies, where he is co-director of the United Nations Intellectual History Project and editor of *Global Governance*.

Margaret E. Crahan is the Dorothy Epstein Professor of Latin American History at Hunter College and The CUNY Graduate Center and a Senior Research Associate of the Institute of Latin American Studies at Columbia University.

John Goering is a Professor at the School of Public Affairs at Baruch College and The CUNY Graduate Center. From 1997 to spring 1999 he served on the staff of the White House Initiative on Race.

Wars on Terrorism and Iraq

Human rights, unilateralism, and U.S. foreign policy

Edited by Thomas G. Weiss,
Margaret E. Crahan, and John Goering

Routledge
Taylor & Francis Group

NEW YORK AND LONDON

First published 2004 by Routledge
29 West 35th Street, New York, NY 10001

Simultaneously published in the U.K. by Routledge
11 New Fetter Lane, London EC4P 4EE

Routledge is an imprint of the Taylor & Francis Group

Typeset in Baskerville by The Running Head Limited, Cambridge
Printed and bound in Great Britain by TJ International Ltd, Padstow, Cornwall

Library of Congress Cataloging in Publication Data
Wars on terrorism and Iraq: human rights, unilateralism, and U.S. foreign
policy/edited by Thomas G. Weiss, Margaret E. Crahan, and John Goering
p. cm.
Includes bibliographical references and index.
1. War on Terrorism, 2001–2. United States–Relations–Iraq.
3. Iraq–Relations–United States. 4. United States–Politics and
government–2001– 5. Human rights. I. Weiss, Thomas George. II. Crahan,
Margaret E. III. Goering, John, 1950–
HV6432.W38 2004
973.93 1—dc22   2003021057

British Library Cataloguing in Publication Data
A catalogue record for this book is available from the British Library

ISBN 0–415–70062–0 (hbk)
ISBN 0–415–70063–9 (pbk)

In memory of those who gave their lives working for peace at
United Nations Headquarters, Baghdad, Iraq, August 19, 2003

Contents

Contributors

José E. Alvarez is a Professor of Law at Columbia Law School. His principal areas of teaching are: international law, especially international organizations; international tribunals; war crimes; international legal theory; and foreign investment. He is also a member of the Board of Editors of the *American Journal of International Law* and of the *Journal of International Criminal Justice*, a member of the Council on Foreign Relations, and Vice-President of the American Society of International Law. Prior to teaching at Columbia he taught at the Georgetown Law Center, George Washington University National Law Center, and University of Michigan Law School. Before entering academia he was an attorney adviser in the Office of the Legal Adviser of the U.S. Department of State.

Mohammed Ayoob is the University Distinguished Professor of International Relations at James Madison College, Michigan State University. A specialist on conflict and security in the Third World, he has taught at the Australian National University, the National University of Singapore, and Jawaharlal Nehru University, and he has held visiting appointments at Princeton, Oxford, Columbia, and Brown Universities. He has published in such journals as *World Politics*, *Foreign Policy*, *Global Governance*, and *Survival*. He has authored, coauthored, or edited eleven books, including *The Third World Security Predicament: State Making, Regional Conflict, and the International System* (1995).

Margaret E. Crahan is the Dorothy Epstein Professor of Latin American History at Hunter College and The CUNY Graduate Center and a Senior Research Associate of the Institute of Latin American Studies at Columbia University. From 1982 to 1994 she was the Henry R. Luce Professor of Religion, Power, and Political Process at Occidental College and from 1993 to 1994 the Marous Professor at the University of Pittsburgh. She currently serves on the boards of the Inter-American Institute of Human Rights and the Democracy Coalition Project of the Open Society Institute. She has done research in Argentina, Brazil, Chile, Colombia, Costa Rica, Cuba, El Salvador, Guatemala, Honduras, Mexico, Nicaragua, Panama, Paraguay, Peru, Spain, Switzerland, and Uruguay on topics spanning the sixteenth through the twentieth centuries in Latin America. She is currently writing a book about female political prisoners and strategies of resistance in Argentina during the 1976–83 military regime. Her books include *Africa and the Caribbean: Legacies of a Link* (1979), *Human Rights and Basic Needs in the Americas* (1982), and *The City and the World: New York's Global Future* (1997).

Jack Donnelly is the Andrew W. Mellon Professor and Associate Dean of the Graduate School of International Studies at the University of Denver, and in 2002–3 the Gladstein Visiting Professor at the University of Connecticut. He previously taught at the University of North Carolina, Chapel Hill, College of the Holy Cross, and Tulane University and at universities abroad. He specializes in human rights, international relations theory, international organization, political theory, and international law. He is the author of *The Concept of Human Rights* (1985), *International Human Rights* (1998), and *Universal Human Rights in Theory and Practice* (2002; 2nd edition). His most recent book is *Realism and International Relations* (2000) and he is currently writing a book on ancient Greek international society.

Tom J. Farer is the Dean of the Graduate School of International Studies at the University of Denver. He is the former President of the Inter-American Commission on Human Rights of the Organization of American States and of the University of New Mexico. In 1993 he served as legal consultant to the United Nations Operations in Somalia. He has served as special assistant to the General Counsel of the Department of Defense, Assistant Secretary of State for Inter-American Affairs, and Senior Fellow of the Council on Foreign Relations and the Carnegie Endowment for International Peace. At present he serves on the boards of several human rights organizations, for which he conducts occasional investigatory missions abroad, and is on the editorial boards of the *American Journal of International Law* and the *Human Rights Quarterly*.

David P. Forsythe is the Charles J. Mach Distinguished Professor of Political Science, and University Professor, at the University of Nebraska–Lincoln. He has held visiting professorships at universities in Denmark, Ireland, the Netherlands, and Switzerland and has been a consultant to the International Red Cross and to the United Nations Office of the High Commissioner for Refugees. He served as President of the Human Rights Committee of the International Political Science Association, Vice-President of the International Studies Association, and a member of the Committee on Scientific Freedom and Responsibility of the American Association for the Advancement of Science. His books include *Human Rights in International Relations* (2000), *Human Rights and Comparative Foreign Policy* (2000; edited), *The United States and Human Rights* (2000; edited), *The United Nations and Changing World Politics*, (2000; 3rd edition), and *Human Rights and Diversity: Area Studies Revisited* (currently in press).

John Goering is a Professor at the School of Public Affairs at Baruch College and The CUNY Graduate Center. From 1997 to spring 1999 he served on the staff of the White House Initiative on Race. He has published articles and books on urban housing, and civil rights issues, including *The Best Eight*

Blocks in Harlem (1979), *Housing Desegregation and Federal Policy* (1986), and *Mortgage Lending, Racial Discrimination, and Federal Policy* (1996), and forthcoming is a coauthored work: *Choosing a Better Life? Evaluating the Moving to Opportunity Experiment.* He has served on the editorial boards of the *Urban Affairs Review*, *New Community, Housing Studies*, and the *Journal of Ethnic and Migration Studies.*

Bruce D. Jones is Deputy Director and Fellow at New York University's Center on International Cooperation. In 2000–2 he served as the Chief of Staff to the United Nations' Special Coordinator for the Middle East Peace Process. He previously worked in the United Nations Office for the Coordination of Humanitarian Affairs. He was a member of the U.N.'s Advance Mission in Kosovo and of the U.N. Department of Peacekeeping Operations' planning team for the U.N. Transitional Administration in East Timor. He earlier worked for a range of nongovernmental organizations involved in conflict response, particularly in central Africa, including CARE, Conciliation Resources, and International Alert. He is the author of *Peacemaking in Rwanda: The Dynamics of Failure* (2001).

Judith Lichtenberg is a research scholar at the Institute for Philosophy and Public Policy and an Associate Professor in the Department of Philosophy, both at the University of Maryland at College Park. She is the editor of *Democracy and the Mass Media* (1990); coauthor of *Getting a Leg Up: Justice and College Admissions* (forthcoming); and author of many articles on international ethics, race and ethnicity, higher education, and the mass media. From 1997 to 2002 she served on the national advisory board of the Poynter Institute. She currently directs the University of Maryland's Committee on Politics, Philosophy, and Public Policy, an interdisciplinary graduate program.

Edward C. Luck is Director of the Center on International Organization and Professor of Practice in International and Public Affairs at Columbia University. Since 2001 he has served as a member of the U.N. Secretary-General's Policy Working Group on the United Nations and Terrorism. A past President of the United Nations Association of the U.S.A. and a specialist in Washington's policies toward the world organization, he is author of *Mixed Messages: American Politics and International Organization, 1919–1999* (1999) and *Reforming the United Nations: Lessons from a History in Progress* (2003).

Chantal de Jonge Oudraat is Senior Fellow at the Center for Transatlantic Relations of the Paul H. Nitze School of Advanced International Studies of The Johns Hopkins University and Adjunct Professor at the Edmund A. Walsh School of Foreign Service, Georgetown University. She is Vice-President and member of the Executive Board of Women in International Security and formerly was co-director of the Managing Global Issues project at the Carnegie Endowment for International Peace; Senior Research Associate at the United Nations Institute for Disarmament Research; and researcher at the Belfer Center for Science and International Affairs, Kennedy School, Harvard University. She is the co-editor of *Managing Global*

Issues: Lessons Learned (2001) and the author of articles in journals such as *Survival, Current History, Washington Quarterly*, and the *European Journal of International Law*.

Mary Robinson is Executive Director of the Ethical Globalization Initiative. She was United Nations High Commissioner for Human Rights (1997–2002) and President of Ireland (1990–7). Before being elected President, she served as a senator in the Irish Parliament for 20 years, during which time she also was Reid Professor of Constitutional Law at Trinity College, Dublin, and practiced before the Irish Bar.

Kenneth Roth is the Executive Director of Human Rights Watch, the largest U.S.-based international human rights organization that investigates, reports on, and seeks to curb human rights abuses in some 70 countries. From 1987 to 1993 he served as Deputy Director of the organization. Previously, he was a Federal Prosecutor for the U.S. Attorney's Office for the Southern District of New York and the Iran–Contra investigation in Washington. He has also worked in private practice as a litigator. He has conducted human rights investigations around the globe, devoting special attention to issues of justice and accountability for gross abuses of human rights, standards governing military conduct in time of war, the human rights policies of the United States and the United Nations, and the human rights responsibilities of multinational businesses.

Thomas G. Weiss is Presidential Professor of Political Science at The CUNY Graduate Center and Director of the Ralph Bunche Institute for International Studies, where he is co-director of the United Nations Intellectual History Project and editor of *Global Governance*. He also was Research Professor at Brown University's Watson Institute for International Studies, Executive Director of the Academic Council on the U.N. System and of the International Peace Academy, a member of the U.N. secretariat, and a consultant to several public and private agencies. He has written or edited some 30 books about multilateral approaches to international peace and security, humanitarian action, and sustainable development.

Foreword

Mary Robinson

I write this Foreword in the sad aftermath of the tragic bombing of United Nations headquarters in Baghdad on August 19, 2003. It took the life of my friend and successor as U.N. High Commissioner for Human Rights, Sergio Vieira de Mello, and of at least 22 others, mainly U.N. colleagues. Among those killed was another friend, Arthur Helton, Senior Fellow for Refugee Studies at the Council on Foreign Relations in New York, who had told me only a week earlier that he was going to Iraq to meet Sergio and assess the refugee situation there.

Will their deaths be the wake-up call that leads to a significant reconfiguration of the U.N. presence on the ground, with broad international military and police support for the establishment of basic human security throughout Iraq? This is an essential precondition for building a peaceful, stable, and—hopefully—democratic country. It is vital to change the current perception of "occupying forces," which can be manipulated by those determined to sabotage any efforts at rebuilding the infrastructure and services of that country.

By the time this book is published we may know if out of this bleak moment came the inspiration, energy, and political will to strengthen the U.N.'s mandate and fully internationalize the military presence in its support. The essays in this remarkable book, written from different perspectives and drawing on a wide range of scholarly and practical expertise, make a powerful case for such a multilateral approach. The work is remarkable precisely because the contributors address with honesty and integrity the deeply difficult nexus among human rights standards, the war on terror, the insecurity in Iraq in the aftermath of the war, and U.S. attitudes toward multilateralism.

Another truly unusual feature of these essays—which attests to the quality of the overall direction by Thomas G. Weiss, Margaret E. Crahan, and John Goering—is that the work was planned many months before the terrible attacks of September 11, 2001, and had to adapt as a work in progress to events that literally changed our world. The initial task, that of appreciating U.S. power in relation to international normative standards, was gradually subsumed into a vastly more complex task. It successfully assesses the war on terrorism, including the war in Afghanistan and its aftermath. It also probes the subsequent regime change brought about by the military invasion of Iraq by coalition forces, along with the implications for the effectiveness of the United Nations and its core moral values expressed in human rights. Fortunately, that initial task has also been addressed by John Shattuck, in his book *Freedom on Fire*,[1] which is an excellent companion to these essays, drawing as it does on his personal experience on the front lines in the Clinton administration as Assistant Secretary of State for Democracy, Human Rights, and Labor.

The editors of this collection managed the transformation of the work by organizing a year-long sequence of seminars and public events focusing on the issues of war, rights, and U.S. foreign policy. A complex range of questions, and sometimes even contradictory sets of issues, are raised; and not all of them can be answered until more of the dust settles, in the region and in Washington. In a constantly changing foreign policy environment, it may be too soon to find clear, unequivocal assessments of the human rights benefits and costs of the war on terrorism. For example, may it have been a strategic error to characterize the attacks of September 11 as requiring a "war on terrorism" rather than as "crimes against humanity" that required intense international military, police, and intelligence cooperation to bring the perpetrators to justice?

Language is crucial in shaping our reactions to critical events. The words that we use to characterize the event may determine the nature of the response. In my view, the tragic attacks on the World Trade Center and on the Pentagon fell within the definition under international human rights jurisprudence of "crimes against humanity," which would have been a more effective rubric under which to organize the fight.

International cooperation and resolve are required under international human rights law to combat such crimes. Within this model are such actions as the adoption by the Security Council of Resolution 1373 that imposed a new international legal obligation on states to cooperate against terrorism, and the subsequent establishment of the Counter-Terrorism Committee to monitor implementation. Also within this approach to deal with crimes against humanity is the necessity of the war in Afghanistan because the Taliban had persistently refused to hand over Osama bin Laden and Al Qaeda, who claimed to be responsible for these crimes.

That the language of being "at war with terrorism" was used from the beginning had direct, and nefarious, implications. It brought a subtle—or not so subtle—change of emphasis in many parts of the world: order and security became priorities that trumped all other concerns. As was often the case in the past during times of war, the emphasis on national order and security frequently involved curtailment of democracy and human rights. An honest debate about the costs and benefits has not yet really taken place. Abrogations in the United States, where there are many checks and balances in the wider society, have been copied with very negative effects for human rights in many countries of the world, as this book so persuasively illustrates. Questions arise as to when, if ever, this war on terrorism will be won. Are we, as the novelist and commentator Gore Vidal has characterized it, embarked on a *Perpetual War for Perpetual Peace*?[2]

Another issue that troubles me deeply and has not yet received adequate analysis: has casting the post-September 11 challenge as a war on terrorism, paradoxically, inflated the perceived status and self-esteem of the terrorists themselves? Whereas being branded as terrible criminals who committed crimes against humanity would make it impossible to invoke a religious justification for such acts, the question arises as to whether being at war—as it would be per-ceived—against the "great Satan" allows a manipulation by religious extremists so that it amounts to a war for a religious cause. As such, and as painful as it may be to ask the question, we need to do so: has the recruitment of impres-sionable, unemployed youths not been facilitated?

While it is impossible at this stage to know for how long the so-called war on terrorism may have to continue, its negative impact on international human rights standards worldwide is already evident. The erosion of civil liberties in the United States itself—the standard-bearer for civil and political rights—has been monitored and criticized by various human rights groups, a troubling theme running through these essays. A recent report by the Lawyers Committee for Human Rights makes sobering reading.[3]

The report highlights a pattern of actions by the administration of President George W. Bush since September 2001 that is at odds with core U.S. and inter-national human rights principles. Central among them is the idea of checks and balances—the long U.S. tradition of separation of powers among the executive, judicial, and legislative branches of government. The Lawyers Committee pro-vides numerous examples of how these safeguards are being undermined by aggressive executive branch actions that are usurping the constitutional powers of the federal courts and Congress.

The report focuses, for example, on the erosion of the right to privacy. There have been a series of initiatives by the executive branch over just the previous six months to collect an unprecedented amount of information on U.S. citizens and non-citizens who are under no suspicion of having committed a crime. These include the military's proposed Total Information Awareness Program, which would create comprehensive data profiles of everyone in the country; the use of expanded search and seizure powers under the U.S.A. Patriot Act to seize library, bookstore, and other records; increased powers to intercept tele-phone and Internet communications; and the lifting of restrictions on the use of special foreign intelligence powers in ordinary criminal prosecutions.

The international effects on civil liberties are equally troubling. Many of us, including several contributors to this volume, are very concerned with the pre-cedents set by the country that has long championed human rights: increasingly harsh treatment of immigrants, refugees, and minorities, such as monitoring, registration, detention, and secret deportation of immigrants against whom no charges have been made; restrictions on visitors and immigrants alike from many parts of the world, and a reversal of the United States' traditional welcome to refugees fleeing persecution abroad.

The international repercussions of the changes in U.S. policy and practice should not be ignored. Repressive new laws and detention practices have been introduced in a significant number of countries, all broadly justified by the new international war on terrorism. The report states it bluntly: "In lowering its own human rights standards, the United States has encouraged other governments, though often inadvertently, to lower the standards of human rights around the world."

This is a country rightly proud of its checks and balances. A vital check is an informed and alert public willing to exercise "eternal vigilance" in protection of its democratic values. In that respect, this book is a timely publication that provides rigorous analyses to reinforce those checks.

The range and depth of issues dealt with by the distinguished contributors, who represent the best of scholarship and advocacy, are well summarized by the editors in their introduction and conclusion. If I had the power to do so, I would make this book compulsory reading for all who exercise political power in our world today! Instead, I will keep my fingers crossed that it will be read by as many members of Congress and of the current U.S. administration as possible, and by a wide cross-section of policy analysts, diplomats, academics, and human rights defenders.

At a time when, in every region of the world, individuals and civil society are relying increasingly on the international human rights framework to hold their governments accountable, it is more vital than ever to move from U.S. exceptionalism back to the kind of leadership on human rights exemplified by Eleanor Roosevelt when she chaired the Commission on Human Rights that drafted the Universal Declaration of Human Rights, which was adopted in 1948. These essays provide a rich resource to support a broad debate about U.S. "exceptionalism." We may be encouraged by some recent judgments of the U.S. Federal Supreme Court, such as the passage from Justice Anthony M. Kennedy in *Lawrence v. State of Texas*, where he cited judgments of the European Court of Human Rights and concluded:

> The right the petitioners seek in this case has been accepted as an integral part of human freedom in many other countries. There has been no showing that in this country the governmental interest in circumscribing personal choice is somehow more legitimate or urgent.[4]

This century began with the commitments made by governments in the Millennium Declaration,[5] which were grounded in respect for international law—including international human rights law—and the values of multilateralism. I believe that it is possible to reconcile the understandable preoccupation with security and the war on terrorism which followed the terrible attacks of September 11, on the one hand, with giving priority to achieving the millennium development goals and addressing human security in a deeper and more holistic way, on the other hand. The groundwork has been laid particularly by three recent reports: *The U.N. Human Development Report* of 2000 and of 2003, which call for mainstreaming human rights and for implementing a compact among nations to end poverty, and the Commission on Human Security's report, *Human Security Now*, which focuses on protecting and empowering people.[6]

We need to build a broad international consensus around the idea of connecting human rights, human development, and human security. To balance the sense of anxiety, fear, and foreboding resulting from the wars on terrorism and Iraq, we need a mood of hope. I find inspiration from Seamus Heaney's "Chorus: The Cure at Troy"[7]:

> History says, Don't hope
> On this side of the grave,
> But then, once in a lifetime
> The longed for tidal wave
> of justice can rise up
> And hope and history rhyme.

Mary Robinson
New York, September 2003

Notes

1 John Shattuck, *Freedom on Fire: Human Rights Wars and America's Response* (Cambridge, MA: Harvard University Press, 2003).
2 Gore Vidal, *Perpetual War for Perpetual Peace* (New York: Thunder's Mouth Press, 2002).
3 Lawyers Committee for Human Rights, "Imbalance of Powers: How Changes to U.S. Law and Policy Since 9/11 Erode Human Rights and Civil Liberties," http://www.lchr.org/us_law/loss/imbalance/powers.pdf.
4 John Geddes Lawrence and Tyron Garner, Petitioners v. Texas, 539 U.S. (2003), p. 16.
5 "Millennium Declaration" available at http://www.un.org/millennium/declaration/ares552e.htm.
6 UNDP, *Human Development Report 2000: Human Rights and Human Development* (Oxford: Oxford University Press, 2000); *idem, Human Development Report 2003: Deepening Democracy in a Divided World* (Oxford: Oxford University Press, 2000); and Commission on Human Security, *Human Security Now* (New York: Commission on Human Security, 2003).
7 In Seamus Heaney, *The Cure at Troy: A Version of Sophocles'* Philoctetes (New York: Noonday Press, 1991).

Preface

Thomas G. Weiss, Margaret E. Crahan, and John Goering

The chapters in this volume are one of the products of a year-long faculty seminar and public forums, held during the academic year 2002–3, sponsored by the Ralph Bunche Institute for International Studies and the Center for Humanities at The Graduate Center of The City University of New York. The Andrew W. Mellon Foundation and its Vice-President Harriet Zuckerman were supportive of this intellectual undertaking and generous in funding the project.

New York has proven to be an ideal, if scarred, location to convene a discussion of the impact of the wars on terrorism and Iraq on issues of human and civil rights. We began our seminars in September 2002, almost exactly a year after the tragic events of September 11, 2001. The issue of terrorism was concurrently on the international, national, and local (New York City) agendas. The war in Iraq was raging during the final sessions of the series after difficult debates in the United Nations Security Council. Current events had a very direct impact on our discussions.

As a result, the conceptualization and focuses of the seminar evolved over time. Our initial overarching theme was the interaction of U.S. policy on state sovereignty and its impact on the enjoyment of human rights both in this country and abroad. As part of the basis for our discussion, we used a definition of human rights common in the national and international human rights communities: that human rights are inherent claims by individuals and groups on states and societies for life with dignity, including the complete and complex range of political, civil, ethnic, social, economic, cultural, intellectual, and religious rights.

Given the subject's inherent breadth, coupled with our desire to engage in intensive analysis and debate, we focused the seminar on three major case studies or issue areas that helped illustrate and reveal the complex interactions of factors shaping the tensions between war, rights, and the dynamics of state sovereignty. The three topics were: the impact of the war on terrorism on human rights both in the U.S. and around the world; the relevance of U.N. activities on the subject of race, including the 2001 U.N. World Conference against Racism, to U.S. domestic and foreign policy; and the impact of U.S. unilateralism since the end of the Cold War on this nation's foreign policy, with particular attention devoted to the Middle East and surrounding regions. The first and the third emphases are clearly intertwined and provide the focus for this book. Challenging the notion that national security and a strong human rights posture are not complementary, the Sawyer Seminar concluded that they are, in fact, mutually supportive. Indeed, the analyses presented during the course of the seminar repeatedly stressed that national security was more likely to be guaranteed by a strong rather than by an enfeebled commitment to human rights domestically and abroad. We are most grateful to the ten contributors to this collection for their timely, incisive, and provocative chapters analyzing the complexities of their topics with a view toward suggesting effective security and rights policies. Their profiles are found at the front of the volume. We are also extremely gratified that Mary Robinson, the former President of Ireland and U.N. High Commissioner for Human Rights who now heads the Ethical Globalization Initiative, agreed to enhance this book with her Foreword.

We would be remiss if we did not mention that a number of other papers were also presented and provided intellectual grist for the mill, which we have been unable to include in this collection. Many of the ideas and criticisms of seminar participants and discussants have also found their way into the chapters or into the Introduction and Conclusion. In particular, the authors and editors benefited from the wisdom of Adolfo Aguilar Zinser, Marcellus Andrews, Penelope Andrews, Zehra Arat, Beth Baron, Anne Bayefsky, Ann Beeson, Mehdi Bozorgmehr, Rhonda Copelon, Julie Fernandes, Paul Heinbecker, Tracy Higgins, James O.C. Jonah, David Malone, Gay J. McDougall, William L. Nash, Giandomenico Picco, Michael Posner, John A. Powell, Anthony C.E. Quainton, Barnett Rubin, Arthur M. Schlesinger Jr., Domna Stanton, André M. Surena, Yvonne Terlingen, Shashi Tharoor, J. Michael Turner, and Marta Varela.

We would also like to express our appreciation to a number of persons who were essential to the creation of this volume. David Nasaw, distinguished Professor of History at The Graduate Center, provided considerable intellectual advice and assistance in the initial formulation of this project. Our colleague from Brooklyn College and The Graduate Center, Mark Ungar, provided intellectual firepower to the undertaking, and helpful comments in framing the volume. Mirna Adjami, a Mellon postgraduate fellow, acted as rapporteur for the workshop; her diligence and insights about international human rights were very helpful in drafting the Introduction and Conclusion. She was a wonderful colleague during the year she spent in New York extracting lessons from her previous experience in the Congo and in pursuing research on universal jurisdiction. María Victoria Pérez-Rios, a Mellon graduate student fellow working on human rights, provided research assistance. Elisa Athonvarangkul cheerfully helped prepare the final manuscript. Nancy Okada, the Administrative Director of the Ralph Bunche Institute for International Studies, contributed good humor and problem-solving skills in overseeing the administrative details of the workshop. We are also most grateful to Danielle Zach for having shouldered a lion's share of the administration of the Sawyer Seminar Series itself and for her attention to every detail of fact-checking and editorial assistance during the preparation of the final manuscript. She is a most promising graduate student in comparative politics and international relations, who was a Mellon Fellow for two academic years. Neither the series nor this volume would have had the same professional tone and quality without her able assistance.

Finally we thank the faculty members, students, and other participants in the seminars and public forums whose interests, fears, questions, and thoughts kept alive our concern for new policy insights.

Thomas G. Weiss, Margaret E. Crahan, and John Goering
New York, September 2003

Abbreviations

AIDS	acquired immune deficiency syndrome
CHR	Commission on Human Rights
ESDP	European Security and Defense Policy
E.U.	European Union
GDP	gross domestic product
G-8	Group of Eight
ICC	International Criminal Court
ICJ	International Court of Justice
ICRC	International Committee of the Red Cross
NAFTA	North American Free Trade Agreement
NATO	North Atlantic Treaty Organization
NGO	nongovernmental organization
OSCE	Organization for Security and Cooperation in Europe
POW	prisoner of war
U.K.	United Kingdom
U.N.	United Nations
UNAMA	United Nations Assistance Mission in Afghanistan
UNESCO	United Nations Educational, Scientific, and Cultural Organization
UNMOVIC	United Nations Monitoring, Verification, and Inspection Commission
U.S.	United States
WEU	Western European Union
WMD	weapons of mass destruction
WTO	World Trade Organization

Introduction

The serendipity of war, human rights, and sovereignty

The case of the United States

Thomas G. Weiss, Margaret E. Crahan, and John Goering

The wars on terrorism and Iraq currently dominate public policy debates in the U.S. and abroad, often reflecting deeply held political and ideological beliefs. In-depth analyses of these issues are much less common. This book aims to fill that gap by analyzing the impact of the wars on terrorism and Iraq on the enjoyment of human rights both nationally and internationally, as well as on the historical competition between unilateralism and multilateralism in U.S. foreign policy. We should state at the outset that this approach does not imply that security or human rights specialists "should focus their attention exclusively on the terrorist threat."[1] Rather, our purpose is to identify factors that should be incorporated into the formulation of policies to respond effectively to the challenges of these wars in both the short and long term.

Our analytic point of departure is the seeming, and much hoped-for-growth of a worldwide commitment to the enjoyment of human rights in ensuring national and international security.

One of the core worries that prompts this volume is whether such rights are sufficiently entrenched that their defense will not—indeed cannot—be undermined by the demand for security in the wars against terrorism and in Iraq. In the 1970s there was debate over the supposed competition between the prerequisites for national security and human rights. By the 1990s there appeared to be substantial international consensus, clearly expressed in the upsurge of multilateral humanitarian interventions, that the observance of human rights was one of the prime guarantees of greater national and international security.

Will human rights ever be entrenched firmly enough to act as fundamental guides to the interests and choices of hegemonic powers? Does an effective war on terrorism require that human rights observance be restricted in fundamental ways, or is there an essential relationship between a high degree of respect for human rights and the prevention of terrorism? In short, what sort of balance is required for effective counter-terrorism policies if respect for human rights is, as international consensus seems to suggest, a prime means of reducing the sources of terrorism?

Since September 11, 2001, it has become clear that responding to the demands of national and international security and those of human rights promotion requires a significant rethinking of both policies and strategies.[2] This is evident in the growing preoccupation with the impact on human rights of measures adopted to combat terrorism in the U.S. and elsewhere.[3] The U.S.A. Patriot Act, the detention of immigrants without charges, together with the designation of the Guantánamo detainees as "non-combatants," rather than "prisoners of war" under the Geneva Conventions, have raised doubts about the capacity of the U.S. to promote human and civil rights while fighting terrorism. Given that the legitimacy of the U.S. government both at home and abroad is deeply rooted in its historical support of democracy and human rights, the answers to the above questions help determine the capacity of the United States to exert moral as well as military leadership on the world stage.

U.S. international leadership is tied to the degree to which other countries recognize the remaining superpower as acting not only in its own interests but also on behalf of broader ones. Serious questions have been raised even by long-standing allies about the effect of unilateralist tendencies in U.S. foreign policy as Washington has focused almost exclusively on the wars on terrorism and Iraq. There has been passionate disagreement about whether Washington's leadership required a predominantly multilateral approach to foreign policy or if, by virtue of its superpower status and the demands of the war on terrorism, it was reasonable to expect and accept U.S. unilateralism. While a good number of commentators have cast U.S. foreign policy, particularly since September 11, as essentially unilateral, several of the authors in this volume suggest that George W. Bush's administration has demonstrated as much multilateralism as previous ones, including Bill Clinton's. In addition, U.S. policy with respect to the Israeli–Palestinian conflict, it is further argued, was more unilateral under Clinton than under the current administration. In short, this book challenges some of the conventional wisdom about the impact of the wars on terrorism and Iraq on U.S. foreign and human rights policies, on its bilateral and multilateral relations, as well as its role within the United Nations.

The debate over the weight of national security in U.S. foreign policy versus the demands of international human rights is hardly new. However, the international context imposes pressure on Washington's policy-makers to devise effective ways to combat terrorism while ensuring that the United States maintains a firm enough commitment to human rights to legitimize its world leadership. The contributors to this volume do a great deal to clarify the basis for sustaining national and international security within a viable rights context. As the United Nations Charter maintained in 1945, broad-based respect for human rights is the best guarantee of international peace and security.

In planning this volume, the editors started with a simpler problematic: we sought to uncover, with the aid of some of the world's leading analysts, a deeper understanding of the linkages between the pressures on governments to ensure their sovereign independence and the inexorably growing pressures—albeit with some backsliding during periods of stress as at present—for greater enjoyment of human rights. More precisely, we sought to understand better the requirements of sovereignty in today's world given human rights claims. We hoped to address, in part, the difficulty of advancing international human rights while the

U.S. continues to maintain a fairly traditional definition of its sovereign independence. As one of our contributors, Edward C. Luck, noted elsewhere, "international law and organization have been expected to express, embody, and extend the American dream, not to challenge or modify it."[4] We also aimed to learn whether or not human rights requires *a priori* the rejection of any political justification for the denial of human rights, including war.

Our planning began nearly a year before September 11, 2001. That tragedy, and the subsequent unfolding war against terrorism, quickly formed a politically and analytically indispensable focus for the issues at the core of this volume. An already challenging task of evaluating U.S. power in relation to international normative standards was made vastly more complex, and difficult. How has the war on terrorism and the ongoing struggle in Iraq reshaped our appreciation of the core values expressed in human rights? Is it true, as some argue, that the U.S. has deeply undercut its capacity for international leadership because of its unwillingness to enforce relevant rights protections for those imprisoned at Guantánamo?[5] And what does U.S. action portend for multilateral institutions such as the United Nations? Has Washington, as suggested by many—including Anne-Marie Slaughter, the President of the American Society of International Law—rung the death knell for the world organization?[6] In the aftermath of the Security Council debate over the Iraq war, David Malone, President of the International Peace Academy, commented: "The Security Council has probably been fatally wounded in terms of its centrality to the U.S. on the use of force around the world . . . The diplomats of Turtle Bay . . . don't fully comprehend the extent of the train wreck in which the Security Council has been involved."[7] Are such assessments valid?

As will become clear, there is nothing straightforward about the answers to any of these questions. Mary Robinson, the former U.N. High Commissioner for Human Rights whose Foreword opens this volume, recently commented: "It is both in the national interest of the United States and in our collective interest to defend, strengthen, and yes, reform, the multilateral system in which we have invested so much so that it can meet the challenges of the twenty-first century."[8] What policies appear most central to enabling the U.S. and the U.N. and its treaty bodies to work together to meet the intertwined challenges of terrorism and needs for human rights protection? How can human security and human rights be best linked? Does war inevitably displace the human rights deemed by the U.N. Charter to be essential for international peace and security? Does a more unilateralist set of policies rather than multilateralism best ensure security? What policies and reforms, if any, appear germane as we assess the human rights benefits and costs of the war on terrorism?

The editors of this collection conceived a year-long sequence of seminars and public events at which the issues of war, rights, and U.S. foreign policy were the centerpieces. Initially, these broad themes were to be explored through a focus on the war on terrorism; U.S. Middle East policy, especially regarding Israel and Palestine; and the impact of race on U.S. foreign policy, particularly pertaining to the debate on reparations and the U.N. World Conference against

Racism. (The latter subject, while treated during the series, was not included in this collection.[9]) We chose, moreover, to address a wide range of political, social, cultural, and philosophical positions in order to maximize the likelihood of transcending narrow, partisan analyses in favor of broader, more innovative approaches. To this end, we assembled contributors with a variety of views, sometimes at odds.

During the planning of the seminar itself, the United States invaded Afghanistan and overthrew the Taliban regime, which had harbored Al Qaeda —the perpetrators of the tragic attacks of September 11. The Bush administration did so with the genuine support of the United Nations and widespread international sympathy. At home, the administration instituted intelligence and law enforcement policies and procedures with the goal of preventing further terrorist activity and prosecuting those suspected of planning, abetting, or undertaking it. As our series began in the fall of 2002, it became clear that the U.S. was opening a third front in its war on terrorism, namely against the regime of Saddam Hussein. So, during the planning and actual conduct of our deliberations, the interactions among the wars on terrorism and Iraq, human rights, sovereignty, and unilateralism versus multilateralism were real and not merely academic concerns.

To better appreciate the complexity of the issues, it would be useful to consider some of the challenges that we faced in framing the discussions. It has now become commonplace to read criticisms of the current administration for "undermining civil liberties."[10] For instance, an investigation by the Office of the Inspector General at the U.S. Department of Justice concluded that there had been "glaring errors" committed by the Federal Bureau of Investigation (FBI) and the Immigration and Naturalization Services (INS) in the treatment of those detained after September 11, 2001.[11] Such analyses occurred well after Congress had granted the executive branch sweeping new powers aimed at curbing terrorism; authority that now appears to constrain, if not erode, civil liberties. The withholding of information from the press, researchers, and even from defendants has become part of the difficulty associated with learning what specific threats are most imminent, where or to whom, and in evaluating what price citizens should be expected to pay to confront them. This problem again manifested itself when the White House refused to declassify sections of the Joint Congressional Inquiry into the September 11 attacks chaired by Senator Bob Graham and Representative Porter Goss.[12]

There is, therefore, need for thoughtful assessments of the possibility that U.S. citizens may lose important—even ostensibly inalienable—rights in the effort to protect the country against current and potential threats. The essays in this book are an important step toward understanding the interactions of threats and rights. Each of the contributors draws upon years of experience in analyzing effective policies for responding to threats to the peace and the best mechanisms by which to implement them, including the U.N. and international human rights system.

This collection therefore includes analyses of the war or terrorism followed by an in-depth look at the consequences of the war in Iraq and the ongoing conflict in the Middle East. The views reflect judgments from practitioners with experience in governmental, intergovernmental, and nongovernmental organizations (NGOs), as well as from academia. All of the authors are U.S. citizens or residents, who explore the consequences of the failure of the United States, a historical advocate of human rights, to conform to international law in the name of combating terrorism. Each strives both to find effective means for appreciating the need for new policies and actions, and to point toward alternatives that might help promote a more stable international order. Among the central themes is the uniqueness of the current moment in terms of U.S. power and policies, with several authors seeing signs of both continuity and change in the current administration.

At the same time, most of the contributors are concerned about the spill-over from Washington's rhetoric and actions. First, there are the worldwide negative reactions to perceived U.S. arrogance in ignoring both enemies and allies and "going it alone."[13] Second, there are possible demonstration effects. As U.N. Secretary-General Kofi Annan said recently: "We are concerned that, under the guise of terrorism, governments all around the world are using the 'T' word— and tagging people with it—to abuse their rights and lock them up in jail and to deal with political opposition. We are seeing an erosion in respect for human rights, which is of concern to all of us."[14]

Before providing an overview of the issues raised in the chapters by individual authors, it would be helpful to recall key elements of the current human rights situation. The following section also introduces shifts in the conceptualization of sovereignty in the modern world. Both of these topics provided a backdrop for subsequent analyses.

The human rights battlefield

Human rights were among the more powerful ideas to emerge from the U.N. Charter—along with peace, national self-determination, and development. After the drafting and adoption of the Universal Declaration of Human Rights in 1948, to which all the countries of the world subscribe, at least rhetorically, the modern international human rights system developed slowly within the constraints of the Cold War. While there remains much to celebrate about the Universal Declaration and collateral human rights treaties, there have also been substantial complications in managing the political organization of such international obligations.

Within the U.N., until the 1980s, the issue of human rights was essentially an ideological football, kicked back and forth in a match between West and East. Western players prioritized political and civil rights, and their Eastern counterparts (usually backed up by southern reserves) economic and social rights. The divide was part of Cold War competition, which left little room for the possibility of joint promotion.

Although change was perceptible earlier, it was only as the Cold War was beginning to thaw that groups concerned with the rights of women, children, refugees, and minorities really entered the match, thus altering the game and playing field in a major way. Since the mid-1980s there has been a surge in official ratifications of human rights conventions. Almost a hundred countries, over half the U.N. member states, have now ratified all six major human rights instruments, and about three-quarters have ratified the covenants on civil and political rights and on economic, social, and cultural rights. Over 80 percent of countries have ratified the conventions on the elimination of all forms of racial discrimination and of all forms of discrimination against women. All but two countries (Somalia and the United States) have ratified the Convention on the Rights of the Child.[15]

Various monitoring and implementing mechanisms evolved under the U.N.'s umbrella, including such agencies as the World Food Programme (WFP), the U.N. High Commission for Refugees (UNHCR), the World Health Organization (WHO), and UNICEF (U.N. Children's Fund), as well as others assigned to both the General Assembly and to the Security Council. Central to the evolution of a worldwide consensus on rights has been the generation of treaties, and affiliated agencies, with specific human rights staffs and obligations. These include agreements to end, for example, racism, torture, and the abuse of women, and to protect children. International norms have thus, over the last half-century, become enshrined in a wide range of legally binding international human rights instruments.[16]

In 1994 the United States ratified the Covenant on Civil and Political Rights and in 1996 the Convention on the Elimination of Racial Discrimination. It was not, however, until the end of 2000 that the U.S. submitted to the U.N. its first official report addressing the state of race relations and civil rights law enforcement within the United States. Such tardy compliance stems partly from a disinclination by the Senate to ratify treaties that imply any conditioning of sovereign autonomy, reinforced by mistrust of the United Nations on the part of some members of Congress.

Nevertheless, a wide range of international norms have been enshrined in legally binding international human rights instruments, and in a growing web of customary international law. Protections were established by treaty for those subjected to torture, for victims of racial discrimination, for children, and for women. As neither the United States nor the Soviet Union deferred fully to this system during the Cold War, the protection of human rights remained more nominal than actual. The sovereign prerogatives of the superpowers trumped rights enforcement, with the U.N. system accepting non-compliance on many occasions.[17]

The end of the Cold War and the elimination of the most serious security threat to the United States abruptly raised expectations that human rights and humanitarian concerns would take center stage in the conduct of international relations. This volume's essays pick up the story in the 1990s when rights became more visible within international forums.

The evolution of sovereignty in the 1990s

The key U.N. Charter article relating to national sovereignty is 2 (7), which holds, "Nothing contained in the present Charter shall authorize the United Nations to intervene in matters that are essentially within the domestic jurisdiction of any state." Major powers, including the United States, along with the least influential states, have at times relied upon this provision to argue that international norms do not necessarily constrain national prerogatives. While the United States has always championed civil and political rights, at least as broad principles, it has also demonstrated a fundamental ambivalence toward international constraints on its freedom of action. The long history of U.S. ambiguity, even antipathy, toward international obligations and commitments dates back to the Founding Fathers' deep unease about foreign entanglements, as much as a strong inclination toward a defense of sovereignty.

The first Gulf war in 1991 suggested the dawn of a more effective multilateral system in the service of enforcing international law, further raising hopes that human rights would emerge as a core foreign policy priority. The 1990s, however, did not fully realize their initial promise. After an ill-fated mission in Somalia (1993), the United States retreated from global leadership on humanitarian issues. The wars in the Balkans flared with uncertain responses from the United Nations, Europe, and the United States. A low point came with the international failure to prevent the genocide in Rwanda in 1994. The U.N.'s incapacity to intervene dampened expectations for a more effective era of human rights and humanitarian intervention.

The 1990s nonetheless witnessed a dramatic transformation in the widespread view that the U.N. Charter is a Westphalian document *par excellence*, that is, what transpires within the borders of one sovereign state is not the concern of persons, institutions, and states elsewhere. The U.N.'s constitution prohibits intrusions into the domestic affairs of member states, but what is considered "domestic" has shrunk. In particular, humanitarian and human rights interventions of the 1990s transformed the debate, which was captured by the International Commission on Intervention and State Sovereignty (ICISS). Its position, as stated in *The Responsibility to Protect*, moves away from the rights of interveners toward the rights of victims and the obligations of outsiders to act.[18] The ICISS essentially endorses what Francis M. Deng, the U.N. Secretary-General's special representative for internally displaced persons, calls "sovereignty as responsibility."[19] It is primarily state authorities whose citizens are threatened that have "the responsibility to protect." Yet a residual responsibility rests with the larger community of states when an aberrant member of their club misbehaves egregiously or simply implodes.

The acute suffering in such failed or failing states as Somalia, the former Yugoslavia, Rwanda, Haiti, and East Timor opened the door to international scrutiny of domestic policies that had led to genocide, massive displacements, and gross abuses of human rights. Such abuses within states are now considered by many to be legitimate "international" concerns. Moreover, the last

two secretaries-general of the United Nations have actively supported the articulation of a fast-evolving human rights regime, with support from the High
Commissioner for Human Rights. That the heads of an intergovernmental
organization have publicly taken such stances against their member states is
remarkable. Such positions reflect those of major internationally focused human
rights NGOs, including Amnesty International, the International Human Rights
Law Group, Human Rights Watch, and the Lawyers Committee for Human
Rights.

The administration of William Jefferson Clinton accepted human rights as
an element of its foreign policy. It raised human rights concerns in its bilateral
relations with several countries and acknowledged the link both between human
rights and democracy and with national and international stability. It partici-
pated actively in multilateral conferences convened by the United Nations that
addressed human rights concerns, such as the Vienna Summit on Human
Rights in 1993, the Beijing Conference on Women in 1995, and the preparatory
meetings for the World Conference Against Racism. The U.S. also played a role
in negotiating the legal standards and procedures for the International Criminal
Tribunals for the former Yugoslavia and Rwanda, as well as the Rome Statute
of the International Criminal Court (ICC). President Clinton signed that treaty,
though he did not send it to Congress for ratification. In sum, his administration's human rights policies appeared supportive of the growing prominence of
mainstream human rights concerns. Sovereignty concerns bowed, however
slightly, to commitments to multilateral rights enforcement.

President George W. Bush entered office in January 2001 with a distinctly
different foreign policy vision from his predecessor. He spoke unabashedly in
traditional terms about state sovereignty, including prioritizing the strengthening
of U.S. military and economic interests both at home and abroad. Observers
waited to see how this would translate into policy initiatives. How would the role
of human rights in foreign policy change in his administration? Did tough talk
on state sovereignty mean that the administration would definitively opt for unilateralism over multilateralism?

Would the "new sovereigntists," who judged international obligations as
"vague and illegitimately intrusive" because they relied on procedures that are
"unaccountable and unenforceable," predominate? Would their view that "the
United States can opt out of international regimes as a matter of power, legal
right, and constitutional duty" be adopted?[20] What precisely is the impact of, in
the title of a recent book, *United States Hegemony and the Foundations of International
Law*?[21]

Thus while there has been a gradual transformation of many states' perspectives about their human rights responsibilities, the U.S. has not adopted a
consistent policy of prioritizing human rights as an essential strategy for guaranteeing international peace and security. Moreover, there has been little
improvement in U.N.-based human rights compliance mechanisms. Debates
are thus justified about how full or empty the glass is at the beginning of the
twenty-first century. On the one hand, Michael Ignatieff and others have popu-

larized a so-called revolution in moral responsibility.[22] David Rieff, on the other hand, questions such optimists because they have not "actually kept a single jackboot out of a single human face."[23]

To state the obvious, there is no "global Bismarck" for human rights any more than there is for other global challenges such as the protection of the environment or reducing unemployment. The United Nations and related treaty bodies do not have enforcement capabilities or even compliance modalities. What does this constrained system for global rights portend for a world confronted with terrorism and the apparent threat of weapons of mass destruction (WMD)? More particularly, how well do multilateralist commitments fare when confronted with the reality of unexpected attacks by groups such as Al Qaeda and the possibility of mass death?

The effect of war?

The authors analyze the underlying tensions, even the direct clash, between universal aspirations and norms for human rights, on the one hand, and the reality that there is only limited authority to ensure the security needed for human rights compliance, on the other. These tensions have been significantly, some would argue irretrievably, exacerbated by events since September 11. In the immediate wake of the attacks on the World Trade Center and the Pentagon, the United States declared a war on the new, singularly important global security threat—terrorism.

The U.S. began its war on terrorism with the invasion of Afghanistan but only after obtaining the approval of the United Nations, and the follow-on activities involved the cooperation of a coalition. Indeed, some commentators are quite unaware of the Security Council's genuinely supportive actions at that time, indeed throughout the 1990s, in the fight against terrorism. Others are ignorant of the General Assembly's long-standing efforts to hammer out international conventions and treaties, even if the definition of "terrorism" has been finessed.[24]

At home, the government rushed into law new measures, particularly the U.S.A. Patriot Act, that were designed to increase the authority of the state with the goal of preventing and prosecuting terrorist activity on U.S. soil. Many human rights NGOs expressed reservations that basic rights were all too likely to be sacrificed if the effort to protect the country was not conscious of the essential role of human rights in undercutting the generation of terrorists. The historical complementarity and tension between national and international compliance in the arena of human rights within the context of the war on terror is unsettling for every contributor to the book, but most notably addressed by those in the first and second sections.

As the authors were outlining their analyses, the United States began planning its war against Saddam Hussein. By the time they finished their rough drafts, the war in Iraq had begun on March 23; and even before chapters were finalized, the war was declared "over" on May 1, 2003—although the violence was certainly anything but over. As contributors were polishing their essays, the bombing of the U.N.'s Baghdad headquarters occurred, killing 23 persons, the largest disaster in the world organization's history. Throughout, domestic and international debate raged about whether and why to wage war, the importance of solidarity, the "end of alliances,"[25] and what role the United Nations should play in the conflict and in rebuilding the country afterwards. Such concerns preoccupy especially those authors in the third section of the volume.

As we go to press, the war has technically ended, while the fitful beginnings of Iraqi independence are taking shape amid almost daily deaths of Iraqi citizens and of U.S. and British military, and U.N. and human rights NGO personnel. The occupation under way promises to continue for months, if not years. Meanwhile, Washington returned to the Security Council in October 2003 to seek an international imprimatur with an accompanying spread of risks and of costs; the result was Resolution 1511.

Part 1, "Framing the debate," contains two essays that introduce the subject matter for the rest of the book: the interplay of U.S. domestic and foreign policies on respect for human rights in the context of tensions between unilateralism and multilateralism in prosecuting the war on terrorism. While current issues are the focus, the authors also place U.S. policy in broader historical, cultural, and philosophical contexts.

Tom J. Farer, the Dean of the Graduate School of International Studies at the University of Denver, begins with a comprehensive look at "The interplay of domestic politics, human rights, and U.S. foreign policy." He argues that U.S. foreign policy, lacking a clearly defined organizing principle since the end of the Cold War, selects from a set of multilateral, bilateral, or unilateral options depending on the task. Both Presidents Clinton and Bush, he finds, have been willing to use force when necessary to defend U.S. security or promote U.S. objectives. However, despite apparent expediency, there are deep social, religious, and cultural forces that underlie the U.S.'s ambivalence toward human rights and multilateralism. Culture, class, and religion are currently construed by neo-conservatives within an evil/good dyad that frustrates subtler and more pragmatic policy options. They may also, as in the case of current policy, frustrate commitments to multilateral institutions and goals.

To explore the roots of the George W. Bush administration's unilateralism, Farer analyzes U.S. exceptionalism. Although unilateralism predominated during the presidency of Ronald Reagan, its roots run deeper. In order to establish its nature, he contrasts traditional realist conservatives and more recent neo-conservatives. The former believe that "the purpose of statecraft is to advance U.S. power and protect material interests in a dangerously competitive and structurally anarchic world." Neo-conservatives, in contrast, have a more expansive vision. The U.S. "is not simply a great power but also a cluster of ideals." Farer concludes that George W. Bush, not unlike his father, embraced a limited realist perspective during his campaign, but that September 11 gave neo-conservative influences increased weight in policy decisions.

Farer's operational definition of multilateral diplomacy is a helpful starting point for later chapters: "The test of a serious commitment to multilateralism is willingness to discuss ends and means and to modify them in order to foster cooperation not only in the instant case, but in a multitude of others that will eventually reach the policy agenda." A key issue for other contributors is assessing how much, and how willingly, the Bush administration's diplomacy in the wars on terrorism and Iraq has modified either means or ends.

Central to the realization of any degree of multilateral engagement is the trade-off between realists, on the one hand, and neo-conservatives who defend a cluster of relatively inviolate "ideals," on the other hand. The rise of the latter has meant that the current Fourth World War, in Farer's terms, pits believers in free peoples and markets against infidels. "It is," Farer argues, "a war between democratic capitalism and its enemies." Hegemonic global control appears as the not quite invisible hand of these otherwise free-market acolytes. Such ideological stances form an essential core of Farer's prediction that war is indeed our future. "As the financial and cultural base of the expansion (sometimes labeled 'globalization'), the U.S. is the inevitable target for all those who, being threatened, resist. And since globalization is not a public policy . . . the U.S. government cannot erase the bull's eye from the nation's flank."

Farer also helps by clarifying the degree to which the corpus of human rights can be confined to a relatively narrow set of rights including those to life, to freedom from torture, and to some highly limited form of due process. War thus notably narrows those rights that any of us have a reasoned basis to expect as inviolate. He ends with a chastening view of policy options. While he concurs with neo-conservatives that the U.S. is "indispensable for any project to mitigate the present and looming humanitarian horrors of the twenty-first century," he is also acutely aware that neo-conservatives have repeatedly failed to protect the basic rights of individuals and the culture in Iraq. It is also these same ascendant policy-makers who indicate unease with multilateral commitments and ideals.

In brief, Farer offers a sociopolitically informed but somewhat alarming view of the future. A question remains as to whether or not he adequately acknowledges the possibility of the emergence of countervailing liberal and critical views that can constrain, if not reverse, the neo-conservative influence in current foreign and human rights policies. Has the human rights movement the ability to challenge and reduce the power of neo-conservative hegemonic views? Will U.S. military shortcomings in Iraq cause a shift away from the current pre-emptive philosophy? He brilliantly dissects the roots and power of conservative views, but he offers less insight into alternative power centers that may reappear as policy pendulums shift and refocus. Finally, Farer reminds us: "However fine a symbol of cosmopolitan sympathies they may be, human rights are not yet connected in the U.S. electorate's mind to a set of foreign policy guidelines. As a symbol, therefore, they remain available for appropriation by advocates of almost any position."

Chapter 2, "Pre-emption and exceptionalism in U.S. foreign policy: precedent and example in the international arena," is by Judith Lichtenberg, research scholar at the Institute for Philosophy and Public Policy and a professor in the Department of Philosophy of the University of Maryland at College Park. She questions whether there is a guiding maxim or principle behind the Bush administration's policy of pre-emptive military intervention. It is unusual in a social science collection to introduce philosophical issues, but the editors thought that it would challenge readers to frame the issues more conceptually and hence facilitate the identification of relevant options. While political scientists and others may have difficulties with her framing of such topics as realism and humanitarian intervention, we urge them to consider carefully her line of inquiry.

Lichtenberg explores a range of principles that might serve as moral and operational maxims justifying the current U.S. policy in the wars on terrorism and Iraq. Her concern is: "What is most troubling about U.S. foreign policy today is the example that it holds up to the world and the precedent that it sets." Taking off from Immanuel Kant's Categorical Imperative and Jean-Paul Sartre's work, she argues that states should act according to universal principles. Even so, after running through a set of principles, she finds that: "The U.S. may engage in actions that other nations may not, such as deciding which foreign regimes are rogues and removing them." This is, clearly, an assertion of U.S. hegemony clothed in exceptionalism. It is also a view of U.S. unilateralism that arrogates "moral rights" to itself. Lichtenberg closes by proposing her own operational principle based on a cost–benefit understanding of what she labels "humanitarian intervention." She argues that states "may intervene militarily in the affairs of other states to prevent or end severe and widespread violations of human rights, when they have very good reason to believe that the benefits of intervention will outweigh the costs."

Her philosophical insights, however, do not offer guidance about how to proceed in the rough and tumble of political, economic, and moral calculations within government, both in the short and longer term. How can benefits and costs be established, especially in the absence of any viable expression of choice by a country's residents? It seems unlikely that quantifiable measures of costs and benefits could be found with sufficient credibility to alter policy choices. Nor does Lichtenberg refer to the continual balancing of the pros ands cons, including budgetary liabilities, associated with traumatic foreign policy events. She nonetheless helps to guide the reader through a set of compelling philosophical choices that lay the basis for a closer examination of foreign policy.

Building upon Farer's historical overview and Lichtenberg's conceptual concerns, Part 2, "Human rights and the war on terrorism," consists of three provocative analyses of the impact of the war on terrorism on human rights. The contributors explore this issue from different perspectives, including a look at whether prior U.S. administrations and the current one have complied with international human rights standards in general, and more specifically in the execution of the wars on terrorism and Iraq.

Chapter 3, "U.S. foreign policy and human rights in an era of insecurity: the Bush administration and human rights after September 11," is by David P. Forsythe, the Charles J. Mach Distinguished Professor of Political Science and University Professor at the University of Nebraska–Lincoln. He begins by reminding us that "no administration has been able to secure a lasting and bipartisan commitment to specific human rights across time, situations, and issues." In part, this is due to the plethora of often hesitant voices addressing rights, but just as importantly to the fact that "situations of war and threat to security correlate negatively with human rights protection." For most of the public, as well as for their elected officials, security trumps rights no matter which party dominates the White House and the Congress. Nonetheless, Forsythe views the Bush administration as ultra-nationalist and unilateralist; it only "cosmetically" makes use of multilateral institutions. He illustrates this with an in-depth look at current policies toward the International Criminal Court, including the current President Bush's decision to "unsign" his predecessor's approval of the Rome Statute.

In addition, Forsythe notes the administration's tendency to give more weight to a traditional prioritization of security over human rights since September 11. "Despite administration rhetoric stressing continuing interest in democracy, human rights, and political reform, the U.S. does not seriously press regimes on these 'liberal' issues when they are deemed crucial for U.S. military and paramilitary operations in places like Afghanistan and Iraq." Support for the U.S. on the broad agenda of anti-terrorism may well insulate some regimes from human rights charges by Washington. "The U.S. endorses international human rights in the abstract," Forsythe writes, "but practices a human rights policy that reflects cultural relativism and national particularity." He cites U.S. policy toward Uzbekistan and Egypt to illustrate his point, but makes clear that it has not only been the current administration that has failed to press aggressively for rights or democratizing reforms.

Forsythe's analysis includes a useful assessment of the failures of virtually every U.S. administration to include welfare rights—including rights to food, shelter, and health care—among the set of basic human rights priorities that are accepted by most other states. This balkanization of "core rights" is a fundamental limit to the viability of human rights campaigns both within the United States and globally. Forsythe notes that "international welfare rights remain the stepchild of the global human rights movement." When such rights are supported, as in U.S. funding for the Millennium Challenge Account, it is typically to ensure that free trade and market-based capitalism are aided. An exception may be U.S. support for global AIDS prevention, which was proposed as part of the President's trip to Africa in mid-2003.

Forsythe is among several contributors who take note of the contradictions within the current administration's security policies. "It remains," he writes, "supremely ironic that in order to pursue war allegedly in part for democracy in Iraq, Washington finds it useful to turn a blind eye to lack of democracy and related humans rights violations in key supporting states." He laments that U.S. promotion of absolute sovereignty assures continued firm opposition to any form of "muscular international law and organization" in support of equitable international human rights observances. Hence, Forsythe concludes, "What is really needed in the twenty-first century is presidential leadership that can re-orient U.S. society to accept limits on state sovereignty and unilateral action."

Chapter 4, "International human rights: unintended consequences of the war on terrorism," is by Jack Donnelly, Andrew W. Mellon Professor and Associate Dean of the Graduate School of International Studies at the University of Denver. His central argument is that the war on terrorism has shifted always limited attention and resources away from human rights. "Since September 11, human rights have not so much retreated from American foreign policy as they have been eclipsed by a focus on terrorism." As a result, "the space in U.S. foreign policy for human rights and democracy has been significantly reduced—not by design, but no less surely."

Donnelly reminds us that for the U.S., as well as for most countries, security comes before either economic or "other" human rights interests in foreign policy. It was the contraction of security concerns accompanying the end of the Cold War that enabled rights to flourish relatively, but not absolutely, and obviously not irreversibly. As a result, attention shifted, in part, from "a largely reactive and remedial emphasis on stopping, and aiding victims of, systematic and often brutal repression" toward "a more positive emphasis on helping to build a human rights culture."

Prioritizing human rights was short-lived. After the events of September 11, human rights were again marginalized. Human rights violations and repressive policies in countries such as Pakistan, Russia, and Israel since September 11 illustrate how security goals have displaced human rights within U.S. foreign policy. Even more worrying for those who see rights as an essential element for success in the war against terrorism, he offers a judgment that "a return to a more active, aggressive, and consistent international human rights policy must await the reopening of the political space currently pre-empted by the war on terrorism."

Donnelly offers an additional explanation for reordering of interests in the war on terrorism, namely the redefinition of the concept of "security" as a "tendency to conceive new threats in moralized terms and to respond with an irrational exuberance for a militarized crusade." September 11 renewed a sharply ideological vision of national security and a sense among some that human rights could be ignored in its defense. Indeed it has created a political circumstance that has resulted in "an increasing tendency to see security and human rights as competing rather than reinforcing concerns." Donnelly argues that the "axis of evil" states— Iraq, Iran, and North Korea—do not represent viable security threats. Despite this critical perspective on current U.S. foreign policy, Donnelly's unintended-interest perspective leaves room for hope that unrealistic security concerns will wane in the future, reopening more space for human rights and democracy concerns to flourish.

Further evaluation of the current administration is provided in Chapter 5, "The fight against terrorism: the Bush administration's dangerous neglect of human rights." Kenneth Roth, a leading advocate in the international human rights movement and the Executive Director of Human Rights Watch, analyzes the ways that the administration is compromising respect for human rights in order to fight its war on terrorism. He worries that weakening the U.S. commitment to human rights and an overall "degrading of international standards threatens to come back to haunt the United States." Central to his argument is his belief that it is really only a strong human rights culture that can serve as an effective "antidote" to the "pathology of terrorism."

While the U.S. has made such efforts as the Millennium Challenge Account, the war on terror has had, he concludes, a negative impact on U.S. human rights policy in three distinct areas. First, the Bush administration has refused to treat its terrorist suspects in accordance with international legal standards. Second, the U.S. has turned a blind eye to human rights abuses by foreign governments that are seen as allies in the war on terrorism. Third, the Bush administration has "intensely opposed the enforcement of international human rights law," exemplified by its opposition to the International Criminal Court.

Roth worries that the current administration is both preventing public and press scrutiny of its detentions, and using the label of "enemy combatant" that "threatens to create a giant exception to the most basic guarantees of criminal justice." These measures suggest that the administration sees international human rights as "an inconvenient obstacle to fighting terrorism that is readily sidestepped rather than as an integral part of the anti-terrorism effort." His sharpest critique is that human rights "are dispensable" for the current Bush administration.

Roth recognizes that both Democratic and Republican administrations have traditionally been skeptical of human rights treaties. But the Bush administration has intensified U.S. "resistance to enforceable human rights standards" since September 11. In addition to its stance against the ICC, the administration has derailed efforts to protect human rights in such U.N. forums as negotiations over the proposed Optional Protocol to the Convention Against Torture, the General Assembly's Special Session on Children, and the Cairo Program of Action on population control. He concludes that the Bush administration's position vis-à-vis treaties undermines the evolution of human rights norms by signaling that they are but grand pronouncements rather than enforceable rights.

Roth foresees two grave consequences of the Bush administration's war on terrorism. First, by failing to abide by international human rights standards, the U.S. is encouraging a "copycat phenomenon" as repressive regimes increasingly justify human rights violations in the name of combating terror. Second, the inconsistent record on human rights undermines U.S. credibility when the administration does speak out against human rights abuses. In sum, "an anti-terrorism policy that ignores human rights is a gift to terrorists." In pointing to this possible "boomerang" effect, Roth proposes stronger human rights as an essential underpinning for security: "A successful anti-terrorism policy must endeavor to build strong international norms and institutions on human rights, not provide a new rationale for avoiding and undermining them."

Part 3, "U.S. unilateralism in the wake of Iraq," consists of five thought-provoking analyses that explore the implications of the decision to go to war in

Iraq as well as the conduct and aftermath of the war. The five contributors challenge popular characterizations of U.S. policy along the spectrum between unilateralism and multilateralism and provide valuable insights into the implications for the future of transatlantic relations and the central issue of conflict management in the Middle East.

Edward C. Luck, the Director of the Center on International Organization and Professor of Practice in International and Public Affairs at Columbia University, explores the possible motivations for the Bush administration's efforts to make use of the United Nations in its planned war upon Iraq. Chapter 6, "Bush, Iraq, and the U.N.: whose idea was this anyway?," investigates why George W. Bush would seek multilateral support from the U.N. at all. That he stood before the General Assembly on September 12, 2002, and called on the world organization to authorize all necessary means to disarm Iraq was considered surprising by some for an administration that had expressed a deep skepticism of the effectiveness of multilateral approaches and a clear preference for avoiding them.

The administration ultimately sidestepped the U.N. and went to war with the support of the United Kingdom and a small coalition. Luck recites basic reasons why the U.S. campaign might have been predicted to be a failure before it began. The world organization, with its built-in power blocs of contending geopolitical interests, was a relatively inflexible and resistant tool for war planning. Resistance existed because many states used the U.N. as a tool "to counterbalance, at least politically, U.S. power." Iraq had "habitually ignored Security Council resolutions about its weapons of mass destruction." On its part, the council looked askance upon U.S. verbal support for multilateralism in the face of what appeared to be an institutionalized distaste for international commitments. More pointedly, Luck reminds us that both the current Secretary-General and his predecessor "solemnly declared that the U.N.—despite its Charter—no longer was in the business of military enforcement."

Despite these apparent institutional and political bases for not making use of the U.N., "the President, shrugging off the diplomatic torpedoes, decided at that point to plunge straight into the U.N.'s icy waters." Luck presents possible alternative explanations for the revived multilateralist inclinations of the President in fall 2002. The four factors usually invoked to explain the President's appeal to the United Nations included pressure from domestic public opinion, Congress, British Prime Minister Tony Blair, or Secretary of State Colin Powell. He finds that while each of these factors influenced Bush's policy marginally, it was ultimately the President's own decision.

Public opinion polls about the war in Iraq indicated that support for the war either remained the same or increased *after*, rather than before, Bush called for U.N. authorization. As for Congress, Luck shows that Democrats did not take a stance opposing a war on Iraq, let alone advocate pursuing multilateral diplomacy. In the same vein, there is insufficient evidence to demonstrate that pressure from either Prime Minister Blair or Secretary of State Powell was decisive in formulating Bush's U.N. policy.

Luck concludes that the President followed his own judgment and instincts in deciding to seek support from the Security Council in order to forcefully disarm Iraq, suggesting that while it would be a stretch to call Bush a "closet internationalist," he nonetheless has some internationalist leanings. Bush possessed an "abiding confidence that he could persuade the world and employ the Security Council to advance his vision of a transformed and disarmed Iraq and of a reinvigorated and more muscular United Nations."

Luck's conclusion differs from most conventional analyses of this moment on the road to Baghdad. He argues that George W. Bush is too easily dismissed "as something of a clumsy and dimwitted country bumpkin" and offers a convincing argument that the President was tactically shrewd in seeking multilateral support, as had his father before him in the Gulf war. Luck's analysis forces the reader to wonder how his staff could have so poorly evaluated the viability of potential Security Council support following Resolution 1441 of November 2002, with a hint that by knowingly allowing the Security Council to fail, the administration greased the skids on the Council's gradual paralysis. Indeed, Bush seemed to have won more than he lost. As Luck reports, "the Security Council's bitter divisions over the use of force in Iraq . . . soured American public support for the United Nations." An ostensible multilateralist move by Bush, in fact, served to reinforce popular unilateralism—surely a long-term goal of the new sovereigntists. In a White House not known for making simple tactical errors, this could have been among their shrewdest political choices to undercut for domestic purposes—even if only in the short run—the Security Council.

Just how much did the Bush administration anticipate and consider the consequences of its decision to proceed with the war on Iraq? Chapter 7, "The war against Iraq: normative and strategic implications," is by Mohammed Ayoob, University Distinguished Professor of International Relations at James Madison College, Michigan State University. He explores how the Bush administration's rhetorical manipulation of normative and strategic justifications for waging war against Iraq affects global perceptions of the United States and regional geopolitics in the Middle East.

Ayoob believes that this administration's unilateralism departs from Washington's position in the 1990s as a "liberal hegemon," in which it willingly and frequently sacrificed "some of its immediate interests in order to promote the legitimacy and credibility of multilateral institutions." By abandoning this stance, the U.S. has risked fracturing the North Atlantic alliance and undermining the moral authority of international institutions. "Unilateralism," he argues, "begets selectivity and, therefore, the charge of hypocrisy thus eroding the moral basis of international order."

Ayoob evaluates the argument that Iraqi weapons of mass destruction justified the war. Within the Arab world, he argues, it was well known that Iraq no longer possessed such weaponry. These weapons, he asserts, "posed no real threat to its neighbors." Equally importantly, and with more credibility, Arabs believe that it is Israel's nuclear capability that poses a far clearer and more present danger to them and the region. The U.S. war on Iraq, therefore, will increase Arab anger toward the U.S., thereby potentially destabilizing pro-Western regimes in the region. Moreover, Ayoob contends that U.S. action has severely damaged the "legitimacy and credibility of the U.N." and will likely lead to further geopolitical competition between the U.S. and its closest allies in Europe.

Arab anger and radicalism, he believes, will be fueled because the war in Iraq will strengthen Arab solidarity with the plight of and perceived injustices toward Palestinians. Even the May 2003 "Road Map" that included provisions for an independent state of Palestine will be viewed as "another half-hearted attempt to assuage the concerns of pro-Western regimes that feel their legitimacy increasingly challenged." The U.S. has demonstrated that it sustains "double standards" in which Israel is free to violate some 32 Security Council resolutions, while Iraq is vigorously sanctioned for similar violations of far fewer supposedly obligatory mandates.

Ayoob asserts the deep perils of engaging in policy initiatives in a region all too inured to scores of prior attempts and failures. In addition, he fears that if Iraqi oil resources become seen as "the overriding goal of U.S. policy," continued regional turmoil is almost certain. He leaves us with a clearly drawn portrait of a region that disputes virtually every postulate of current U.S. policy toward Iraq and the Middle East. He offers a sobering depiction of the geopolitical limits of the war in Iraq and its consequences for the United Nations, the region, and Washington's credibility as an international standard-bearer for human rights. If Ayoob is correct, U.S. dominance through Israeli regional hegemony will further fuel the clash between Islamic Arabs and the Judeo-Christian West: "In order to guarantee U.S. hegemony in the short run through unilateral measures, the Bush administration may well have ended up damaging the chances of prolonging America's legitimate pre-eminence in the international system over a more extended period."

Chantal de Jonge Oudraat, Senior Fellow at the Center for Transatlantic Relations at the Paul H. Nitze School of Advanced International Studies of The Johns Hopkins University and Adjunct Professor at the Edmund A. Walsh School of Foreign Service of Georgetown University, offers an analysis of "The future of U.S.–European relations" in Chapter 8. She begins by examining the views of the "establishment school of thought," which maintains that no fundamental problems exist in U.S.–European relations. She then scrutinizes the "estrangement school," of which Ayoob is an example, which contends that the U.S. and Europe are inexorably drifting apart.

Oudraat believes that both are off the mark. Nevertheless, she sides with the establishment school by arguing that the fundamentals of the transatlantic relationship are strong. The United States and Europe continue to share basic and fundamental values such as democracy, free trade, and human rights. Furthermore, economic disputes between Washington and the continent are not serious enough to threaten the fundamentals of the partnership. However, she is clear that NATO will no longer be the centerpiece of the transatlantic security partnership, but that the U.S. and Europe continue to face common extra-regional security threats. NATO, she argues, is gradually "withering away." Part of the explanation undoubtedly reflects the fact that European states have a pronounced aversion to the use of force "as a tool of international relations." At the same time, she sees Kosovo as a "watershed" in that the U.S. learned that "war by multilateral committee is a bad idea" and that "the U.S. could do it alone."

Generalized security threats will require capabilities that NATO does not have. Rather than view the transatlantic partnership as we know it as either dead or alive, Oudraat believes that U.S. and European relations will become a web of alliances, what she calls a new "transatlantic security network." This network has several key defining characteristics including that ties within it will likely be dynamic and issue-specific, and that individual states will be closely engaged in bilateral ties to Washington. This new U.S.–Europe network will likely cooperate with other international and multilateral organizations on security issues alone, largely independent of other areas of transatlantic diplomacy. Most critically for those concerned with oversight and transparency, she believes that this new set of alliances will develop outside of public scrutiny because of the nature of countering terrorism and WMD.

She concludes by specifying a set of conditions that would enable this new version of a transatlantic alliance to flourish, many of which are daunting. Included is the requirement that the U.S. and Europe "build an international consensus regarding the basic rules that govern the network." It was, however, this very challenge that so quickly paralyzed the Security Council in confronting Iraq. There is little evidence that such a consensus will quickly or easily emerge. Although the form of the future network is still to be determined, Oudraat assures us at least that the wars on terrorism and Iraq have not totally shaken the fundamentals of the transatlantic partnership.

Foreign policy differences between Europe and the United States go beyond the realm of security. In Chapter 9, "Legal unilateralism," Columbia University's Professor of Law, José Alvarez, explores the legal dimension of the U.S. preference for unilateralism and the European penchant for multilateralism. The Bush administration's decision to wage war on Iraq displayed only the most recent rift between European and U.S. visions of a global order based on international law. The continent and the United States, Alvarez argues, "may be growing farther apart with respect to their attitudes toward the rules and institutions of public international law." His view of legal perspectives differs from Oudraat's interpretation of the fundamental solidity in values on the two sides of the Atlantic.

Notable differences in legal philosophy and commitments exist between European and U.S. international lawyers as exemplified by wide divergences over the legitimacy of the death penalty and the importance of ratifying and implementing a range of international treaties. European lawyers have been especially critical of the Bush administration's new doctrine of pre-emptive defense. Differences are neither incidental nor marginal to national interests but rather have evolved into a fundamental choice because, in contrast to their

U.S. counterparts, "Europe's positivistic international lawyers take multi-lateralism more seriously." The legal obligation to cooperate is, for them, absolutely fundamental; "their civic religion is multilateralism."

U.S. legal thought, in comparison, turns rather to concerns about the effectiveness of international legal systems, including for many the "blatant ineffectiveness" of the U.N. Charter. "International human rights are essentially for export" reveals an underlying belief in exceptionalism; the purpose of law is to protect U.S. values, interests, and political order. In the process of narrowing the relevance of international commitments, the U.S. is now seen, by many in Europe, as fundamentally uninterested "in using the Council to define or defend coherent international rules applicable to all." Arab and Muslim governments, as well as European international lawyers and their governments, reach relatively comparable conclusions from very different starting points.

Alvarez places European reactions to the U.S.'s attempt to obtain Security Council authorization for the use of force against Iraq in this context of differing legal cultures. After the first Gulf war, the Security Council passed Resolution 687, which stipulated boundary demarcations and imposed duties on Iraq to destroy its weapons. In Alvarez's view, "Resolution 687 effectively put Iraqi sovereignty in receivership," criminalizing the Iraqi regime along the lines of the Treaty of Versailles. As the effectiveness of this effort came into question during the 1990s, Europeans became increasingly uncomfortable with the notion of collectively punishing the Iraqi people. The current Bush administration's enthusiasm for the logic of the "mother of all resolutions" led to calling on the U.N. for authorization for the military invasion of Iraq in order to effect regime change. This episode became yet another case in which the U.S. treated the U.N. and international law "as mere politics."

Concluding this third section, New York University's Bruce Jones makes use of his experience as Chief of Staff to the U.N. Special Coordinator for the Middle East Peace Process to assess U.S. preferences for unilateral or multilateral diplomacy in the region. His analysis points toward a pragmatic rather than an ideological approach to foreign policy, thereby disagreeing with Ayoob and, to a degree, Farer. Chapter 10, "Tactical multilateralism: U.S. foreign policy and crisis management in the Middle East," begins by describing factors that remained constant throughout both the current and preceding administrations. In his view, "the record suggests a 'tactical multilateralism'" in which there is "use of multilateral instruments when they help achieve U.S. goals, tolerance of multilateral approaches where they do not impede U.S. objectives, and avoidance of multilateral institutions when they threaten to constrain U.S. policy." Jones reminds us that all multilateral instruments really only "work effectively when they balance core principles with a constructive relationship with U.S. power." It is therefore futile to seek ideological moorings because foreign policy calculations are necessarily tactical and not philosophical. He notes that "the pros or the cons of [a] policy lie not in whether the approach is unilateral or multilateral, for the form of engagement does not particularly shape the nature of policy."

Jones illustrates this view by examining the evolution of U.S. policy on the Middle East peace process and the Arab–Israeli conflict. He documents the Clinton administration's approach of "engaged unilateralism," which insisted upon exclusive U.S. leadership of any peace initiatives at the expense of any multilateral approach. In contrast, and distinct from the conventional wisdom, Jones finds evidence of modest tactical multilateral engagement by the current Bush administration, especially through the Quartet in which coordination of efforts has relied upon the U.N., the European Union (E.U.), and Russia.

In Afghanistan, the Bush administration was able to pursue its policies, devised to reflect its interpretation of the national interest, through multilateral channels. By contrast, in Iraq, once it became clear that the Security Council would not pass a resolution tailored according to U.S. specifications or on the schedule deemed necessary, the U.S. opted to pursue its strategic objectives by skirting the U.N. and building an ad hoc coalition. Jones points out that the rift between the U.S. and the Security Council members who opposed approving the war in Iraq was a "false debate." The Bush administration's ethical appeal to the world organization to authorize force against Iraq in order to strengthen the U.N. by proving its willingness to enforce resolutions was regarded by some as disingenuous. French, German, and Russian objections were similarly considered unprincipled.

Jones concludes by examining the potential implications of U.S. policy for the Middle East and the United Nations, which is especially pertinent in thinking through the implications for the "Road Map" that was finally put on the table in late spring 2003. He disagrees with those who believe that the Security Council has been irreparably damaged. For instance, he notes a series of actions taken both by the Security Council, as well as by the current administration, that have helped bridge the harsh divide that appeared in March. Nonetheless, he believes that "there is also room for a great deal of skepticism about whether the U.N., as currently configured, can realistically be expected to play a credible role in managing key contemporary threats to international security." It is with only "deep and sustained reform" that the U.N. security apparatus might grow to have a more substantial and consistent role in restraining future wars. Rather than ask what the impact of U.S. policy will be on the United Nations, Jones suggests that the better question for the future of the world organization is whether it can evolve to meaningfully adapt to the current global power balance and to new challenges to international peace and security.

Looking toward conclusions

There are numerous issues and questions that readers should keep in mind as they proceed through the following essays. The first concerns the relative weight of fundamental rights. While security pressures and fears historically have often overridden human rights, what have we learned from this most recent contest among war, terrorism, and human rights?

The second is the actual trajectory in the evolution in human rights. Have they gradually assumed a more central role in international relations? Do human rights constitute an enforceable diplomatic prerequisite for the legitimacy of any government, especially one exercising international leadership? Are there domestic implications within the U.S. of the tension between war and human rights?

A third issue regards the caricature that juxtaposes the extremes of a fully multilateralist engagement versus a unilateralist posture, which may not accurately describe U.S. foreign policy decisions. Even within an administration often espousing a unilateralist approach, multilateralism may emerge as a tactical option. Under what circumstances should tactical multilateralism kick in? Given the intensity of the commitment to sovereignty, what are the prospects for the stability and growth of rights based on U.N. conventions and treaties? To what extent is it realistic to expect the remaining superpower to engage in more than tactical multilateralism?

A closely related set of issues concerns the health of intergovernmental institutions. In the post-World War II era, all presidents and their administrations have selectively made use of alliances and intergovernmental institutions in the pursuit of foreign policy goals. To what extent have the wars on terrorism and Iraq damaged international organizations, most notably the United Nations? Conversely, have these wars engendered an enthusiasm for the restructuring or reform of multilateral instruments as a safeguard against the potential excesses of hegemonic states?

We will return to these questions in the final chapter but readers are first invited to appreciate the expertise and insights in the following chapters.

Notes

1 Michael E. Brown, ed., *Grave New World: Challenges in the 21st Century* (Washington, D.C.: Georgetown University Press, 2003), p. ix.
2 For indications of the thinking under way, see two collections coordinated by the Social Science Research Council: Eric Hershberg and Kevin W. Moore, eds., *Critical Views of September 11: Analyses from Around the World* (New York: The New Press, 2002); and Craig Calhoun, Paul Price, and Ashley Timmer, eds., *Understanding September 11* (New York: The New Press, 2002). See also James F. Hoge Jr. and Gideon Rose, eds., *How Did This Happen? Terrorism and the New War* (New York: Public Affairs, 2001).
3 For an overview, see Richard C. Leone and Greg Anrig Jr., eds., *The War on Our Freedoms: Civil Liberties in an Age of Terrorism* (New York: Public Affairs, 2003).
4 Edward C. Luck, *Mixed Messages: American Politics and International Organization 1919–1999* (Washington, D.C.: Brookings, 1999), p. 16. Michael Ignatieff argues that "the very idea that American justice should be brought before the bar of international standards seems, to many Americans, to be impudent, unpatriotic, or irrelevant." In Michael Ignatieff, "The Rights Stuff," *New York Review of Books*, June 13, 2002.
5 See, for example, Philip Shenon, "Report on U.S. Patriot Act Alleges Civil Rights Violations," *New York Times*, July 21, 2003, p. A1.
6 Anne-Marie Slaughter, "Good Reasons for Going around the U.N.," *New York Times*, March 18, 2003, p. A33.

7   Quoted by James Traub, "The Next Resolution," *New York Times Magazine*, April 13, 2003, p. 51.

8   Mary Robinson, "Shaping Globalization: The Role of Human Rights," Fifth Annual Grotius lecture, American Society of International Law, April 2003, Washington, D.C., http://www.eginitiative.org/documents/grotius.html.

9   After careful consideration, the editors eliminated this topic from the volume. While the wars on terrorism and in Iraq are distinct events, they are intimately linked in public and intellectual discourse. Thus focusing only on these two events made for a more cohesive volume. For published overviews by participants in the seminar, see Gay McDougall, "The World Conference Against Racism: Through a Wider Lens," *Fletcher Forum of World Affairs* 26, no. 2 (Summer 2002), pp. 133–49; and J. Michael Turner, "The Road to Durban—and Back," *NACLA Report on the Americas* XXXV (May–June 2002), pp. 31–5. See also "Anti-racism summit ends on a hopeful note: progress amid controversy," *Human Rights Watch World Report 2001* (New York: Human Rights Watch, 2001).

10 Adam Nogourney, "For Democrats Challenging Bush, Ashcroft Is Exhibit A," *New York Times*, July 13, 2003, p. 14.

11 See U.S. Department of Justice, "The September 11 Detainees: A Review of the Treatment of Aliens Held on Immigration Charges in Connection with the Investigation of the September 11 Attacks," April 2003, Office of the Inspector General, http://www.usdoj.gov/oig/special/03-06/index.htm; Eric Lichtblau, "U.S. Report Faults the Roundup of Illegal Immigrants after 9/11," *New York Times*, June 3, 2003, p. A1; Mike Allen, "Former INS Head Warns of Rights Abuses," *Washington Post*, June 15, 2003, p. A12.

12 The House Permanent Select Committee on Intelligence and the Senate Select Committee on Intelligence, *Report of the Joint Inquiry Into the Terrorist Attacks of September 11, 2001*, July 24, 2003, http://news.findlaw.com/hdocs/docs/911rpt/index.html.

13 For a collection of views from around the world, see David M. Malone and Yuen Foong Khong, eds., *Unilateralism and U.S. Foreign Policy: International Perspectives* (Boulder, CO: Lynne Rienner, 2003). For a slightly different take, see Stewart Patrick and Shepard Forman, eds., *Multilateralism and U.S. Foreign Policy* (Boulder, CO: Lynne Rienner, 2002).

14 "Transcript of Press Conference by Secretary-General Kofi Annan at United Nations Headquarters, 30 July 2003," Press Release SG/SM/8803, p. 7.

15 For more, see Thomas G. Weiss, David P. Forsythe, and Roger A. Coate, *The United Nations and Changing World Politics*, 4th edition (Boulder, CO: Westview, 2004), Chapters 5–7.

16 This point is documented in the first two sections. On race, see Michael Banton, *International Action against Discrimination* (Oxford: Clarendon Press, 1996) and *idem*, The *International Politics of Race* (London: Polity Press, 2002).

17 See the argument by Robert Drinan, *The Mobilization of Shame: A World View of Human Rights* (New Haven, CT: Yale University Press, 2001).

18 International Commission on Intervention and State Sovereignty, *The Responsibility to Protect* (Ottawa: ICISS, 2001).

19 Francis M. Deng, *Protecting the Dispossessed: A Challenge for the International Community* (Washington, D.C.: Brookings, 1993); Francis M. Deng et al., *Sovereignty as Responsibility* (Washington, D.C.: Brookings, 1995); and Francis M. Deng, "Frontiers of Sovereignty," *Leiden Journal of International Law* 8, no. 2 (1995), pp. 249–86.

20 Peter Spiro, "The New Sovereigntists: American Exceptionalism and Its False Prophets," *Foreign Affairs* 79, no. 6 (November–December 2002), pp. 9–10.

21 Michael Byers and Georg Nolte, eds., *United States Hegemony and the Foundations of International Law* (Cambridge: Cambridge University Press, 2003).

22 See Michael Ignatieff, *Human Rights as Politics and Idolatry* (Princeton, N.J.: Princeton University Press, 2001), edited with an introduction by Amy Gutman.

23 David Rieff, *A Bed for the Night: Humanitarianism in Crisis* (London: Vintage, 2002), p. 15.
24 For historical overviews and discussions of the current context, see Chantal de Jonge Oudraat, "The role of the Security Council," and M.J. Peterson, "Using the General Assembly," in Jane Boulden and Thomas G. Weiss, eds., *Terrorism and the U.N.: Before and After September 11* (Bloomington, IN: Indiana University Press, 2004), Chapters 7 and 8.
25 Rajan Menon, "The End of Alliances," *World Policy Journal* XX, no. 2 (Summer 2003), pp. 1–20.

Part 1
Framing the debate

1 The interplay of domestic politics, human rights, and U.S. foreign policy

Tom J. Farer

However fine a symbol of cosmopolitan sympathies they may be, human rights are not yet connected in the U.S. electorate's mind to a set of foreign policy guidelines. As a symbol, therefore, they remain available for appropriation by advocates of almost any position. The contributors to this volume share the conviction that it is possible to anticipate, however provisionally, the human rights consequences of today's foreign policy projects and their associated grand strategies. This essay is a nascent effort to clarify the substance, purposes, and sources of the doctrines and strategies that have been competing for dominance over U.S. foreign policy.

During the 12 years between the destruction of the Berlin Wall and the destruction of the World Trade Center on September 11, 2001, the foreign policy of the George H.W. Bush and Bill Clinton administrations lacked an overriding theme, possibly because it lacked an organizing Manichaean focal point. Themes were indeed debated by politicians and commentators, usually in dyadic terms: unilateralism v. multilateralism, humanitarian intervention v. national self-restraint, realism v. idealism, coercive v. persuasive diplomacy, and the West v. the rest. There were also values like human rights and democracy airily invoked but ambiguously and controversially expressed in the quotidian details of policy.

September 11 and the subsequent war on terrorism provide a new, thoroughly Manichaean policy template with implications for domestic as well as foreign affairs. But within that template the existing dyads and values continue to color debate. Should we organize coalitions of the willing or act through the United Nations? Should we ethically sanitize any government that aspires to join the war on our side or seek ideological coherence among our allies? Should we succor failed and failing states or simply quarantine them and deter export of their pathologies? And what restraints should human rights impose on our means? In short, September 11 does not absolve us from dealing with old issues. The context has arguably changed; the traditional divisions within the community of foreign policy analysts and practitioners have not.

The post-Cold War debate over grand strategy

As soon as the Cold War became history, analysts, practitioners, and politicians began debating four grand strategies.[1] One, often labeled "neo-isolationism," called for withdrawal from overseas military commitments and a corresponding reduction in defense expenditures. Its advocates were a curiously mixed crew. There were the libertarians, who championed a minimalist foreign policy that would in turn help make minimalist government possible, and were confident that two oceans, nuclear deterrence, weak neighbors, non-existent competitors for global power, and regional balances of power outside the western hemisphere made minimalism safe, indeed safer to the extent that it discouraged U.S. involvement in other peoples' quarrels.[2] Libertarians are not provincial in their sympathies; they believe that free markets and the U.S. example make the world a better place.

Starting with similar security premises but rather more provincial values, basically the traditional conservative conviction that duties are owed only to members of one's own national tribe, the shrinking band of paleo-conservatives, led by the perpetual presidential candidate Patrick Buchanan, arrived at roughly the same general policy preference.[3] Despite its contrastingly cosmopolitan view of human obligation and sour view of American society, so did the old left (epitomized by Noam Chomsky),[4] driven by the conviction that the structure of social power assures that the U.S. will generally act ungenerously. Thus it joined some odd bedfellows in urging minimal engagement with the rest of the world albeit for the sake of the world.

Selective engagement, the second grand strategy, also had its adherents. While they too were generally sanguine about the U.S.'s long-term security position, they regarded regional power balancing as sufficiently problematic to require monitoring and occasional intervention either to restore or to reinforce local power balances in regions or sub-regions of real importance to the United States. One advocate, the European commentator Josef Joffe, called explicitly for a foreign policy of "offshore balancing."[5]

Since the importance of different regions and sub-regions is likely to vary over time and since reasonable people can and will differ in their perceptions of the need for U.S. intervention to prevent the emergence of regional hegemons, selective engagement invariably slides toward the two other competitors for doctrinal dominance: unilateral and multilateral global engagement. Adherents of these last two had much in common. They believed that developments worldwide can have a serious impact on the security and welfare of the American people and that a relatively benign global political, economic, and military environment requires unremitting involvement. They differed, however, in at least two respects: in the way they prioritized threats and, more importantly, in basic ideas about remedies.

Global unilateralists, like selective engagers, emphasized classical political–military threats, precisely those that are most amenable to mitigation by military power, the resource that the United States possesses in singular abundance.[6]

Global multilateralists, while they would not eliminate, would at least flatten the hierarchy, thus reducing the steep distinction between threats that often yield to coercive diplomacy and threats like pandemics, global warming, destruction of the seas' living resources and the rain forests, and volatility in the global economy that are not amenable to military remediation.[7] Nor, of course, will they yield to any other form of unilateral action.

There is something less here than a simple policy polarity. Specifying a pure example of either the unilateralist or multilateralist is not easy. There is a continuum of attitudes and a tendency for policy-makers to position themselves rhetorically near what they believe the U.S. electorate will perceive as the center. For example, it is virtually a cliché to describe the Bush administration as "unilateralist." Yet when pressed on this point, senior officials reject the designation. They invoke their efforts to construct different coalitions for different tasks.[8] In the war in Iraq they have been at pains to publicize the numbers of cooperating states (including those preferring to remain anonymous) many magnitudes larger than those directly engaged in the fighting.[9] So, they argue, they cannot be categorized as unilateralists; they simply are not in favor of multilateralism for the sake of multilateralism, as one senior official put it in a private meeting or, in the words of another still higher official speaking semi-privately, they are not "lowest-common-denominator" multilateralists.[10]

By comparison, the Clinton administration was widely seen as distinctly multilateralist. The President struggled to secure appropriations from Congress to pay U.N. arrears. He signed global environmental agreements and the treaty establishing an International Criminal Court (ICC). And in the case of Somalia, he antagonized conservatives by placing U.S. troops at least notionally under the direct authority of the U.N. Secretary-General.[11] Yet following the lethal firefight in the streets of Mogadishu, Clinton authorized U.N. Ambassador Madeleine Albright to deliver a lecture at the National War College declaring readiness to use force without reference to or even in defiance of the world organization's Charter. In an address that could as easily have been written by her Reaganite predecessor, Jeane Kirkpatrick, the future Secretary of State remarked that the United States would approach international conflicts on "a case by case basis, relying on diplomacy whenever possible, on force when absolutely necessary."[12]

Although the rhetoric of more-or-less liberal Democratic and of plainly conservative Republican officials often seems indistinguishable insofar as multilateralism is concerned, right-wing commentators perceive a qualitative difference between the real attitudes of themselves and liberals of all stripes. One way of getting at that difference is through an operationally meaningful definition of multilateralism. If it includes everything from ad hoc coalitions of the willing—even if the will be bought or coerced—to world government, in policy terms it means nothing. But if it attaches substantial value to the institutionalization or the "normalization" of cooperation by means of legal rules and intergovernmental bureaucracies, then real differences quickly emerge.[13]

One good indicator of a serious commitment to multilateralism is unintentionally found in Albright's War College speech in which she proposes that the

U.S. should use multilateral institutions only instrumentally. That proposition is deaf to the possibility that one end might be strengthening multilateral institutions precisely because they facilitate cooperation. If institutions are used only when they abjectly serve immediate purposes, we weaken them by implicitly announcing a lack of commitment to cooperation on any terms other than our own. Who needs institutions if our intention is to determine our ends and means independently and then bludgeon others to help shoulder the costs? The test of a serious commitment to multilateralism is willingness to discuss ends and means and to modify them in order to foster cooperation not only in the instant case, but in a multitude of others that will eventually reach the policy agenda.

Unilateralism in historical context

Throughout the Cold War era, a defining characteristic of the right wing in U.S. politics has been hostility to international organizations and the integrally related encumbrance of international law. To the extreme right, international organizations were part of a left-wing if not fully communistic threat to U.S. sovereignty and culture. In recent years the basic hostility, particularly to international institutions but also to international law in its current form, has emerged from provincial fortresses into segments of polite society, acquiring on the way the sophisticated accent of high-gloss policy journals[14] and the leading business newspaper.[15] Of course, unease about foreign entanglement has a venerable historical pedigree, extending back to the generation of the Founding Fathers.[16] Reluctance to take sides in the clashes of the Europeans did not, however, coincide with hostility to international law. After all, the nineteenth-century legal order, premised on the equal right of states large and small to govern their internal affairs, to use oceanic trade routes on the same terms, and to be neutral in relation to the conflicts of third parties, was peculiarly beneficial to weak states. In order to defend its self-perceived rights under international law the new country even fought against Great Britain in the War of 1812.

The sense that legal restraints on the use of national power served national interests did not expire when the U.S. itself joined the club of the powerful at the end of the nineteenth century. On the contrary, the then small foreign policy establishment, manned largely by East Coast bankers and lawyers, became leading advocates of legal restraints on the use of force, clashing fiercely with their German counterparts at The Hague Peace Conferences of 1897 and 1904.[17] Charles Evans Hughes, a Republican and a conservative in the idiom of the time, spearheaded the U.S. effort. While Senator Henry Cabot Lodge played the leading role in blocking U.S. participation in the League of Nations after World War I, overall foreign policy elites sustained the turn-of-the-century commitment to international law during the interwar period.[18] The U.S. prominently backed and signed the Naval Limitation Treaty and the Kellogg–Briand Pact ostensibly outlawing war for purposes other than self-defense, a restraint that went well beyond the language in the League of Nations Covenant.[19]

This tradition of upper-class commitment to international law as a vehicle for advancing national interests reached its apogee during and immediately following World War II with the drafting and ratification of the U.N. Charter, the creation of the Bretton Woods institutions, and the adoption of the Universal Declaration of Human Rights.[20] Nor did it end there. In 1956, when France and the United Kingdom colluded with Israel to invade Egypt, it was the Republican administration of Dwight D. Eisenhower that used the Security Council to declare that, whatever their grievances, the invaders could not seek amelioration through acts of violence incompatible with the Charter of the United Nations.[21]

But even as this was occurring, the split within the Republican Party that would ultimately help restructure the U.S. foreign policy elite was already apparent.[22] Passage of the Republican scepter from Eisenhower to Richard Nixon signaled the beginning of the end of the eastern elite's domination of the Republican Party and American foreign policy. Richard Nixon, who had made his political ascent first by accusing his opponents of ties to international communism and then by leading the Congressional inquiry that would culminate in the perjury conviction of Alger Hiss, opened the party to southerners who had abandoned the Democratic Party when, during Harry Truman's presidency, it had abandoned its tolerance of racial autocracy south of the Mason–Dixon line. In the name of local rights against federal power and of freedom from regulation, Nixon made the Party of Lincoln relatively comfortable for bigots although he did not attempt to roll back the gains of black Americans.[23] In a Republican Party increasingly tilting to the culture and society of the south, the southwest, and the Rocky Mountains, Faulkner's Mississippi Snopes met their Orange County counterparts and found common cause.[24]

Nixon, not unlike Lyndon Johnson, presided over the transition from an eastern-based elite to southern and western populism in league, however unconsciously, with corporate power.[25] But, whatever the cultural emanations and rhetoric, his generally centrist domestic policies and on the whole cautious foreign ones were much more in line with those of northeast Republicanism than the preferences of the right-wing populist forces who were assuming control of the party's base. They had signaled their power in 1964 with Barry Goldwater. Nixon could express their resentments in his self and his language, but not in his policies. For the complete package, or at least what seemed to be the complete package, they had to await Ronald Reagan with his "welfare queens" and "evil empires" and calls for victory in the Cold War in place of the Nixon–Ford–Kissinger experiments with détente.[26] George H.W. Bush was a compromise, the Brahmin gone but not bred south. The grass roots would have to wait for the son who, in migrating with his family to the new heartland of Lincoln's party, had found God and a local culture consistent with what appears to be his personal one.

Right-wing populism and U.S. foreign policy

As competitive symbols, "multilateralism" and "unilateralism" connote more than disagreement about the instrumental value to the national interest of intergovernmental institutions and international law. They suggest the collision of identities and deep cultural attitudes about the use of force, the extent of individual and collective moral responsibilities, the limits of tolerance and the hierarchy of virtue, and faith versus reason. They stand on opposite sides of the abyss that separates fundamentalist from cosmopolitan Protestantism.[27]

Populism is a movement that seeks to mobilize masses among the middle- and lower-middle income peoples.[28] Left populism mobilizes largely on the basis of class resentments stemming from a material inequality. Right populism emphasizes cultural or racial resentments. However, the two can merge where a minority enjoys disproportionate affluence or where a segment of the upper class can be identified with the rebellious struggles of a traditionally despised minority. As the experience of European fascism suggests, right-wing populism normally becomes powerful only when its entrepreneurs can form a strategic alliance with portions of the upper classes, a scenario familiar to every student of Adolf Hitler's rise to power.[29]

We do not, however, need to look abroad. A coalition of the black and white poor at the turn of the twentieth century would have overthrown the system of upper-class rule and working-class poverty. If at that point federal power had been deployed to enforce the black population's constitutional right to vote, such a coalition might have coalesced. Instead, political entrepreneurs in most states mobilized white voters in defense of racial hierarchy and the status quo.[30]

Obviously the uses and character of right-wing populism evolved, so that in the second half of the twentieth century it was far more complex than it had been in the south at the turn of that century. But it retains its inherent character in domestic politics as a political strategy to bond people of modest means with very rich people and corporate managers who, by virtue of possessing great economic power, have material interests that conflict with those of their lower-class partners. There needs to be a cultural bond, an "other" or "others" against whom to relate. In an earlier era, African-Americans and Jews were prominent among the perceived "others."[31] The former still play that role to varying degrees in some parts of the country, although in others they have been largely, if not entirely, phased out. The latter have been almost uniformly released from the realm of the "other" and admitted wholesale to the imagined community of true Americans. If "Jewish bankers" no longer serve as "the other" in the negative pantheon of populism, who has replaced them?

The new "other" has less well-defined features. It is all those who do not respect the national tradition of virile religiosity, who have pushed prayer from the public schools and replaced it with sex education, who sully the immaculate view of U.S. history, who take notice of slums in the City on the Hill, who would take from ordinary citizens their right to bear arms and to dispense Old Testament justice in the form of capital punishment, and who question the proposition that success is a function of virtue not luck.

The "other" is liberal, urbane, financially comfortable, cosmopolitan, secular, and unpatriotic in the sense of being unappreciative of the splendid singularity of America, uneasy with the rituals of patriotism, ready to expend national treasure on behalf of obscure peoples in remote places, and eager to subject national sovereignty to rules made by and institutions run by other peoples, including enemies of the U.S. way of life.[32] Coincidentally, he or she worries about inequality in income and wealth and does not believe that markets are self-policing or can produce all necessary public goods.[33]

Like many caricatures, this clustering and generalizing of characteristics is not wholly unconnected to reality. People who worry about inequality and the environment, who believe in the careful monitoring of private markets by public institutions, who favor restricting matters of faith largely to the private sphere, and who find much to condemn in U.S. history tend also to be the people who favor multilateralism. And they are the people who tend to staff and support the principal human rights nongovernmental organizations (NGOs) and to pressure the U.S. government to use statecraft in defense of human rights around the globe.[34]

The majority resides at multiple points on a continuum between irreducible hostility to every restraint on U.S. power and theological support for the U.N. and the values in its Charter. Otherwise, the national Democratic Party would not have won an election in the last 50 years, or it would be entirely indistinguishable in its platform from the Republicans. Since the 1970s, polling data has regularly provided evidence of a large majority sympathetic to U.S. participation in the U.N. and at least a mild multilateralist orientation.[35] But public opinion is volatile. For months prior to the invasion of Iraq, a majority of Americans favored war only with U.N. approval.[36] By the eve of the invasion, the majority endorsed invasion irrespective of a legitimizing resolution.[37]

In a political system with multiple points for the insertion of influence, where money is trumps and legislative power widely dispersed, impassioned minorities can often defeat a diffuse majority's mild policy preferences. To understand how the character of domestic politics can influence the outcome of policy conflicts within the foreign policy elite over multilateral versus unilateral engagement, one therefore needs to recognize the political importance of the minority that understands itself as the conservators of traditional values and the opposite of the cosmopolitan "other." It is naturally sympathetic to foreign policy arguments couched in Manichaean terms, dismissive of the views of other countries, and in favor of coercive diplomacy.[38] It is, however, important to recall that those who form the populist right wing have not traditionally favored overseas adventures. Like the majority of Americans in the 1930s, they could not be aroused to support preventive action against Hitler or the Japanese until the attack on Pearl Harbor and Germany's ensuing declaration of war.[39] Certainly in the past their instincts and general convictions would seem to have placed them in the paleo-conservative more than the global engagers' camp.

There is a second caveat when trying to assess the domestic political arena in which advocates of multilateral policies compete with unilateralists. Some of the convictions that resonate powerfully with the populist right also engage more cosmopolitan types. The "City on the Hill" is an image that precedes by two centuries the country's founding and has never been restricted to provincial constituencies.[40] Many Americans far removed from the Moral Majority also are receptive to the view that there are evil people who understand only the language of force and who mean to do us harm for crimes of which we are innocent or for acts which in our judgment are not crimes at all.

Certain enduring features of our history and society help to illuminate the struggle between elites over how the United States should engage globally. One is religiosity. Periodic surveys of the intensity of religious sentiment in the main industrial democracies reveal a continuum, with the U.S. almost alone at one end and Japan at the other with European states much closer to Japan.[41] Intense monotheistic religious beliefs predispose adherents to see the world in stark Manichaean terms. The Calvinist version of Christianity, the country's dominant monotheism, which deeply insinuated itself into U.S. culture at the very outset of our national adventure, predisposes adherents to see success, national as well as personal, as a sign of divine will.[42]

A second key background feature is the failure of the working and intellectual classes to bond ideologically.[43] Christian democracy, with its natural cosmopolitanism and communitarianism, as well as its emphasis on responsibility of the successful for the poor of the community, also failed to take root here. The language of reform has been liberalism with its emphasis on restraining power for the benefit of the striving meritorious individual.

The third background feature, the constitutional culture, reinforces a cultural emphasis on the individual's rights and a suspicion of governmental power except where it is employed in the name of national security against other, less morally inspired communities.[44] The constitutional culture has provided a core sense of national identity just as intense, and hence potent, as the sense of being a blood community, literally an extended family, which is characteristic of strongly nationalistic states.

A fourth background feature, intimately connected to the ones enumerated, is the ideological supremacy of *laissez-faire* capitalism. The mental soil of the U.S. is far more receptive than its European counterpart to a politics of either isolation or episodic self-assertion in foreign policy and acquisitive individualism in the domestic realm. At the same time, the U.S. is less receptive to a cosmopolitan foreign policy and a domestic one that champions greater equality of results or special benefits for historically disadvantaged groups.[45] In politics, therefore, liberal cosmopolitans swim a bit against the tide, and their projects are in general limited by a need to use the dominant discourse to overcome cultural resistance.

This account of the cultural and ideological background of contemporary U.S. politics simplifies a more complex or ambiguous reality, certainly in comparison with Europe before World War II. Prewar European conservatism, at least on the continent, was hierarchical in its view of the good society, qualified in its commitment to majority rule, and racially and ethnically intolerant.[46] It valued faith and tradition over utilitarian reason and extolled the interests of the state in foreign policy, regarding war, therefore, as an inevitable instrument of statecraft, and imperialism as the natural condition of the world.[47] Whatever their differences, reformist liberals and social democrats were largely united in rejecting everything that conservatives affirmed. In the wake of World War II, the right cut loose from its ideological moorings and moved toward the center where it now encounters a left with whom it largely shares a rational, secular, cosmopolitan, and moderately communitarian outlook.[48]

Since the defeat of the South in the Civil War, the division between left and right never has had the same clarity in the U.S. that marked prewar Europe. Liberal individualism has been the principal normative idiom of the political leaders of both major parties.[49] Each has evoked utilitarian instrumentalism to defend its favored domestic policies and has defended foreign policy with a mix of idealism and national self-interest. To be sure, the wealthy did in general resist virulently the effort to soften the rough edges of corporate capitalism and to provide a modest amount of income security for the white working class.[50] But when, after 20 years of Democratic rule, the Republicans again captured the White House in 1952, the party made its peace with the regulatory and social security structures erected during the era of reform. And so on the eve of war in Vietnam, sociologist Daniel Bell pointed to the end of ideological conflict in the U.S. and the Western world more generally.[51] What remained were technocratic differences of opinion over incremental adjustments in a consensus-based, moderately regulated capitalist economy.

But that view was a bit myopic. A convergence took place within the political, social, and economic elite and in presidential behavior, since presidents had to appeal to and at least appear to come from the broad centrist majority. But Bell saw fuzzily, if at all, the half-slumbering conservative minority and the substratum of conservative feeling that had varying degrees of resonance in the wider electorate. This view ignored power sources that could be activated by contingent events and tectonic adjustments in social and economic conditions and then employed by ambitious political entrepreneurs in the name of defending authentic U.S. values against the "other." Vietnam was the main event, a war not of destiny but of choice. The accelerating struggle for African-American civil rights had more the character of a tectonic adjustment to accelerating pressure in deep societal structures.

The coincidence of a sanguinary war of choice and a predestined struggle by a substantial minority to complete its emancipation helped precipitate a decade of disorder and polarization. They were not, however, the only factors at work. Economic growth and changes in the location and composition of industrial and commercial activity and corresponding changes in transportation networks and planning policies were driving internal migration from small rural communities to sprawling suburbs. Hence people with traditional religious and moral views and uncomplicated iconographic appreciation of the U.S. past encountered public-school systems staffed on the whole by persons with more secular, morally permissive, and iconoclastic world views.[52] Decisions of the federal courts in favor of strict separation of church and state in education, as in the public sector more generally, also were disturbing.[53]

The long-growing strength of secular and utilitarian views in the broader society and a coincident relaxation of traditional moral perspectives undoubtedly were accelerated by the breakup of traditional families and communities and the vast expansion of higher education after World War II. The Supreme Court's decision in *Rowe v. Wade* and the gradual extension of the civil rights movement to include homosexuals further aggravated the traditionalists' sense of being under siege.

Meanwhile, parts of the population with relatively more relaxed views about morality and culture had their own sources of angst. One was the disorder in the universities that occasionally spread into the streets with its quasi-revolutionary rhetoric. A second was the integration of public schools. And a third was the spread of violent crime beyond its traditional locus in the precincts of the poor.

The rise of neo-conservatism

The wider electorate sets limits to and is arguably the ultimate arbiter of disputes among insiders over foreign policy issues, but it does not define them. In all countries that is the work of a relative few. And while—at least in a democratic country—that few has a more or less vital connection to the wider society, elites have their own histories.

In the face of the near-insurrectionist style of some student protests and the rise and spread of anomic social violence, the bulk of the intellectual class remained liberal-to-social democratic in its politics. But under the flag of "neo-conservatism," a minority seceded.[54] They were alienated by what struck them as an acute threat to traditional liberal politics—incrementalism, compromise, and technocratic reform. A credible if wildly exaggerated assault on liberal values traditionally construed was not, however, the only factor encouraging ideological secession from the main body of the intellectual class. Within that class there were fault lines dating from the early Cold War. For most of the century intellectuals had had a distinctly leftist tilt in comparison to the rest of U.S. society.[55] By the 1960s, however, the affluence and individual freedom manifest in the developed capitalist states in contrast to the disjunction between Marxist visions and reality in the Soviet Union had persuaded many intellectuals that the Soviet dystopia stemmed not from the peculiarities of Russian history or the accident of bad leaders but rather from the very nature of the sociopolitical model implicit in Marxism and actualized in the Leninism practiced by states.[56]

What followed among that cluster of leftists moving right was a corresponding embrace of capitalist development and generalized hostility not only to Marxist regimes but to movements that identified themselves as Marxist in their inspiration, or advocated a state-dominated economy, or received assistance from Marxist regimes. They became, in short, enemies of revolutionary movements in principle, as most famously articulated by Jeane Kirkpatrick.[57] Revolutionary regimes were totalitarian in principle and thus could not evolve in a democratic direction, while authoritarian governments of the right did have a democratic potential. By contrast, the bulk of liberal-to-leftist intellectuals felt that in developing countries with extreme and embedded inequalities sustained by remorseless repression, virtually any movement that challenged the status quo was worthy of conditional encouragement. Moreover, the popular mobilization encouraged by revolutionary movements and, following their victory, a radical change in property relationships carried out by a strong state were necessary preconditions for the evolution of freer and fairer societies.

Ethnic identities and interests also played a role in the emergence of neo-conservatism, helping to crystallize divisions over foreign and domestic policy. Americans of Jewish extraction had played (as they continue to play) a prominent role in every dimension of the country's intellectual and artistic life and also in the struggle for civil rights and civil liberties. In domestic conflicts, Jews and African-Americans were the main elements of the coalition battling to complete the emancipation announced almost a century earlier, and provided many of its leaders.[58] Civil rights legislation had demolished the formal and also the most palpable de facto barriers to upward social movement. The victory of the civil rights coalition opened doors through which the talented and well-prepared could pass. That high percentage of the Jewish minority that was university educated or already in the middle-to-upper classes surged through. African-American university graduates also benefited, but a large number could not get through the newly opened doors or could do so only with some form of assistance.[59] For many, poverty replaced race as the principal barrier to social mobility.

One result for relations between Jews and African-Americans was erosion of the common interests which, along with liberal values, had bonded their coalition. Many African-American leaders, accurately invoking a historical experience comparable in its trauma only to that of Native Americans, began calling for affirmative action by the state and by large private entities like corporations and universities to shrink the existing barriers and to compensate for the traumatic legacy.[60] Affirmative action could take quite a variety of forms but, to the extent that it was construed to mean race-based preferential access to jobs and opportunities like seats in selective universities or positions in public service and the professions, it jammed up against the interests of those ethnic groups, like Jews, who had broken discriminatory barriers in part by excelling in the tests of merit devised by the old White Anglo-Saxon Protestant (WASP) majority. Despite this emerging conflict, many Jewish intellectuals supported affirmative action. But for some among them, it contributed to the confluence of events and issues pushing them to the right.[61]

Perhaps hastening that move was a coincident movement within a part of the African-American community of what is sometimes called "nationalism," a felt need to assert a distinctive identity and to build ethnically homogeneous social and political action organizations. At one point, a small minority within one of the established civil rights organizations—the Student Nonviolence Coordination Committee (SNCC)— even considered the exclusion of whites, which to a considerable extent meant excluding Jews.[62] For some Jews who had seen themselves as champions of black interests, the increased edginess in relations between the two groups and more generally between black and white liberals was disillusioning.[63]

Two other developments encouraged the rightward float of a portion of the Jewish intelligentsia. One was increasing friction between the communities at their socioeconomic bases.[64] The second was growing identification of the African-American intelligentsia with the views and interests of the Third World, particularly with respect to the issue of "national liberation" for the peoples who had been colonized.[65] By the 1970s most colonial territories had become sovereign states and U.N. members. The refusal by the U.S. and a number of its European allies to reduce their economic relations with South Africa, and a U.S. style of diplomacy that seemed dismissive of the Third World generally,[66] led to polarization at the world organization.

One notorious outcome was 1975 General Assembly Resolution 3379 equating Zionism with racism. U.S. Permanent Representative Patrick Moynihan voiced the outrage of the U.S. Jewish community (and, to be sure, many others)[67] and committed himself to confronting the Third World on this and every other issue construed as inimical to U.S. interests and values, a position that added to the polarization at the U.N. and would later help catapult him into the Senate.[68]

Hostility by the Third World majority in the General Assembly to Israeli policy or, as many saw it, to Israel itself and to U.S. interests and values more generally induced a reciprocal hostility toward the U.N. that spread beyond the confines of the far right. It became one of the distinguishing features of neoconservatives and further distanced them from African-American leaders.[69] The latter did not endorse the Zionism-as-racism position, but at least some could not help feeling a certain sense of identity with Palestinians living without political rights and without even well-protected civil rights in the territories occupied by Israel in 1967.[70] They naturally sympathized with whomever sought to overturn white racist rule in South Africa, and felt some affinity with those demanding a fairer economic deal for poor countries and some form of redress for past exploitation.[71] A General Assembly in which African states formed the largest bloc meant that the African-American intelligentsia could not in general share the hostility toward the U.N. present among their conservative Jewish counterparts, particularly among those moving right for other reasons as well.

In addition, there were two other exacerbating factors specifically related to events in the Middle East. One stemmed from choices Israel made following its victory in the 1967 war. The government took the fateful decision to annex east Jerusalem, the Gaza Strip and the West Bank as well as to suppress political activities in other territories and to begin planting Jewish settlements in them.[72] The seemingly permanent denial of political and many civil rights to the population of these territories was so in conflict with liberal democratic values that it was bound to threaten the hitherto broad base of support for Israel among liberal elites in the West.

The 1973 war also helped, however indirectly, to shape the neo-conservative project. After the easy triumph of 1967, the early days of the 1973 war were frightening as Israeli forces suffered serious casualties and ultimately needed rapid resupply from the United States. Although the war ended in another defeat for the Arabs, it restored the sense of vulnerability that the triumph of 1967 had sharply reduced. In addition, the unprecedented show of Arab unity in withholding oil from the market, not solely to benefit oil-producing states but also to advance political ends, conveyed a message of Israeli and Western vulnerability. Was there not a danger of Western countries forcing Israel to accommodate Arab demands, if the backing for Israel was only sentimental or moral? However, if Israel could appear as a strategic partner, a protector of Western or at least U.S. interests in the Middle East, Israel would be safer. Is it merely coincidental that emphasis on Israel's strategic value and disparagement of Arab regimes is a prominent feature of the neo-conservative canon?

Traditional conservative realists and neo-conservatives: conflict and reconciliation

Henry Kissinger and James Baker—foreign policy stalwarts in the administrations of Richard Nixon, Gerald Ford, Ronald Reagan, and George H.W. Bush —epitomize the realist conservative. For them, the purpose of statecraft is to advance U.S. power and protect material interests in a dangerously competitive and structurally anarchic world; the promotion of democracy and the defense of human rights is incidental.[73] One result of this world view is a readiness to strike deals with regimes seemingly of any ideological stripe or level of brutality in the treatment of their own people so long as those deals appear to advance national interests. Another is a certain measure of restraint in the exercise of power because the United States should not slay dragons that have no capacity or incentive to threaten either the country or its allies.[74]

Jeane Kirkpatrick, Ronald Reagan's first Ambassador to the United Nations, and Elliot Abrams, who became Assistant Secretary of State for human rights and humanitarian affairs early in the Reagan administration, epitomize the foreign policy views of neo-conservatives. For them, the realpolitik statecraft of Kissinger and Baker is too limited in its goals and too restrained in its means. The United States, for them, is not simply a great power but also a cluster of ideals. And by a marvelous, even divine, coincidence, pursuit of those ideals can only enhance the country's power, wealth, and security. In praising Reagan as the defender of liberal values, Kirkpatrick enunciated the core vision of the neo-conservative.[75]

"Liberal" was not, however, a description that Reagan's first Secretary of State, General Alexander Haig, would have welcomed. Underscoring the differences between the defeated Democratic administration of Jimmy Carter and Reagan's, Haig announced that human rights was off the agenda.[76] Suiting deed to word, he purged from the diplomatic corps those ambassadors most closely identified with Carter's human rights policies.

This remained the declared position of the administration until, still early in his first term, President Reagan accepted Secretary of State Haig's resignation. Shortly thereafter, Elliot Abrams became Assistant Secretary. His accession roughly coincided with a sea change in administration rhetoric. Until Haig left, there was dissonance between the Reaganite characterization of the relationship with the Soviet Union—a struggle between the free world and the "evil empire"—and hostility to Carter's human rights legacy. After Haig, the rhetoric segued into harmony by equating the defense of human rights with the promotion of democracy defined narrowly in terms of elections that were not grossly fraudulent.[77] This was a conspicuous departure from Carter administration policy that had been deeply concerned with torture and summary execution in the Third World even when perpetrated by such dependable U.S. clients as right-wing military governments in Latin America.[78]

The post-Haig State Department responded by minimizing, denying, or rationalizing delinquencies and urging elections while opposing negotiated power-sharing arrangements in cases where massive human rights violations were entangled with civil wars between military governments and left-wing guerrillas.[79] Thus policy incorporated the view announced by Kirkpatrick before the administration assumed office, namely a categorical hostility to regimes and movements of the left.

After Haig's departure, latent tensions between realists and neo-conservatives rarely surfaced conspicuously. Whatever the differences in motives—between the conservative aim of maintaining unchallenged U.S. hegemony in the western hemisphere and the additional neo-conservative one of maintaining ideological purity by pulverizing left-wing authoritarian regimes—both supported ruthless right-wing regimes in El Salvador and Guatemala and efforts to overthrow a leftist one in Nicaragua. Conflicts over relations with Moscow lost their edge once Mikhail Gorbachev assumed office and initiated multi-faceted policies that would, with astonishing speed, liquidate Moscow's empire and then the Soviet Union itself. But once George H.W. Bush took office and put James Baker in charge of foreign policy, discord re-emerged, particularly over the failure to use the occasion of the first Gulf war to eliminate Saddam Hussein and to engineer a viable settlement of the Arab–Israeli dispute.[80] Modest pressure on Israel for concessions to Palestinian nationalism, including for the first time in years a hint of material sanctions, evoked a furious assault from neo-conservatives even to the point of implying that Baker was a hidden anti-Semite.[81]

Beyond factional conflict over particular issues lay the broader difference of world views. In a seminal statement of neo-conservative goals for the post-Cold War era, Charles Krauthammer caught the policy community's eye with an article calling for full exploitation of the "unipolar moment."[82] Concretely the U.S. was to employ its unrivaled power to shape a world reflective of American values, elected governments, and free markets. Neither the cautious democracy-promoting efforts of realists nor their strategy of positive engagement with the nominally communist regime in China came close to satisfying this vision. And so the neo-conservatives noisily nursed their dissatisfactions, seemingly as disappointed as right-wing Christian groups with an administration so plainly indifferent to the excited ambitions and cultural sensibilities of both factions.[83]

Whatever their sour disappointment with the first President Bush, it was as nothing to the fury and contempt evoked by William Jefferson Clinton, the incarnation of the detested countercultural life-style, and his First Lady, a feminist icon. Hardly friends of Clinton's easy virtue and broad tolerance, the neo-conservatives were even more enraged by the dissipation of U.S. opportunity and power. Realist conservatives could make common cause with neo-conservatives and the religious right, their sometime allies in the broad conservative coalition, because they disliked Clinton's stance on humanitarian intervention and state-building.

To the limited extent that the 2000 presidential campaign debates engaged foreign policy, George W. Bush sounded the themes of the realists. On his watch, U.S. troops would be used as soldiers, not as humanitarian handholders.[84] He would not waste the U.S.'s human and material resources on errant adventures in nation-building or to rescue feckless peoples. Asked what he would have done had he been faced with the Rwandan genocide, he replied that he would have encouraged U.N. action but not sent U.S. troops.[85] Presumably to propitiate the Jesse Helms wing of his own party, he also criticized placing American forces under U.N. command, as had happened briefly in Somalia, a position Clinton himself seemed to have adopted after October 1993.[86] Beyond that, Bush actually mirrored Clinton by deploring his father's accommodationist behavior toward China and intimated that he would shift to a much cooler tone.[87] In brief, nothing in the rhetoric of George W. Bush's campaign or in his selection of two apparently realist conservatives, Colin Powell and Condoleezza Rice, to be his top foreign policy advisers augured a major change in foreign policy. Still, given the number of neo-conservatives who were slated for important posts, the role of the Christian right (now in close alliance with the neo-conservatives), the volatility of the Middle East, and the existence of Al Qaeda with its expressed determination to drive the U.S. out of the Middle East, it would not have taken clairvoyance to imagine circumstances that would open the door for a quite dramatic policy departure.

From the inauguration in January 2001 until September 11, 2001, the Bush administration complied roughly with the expectations that the President had cultivated while he was a candidate. Even his curt dismissals of U.S. participation in international treaty regimes like Kyoto, the ICC, and the supplemental enforcement protocol to the Biological Weapons Convention were hardly at odds with his general approach to national security policy. Then the attacks on the World Trade Center and the Pentagon opened a world of risk previously envisioned only by some of the national security cognoscenti. Neo-conservatives alone had a grand strategy of response, one that in its very ambition and vision corresponded to the shock and fury of the U.S. public and to its congenital sense that wars should end in glorious, transformative victory.

The neo-conservative project

Hegemony, as neo-conservatives argued in the 1990s, is not the mere possession of dominating power, but also the will to use it on behalf of a coherent project. In the Clinton years, hegemony was only latent. The catastrophe of September 2001 created the circumstances in which it could be made real.

Although there is not a single comprehensive statement of the neo-conservative project and its premises, out of the particular policies advocated by its high priests and house organs, as well as the thicket of argument surrounding them, project and premises materialize.[88] Having won the Third World War, conventionally called the "Cold War" although it had many hot incidents, we are now by dint of circumstance launched into a fourth. Like the second and third ones, it stems from a conflict of values and not of mere interests. It is a war between believers in free peoples and markets, on the one hand, and infidels, on the other; it is a war between democratic capitalism and its enemies. The former is expanding, not at the end of a bayonet but in response to the desire of people everywhere to receive it or at least its blessings. It expands, in other words, by pull and not push. And that expansion is coterminous with the expansion of individual freedom.

The expansion coincidentally threatens, where it does not immediately demolish, the practices, beliefs, and institutions that thrive only where freedom is alien and can be made to remain so. As the financial and cultural base of the expansion (sometimes labeled "globalization"), the U.S. is the inevitable target for all those who, being threatened, resist. And since globalization is not a public policy but the summation of millions of private initiatives, the U.S. government cannot erase the bull's-eye from the nation's flank by any policy other than attempting to remake the country in the image of its enemies, a closed society. For political reasons, the government could not do that; for moral ones, it should not try even if the political obstacles were to diminish.

So war is our fate. A conventional war would be a minor affair for a country with such military power. But in the epoch of globalization, we must contend with asymmetrical war. Since the enemies of the open society cannot stand up to our armies, they turn to such soft targets as civilians and the infrastructure that supports them. Here our enemies find vast vulnerabilities springing from the very nature of our open society and the delicate systems of communication and movement and energy generation that sustain quotidian life. The destruction of the World Trade Center illustrated the lethal potential of asymmetrical war even when waged without benefit of weapons of mass destruction. With unconventional weapons in the mix, images of unspeakable catastrophe are summoned.

As the U.S. is the center of expanding liberal capitalist democracy, the Islamic world, particularly its Arab sector, is the center of violent opposition precisely because the dynamism, pluralism, and instrumental rationalism of liberal capitalism challenge deeply rooted social arrangements. And this challenge occurs against a backdrop of nearly a millennium of armed conflict between the West and the various Islamic polities on the southern side of the Mediterranean and, in recent centuries, a succession of devastating military defeats and political humiliations for the latter. Added to this dangerous mix is a strain of sacrificial violence in contemporary, if not original, Islamic thought which leads to the suicide bomber.

What, then, is to be done? A first step is to seek out and destroy immediate threats and demonstrate that U.S. power is now driven by an implacable will and a universal capacity to revenge every injury by inflicting greater ones. Being hated is not good; being hated without being at the same time feared is far worse. In destroying the Taliban regime and killing or incarcerating various Al Qaeda members, the first step was taken. Going after Saddam Hussein also has had demonstrative value. For the Taliban were barely a regime, virtually unrecognized and not fully in control of the country they misruled. Destroying the long-established regime in Baghdad, one not credibly connected to September 11, was a dramatic expansion of the anti-terrorist project, calculated to be a qualitatively more potent demonstration of Washington's will and power.

If one is to take neo-conservatives at their word, however, the overthrow of Saddam Hussein also created the conditions for installing a capitalist democracy in the once most formidable and technologically advanced country in the Arab world.[89] This too would be done in part for its hopefully contagious effects on the surrounding Arab states. This hope flows from a key, if not always clearly declared, premise of neo-conservative grand strategy: given the opportunity, ordinary people will prove to be *Homo economicus*, rational maximizers of their material well-being. To serve its interests and theirs, the United States should provide the opportunity, as it provides the quintessential model: strict limits on state power, the rule of law including transparency of the public realm, an independent judiciary, extensive rights to private property associated with constitutional limits on the confiscatory power of the state, and free elections to sustain the rest.

The individual, being protected from depredations of the state, is thereby liberated to pursue material well-being. The ethic of consumption will trump all other ends. An electorate of economic strivers will disown projects that conscript their wealth; they will find dignity and meaning in the struggle to produce and sufficient pleasure in the satisfaction of their appetites. That is why liberal democracies do not war with each other. To be sure, fanatics immune to the ethic of material consumption will not altogether disappear. But they will no longer be able to multiply themselves so easily. And liberal democratic governments, driven by the coercive power of elections to mirror the interests of their electors, will cooperate with the U.S. to extirpate fanatics.

Neo-conservatives do not rely exclusively on a contagion of democracy springing from the demonstration factor of Iraq. The evidence of freedom, peace, and affluence in Iraq will weaken from within the stagnant autocracies of surrounding Arab states like Syria and Saudi Arabia. Meanwhile the U.S., with as many of its industrialized allies as it can muster, will encourage them with positive and negative incentives to manage a transition to open societies for the benefit of the Arab people in general and for ours. And for Israel's too because citizens of open societies will no longer have grounds to rage at their fate—rage which today's Arab governments deflect to Israel first and then to the United States.[90]

After September 11's demonstration of U.S. vulnerability to asymmetrical warfare, this vision, to the extent that it is credible, could draw support from traditional conservatives concerned primarily with maximizing the country's security and wealth, as well as those who *a priori* equate U.S. and Israeli security interests. Should it not appeal as well to human rights activists and to the wider universe of liberals and social democrats? Can one believe in the universality of human rights and not embrace a strategy that purports to merge realism and idealism in the cause of freedom? Apparently so. Most of the established organs and prominent advocates of liberalism and social democracy and most of the leading figures and institutions in the international human rights world have reacted along a spectrum ranging from intense skepticism through selective criticism to comprehensive hostility toward the Bush administration's grand strategy.[91]

Grounds for doubt: a human rights perspective

Is the skepticism a merely visceral response to the conservative messenger? Or are there reasoned grounds, rooted in liberal values and the deep essence of human rights, for rejecting this message? Actually, taking the messenger's identity into account is entirely reasonable, part of the seasoned wisdom of everyday life. We do not entrust things that we value except to persons who have created grounds for trust. And there are essentially two reasons why we trust people. One is that they have a record of fulfilling their commitments, and the other is that we have common values. The latter is particularly important when the mission we are called upon to entrust to the messenger has as its very purpose the advancement of our values.

If our end is the broader realization of human rights, there are substantial reasons to distrust the right-wing executors of contemporary foreign policy. The first is that they are what they claim to be, namely conservatives. One of the defining characteristics of conservative American elites is hostility to the use of government to moderate inequality both by positive measures and by restraining the rich from leveraging their social and economic advantages in order to augment them. Thus they are ideologically disabled from pressing for exactly the kinds of change required in most developing countries to lend substance to democratic forms and to create societies in which human rights can advance. Ideological choices, like conceptions of the national interest, are not accidental. They are related to a core sensibility, to one's capacity or incapacity to experience vicariously the agony of ordinary people in far-off places. They relate, in other words, to the breadth of one's moral imagination. As noted above, when George W. Bush sought the presidency, he disowned use of the coercive power of the U.S. where the only potential gain in a given case would be protection of human rights. This was also the position of his national security adviser.[92] Moreover, his Secretary of Defense had served as special envoy to Saddam Hussein when the U.S. was assisting the monster in his frantic attempts to prevent his aggression against Iran from turning into a military debacle.[93] During this period Saddam Hussein employed chemical weapons against both the Iranians and the Kurdish population of Iraq without in any way compromising Washington's support for his regime.

Many senior members of the current administration served in the earlier Bush administration when it stood idly by as Yugoslavia disintegrated and Serbia initiated mayhem in Croatia and Bosnia. To be fair, they do not have more to answer for morally than the Clinton administration, which also wrung its hands as Slobodan Milošević and his colleagues murdered their way around the Balkans and as Rwanda's slow-motion genocide took place.[94] But Clinton never promised us a no-holds-barred crusade for liberal democracy and did not ask the country to entrust him with wartime power to spread the American Way.[95]

One could, moreover, argue that, if we are going to ground skepticism on past words and performance, we need to disaggregate realist conservatives like Rumsfeld and Rice from neo-conservatives like Deputy Secretary of Defense Paul Wolfowitz or the National Security Council's Elliot Abrams, or pundits like Charles Krauthammer.[96] Even if it is hard to credit the traditionalists with an epiphany in September 2001, have the neo-conservatives not been at least rhetorically consistent? Indeed, is not a declared commitment to Wilsonianism with fixed bayonets a defining feature of neo-conservatism?[97] Thus the problem seems less one of the messenger's sincerity than it is of the humanitarian implications of the message itself.

A crusade for democracy, even full-blown liberal democracy, overlaps but is not synonymous with a crusade for human rights. Moral criteria for evaluating the exercise of power stretch into the remote past.[98] So does the idea of possessing rights in relationship to power holders. But the idea of rights held in common not just by all members of the same class, profession, guild, race, religion, or nation, but by every human being simply by virtue of being human, is a modern idea. And just as it is not synonymous with liberal democracy, it is not synonymous with general human welfare.

A common conception of human rights is that they are categorical claims on human beings and institutions, primarily on governments to act or refrain from acting in ways injurious to the exercise or experience of the right.[99] At least the so-called first generation of civil and political rights that have evoked the widest consensus about their imperative quality are focused on the individual, not the wider community. More than that, they are claims that the community cannot trump or be subordinate to some presumed general good which, while causing injury to a few, enhances the welfare of the many.

Actually, even in the case of civil and political rights, this is something of an overstatement in the sense that during periods of emergency the community for its collective welfare can temporarily suspend the great majority of rights.[100]

Many national constitutions so provide, as does the International Covenant on Civil and Political Rights.[101] But some rights cannot be abrogated under any circumstances. Among them are the right to life, not to be tortured, and not to be punished except as a result of a finding of guilt after a fair legal process.[102] It is conceivable that a good-faith effort to implant liberal democracy throughout the Middle East and in other areas where it is largely absent, an effort carried out in part by war, armed subversion, assassination, and other instruments of coercive statecraft, might in the long course of history enhance human well-being beyond anything that could be achieved through such nonviolent means as education, economic incentives, financial and technical assistance to democratic movements, and improving the welfare consequences of democracy so as to increase its attractions.

But even if we could be certain that human welfare would in the long term be better served by violent statecraft, if one were committed to the view that human rights are trumps, then one might still oppose a crusade for democracy. Taking of innocent lives is among the probable features of a violent crusade for whatever end. One particularly awful instance occurred during the invasion of Iraq, when a missile flying off course struck an apartment complex, wiping out a child's immediate family, ripping off his arms, and crisping his body.[103] Since civilians were not targeted—on the contrary it appears that the U.S. military made an unusual effort to minimize civilian casualties[104]—this child's horror was entirely within the boundaries of the humanitarian laws of war.[105] Moreover, given the Security Council resolutions violated by Saddam's regime, its chronic violations of human rights, and the loss of life arising from Iraq's aggressions against Iran and Kuwait, a not entirely implausible just-war argument could be made in favor of the U.S.-led invasion.[106] That being so, the just-war tradition would absolve the U.S. and its allies from guilt with regard to civilian deaths and injuries, since serious efforts were made to avoid them.

Nevertheless, pain and death inflicted predictably, albeit unintentionally, on the innocent rubs against the grain of human rights in any war of choice rather than self-defense. And that would be the case whether the choice is made for the purpose of preserving U.S. freedom of action or extending the incidence of democracy. Human rights concerns were a secondary justification for the invasion of Iraq. The Bush administration defended it primarily on the grounds of national security and of legitimate enforcement of Security Council resolutions.[107] Hence the occupation of Iraq may well not herald further wars against authoritarian regimes. But nothing in the premises and values of neo-conservatism precludes them. And the ease with which Iraq fell may encourage them. Neo-conservatives are prepared to make war not simply for the immediate purpose of installing elected governments, but also for the more general one of maintaining U.S. hegemony indefinitely as is now enshrined in the National Security Strategy of September 2002.[108] A hegemonic United States will assure, or is at least the best means of assuring, the long-term triumph of liberal democracy and hence the greater good of humanity.[109] Of course, for traditional conservatives, hegemony needs no justification beyond the influence and wealth and presumably the security brought to one's own country. For them the tribal good does not have to be wrapped in the politically correct colors of the general good.

Is there any tension between the traditional realist and the neo-conservative world views? And if there is, should those who define the good in terms of the more effective defense and promotion of human rights prefer the triumph of the traditionalists or the crusaders? Prominent traditionalists like Henry Kissinger and Brent Scowcroft either supported without enthusiasm or opposed the Iraq war.[110] So did some of their ideological brethren in academia.[111]

In a state that for good reason feels the tide of history running against it, a state that feels geopolitically insecure, as Germany did when it ignited World Wars I and II, realists may be risk takers.[112] And few risks are consistently greater than the risk of war. But in a country like the United States—wealthy, cohesive, and without any rival in sight—realism generally operates as a restraint on military adventures.

The one thing certain about armed intervention is the death and mutilation of the innocent.[113] Because the core human rights are imperative claims by individuals not open to trumping by some supposed long-term general good, a crusade to defend them has built-in restraints that a crusade for the general expansion of democracy does not. In the former case, we are constrained at least to balance the lives hopefully saved against those we will take in order to save them. But if democracy alone is the end, then as long as we are confident that some will survive to hold free and fair elections what could matter more than the lives of our own troops? This may seem like an unfair *reductio ad absurdum*, carrying the logic of the neo-conservatives' position beyond the point that most of them would probably go. Yet, in fact, it is grounded in experience such as Central America in the 1980s.[114]

Conclusion

The greatest humanitarian risk from the neo-conservatives' tendency to discount the particulars of collateral damage in favor of the general goal of promoting democracy may lie in Asia rather than the Middle East. China, with its authoritarian government and 1.25 billion people, is a natural target for their zeal. Anyone who cares for human rights hopes to see China evolve into a state where rotation in office achieved through fair elections at all levels of government helps to make elites accountable and to widen the scope of personal freedom. The progressive dismantling of Maoist structures since 1979 and the corresponding growth of a market economy open to foreign investment and transnational cultural forces have already effected both a measure of personal liberation and a remarkable reduction in poverty.[115]

Whether the further openness to transnational economic forces implied by China's accession to the World Trade Organization will lead eventually to some form of political pluralism and effective constitutionalization of civil liberties remains to be seen.[116] For most of the twentieth century, it was zealots identified with or invoked by the Republican Party who claimed a virtual coincidence of free markets and free people;[117] liberals and social democrats had their doubts that the latter followed necessarily from the former. These days the doubt seems more intense among various factions of the right within the U.S. policy spectrum. Politicized Christian fundamentalists, the neo-conservatives' erstwhile allies within the Party, have ardently opposed normalization of trade relationships with China and seem committed to a strategy of confrontation.[118] Writers and journals in or on the fringe of neo-conservatism tend to disparage the views that China is moving toward human freedom and can become a useful participant in the processes of decentralized global governance.

Organizations like Human Rights Watch have consistently exposed human rights violations in China as elsewhere.[119] That those violations are serious and should be part of the diplomatic discourse between Beijing and Washington is not in dispute among rightists and human rights advocates. However, persons in the human rights community and centrists and liberals more generally have no uniform view of how best to encourage the protection of human rights in China. In general, whether in the case of China or other authoritarian countries like Cuba, they are pragmatists about means. They believe that the efficacy of means is a function of circumstance and that in the choice of means, the governing criterion is how best to mitigate the suffering of identifiable human beings rather than how to execute an abstract project. That is one reason why they are not found in the forefront of those who, though knowing it could lead to war between Taiwan and the mainland and to armed confrontation between China and the United States, would nevertheless encourage Taipei to declare its independence.

Imagining a greater calamity for human rights and welfare than a military conflict between the U.S. and China is difficult. Even something less than armed conflict, a renewed Cold War, for instance, seems certain to limit sharply the relative freedom of people in today's China. Moreover, by deflecting additional resources into an arms buildup and reducing foreign involvement in China's economy, a Cold War would reverse the trend toward the reduction of poverty in that huge country. In addition, a Sino-American Cold War would dim any prospect of the U.S.'s investing significant resources in humanitarian activities unrelated to the conflict—for instance to mitigate intercommunal wars and the ravages of AIDS in Africa. Conversely, one could anticipate the same cynical *laissez-passer* for friendly but brutal regimes that often marked U.S. policy during the last Cold War.

Does it then follow that human rights advocates should, at least in the case of China and possibly more generally, look to the conservative realists as allies, albeit allies of convenience? Probably not. In the first place, realists come in two forms, the prudent and the adventurous, or, in academic discourse, the defensive and the offensive, the latter believing that states generally do and in all cases should seek to maximize their power, that the idea of a mere "sufficiency" of power is absurd.[120] The first type of realist, epitomized today by former Secretary of State Henry Kissinger and the former national security adviser,

General Brent Scowcroft, is sensitive to the risks of trying to reshape the international system's norms and actors. They are seemingly aware of the danger, among others, of provoking a hostile coalition of states which, were it not for their shared opposition to domination by an ambitious hegemon, would have relatively little in common. And in a world of potentially catastrophic terrorism, they are cautious about swelling the pool of recruits for the terrorist project and making the United States its favored target.

This ideological difference explains why defensive realists grudgingly supported the war in Iraq. In common between defensive realists and human rights advocates is that both support constructive engagement with China through trade and other exchanges. Yet trade and foreign investment help drive China's rapid economic growth that in turn helps sustain political stability. If rapid growth continues for another 20 years, China will be the only state capable of challenging U.S. hegemony in Asia. For that very reason the leading academic offensive realist, John Mearsheimer, urges adoption of economic measures that would slow China's growth, but he stops short of celebrating pre-emptive war.[121] Kissinger's advocacy of engagement, both bilateral and multilateral, implies belief that the United States and a more developed China are not inevitably enemies, and that they have far greater common interests than differences. In short, Kissinger's China policy is more easily reconciled with non-realist theories that attribute causal value to institutional arrangements and subscribe to the idea that national interests are not given but rather constructed through the interaction of state elites.

But there is another species of realist, personified by Secretary of Defense Donald Rumsfeld and Vice-President Dick Cheney, who apparently join the neo-conservatives in discounting the danger of flouting long-established practices and norms and magnifying the decisive effect of military power. Today, when their focus is on terrorism, they are seemingly happy to accept China as a cooperative state. But given the centrality of military power in their world view, if and when the present sense of immediate danger passes, they could be as susceptible as the neo-conservatives to a policy of confrontation with China.

Should the costs of Iraq's occupation continue to mount and its inhabitants obdurately resist forms of governance and policy congenial to the occupier, the balance of persuasive power in Washington might shift to cautious realists led by Colin Powell. They were, at least initially, skeptics about the enterprise and the grand vision of a transformed Middle East. If constraining U.S. power were the optimal strategy for promoting humanitarian ends, human rights advocates might reasonably seek an alliance with resurgent realists in the Kissinger–Powell mode. But surely it is not. For realists of all stripes tolerated butchery in Bosnia, genocide in Rwanda, and ethnic cleansing in Kosovo. The Congo's agony and Liberia's bloody convulsions have little purchase on their moral imagination because they have no place in their grand strategy, any more than does a renewed Afghanistan as opposed to one where sufficiently accommodating commercially minded warlords regulate the rubble. The neo-conservatives are certainly right about one thing: U.S. leadership is indispensable for any project to mitigate the present and looming humanitarian horrors of the twenty-first century.

In that they are in accord on that point, would it not be useful for liberal humanitarians to reconcile with neo-conservative militants? Alas, the prospect for accord must be judged dim. For what does the past tell us about the nature of these militants? It was said of Charles de Gaulle that he loved the idea of France but not the French. Similarly, neo-conservatives betray love of the idea of liberty with their indifference to the fate of the liberated.

Neo-conservatives invoked Saddam Hussein's savagery as one justification for invading Iraq. In doing so, they struck a sympathetic chord in liberal hawks, including the author, who have favored intervention in cases of gross inhumanity where the predictable collateral damage seemed small compared to the human costs of inaction. But what credibility can claims of humanity summon when those who make them fail to protect the purported beneficiaries of their concern?

To invade Iraq without preparing to deploy immediately and instruct properly the forces necessary to establish order, protect the inhabitants' rich cultural legacy, and safeguard the material infrastructure of government and the health system is hardly to evince concern for real people as distinguished from abstract ideas. Nor is a determination not to tally at least the civilian Iraqi dead and maimed, the collateral damage, as it were, of liberation. Nor is leaving Afghanistan in shambles the better to pursue a war of choice and opportunity but hardly necessity in the Middle East. Nor is willed amnesia about the fate of the Central American countries where, in the name of democracy during the Reagan years, neo-conservatives championed war rather than fostering compromise and leveraging the social change that might have given substance to democratic forms. But all of these acts and omissions are entirely consistent with a cynical power-sharing compromise with the hard proponents of an unadorned chauvinism. And they are consistent as well with a sentiment that administration realists and neo-conservatives appear to possess jointly, which is indifference to what liberal humanitarians deem essential: due regard for the opinion of our old democratic allies and due concern for the lives of the peoples we propose to democratize.

Notes

1 Barry R. Posen and Andrew L. Ross, "Competing Visions for U.S. Grand Strategy," *International Security* 21, no. 3 (Winter 1996–7), pp. 5–53. For a slightly idiosyncratic, seven-fold categorization, see Robert J. Art, "Geopolitics Updated: The Strategy of Selective Engagement," *International Security* 23, no. 3 (Winter 1998–9), pp. 79–113.

2 See, for example, Earl C. Ravenel, "The Case for Adjustment," *Foreign Policy* 81 (Winter 1990–1), pp. 3–20.

3 See, for example, Andrew J. Bacevich, "Bush's Grand Strategy," *The American Conservative*, November 4, 2002, http://www.amconmag.com/11_4/bushs_grand_ strategy.html; and Pat Buchanan, "The Unintended Consequences of War," *The American Conservative*, February 24, 2003, http://www.amconmag.com/02_24_03/ buchanan.html.

4 See Noam Chomsky, *Rogue States: The Rule of Force in World Affairs* (Cambridge, MA: Southend Press, 2002). For his views on the recent war with Iraq, see his "Drain the Swamp . . . No More Mosquitoes," *Toronto Star*, October 20, 2002, p. B1.

5 Josef Joffe, "How America Does It," *Foreign Affairs* 76 (September–October 1997), pp. 13–27. See also Robert Art, "Geopolitics Updated."

6 See Charles Krauthammer, "The Unipolar Moment Reconsidered," *The National Interest* 70 (Winter 2002–3), pp. 5–27; Robert Kagan, "The Benevolent Empire," *Foreign Policy* 111 (Summer 1998), pp. 24–35; *idem*, "Power and Weakness," *Policy Review* 113 (June–July 2002), pp. 3–28; and John Bolton, "Should We Take Global Governance Seriously?" paper presented at the conference "Trends in Global Governance: Do They Threaten American Sovereignty?" at the American Enterprise Institute, Washington, D.C., April 4–5, 2000.

7 See, for example, Jessica Matthews, "Power Shift," *Foreign Affairs* 76 (January–February 1997), pp. 50–66.

8 See, for example, Donald Rumsfeld, "A New Kind of War," http://www.defenselink.mil/speeches/2001/s20010927-secdef.html.

9 Remarks by President George W. Bush at the Cincinnati Museum Center, October 7, 2002, http://www.whitehouse.gov/news/releases/2002/10/20021007-8.html. See also Paul W. Schroeder, "Iraq: The Case Against Preemptive War," *American Conservative*, October 2, 2002.

10 The author was present at both meetings. Others associated with the Bush administration have made similar declarations. For example, Richard Haass, formerly head of the State Department's Policy Planning Staff, has defined the administration's policy of selective engagement as "à la carte multilateralism." See Irwin M. Stelzer, "Is Europe a Threat?" *Commentary* 112 (October 2001), pp. 34–42.

11 For example, Senator Trent Lott of Missouri wrote that "placing U.S. military forces under U.N. command and in harm's way to create government where none exists, is poorly conceived and ill-defined." Sen. Trent Lott, "U.N. Must Not Direct U.S. Troops," *Christian Science Monitor*, November 16, 1993, p. 20.

12 Thomas W. Lippman, "Clinton Struggles to Define World Vision," *Chicago Sun Times*, September 30, 1993, p. 30.

13 See John Mearsheimer "The False Promise of International Institutions," *International Security* 19, no. 3 (Winter 1994–5), pp. 5–49.

14 See, for example, Clifford D. May, "U.N.done: It's Time to Reform International Institutions and Alliances," *National Review*, March 25, 2003, http://www.nationalreview.com/may/may032503.asp; Martin Hutchinson, "Unmitigated Disaster: Next Time, Ignore the U.N.," *National Review*, March 7, 2003, http://www.nationalreview.com/comment/comment-hutchinson030703.asp; and John C. Hulsman, David Polansky, and Rachel Prager, "The Rebirth of Realism: The Kantian Trap—Utopianism in International Affairs," *In The National Interest*, http://www.inthenationalinterest.com/Articles/Vol1Issue10/Vol1Issue10Hulsman1.html.

15 See, for example, George Melloan, "Global View: Will There Be a New World Order after Iraq?" *Wall Street Journal*, March 18, 2003, p. A17.

16 See Joseph J. Ellis, *Founding Brothers: The Revolutionary Generation* (New York: Knopf, 2002); David McCullough, *John Adams* (New York: Simon and Schuster, 2001).

17 Peter H. Maguire, *Law and War* (New York: Columbia University Press, 2001), pp. 47–9.

18 Dexter Perkins and Oscar Handlin, *Charles Evans Hughes and American Democratic Statesmanship* (Westport, CT: Greenwood Publishing Group, 1978).

19 See Treaty on Naval Armament Limitation, April 22, 1930, 46 Stat. 2858, T.S. no. 830; and Renunciation of War as an Instrument of National Policy (Kellogg–Briand Peace Pact or Pact of Paris), August 27, 1928, 46 Stat. 2343, 94 L.N.T.S. 57.

20 Robert Skidelsky, *John Maynard Keynes: Fighting for Britain, 1937–1946* (New York:

Viking Press, 2001); Richard N. Gardner, *Sterling–Dollar Diplomacy*, 2nd edition (New York: McGraw-Hill, 1969).

21 Richard H. Immerman, *John Foster Dulles: Piety, Pragmatism, and Power in U.S. Foreign Policy* (Wilmington, DE: Scholarly Resources, 1999), pp. 154–5.

22 Stephen Ambrose, *Eisenhower* (New York: Simon and Schuster, 1983); Michael Bromley, *William Howard Taft and the First Motoring Presidency, 1909–1913* (Jefferson, N.C.: McFarland and Company 2003).

23 Jonathan Aitken, *Nixon: A Life* (Washington, D.C.: Regnery Publishing, Inc., 1993), p. 394.

24 In his Snopes trilogy, *The Hamlet* (1940), *The Town* (1957), and *The Mansion* (1959), Faulkner traced the rise of the insidious Snopes family to positions of power and wealth in the face of the decline in wealth and prestige suffered by the Southern aristocratic families following the end of the war.

25 See Robert A. Caro, *The Path to Power: The Years of Lyndon Johnson*, vol. 1 (New York: Vintage Books, 1990); *Means of Ascent: The Years of Lyndon Johnson*, vol. 2 (New York: Vintage Books, 1991); and *Master of the Senate* (New York: Vintage Books, 2003).

26 Peter J. Wallison, *Ronald Reagan, the Power of Conviction and the Success of His Presidency* (Boulder, CO: Westview, 2002), pp. 64–73; Edmund Morris, *Dutch: A Memoir of Ronald Reagan* (New York: Random House, 1999), pp. 434–8.

27 See William Martin, *With God on Our Side: The Rise of the Religious Right in America* (New York: Broadway Books, 1996).

28 Michael Kazin, *The Populist Persuasion: An American History* (Ithaca, N.Y.: Cornell University Press, 1998).

29 See James Cross Giblin, *The Life and Death of Adolf Hitler* (New York: Clarion Books, 2002); Ian Kershaw, *Hitler, 1889–1936: Hubris* (New York: W.W. Norton and Company, 1999).

30 See C. Vann Woodward, *The Strange Career of Jim Crow* (Oxford: Oxford University Press, 2001), Chapter 3.

31 Kazin, *The Populist Persuasion.*

32 Pat Buchanan, *Right from the Beginning* (Washington, D.C.: Regnery Publishing, Inc., 1990). See also Tom Wolfe's *Radical Chic and Mau-Mauing the Flak Catchers* (New York: Farrar, Straus and Giroux, 1970).

33 See, for example, Thomas Frank, "The Rise of Market Populism," *The Nation*, 271 (October 30, 2000), pp. 13–17; William Greider, "Global Agenda," *The Nation*, 270 (January 31, 2000), pp. 11–15.

34 See Aryeh Neier, *Taking Liberties: Four Decades in the Struggle for Rights* (New York: Public Affairs, 2003).

35 The Chicago Council on Foreign Relations has regularly conducted polling on "American Public Opinion and U.S. Foreign Policy" since the late 1970s. The latest report (1999) is available at http://www.ccfr.org/publications/opinion/opinion.html.

36 Martin Merzer, "Poll: Majority of Americans Oppose Unilateral Action against Iraq," Knight Ridder Newspapers, January 1, 2003.

37 Adam Nagourney and Janet Elder, "More Americans Now Faulting U.N. on Iraq, Poll Finds," *New York Times*, March 11, 2003, p. A1.

38 Former Senator Jesse Helms exemplified these views. For the text of his speech before the U.N. General Assembly on January 20, 2000, see "Senator Jesse Helms Rebukes the U.N.," *Newswatch Magazine*, June 1, 2000, http://www.newswatch-magazine.org/jun00/helms.htm.

39 See, generally, Arthur Schlesinger, *The New Deal in Action* (New York: Macmillan, 1940), pp. 60–8.

40 This view was definitely inspired by the writings and teachings of the earliest Puritan New Englanders. See Perry Miller, ed., *The American Puritans: Their Prose and Poetry* (Garden City, N.Y.: Doubleday Anchor, 1956).

41 The International Social Survey Program conducted cross-national surveys of religious belief in 1991 and 1993. See "The ISSP Cross-National Religion Survey," *The Public Perspective* 5 (March/April 1994), pp. 21–5.
42 Miller, *American Puritans*.
43 Werner Sombart, *Why Is There No Socialism in the U.S.?* (Armonk, N.Y.: M.E. Sharpe, 1978). See also Michael Harrington, *Socialism: Past and Future* (New York: Mentor Books, 1992).
44 See Samuel Huntington, "American Ideals versus American Institutions," *Political Science Quarterly* 97, no. 1 (Spring 1982), pp. 1–37.
45 Ibid., pp. 1–2.
46 Kevin Passmore provides a good overview of prewar European conservatism and its relationship with various forms of fascism. *Fascism: A Very Short Introduction* (New York: Oxford University Press, 2002), pp. 72–86.
47 In the words of Heinrich von Treitschke, "War and conquest . . . are the most important factors in State construction." *Politics*, vol. 1, trans. Arthur James Balfour (London: Constable and Company, 1916), p. 108. See also pp. 597–600 of volume 2.
48 For a description of the evolution of the contemporary left, see Anthony Giddens, *The Third Wave and its Critics* (Cambridge: Polity Press, 2000).
49 See Louis Hartz, *The Liberal Tradition in America*, 2nd edition (San Diego, CA: Harvest Books, 1991).
50 See Schlesinger, *The New Deal in Action*.
51 Daniel Bell, *The End of Ideology: The Exhaustion of Political Ideas in the Fifties* (Cambridge, MA: Harvard University Press, 2000).
52 See Martin, *With God on Our Side*.
53 The Supreme Court has ruled that one public high school district's use of "invocations" or "benedictions" before football games is unconstitutional. See *Santa Fe Independent School District v. Doe*, no. 99–62. Argued March 29, 2000; Decided June 19, 2000. See also *Lee v. Weisman*, prohibiting prayer at graduation ceremonies, 505 U.S. 577; 112 S. Ct. 2649 (1992); *Abington School District. v. Schempp* 374 U.S. 203; 83 S. Ct. 1560 (1963) banning mandatory Bible readings and *Wallace v. Jaffree* 472 U.S. 38; 105 S. Ct. 2479 (1985) invalidating voluntary prayer and moments of silence.
54 Norman Podhoretz is perhaps most exemplary. See his *Making It* (New York: Random House, 1967) and *Breaking Ranks: A Political Memoir* (New York: Harper and Rowe, 1979). Rosenberg and Howe contended that Podhoretz's editorship of *Commentary*, however, was not part and parcel of the development of a new conservative ideology as it was "against recent versions of what Podhoretz takes to be vulgarizations of liberalism." See Bernard Rosenberg and Irving Howe, "Are American Jews turning toward the right?" in Lewis A. Coser and Irving Howe, eds., *The New Conservatives: A Critique from the Left* (New York: Meridian, 1976).
55 Sidney Hook and Irving Howe are prime examples. On Hook, see Christopher Phelps, *Young Sidney Hook: Marxist and Pragmatist* (Ithaca, N.Y.: Cornell University Press, 1997). On Howe, see Edward Alexander, *Irving Howe: Socialist, Critic, Jew* (Bloomington, IN: Indiana University Press, 1998) and Gerald Sorin, *Irving Howe: A Life of Passionate Dissent* (New York: New York University Press, 2003).
56 In an interview with Michele Norris on National Public Radio's *All Things Considered* about his upcoming book, *An Execution in the Family*, Robert Meeropol, the younger son of Julius and Ethel Rosenberg, contends that revelations about the horrors of Stalin's rule that emerged after his death precipitated the largest single decline in membership in the U.S. Communist Party, from 30–40,000 members to less than 10,000. At the height of its popularity in the 1930s, membership was around 100,000 (June 19, 2003).
57 Jeane Kirkpatrick, "Dictatorships and Double Standards," *Commentary* 68 (November 1979), pp. 34–45. For a critical analysis, see Tom J. Farer, "Reagan's Latin America," *New York Review of Books* 28, no. 4 (March 1981), pp. 10–16.

56   *Tom J. Farer*

58 See Julian Bond's comprehensive overview of this history in the Introduction to Maurianne Adams and John H. Bracey, eds., *Strangers and Neighbors: Relations between Blacks and Jews in the United States* (Amherst, MA: University of Massachusetts Press, 1999).
59 See Andrew Hacker, "American Apartheid," *New York Review of Books* 34, no. 19 (December 1987), pp. 26–33.
60 Glenn C. Loury cites the problem of African-Americans' employment of a form of "comparative victimology"—especially equating the suffering and consequences of chattel slavery with the Holocaust—as a significant source of the split between the two groups. See "Behind the Black–Jewish Split," *Commentary* 81 (January 1986), pp. 23–7.
61 The 1978 Bakke–Regents of the University of California case was the font of many of the earliest formulations of "affirmative action quotas" which caught the attention of some Jewish commentators (see, for example, Joseph Adelson, "Living with Quotas," *Commentary* 65 (May 1978), pp. 23–9) and black intellectuals such as Thomas Sowell (see, for example, "Are Quotas Good for Blacks?" *Commentary* 65 (June 1978), pp. 39–43. See also the special issue of *Commentary* (vol. 69, January 1980) entitled "Liberalism and the Jews: A Symposium."
62 This was during the particularly divisive period of 1966–7. The proposal came from a local chapter operating in Georgia. The leader of the SNCC, Stokley Carmichael, never actually endorsed the exclusion of whites from the organization.
63 See Morris Abrams's autobiography, *The Day is Short* (New York: Harcourt, 1982). Abrams's trajectory from a prosecutor at the Nuremberg Trials, to champion of the civil rights movement in the U.S., to embittered neo-conservative is exemplary. Abrams died in 2000.
64 For a historical account of the Ocean Hill-Brownsville Crisis, see Jerald E. Podair, "The Ocean Hill-Brownsville Crisis: New York's *Antigone*" (paper prepared for the 2001 Gotham History Festival, sponsored by the Gotham Center for New York City History, available at http://www.gothamcenter.org/festival/2001/ confpapers/podair.pdf). For an account from a sociological perspective, see Jane Anna Gordon, *Why Couldn't They Wait? A Critique of the Black–Jewish Conflict Over Community Control in Ocean Hill-Brownsville (1967–1971)* (New York: Routledge, 2001).
65 Randall Robinson, the founder of the TransAfrica Forum, is an exemplary and key figure in the reparations movement, not only for African-Americans, but also in the form of North–South transfers for the injustices of African colonialism.
66 See, for example, Walter Isaacson, *Kissinger: A Biography* (New York: Simon and Schuster, 1992), p. 675.
67 Paul Hofman, "Moynihan's Style in the U.N. Is Now an Open Debate," *New York Times*, November 21, 1975, p. A3.
68 See Moynihan's "The United States in Opposition," *Commentary* 59 (March 1975), pp. 31–44.
69 Ibid. See also the special issue of *Commentary*, "Liberalism and the Jews" 69 (January 1980), *passim*.
70 The 1967 war is considered by some to be decisive in the Black–Jewish split because it was widened to include foreign policy. See Huey L. Perry and Ruth B. White, "The Post-Civil Rights Transformation of the Relationship between Blacks and Jews in the United States," *Phylon* 47, no. 1 (1986), pp. 51–60. They quote heavily from Nathan Glazer's *Ethnic Dilemmas: 1964–1982* (Cambridge, MA: Harvard University Press, 1983).
71 This was the movement begun by the Group of 77 and the Non-Aligned Movement, starting first within the U.N. Conference on Trade and Development (UNCTAD) and culminating in the Sixth Special Session of the General Assembly's adoption of the Program of Action on the Establishment of a New International Economic Order and the Charter of Economic Rights and Duties of States in 1974. The most

recent articulation of the issue of redress was at the 2001 World Conference on Racism, held in Durban, South Africa. The Declaration adopted at the Conference is at http://www.unhchr.ch/pdf/Durban.pdf.

72 See Ian Lustick, "Israeli State-Building in the West Bank and Gaza Strip: Theory and Practice," *International Organization* 41, no. 1 (1987), pp. 151–71.

73 See especially Michael J. Smith, "Henry Kissinger: realism in power," in his *Realist Thought from Weber to Kissinger* (Baton Rouge, LA: Louisiana State University Press, 1986), pp. 192–217.

74 With reference to the rapidly deteriorating situation in the Balkans in the early 1990s, Secretary of State James Baker was quoted as telling George H.W. Bush, "we don't have a dog in that fight." Max Boot, "Paving the Road to Hell: The Failure of U.S. Peacekeeping," *Foreign Affairs* 79 (March–April 2000), p. 146.

75 Kirkpatrick basically wrote the blueprint for what would become Reagan's Latin America policy—especially with respect to Central America—in her "U.S. Security and Latin America," *Commentary* 71 (January 1981), pp. 29–40. For other expositions of Kirkpatrick's policy on Latin America, see her collection of speeches: *The Reagan Phenomenon and Other Speeches on Foreign Policy* (Washington, D.C.: AEI Press, 1983). Elliot Abrams—as Assistant Secretary of State for Human Rights and Humanitarian Affairs, and later as Assistant Secretary for Inter-American Affairs— would become deeply enmeshed in the Iran–Contra scandal.

76 James Reston, "The Reagan Show," *New York Times*, February 1, 1981, p. E21.

77 See Robert H. Johnson, "Misguided Morality: Ethics and the Reagan Doctrine," *Political Science Quarterly* 103 (1988), pp. 509–29.

78 See Lars Schoultz, *Human Rights and United States Policy Toward Latin America* (Princeton, N.J.: Princeton University Press, 1981).

79 In late 1980 four American Maryknoll nuns were killed by U.S.-backed Salvadoran soldiers during the civil war against the Frente Farabundo Martí para la Liberación Nacional (FMLN). At the time, Kirkpatrick remarked, "they were not just nuns . . . they were political activists on behalf of the Frente." Flora Lewis, "Keeping it Honest," *New York Times*, March 27, 1981, p. A27. Also notorious was the administration's involvement in concealing the truth about the El Mozote massacre of December 1981, in which over 750 Salvadoran men, women, and children were killed by a U.S.-trained unit of the Salvadoran Army. See Mark Danner, *The Massacre at El Mozote: A Parable of the Cold War* (New York: Vintage Books, 1994). See Alan Riding, "Duarte's Strategy May Work Better in U.S. than in Salvador," *New York Times*, September 27, 1981, p. E5.

80 William Safire, "Bush's Moral Crisis," *New York Times*, April 1, 1991, p. A17.

81 This was primarily a result of the administration's decision to temporarily suspend loan guarantees to Israel in order to halt expansion of Jewish settlements in the West Bank. For an account of the fallout, see Jay P. Leftkowitz, "Does the Jewish Vote Count?" *Commentary* 111 (March 2001), pp. 50–3.

82 Charles Krauthammer, "The Unipolar Moment," *Foreign Affairs* 70 (Winter 1990–1), pp. 23–33.

83 See, for example, Michael Isikoff, "The Robertson Right and the Grandest Conspiracy," *Washington Post*, October 11, 1992, p. C3.

84 While referring to Somalia during the October 11, 2000 Presidential Debate at Wake Forest University, Bush said, "I don't think our troops ought to be used for what's called nation-building. I think our troops ought to be used to fight and win war." The text is available at http://www.issues2000.org/Archive/Wake_Forest_debate_Foreign_Policy.htm

85 Ibid.

86 This criticism was levied on Bush's presidential campaign website, georgewbush.com, "Issues: Policy Points Overview (April 2, 2000).

87 When asked by the TV personality Larry King, "What area of international policy

would you change immediately?" Bush's response was, "Our relationship with China. The President has called the relationship with China a strategic partnership. I believe our relationship needs to be redefined as competitor . . . [W]e must make it clear to the Chinese that we don't appreciate any attempt to spread weapons of mass destruction around the world, that we don't appreciate any threats to our friends and allies in the Far East." *Larry King Live* Show, February 15, 2000.

88 See, for example, Krauthammer, "Unipolar Moment"; Mark Helprin, "What Israel Must Do to Survive," *Commentary* 112 (November 2001), pp. 25–8; Daniel Pipes, "Who is the Enemy?" *Commentary* 113 (January 2002), pp. 21–7; Norman Podhoretz, "How to Win World War IV," *Commentary* 113 (February 2002), pp. 19–29. For a critical view, see Nicholas Lemann, "The Next World Order," *New Yorker*, April 1, 2002, pp. 42–8.

89 Alan Murray, "Bush Officials Scramble to Push Democracy in Iraq," *Wall Street Journal*, April 8, 2003, p. A4; Lawrence Kaplan, "Regime Change," *New Republic* 228, March 3, 2003, pp. 21–3.

90 See Thomas Carothers, "Promoting Democracy and Fighting Terror," *Foreign Affairs* 82 (January–February 2003), pp. 84–97.

91 The Lawyers Committee for Human Rights in particular published "A Year of Loss: Examining Civil Liberties Since September 11" (September 2002), and its update, "Imbalance of Powers: How Changes to U.S. Law and Policy Since 9/11 Erode Civil Liberties" (April 2003). These reports are available online at http://www.lchr.org/us_law/loss/loss_main.htm.

92 See, for example, Condoleezza Rice, "Promoting the National Interest," *Foreign Affairs* 79 (January–February 2000), pp. 45–62.

93 Christopher Dickey and Evan Thomas, with Mark Hosenball, Roy Gutman, and John Barry, "How Saddam Happened," *Newsweek*, September 3, 2002, pp. 34–40.

94 See Samantha Power, *A Problem from Hell: America and the Age of Genocide* (New York: Basic Books, 2002), Chapters 9 and 10.

95 This was due mostly to Clinton's emphasis on domestic—especially economic—policy. David Halberstram, *War in a Time of Peace: Bush, Clinton and the Generals* (New York: Scribner, 2001), pp. 158, 167–8.

96 See, for example, Ramesh Ponnuru, "Getting to the Bottom of this 'Neo' Nonsense," *National Review*, June 16, 2003, pp. 29–32; and *idem*, "The Shadow Men," *The Economist*, April 26, 2003, pp. 21–3.

97 Or even, "Wilsonianism in boots." See Stanley Hoffman, "The High and the Mighty: Bush's National Security Strategy and the New American Hubris," *American Prospect* 13, January 13, 2003, http://www.prospect.org/print/V13/24/hoffmann-s.html.

98 See Micheline Ishay, *Human Rights Reader: Major Speeches, Essays and Documents from the Bible to the Present* (London: Routledge, 1997).

99 Jack Donnelly, *Universal Human Rights in Theory and Practice* (Ithaca, N.Y.: Cornell University Press, 2002), p. 35.

100 For example, Chile's 1925 and 1980 constitutions permitted suspending certain rights under the Constitution during States of Emergency. Edward C. Snyder, "The Dirty Legal War: Human Rights and the Rule of Law in Chile: 1973–95," 2 *Tulsa Journal of Comparative and International Law* 253 (Spring 1995), pp. 253–85.

101 International Covenant on Civil and Political Rights, G.A. res. 00A (XXI) 21 U.N. GAOR Supp. (no. 16) at 5 U.N. Doc. A/6316 (1966), 999 U.N.T.S. 171 entered into force March 3, 1976, Article 4.1.

102 Ibid., Article 4.2

103 Samia Nakhoul, "Boy Bomb Victim Struggles Against Despair," *Daily Mirror*, April 8, 2003.

104 See George F. Will, "Measured Audacity," *Newsweek* 141, April 14, 2003, p. 66.

105 The primary treaties of humanitarian law governing international armed conflict are the 1907 Hague Convention, the 1949 Geneva Conventions and the 1977 Additional Protocol 1 to the Geneva Conventions. Taken in concert, the provisions of these treaties require that military attacks must be directed at military targets and that the rules of necessity and proportionality be followed, but it does not mean that there cannot be civilian casualties. See Michael Bothe *et al.*, *New Rules for Armed Conflicts* (Dordrecht: Kluwer Law International, 1982), pp. 304–5.
106 The White House claimed that Saddam Hussein repeatedly violated 16 United Nations Security Council resolutions designed to ensure that Iraq does not pose a threat to international peace and security. A list of those resolutions can be found in the White House briefing paper, "Iraq, A Decade of Deception and Defiance," http://www.whitehouse.gov/news/releases/2002/09/20020912.html. See, for example, "Iraq: Witnesses Link Mass Graves to 1991 Repression," "The Mass Graves of al-Mahawil: The Truth Uncovered," "Mass Graves Hide Horror of Iraqi Past," and "Human Rights Testimony on Prosecuting Iraqi War Crimes," all available on the Human Rights Watch website, http://humanrightswatch.org/. More than one million people were killed during the Iran–Iraq war. Dilip Hiro, *The Longest War* (New York: Routledge, 1991), p. 1. The U.S. State Department reports that a thousand Kuwaitis were killed during the Iraqi invasion and subsequent occupation in 1990–1. See http://usinfo.state.gov/regional/nea/iraq/crimes/. The reader may wish to compare the above with the "Special Report" published by the United States Institute of Peace after a December 2002 symposium to address the question "Would an Invasion of Iraq be a 'Just War?'" Available at http://www.usip.org/pubs/specialreports/sr98.pdf.
107 David E. Sanger, "Bush Sees 'Urgent Duty' to Pre-empt Attack by Iraq," *New York Times*, October 8, 2002, p. A1.
108 The National Security Strategy is available at http://www.whitehouse.gov/nsc/nss.html.
109 See, for example, William Kristol and Robert Kagan, "Toward a Neo-Reaganite Foreign Policy," *Foreign Affairs* 75 (July–August 1996), pp. 18–32.
110 Henry Kissinger, "Phase II and Iraq," *Washington Post*, January 13, 2002, p. B7; Brent Scowcroft, "Don't Attack Saddam," *Wall Street Journal*, August 15, 2002, p. A12.
111 See, for example, John Mearsheimer and Stephen Walt, "An Unnecessary War," *Foreign Policy* (January–February 2003), pp. 51–60.
112 See generally Gordon A. Craig, *The Germans* (New York: Meridian Books, 1991); William Shirer, *The Rise and Fall of the Third Reich* (New York: Simon and Schuster, 1960).
113 Stuart Taylor Jr., "In Wake of Invasion, Much Official Misinformation by U.S. Comes to Light," *New York Times*, November 6, 1983, p. A20. The invasion of Panama resulted in the deaths of 300 Panamanians. Adam Isaac Hasson, "Extraterritorial Jurisdiction and Sovereign Immunity on Trial: Noriega, Pinochet, and Milošević—Trends in Political Accountability and Transnational Criminal Law," *Boston College International and Comparative Law Review* 125 (Winter 2002), pp. 125–58.
114 For a discussion, see Danner, *El Mozote*; David K. Shipler, "Senators Challenge Officials on Contras," *New York Times*, February 6, 1987, p. A3; Marlene Dixon, *On Trial: Reagan's War Against Nicaragua* (San Francisco: Synthesis Publications, 1985); and Howard J. Wiarda, "Europe's Ambiguous Relations with Latin America: Blowing Hot and Cold in the Western Hemisphere," *Washington Quarterly* 13 (Spring 1990), pp. 153–67.
115 Albert Park, "Growth and Poverty Reduction in China," World Bank Presentation at the University of Michigan, June 17, 2002, http://poverty.worldbank.org/files/12398_APark-Presentation.pdf.

116 The U.S. Trade Representative during the Clinton administration, Charlene Barshefsky, said with regard to China's entry into the World Trade Organization, "I am cautious in making claims that a market-opening agreement leads to anything other than opening the market." William Shultz, *In Our Own Best Interest: How Defending Human Rights Benefits Us All* (Boston, MA: Beacon Press, 2001), p. 71. For another perspective, see Martin Lee, "Free Trade with China? Yes, It Will Spur Reform," *Wall Street Journal*, May 18, 2000, p. A26.

117 Milton Friedman and other Hayekian-inspired "free traders" immediately spring to mind. Friedman's *Capitalism and Freedom* (Chicago, IL: University of Chicago Press, 40th anniversary edition, 2002) is exemplary.

118 For an overview of conservative Christian views on the topic of U.S–China trade relations (pre-WTO), see Julie Kosterlitz, "Conservatives clash over China," *National Journal* 30, July 18, 1998, p. 1693.

119 Human Rights Watch has published scores of topical reports on human rights in China and Tibet over the years. Many are available at http://www.hrw.org/asia/china.php.

120 See generally John J. Mearsheimer, *The Tragedy of Great Power Politics* (New York: W.W. Norton, 2001) and Glen H. Snyder's review of the book in *International Security* 27, no. 1 (Summer 2002), pp. 149–73.

121 John Mearsheimer, "The Future of the American Pacifier," *Foreign Affairs* 80, no. 5 (September–October 2001), pp. 46–61.

2 Pre-emption and exceptionalism in U.S. foreign policy

Precedent and example in the international arena

Judith Lichtenberg[1]

> When a man commits himself to anything, fully realizing that he is not only choosing what he will be, but is thereby at the same time a legislator deciding for the whole of mankind—in such a moment a man cannot escape from the sense of complete and profound responsibility . . . Everything happens to every man as though the whole human race had its eyes fixed upon what he is doing and regulated its conduct accordingly.
>
> Jean-Paul Sartre, "Existentialism Is a Humanism"[2]

> It is not in the American national interest to establish pre-emption as a universal principle available to every nation.
>
> Henry Kissinger, August 11, 2002[3]

What is most troubling about U.S. foreign policy today is the example that it holds up to the world and the precedent that it sets, conjoined with its disregard for the significance of both example and precedent. The United States legislates, dangerously, for the whole of humankind, while simultaneously refusing to acknowledge that role—thereby escaping, as Jean-Paul Sartre says one cannot do, from its "complete and profound responsibility." Of course, states and their governments are not in every way analogous to individual human beings. But in the most important respects, governments are agents whose actions and policies have just the kind of precedential and exemplary significance that individuals' actions do—even more so, I shall argue, because of their inescapably public nature.

Sartre's claim that every agent legislates for all humanity derives from the "Categorical Imperative," Kant's fundamental principle of morality. According to Immanuel Kant, an agent ought to "act only according to that maxim by which . . . [one] can at the same time will that it should become a universal law."[4] This formulation of the Categorical Imperative (one of three that Kant offers) has been subjected to much scrutiny over the years. Contemporary philosophers have found it difficult to interpret it in a way that achieves everything Kant intended. Yet the germ of Kant's idea captures something that goes deep in our thinking about the moral requirements of conduct, and the same or similar conceptions can be found in a variety of other moral theories and systems. The intuitive idea is that in deciding how to act, an agent must consider whether he would be willing for everyone to act according to the same principle (Kant used the term "maxim"). At the very least, unless an agent is willing to accept the universal adoption of his principle of action, the action is impermissible.[5] Universalizability should be understood in terms of consistency: what is right for me is right for anyone similarly situated.

Sartre appears to be expressing the same idea. But whereas Kant argues that one *ought* to employ the Categorical Imperative—acting only on those principles which one would be willing that everyone act on—Sartre makes the bolder point that whether we like it or not, whether we choose it or not, in acting we *inevitably* legislate for all of humanity.[6] My action sets an example; what I do others will conclude that they may do too.

Why does my action set an example? Why this inevitable universalizing feature? Lying behind the universalizability requirement is a postulate of human equality. No person can claim a privilege to act simply by virtue of who he or she is; no one can set himself or herself apart as a special case. If I am justified in acting in a certain way it is because of features of my situation that, if possessed by others, would justify them in so acting as well. These "features of the situation"—the phrases "anyone in the same circumstances" and "anyone similarly situated" get at the same idea—are embodied in the principle or maxim implicit in one's proposed course of action.

Two questions immediately confront us. The first concerns the analogy between states and individuals. Is it plausible to think that nation states, or their governments, are moral agents subject to the requirement of universalizability in the way we suppose individuals are? The second is a question familiar to students of Kant. Assuming we can make the analogy between states and individuals, how do we identify the maxim or principle according to which a state acts? More specifically, what is the maxim or principle that correctly characterizes the preemptive military intervention characteristic of current U.S. foreign policy? I begin with the second, more concrete question before turning to the first.

Possible principles of action

What principle does the U.S. government invoke or imply in its wars against terrorism and against Iraq? Students of Kant know that identifying the relevant principle at work in an agent's proposed course of action is rarely easy. Here are several possibilities, in increasing order of narrowness and specificity.

Principle One. States may engage in wars of conquest. This principle would represent a giant step backward into barbarism and would violate the U.N. Charter. It would justify Hitler's launching of World War II and Saddam Hussein's annexation of Kuwait. Clearly this crude principle is not the one at work in U.S. foreign policy today.

Principle Two. States may engage in preventive wars against those who might potentially attack them. This principle narrows the scope of the policy to preventive acts against potential enemies. But it remains far too broad. During the Cold War it would have justified either a U.S. or a Soviet first strike against the other; today it would justify first strikes by India and Pakistan against each other. There are those troubling words "might" and "potentially." Depending on the degree of probability assigned and the length of the time frame, any state could use the principle to launch a war against its geopolitical adversaries. The deep problem with Principle Two is that it actually *makes* states into potential threats to each other by permitting preventive conquest of potential adversaries. Principle Two would lead to perpetual international conflict.

Principle Three. States may engage in preventive wars against states possessing weapons of mass destruction (WMD). This principle licenses pre-emptive attacks against the United States, the world's largest holder of nuclear weapons and poison gas. Clearly it is not what the current Bush administration has in mind.

Principle Four. States may engage in preventive wars against rogue states possessing weapons of mass destruction. The best definition of a rogue state is one that disregards principles of world order and international law and launches aggressive attacks against others, sometimes by covert means. The trouble with this definition is that once we show ourselves prepared to conquer nations we dislike, we become a rogue state with WMD—hence a legitimate target of attack.

That is absurd, of course. We know we are not a rogue state—and we know that Iraq was. But how do we argue the case to states suspicious of U.S. motives? Without some neutral definition, "rogueness" is in the eye of the beholder. Who decides when another country's "elected" leader is really a dictator and a rogue? Does India get to declare General Pervez Musharraf a rogue and attack him? Perhaps the decision could be made by some multilateral body, like the U.N. Multilateralism might make Principle Four more palatable to the rest of the world, but it will certainly not be acceptable to U.S. interventionists. They do not want a worldwide referendum on Iraq's rogue status.

Principle Five. Superpowers may engage in certain actions that other nations may not, such as deciding which foreign regimes are rogue states and removing them. If this is the principle according to which the U.S. acts, then it is committed to the following view: if X is a superpower, then X may engage in actions that other nations may not. It just so happens that the U.S. is the only superpower in the world today, but that is incidental to the argument. The principle is a general one. It would apply to other superpowers if there were others, and it would hold if the U.S. were not a superpower. Perhaps the central question, then, is whether the U.S. would be willing to accept Principle Five if it were not a superpower. Clearly, it would find Principle Five no more acceptable than 190 other states do at this moment.

Principle Six. The U.S. may engage in actions that other nations may not, such as deciding which foreign regimes are rogues and removing them. The presence of a proper name, the U.S., tells us that with Principle Six we have left the realm of principle. According to this "anti-principle," a double standard—one for the United States and one for the rest of the world—is the right standard, in keeping with "American exceptionalism." Throughout history, realists remind us, the world's superpowers have invariably written their own rules; others go along because they have no choice. The U.S., according to this view, does not need a general principle. If it wants to choose governments for other countries, it has the right to do so. If other states claim the same right, they cannot have it.

Principle Six is not a principle but rather a straightforward rejection of the Kantian and Sartrean standpoints from which we began. But that is not enough to condemn it. Could this way of reasoning, and acting, be justified? It depends at least in part on whether the Kantian and Sartrean standpoints apply to anything other than individuals.

Are states moral agents?

The question, then, is whether states can be moral agents subject to the demand that they conform their behavior to the requirement of universalizability. If not, the foregoing criticism of U.S. foreign policy is inappropriate and unjustified.

Consider two general arguments against the view that states can be moral agents. The first might be called the *anthropomorphism argument*: to believe that states can be moral agents is to attribute human qualities to nonhuman things. To be morally responsible requires, at the very least, having a mind, and states do not have minds.

This argument is flawed on several grounds. We often hold collective entities, such as corporations and agencies, responsible both morally and legally, although they too lack minds. The anthropomorphism argument, if taken seriously, would not permit us to hold any corporate entities responsible and would thus contradict important bodies of law and common practice. If it were not possible to identify such corporate entities with the behavior of individuals, this argument would be worth taking seriously. But we can and do identify states and other corporate entities with the actions of particular individuals—typically their political and military leaders, their executives, and chief officers, and sometimes others under their command who are responsible for making and carrying out decisions. Of course, it can be difficult to assign blame to particular agents, because responsibility is dispersed and diffuse. In the case at hand, we might disagree about who *all* the responsible agents are. But we will have no trouble agreeing about who *some* of them are.

The anthropomorphism argument is closely related to, and may ultimately depend on, the claim of methodological individualism, a view frequently discussed in the philosophy of the social sciences. According to methodological individualism, only individuals exist and all talk of corporate or group entities must be ultimately reducible to the language of individual behavior. We need not enter here into the debate about the merits of this view, because the attribution of agency to states requires no more than the conjoined agency of individuals. States may be obscure entities, but the moral agency with which we are concerned here inheres in governments or regimes.

The more familiar argument for the belief that states (or governments or regimes) are not moral agents is realism, or realpolitik. Realism says that morality is irrelevant to the conduct of states, and that moral criticism and evaluation are therefore also irrelevant. Realism comes in two varieties, which are not often clearly distinguished. According to the first, states *do not* act on the basis of moral considerations. According to the second, states *ought not* act on the basis of moral considerations.

No one would dispute that there is much truth in the first claim. States typically, if not always, act on the basis of their perceived national interests, and moral considerations play, at best, a distinctly secondary role. This fact does not, however, let them off the moral hook. Some individuals act mainly or purely on the basis of their perceived self-interest, but we do not think that they are thereby relieved of moral responsibility.[7]

Implicit in the first realist thesis is an assumption about the motives of state actors. The question of motive—in state action as well as in individual action—is a complex and difficult one. How can we know an agent's actual motives? Under what circumstances is it reasonable to expect an agent (whether an individual or a state) to act against self-interest? How do we factor into the moral equation the presence of multiple motives? These questions are fascinating and important, but attempting to answer them would take us beyond the scope of this essay. And they are not, I believe, ultimately relevant. We should for the most part ignore questions about the motives of states or governments and focus instead on the justifiability of their actions. From that point of view, the realist claim that states do not act according to purely moral considerations is irrelevant even insofar as it is true. Whatever their motives, the actions of states must be able to withstand moral scrutiny. Our interest is not in the moral virtue of states but in the legitimacy of their actions and policies.

This view may seem less plausible if we move from the first realist view to the second—from "states do not act on the basis of moral considerations" to "states ought not to act on the basis of moral considerations." For it may seem odd to say simultaneously that an agent ought not to pay attention to certain sorts of consideration (that is, moral ones) but that its behavior will be subject to evaluation on the basis of whether it conforms to such considerations. If indeed these two ideas are incompatible, that is sufficient reason to reject the second realist view. For nothing could be clearer than that we—individuals, governments, peoples everywhere—continually engage in the moral evaluation of the behavior of states and their governments. Both public opinion and international law hold states responsible for their actions. So either realism is false (on either of its two interpretations), or it is not incompatible with the requirement that states justify their behavior.

Are states equal moral agents?

Even if states are moral agents that must justify their actions, it might be argued that states are not equal in the way that we suppose individual human beings are equal, and that this inequality allows or even requires different standards for different states. These different standards apply both to states *as agents* and to states that are *acted upon*.

Evaluating this argument seems to presuppose that we have a good understanding of what it means to say that individual human beings are equal. But this claim is at best unclear and at worst untrue. We know that human beings are not equal along any dimension that we can name: strength, beauty, intelligence, energy, happiness, sociability, or accomplishment. Nor are they "morally equal" in the most obvious meaning of that term—that is, equally inclined to morally acceptable motives or behavior.

In light of these facts, philosophers typically analyze human equality in terms of the idea that human beings are entitled to "equal consideration" or to "equal concern and respect." Equal consideration or equal concern and respect does not imply that all people should be treated the same, but rather that treating people differently requires providing relevant reasons.[8] Treating a vicious murderer differently from a law-abiding citizen and treating a hungry person differently from a well-fed one are, in this analysis, compatible with treating people with equal concern and respect.

This is admittedly a thin conception of equality, one that does not imply egalitarianism in the usual sense and is compatible with a great deal of inequality. Some will seek a more robust conception. But this one will suffice for our purposes. In demanding that different treatment requires relevant reasons, the principle of equal consideration is very close to (perhaps even identical with) the Kantian and Sartrean requirement of universalizability. In expressing one's principle of action, one is at the same time describing the circumstances under which actions of that kind are justified, for oneself and others. Making a distinction between two agents or two actions requires articulating a relevant difference (or more than one) between them.

What makes a difference relevant? Why should I be permitted to do this and you not? Why should the U.S. be permitted to act in this way and other countries not? We may despair of finding objective criteria of relevance. But the requirement that one be willing for all to act on the principle underlying one's own action is an excellent proxy. It requires only that one answer in good faith. As John Rawls explains, each

> will be wary of proposing a principle which would give him a peculiar advantage, in his present circumstances . . . Each person knows that he will be bound by it in future circumstances the peculiarities of which cannot be known, and which might well be such that the principle is then to his disadvantage.[9]

States, governments, and the peoples whom they govern are unequal in a variety of respects, as are individuals. They differ in physical size, population, riches, power, culture, and technological advancement. Perhaps most important for our purposes is that some states are illegitimate, by virtue of the relationship that they have (or lack) with the people within their borders. Although a democratic form of government is not a necessary condition of legitimacy, some degree of popular support is. Illegitimate states lack the rights of political sovereignty and territorial integrity that international law and custom normally accord states. Just as we may treat criminals, in light of their conduct, differently from other people, so we may treat illegitimate states differently from other states.

But facts such as these do not contradict the idea that the acceptability of a state's proposed course of action must be decided by articulating the principle underlying its action and seeing whether it can be universalized. The illegitimacy of a state, for example—either one that acts or one that is acted upon—will figure in the principle of action. The inequalities between states that make a moral difference are not left out of account in reckoning the legitimacy of actions and policies—*by* states and *toward* states.

This view may appear to suggest a reified conception of states, or one that accords them undue respect. According to the criticism, the analogy between states and individuals is at best highly misleading. Even though differences between individuals justify differences in their treatment, still there is a sense in which individuals possess some kind of inviolability that states do not. What Michael Walzer calls the "legalist paradigm,"[10] according to which states possess rights to political sovereignty and territorial integrity, is in this critical view misguided and mistaken. The legalist paradigm is enshrined in Article 2 of the U.N. Charter, which asserts the "sovereign equality" of member states and their right to territorial integrity and political independence. From the legalist paradigm it follows that states may do what they like within their own borders, or at the very least that outsiders have no right to intervene. But according to this critical view state sovereignty is, if not altogether an illusion, at least an exaggeration. If this is so then the notion of states as entities like individuals who are presumptively equal is also a mistake. How then can one make the analogy on which this argument rests?

I agree with those who believe state sovereignty is overrated as a morally basic concept.[11] At best, state sovereignty is a useful proxy for the rights that a state (in effect, a government or regime) holds in virtue of its relationships with those within its borders—specifically, for the principle of nonintervention in that state's internal affairs. The more positively a regime is related to its people, the more it makes sense to say that state is sovereign and possesses a right to nonintervention. A democratic state is more positively related to its people, we may suppose, than an undemocratic state. But the term "democratic" covers a multitude of possibilities that themselves vary in ways relevant to sovereignty. More fundamentally, the degree of a state's sovereignty, and thus the extent to which the principle of nonintervention holds with respect to it, depends upon how much the regime reflects the ability of people within its borders to choose freely—or determine themselves—consistent with the rights of others. I return to this point in the last section.

Principle and prudence

Kant's Categorical Imperative has counterparts in other moral theories, and it resonates with popular ideas like the "golden rule." It is not an exaggeration to say that something similar to this core idea can be found in most moral systems.

The core idea is sometimes summed up in the question "what if everybody did that?" The hard work, Kant shows, is to figure out what the *that* refers to. As we have seen, the description of the *that*—the appropriate principle underlying what one proposes to do—has important implications for the legitimacy of the action or policy in question.

"What if everybody did that?" suggests another central issue as well. A common answer is that not everybody will. Although this response did not impress Kant, or many who are sympathetic to his approach, others of a more practical bent have found it worth taking seriously. If the act that I am proposing will not affect what others do, why should I be moved by the argument that *if* others did it the consequences would be unacceptable? If everybody plucked flowers from the public garden, the garden would have no flowers—a result, we may suppose, that is unacceptable to me. But what if I can be confident that most people will not follow my example, and that my flower plucking makes little difference to the garden's beauty and well-being?

We know Kant's answer: it is not a matter of mere consequences, but of consistency. It is wrong to treat yourself as special unless you can show that your circumstances are different in some relevant way—some way that legitimizes your acting in this way while others may not. The question is not whether people will actually follow your lead.

Still, when the hypothetical fails to be met (most people do not pluck the flowers from the garden), we may be less satisfied with the answer. This brings us back to a point hinted at earlier, which must now be developed. Kant insists that moral beings act only on those principles that they can universalize; or, in other words, that persons *ought* to act only on such principles. Sartre's idea is slightly different. He asserts that when a person acts, he *does*—whether he likes it or not—legislate for all humanity, and indeed that everything "happens to every man as though the whole human race had its eyes fixed upon what he is doing and regulated its conduct accordingly."

Such a statement sounds hyperbolic in the circumstances in which we are most likely to consider it. Most of the examples used to illustrate universalizability center on the private actions of individuals. The whole human race does not have its eyes fixed on a single individual in most of the circumstances in which he or she acts. And so we do not have to worry about the world regulating its conduct accordingly. Shall I (to use Sartre's famous example) join the resistance or stay home and take care of my aged mother? Shall I break my promise to meet my friend for lunch because a more attractive offer appears? Shall I walk across the lawn instead of on the path? Shoplift once in a while? Who will know?

Some will know, of course, and they may adjust their behavior accordingly. My loose attitude toward keeping promises may get around among my acquaintances, and they may take my promises less seriously or even take their own promises to me less seriously than they otherwise would have. But the idea that everyone everywhere—all of humanity—is watching closely and drawing conclusions from my behavior seems in these contexts absurd.

This is not so in the international arena, however, and certainly not in the era of instantaneous mass communications. What ancient Rome might have gotten away with Washington may not. Political action today takes place on a global stage. Everyone sees. And many ask, in the wake of American action, "what makes them different? What gives them the right to do this? If they can, why can't we?"

It is possible that these observers are wrong. The U.S. might be relevantly different from other countries so that it would be justified in acting in ways that they would not. Earlier we examined some possible grounds for differences and found them wanting; we will return to this subject again. Nevertheless, the highly public nature of international political and military action in contemporary times provides a powerful reason to proceed with the greatest of care—a reason over and above Kant's purely moral one. Peoples and states around the world are suffused with the ideas of equality, self-determination, and national pride. To assert one's own superiority and one's rights to do what they may not is insulting and humiliating. Speaking purely in terms of consequences and not principles, it is hard to see how good can come of it.

No one likes to be confronted with another's flagrant assertion of superiority, even if the assertion is warranted. Countries are no different, and it has always seemed surprising when U.S. leaders such as President George W. Bush think nothing of announcing that the country is "the greatest nation on earth" within earshot of the rest of the world. At the very least, it is bound to create animosity. What else we should say about it depends on what it means. That the U.S. is the richest? The strongest? These claims are true. But the suggestion is of something more: we are morally superior, or somehow at least more important.

Similarly, when Washington's official policy asserts, "Our forces will be strong enough to dissuade potential adversaries from pursuing a military build-up in hopes of surpassing, or equaling, the power of the United States,"[12] it is not hard to see why other nations might object. That no one should be our superior may be an acceptable aim; that no one is permitted to be our equal—as asserted in the September 2002 "National Security Strategy"—is another matter.

"American exceptionalism," an idea often credited to Alexis de Tocqueville, has been defined as the view that "the United States was created differently, developed differently, and thus has to be understood differently—essentially on its own terms and within its own context."[13] The concept has been employed mostly to explain why throughout its history the U.S. has not had a significant labor or socialist movement.[14] One might complain that the claim of exceptionalism is confused. Every country is unique, after all. But perhaps some are more unique than others. In any case, U.S. exceptionalism has traditionally been employed as a way to explain why the country does not conform to explanatory models appropriate to other countries, not as a license for action. Today, however, U.S. exceptionalism seems to describe not so much the explanatory framework appropriate to understanding the historical development of the United States, but the moral rights that it has arrogated to itself.

Principles of humanitarian intervention

An argument for military action in places like Iraq that we have not considered invokes a principle of what some call "humanitarian intervention." A rough approximation of such a principle might look something like *Principle Seven: States may intervene militarily in the affairs of other states to prevent or end severe and widespread violations of human rights.*

We did not consider this principle earlier because it was not, according to credible accounts, the central reason for U.S. intervention in Iraq; rather it seemed to function as a by-product or perhaps a secondary reason. Up until the war began, the arguments made for intervention had to do primarily with U.S. national security and self-defense. More recently, however, the argument based on Iraqi liberation has assumed greater prominence as hard evidence for WMD and links to Al Qaeda has not materialized.

The humanitarian and prudential arguments are intertwined. Iraqi freedom and democracy are good not only for Iraqis but, as Washington now seems to argue, for U.S. interests as well. There are reasons to doubt the second claim. According to recent polls, more than 90 percent of the people in Arab and Middle Eastern countries are hostile to or disapprove of the United States.[15] If these states become more democratic, thereby better representing popular opinion, it is not easy to see how narrowly defined U.S. interests will benefit. Leaving this large problem aside, few would disagree that Saddam Hussein was a brutal and repressive tyrant responsible for gross violations of human rights. Two conclusions seem to follow: that the Iraqis would be well rid of Saddam Hussein and that he has no right to rule Iraq.

Many liberals who favored military action in places like Bosnia, Kosovo, Somalia, and Rwanda found themselves forced to refine their understanding of the principle of humanitarian intervention when it came to Iraq. If Saddam Hussein was so bad, why was war not justified to overthrow him? If liberal distrust of the Bush administration concerning Iraq was justified, what did that say about the legitimacy of the principle of humanitarian intervention? Was liberal hypocrisy at work in the decision about which oppressive states to fight?

At least two factors underlay the widespread doubts about humanitarian intervention as a principle justifying war in Iraq. One had to do with motive, the other with the prospects of success. These doubts too are intertwined.

Many people here and abroad doubted that humanitarian considerations were the primary or even a significant motive in the decision to invade Iraq. Let us suppose that their skepticism was justified. What difference does this fact make? I argued earlier that it is extremely difficult at best to know the motives of states, and better for that reason and others to avoid inquiries that require knowledge of motives. Yet how can we decide whether the principle of humanitarian intervention would justify war in Iraq without knowing whether this was the principle—or at least *a* principle—underlying U.S. action?

To answer this difficult question it is helpful to examine the other source of doubt about the principle of humanitarian intervention, which concerns the prospects of success. Much has been written on this subject specifically about Iraq, and many people have argued that winning the war was the easiest part of the undertaking. Probably the two biggest problems cited are the inherent difficulty of imposing democracy, liberty, and respect for human rights from outside, and the negative effects of U.S. intervention on the beliefs and attitudes of people in Iraq and elsewhere in the region and beyond. It is probably still too early to say whether or to what extent these fears will be borne out sufficiently to undermine any potential positive effects of intervention.

Such concerns make clear that an acceptable principle of humanitarian intervention must be more refined than the crude one proposed as Principle Seven. For one thing, the probability of success must be fairly high to justify intervention. Thus the agent must have weighed the risks and costs of intervening against the benefits and must have been warranted in concluding that the benefits outweighed the risks. That in turn requires a firm commitment on the part of the agent to ensure that the risks of failure do not come to pass. So, for example, if one's aim were to bring democracy to a region where democracy has not existed, a long-term commitment to nation-building would seem to be required.

Even if a state would be well rid of its leader and even if he has no right to rule (certainly true of Iraq and Saddam Hussein, respectively), it does not follow that all things considered it would be sensible to intervene militarily to bring about the dictator's downfall and other desired outcomes. An enormously significant factor is the will of the people in whose country one is proposing to intervene. In the paradigm case of justified intervention, oppressed or persecuted people seek help from sympathetic outsiders to help determine their destiny. Of course, when people are sufficiently oppressed and persecuted, they will not necessarily be able to communicate their wishes freely, making it difficult to discern their will. But a central question must always be whether the people inside desire the involvement of outsiders. If they do not, the term "humanitarian intervention" will be highly suspect.

These considerations help to bridge the gap between the two concerns raised by critics of such humanitarian intervention: motive and probability of success. We should not judge the legitimacy of a state's action based on its motives, but its motives will inevitably figure indirectly in the principles that characterize its actions.

In light of these remarks, a better principle than Principle Seven would be Principle Eight, which adds a crucial clause: *States may intervene militarily in the affairs of other states to prevent or end severe and widespread violations of human rights, when they have very good reason to believe that the benefits of intervention will outweigh the costs.* A full understanding of the meaning of this principle would require spelling out the possible benefits and the possible costs, among other things. There will be disagreement here both about their nature and about their probability. In addition, the agent must have *good reason to believe* the benefits will outweigh the costs—an objective condition that must be satisfied.

This statement of the principle is attractive partly because it avoids the need

72   *Judith Lichtenberg*

to inquire directly into the motives of agents, while building in the relevant questions in an appropriate way. If the U.S. had had good reason to believe that the benefits of intervention would outweigh its costs (and assuming we could reach agreement on the meaning and truth of this claim), it would have been justified in invading Iraq, whether or not humanitarian intervention was its motive. Principle Eight satisfies (or in any case comes closer than any of the other principles to satisfying) both Kant's question and Sartre's: what if everybody did that? What if everybody saw you doing that?

Notes

1 I am grateful to David Luban and Sam Kerstein for comments and suggestions on an earlier draft.
2 Quoted in Walter Kaufmann, ed., *Existentialism from Dostoevsky to Sartre* (Cleveland, OH: Meridian Books, 1956), pp. 292–3.
3 Henry Kissinger, "Iraq Is Becoming Bush's Most Difficult Challenge," *Chicago Tribune*, August 11, 2002.
4 Immanuel Kant, *Foundations of the Metaphysics of Morals*, trans. Lewis White Beck (Indianapolis: Bobbs-Merrill, 1959), p. 39.
5 Kant intended the Categorical Imperative in a stronger sense. He believed that for some actions, "their maxim cannot even be *thought* as a universal law of nature without contradiction"; for others, although "this internal impossibility is not found . . . it is still impossible to *will* that their maxims should be raised to the universality of a law of nature" (ibid., pp. 41–2). These are very strong claims, in keeping with Kant's aim of establishing objective moral requirements. As many commentators have argued, it doubtful that they can be met. A weaker, more subjective interpretation that nevertheless has important implications for morality is the one given here, according to which agents must assess the legitimacy of their actions by their willingness to accept the universalized versions of the maxims that describe their reasons for acting.
6 The existentialists' emphasis on the centrality of choice may seem to make this interpretation implausible. But that conclusion fails to appreciate existentialism's central paradox that the only thing you cannot choose is not to choose; you have no choice but to choose. "Man makes himself . . . by the choice of his morality, and he cannot but choose a morality, such is the pressure of circumstances upon him" (Sartre, "Existentialism Is a Humanism," p. 306).
7 Some argue the precise analogue of the realist thesis with regard to individuals. Psychological egoism is the claim that individuals always act only to advance their own perceived self-interest. Philosophers have argued convincingly that this view is either tautological or false.
8 Our focus here is on public policy and not all forms of interpersonal behavior. Perhaps a person does not need a reason to treat one friend differently from another (although from a certain point of view having a reason to act differently in one case rather than another seems almost a requirement of rationality).
9 John Rawls, "Justice as Fairness," *Philosophical Review* 67, no. 2 (April 1958), pp. 164–94 at p. 171.
10 For a discussion of this view see Michael Walzer, *Just and Unjust Wars*, 3rd edition (New York: Basic Books, 2000), pp. 61–2.
11 See David Luban, "Just War and Human Rights," *Philosophy and Public Affairs* 9, no. 2 (Winter 1980), pp. 160–81; and Allen Buchanan, *Justice, Legitimacy, and Self-Determination: Moral Foundations of International Law* (New York: Oxford University Press, forthcoming).

12 National Security Strategy of the United States of America, http://www.whitehouse.gov/nsc/nss9.html.

13 Byron Shafer, ed., *Is America Different?* (New York: Oxford University Press, 1991), p. v. See Alexis de Tocqueville, *Democracy in America*, vol. II (New York: Random House, Inc., 1970), pp. 36–7: "The position of the Americans is therefore quite exceptional, and it may be believed that no democratic people will ever be placed in a similar one. Their strictly Puritanical origin, their exclusively commercial habits, even the country they inhabit, which seems to divert their minds from the pursuit of science, literature, and the arts, the proximity of Europe, which allows them to neglect these pursuits without relapsing into barbarism, a thousand special causes, of which I have only been able to point out the most important, have singularly concurred to fix the mind of the American upon purely practical objects . . . Let us cease, then, to view all democratic nations under the example of the American people, and attempt to survey them at length with their own features." I thank Laura Hussey for directing me to this passage and for help on this section.

14 See Seymour Martin Lipset, *American Exceptionalism: A Double-Edged Sword* (New York: W.W. Norton and Company, 1997).

15 See Shibley Telhami, "Arab Public Opinion—A Survey in Six Countries," *San Jose Mercury*, March 16, 2003.

Part 2

Human rights and the war on terrorism

3 U.S. foreign policy and human rights in an era of insecurity

The Bush administration and human rights after September 11

David P. Forsythe

Human rights has a most ambiguous position in routine U.S. foreign policy. The subject in general is firmly fixed on the agenda, but its specific importance varies enormously across administrations and within the same administration at different times and on different issues. Even before the attacks on September 11, 2001, the George W. Bush administration had demonstrated a unilateralist and ultra-nationalist approach to most foreign policy issues, including human rights. As a general rule, security crises or the perception of national insecurity drives human rights lower among policy priorities. Thus as we would expect after the tragic attacks on New York City and Washington, the administration reduced its support for international human rights issues such as criminal justice, democracy promotion, and welfare rights. It also continued a strong unilateralist and ultra-nationalist approach to these issues.[1]

Human rights and routine foreign policy

Before we can say what has changed, if anything, on human rights in U.S. foreign policy after September 11, we need at least a cursory understanding of the subject in routine times. Starting in the mid-1970s, when Congress insisted that U.S. foreign policy pay considerable attention to human rights, all administrations have listed human rights among the official priorities of their foreign policy. Nevertheless, no administration has been able to secure a lasting and bipartisan commitment to specific human rights across time, situations, and issues. Neither the supposedly most realist administration (Richard M. Nixon's) nor initially the most liberal (Jimmy Carter's), nor any other came up with a white paper on human rights that both commanded broad support and had a serious policy impact.

This situation obtains because certain ideologies or ideational traditions regularly compete for dominance in thinking about human rights and foreign policy, but none of them consistently dominates. I speak primarily of two cultural ideologies: exceptionalism and isolationism reborn as unilateralism; and two intellectual ideologies, liberalism and realism.

U.S. exceptionalism—the notion that the U.S. reflects a great nation that is not ordinary but rather is divinely inspired to lead the world to greater freedom—comes closest to being the dominant ideology. But as articulated most clearly in modern times by Ronald Reagan, it does not easily give insights into particular policies. Blended with a crusading or militant internationalism by Reagan to roll back communism, U.S. exceptionalism has also been linked to an American isolationism that seeks to lead by example at home (by perfecting U.S. society and thus providing "the shining City on a Hill" for others to emulate).[2]

The current administration shows many similarities to the Reagan period. U.S. exceptionalism, for example, contributed to the pronounced pique directed mainly against France for opposing the use of force to topple Saddam Hussein. In Washington there was deep resentment against Paris for having the audacity to lead the opposition against what the U.S. desired. Bush's evident tendency to see himself and the U.S. as on the side of the angels against the butcher of Baghdad was reminiscent of President Reagan's speech about the Soviet Union as an evil empire. These moralistic inclinations are historically grounded in the U.S. self-image of an exceptionally good nation that is inherently worthy of support by all right-thinking persons.[3]

Unilateralism, easily blended with U.S. exceptionalism, is the preferred course of action for many policy-makers, since it allows Washington to walk away from inconvenient situations, such as genocide in Rwanda in 1994, thus displaying its historic links to isolationism.[4] Liberalism, usually associated first with Woodrow Wilson's foreign policy, emphasizes the possibilities of peaceful change through reliance on international law, organization, and human rights. It also tends to emphasize multilateral arrangements like collective security.[5] At the same time, realism, a foreign policy idea associated more recently with Henry Kissinger and perhaps historically with Theodore Roosevelt, places emphasis on states and their use of force in a hostile and primitive setting.[6] Realism is predicated on a hostile international environment either because of the "nature of man" or because of systematic insecurity involving the absence of international government.

Nixon aside, most presidents—especially former governors without wide foreign policy experience—have not thought deeply (or sometimes at all) about which of these ideational traditions, or which combination, best explains the past or is best suited to approaching international relations. Carter admitted this in his memoirs with regard to human rights, and the same is patently the case with reference to Ronald Reagan, Bill Clinton, and George W. Bush. Granted that Reagan and George W. Bush came into office with an intuitive commitment to U.S. exceptionalism, it is still the case that they did not display a carefully considered position on whether this type of nationalism could or should be combined with unilateralism or multilateralism, or with the more optimistic liberalism or the more pessimistic realism. Was Wilson or Teddy Roosevelt the model to emulate, or perhaps someone like Franklin D. Roosevelt, who displayed both liberal and realist orientations?

These ideational tensions leave us with considerable uncertainty about the George W. Bush administration and human rights in foreign policy after September 11. Given that its basic orientations are toward exceptionalism, unilateralism, and realism, it is well worth asking to what extent this administration can be brought to recognize the practical need for multilateralism in support of a basically liberal world order. After military victory in Iraq, will the administration increasingly turn to the United Nations in order to broaden its legitimacy and practical support? For the same reasons, will it be scrupulous in its respect for the Fourth Geneva Convention of 1949 regulating the occupation of foreign territory? In efforts to construct a new and democratic Iraq, how much serious attention will the current administration give to international standards on such matters?

Compounding the problem of ideational competition and initial lack of clarity about how to lead a superpower (now the only hyperpower, as the French say) is a broad and diffuse policy-making process. In routine times presidents have great difficulty in controlling the foreign policy agenda, let alone outcomes. Individual members of Congress like Jesse Helms or Henry Jackson, or factions like the Black Caucus (at least on Haiti) or Christian conservatives (at least on religious freedom) can exercise great influence, as can interest groups, bureaucratic entities, and the communications media. The result is that different views prevail on different issues at different times. Nixon and Kissinger had to make adjustments to their realist policy of détente with European communists in order to make more space for human rights in the Helsinki Process. Clinton had to make more room for attention to religious freedom, at the expense of more complicated relations with certain allies like Saudi Arabia.

At the time of writing, the Bush administration has not had to face determined and effective opposition from Democrats in Congress on matters under review here. While a few individuals like Senator William Byrd of West Virginia were caustic in their criticisms of foreign policy, most Democrats in either house were not. Once the major combat operations went well in both Afghanistan and Iraq, and with public support at approximately 70 percent, the Bush administration was spared effective critique. Republican critics of Bush foreign policy, such as Senator Charles Hagel of Nebraska, placed their criticisms within a broader party loyalty and showed general support for the President.

Two further points are now especially relevant to a discussion of why U.S. foreign policy on human rights shows so much ambiguity. Social science research can demonstrate both that human rights in foreign policy are more a Democratic than a Republican issue,[7] and that situations of war and threats to security correlate negatively with human rights protection.[8] Thus there is a great probability that the importance of human rights abroad will vary according to which party controls power in each branch of government, and whether security threats are more or less perceived and emphasized. Given that Republican administrations are prone to emphasize traditional national security and the pursuit of economic interests rather than human rights under normal circumstances, only a quite exceptional Republican administration would make international human rights a high priority when the country has been physically attacked.

Finally, it is relevant that when a president is determined to use military force abroad, the Congress cannot say "no" in the short term.[9] This has been true of all presidents since Harry Truman and the Korean War, and it was certainly true for Reagan in Lebanon (and the Caribbean and Central America), and for Clinton in the Balkans. It is only after a policy of force is going off the rails that Congress can generally muster a consensus to say "no" to a president. This was one of the lessons of Vietnam, and in an incipient way it was brought home to Reagan regarding Lebanon and Clinton regarding Somalia. When the president is determined to use force abroad in the name of national security, the role of Congress is reduced, at least in the short term, and along with it the attention to various specific human rights that many members of Congress would pursue in more routine times.

Prior to September 2001, the ultra-nationalist and unilateralist preferences of the Bush administration were evident, contradicting the Bush campaign promise to be "humble" in foreign policy. Examples of U.S. exceptionalism permeated the Inaugural Address.[10] On the first anniversary of September 11, the President stated that "we know that God had placed us together in this moment . . . our cause is even larger than our country. Ours is the cause of human dignity . . . this ideal of America is the hope of all mankind."[11] When the U.S. for the first time was not elected to the U.N. Human Rights Commission, the President—overlooking the U.S. role in human rights violations in many countries such as Chile and Indonesia during the Cold War—asked with apparently genuine astonishment how the world organization could possibly have a Human Rights Commission without the U.S. At West Point the President referred to the country as the "single surviving model of human progress."[12] When the U.N. High Commissioner for Human Rights, Mary Robinson, publicly raised questions about U.S. commitment to human rights in places like China, the Bush administration lobbied for her removal (just as the Reagan administration had successfully pressed for the removal of U.N. Director for Human Rights Theo van Boven, after he had proven inconvenient in pressing Argentina in the 1970s, then a U.S. ally, to clean up its Dirty War). The Bush administration also moved brusquely to unilaterally replace other persons whose views did not accord with administration policy, such as the head of the Organization for the Prohibition of Chemical Weapons and the head of the Intergovernmental Panel on Climate Change.[13]

Later the President was to say that Saddam Hussein had been "stiffing the world" on arms control in Iraq.[14] This was in the face of the U.S.'s refusal to support international agreements relating to the International Criminal Court (ICC), global warming, trade in light weapons, improvements to treaties on biological weapons, children's rights, women's rights, and the future of the missile defense treaty. On these (and other) subjects many countries wanted continued, if not more, international regulation. The Bush administration rejected these views and in most cases offered no new ideas about how to cope with evident international problems. Thus the administration rejected the Kyoto Protocol, but offered no serious alternative for dealing with global warming, walked away from the conference on trade in light arms without apparent concern for the basic problem (perhaps because of its status as the world's leading arms exporter), and refused to ratify the Convention on the Rights of the Child despite unanimous endorsement from all existing governments.

Many centrist commentators noted this pattern, characterizing Bush foreign policy as one of "insolent exceptionalism," or "arrogant," or objectionable and self-defeating in its self-serving "double standards."[15] An early summary judgment by the syndicated columnist William Pfaff is worth noting :

> The motivation of the new decision-makers in Washington is quite simple. They want the United States to have its way. They do not want to rule the world . . . They believe that the United States is the best of all countries, with the right ideas; that it deserves to prevail in international disputes because it is right.[16]

Said Ramesh Thakur wrote in the *International Herald Tribune,* "But Washington cannot construct a world in which all have to obey universal norms and rules, while it can opt out whenever, as often, and for as long as it likes."[17] It bears emphasizing that these commentators are not known for persistent U.S.-bashing. They are widely read and generally respected in the West.

There were, of course, many commentators who supported the administration's approach to foreign policy, including to international human rights.[18] There were also elements of a cosmetic or superficial multilateralism. For example, the Bush administration announced the intention to rejoin the United Nations Educational, Scientific, and Cultural Organization (UNESCO). But this announcement came at a time when the administration was under broad attack for its unilateralism, and was essentially a sop to this criticism. UNESCO, moreover, does not loom large in Bush foreign policy. True, Secretary of State Colin Powell persuaded the President to take the issue of Iraq to the U.N., but the President made clear from the beginning of this demarche that the U.S. would use force against Iraq regardless of the position taken by the Security Council, which is exactly what transpired.

Given the nature of U.S. foreign policy in general, and concomitantly a "made in America" approach to many human rights issues, it was perplexing to think that better packaging and marketing would lead to more deference abroad—although a panel under the aegis of the venerable Council on Foreign Relations recommended a better sales pitch. The fundamental problem was more in the message than in the delivery.[19] No less than the President of the Carnegie Endowment for International Peace branded the Bush administration as "an aggressive new Rome."[20]

International criminal justice after September 11

The Bush administration inherited strong Washington opposition to the new International Criminal Court. The Clinton administration had belatedly signed the Rome Statute of 1998 creating the first permanent international criminal court. But strong opposition from the Pentagon and from a broad bipartisan coalition in Congress meant that Clinton was never able to really endorse the ICC or send the Rome Statute forward for the advice and consent of the Senate. Clinton could not guarantee to the ICC's critics that Americans would never have to appear as defendants before it. Beneath various smoke screens about a rogue prosecutor and politically motivated charges, arguments that were discounted by most international legal experts and human rights organizations in the U.S., lay U.S. exceptionalism and unilateralism—along with enormous power.

True, what was at issue was the semi-revolutionary idea that national leaders should have to answer to an international court for charges of war crimes. This was not a completely new idea, given the Nuremberg and Tokyo Tribunals of the 1940s, and the U.N. tribunals of the 1990s for the former Yugoslavia and for Rwanda. Still, the notion that U.S. elected leaders, and top policy-makers approved by democratically elected leaders, should have to answer to an international criminal tribunal was not exactly seen with great enthusiasm across the political class. What was semi-revolutionary was the notion that U.S. citizens were not exceptional, but were to be potentially judged like the rest.

The Bush administration took the truly unusual step of "unsigning" the Rome Statute. It blocked further movement on all U.N. peacekeeping matters until the Security Council granted a one-year guarantee that U.S. personnel would be exempted from any charges before the ICC while serving in U.N.-approved deployments of force—a guarantee that was renewed for another year in June 2003. It pressured states to grant bilateral agreements guaranteeing that no U.S. citizen would be turned over to the ICC for any charges arising from events in that particular state. It engaged in public disputes with the European Union over this issue, with unhappy applicants to the E.U. caught in the middle of conflicting threats and pressures. Thus in various ways adding up to what the *New York Times* accurately termed an "ugly overreaction,"[21] the Bush administration tried to ensure that the ICC would not be able to exercise its jurisdiction and authority over any U.S. citizen. All of this had the strong support of members of Congress, including many Democrats, who passed the American Servicemen's Protection Act, which among other things authorized the president to use force to liberate any American detained in relation to the ICC (the so-called Hague Invasion Act).

Some perspective is in order. The ICC only exercises its complementary authority if and when a state fails to properly investigate, and if prosecution is warranted in relation to war crimes, crimes against humanity, and genocide. States retain primary responsibility in these matters. If the U.S. properly addresses such subjects, the ICC stays on the shelf. A prosecutor who wishes to advance an indictment must first get the approval of a three-judge chamber of the court. Thus the prosecutor is not free to do as he or she wishes. Moreover, all North Atlantic Treaty Organization (NATO) allies, including some like Britain and France that have frequently used force abroad, have ratified the Rome Statute. The total number of ratifications in mid-2003 was almost 90.

There are few, if any, independent legal scholars or respected human rights organizations that think that there is a high probability of U.S. citizens serving as defendants in the ICC in politically inspired trials.

Finally, under the notion of universal jurisdiction that attaches to grave breaches of international humanitarian law, crimes against humanity, and genocide, U.S. citizens can already be arrested and tried by any state. The ICC at least gives the U.S. the right to initiate its own proceedings when and if charges are filed. The ICC also offers improved guarantees of a fair trial compared to many states that theoretically might arrest Americans under the principle of universal jurisdiction. Moreover, the U.S. Constitution does not travel abroad with U.S. citizens; those arrested and tried in a foreign jurisdiction have no recourse to U.S. laws. The ICC makes no change in this situation. Furthermore, U.S. citizens court-martialed for war crimes are tried in military courts that do not have trial by jury as known in civilian courts.

Nevertheless, the Bush administration has been as adamantly against the ICC as was Jesse Helms before his retirement from the Senate. John Bolton, formerly an official in the Reagan administration and on record with the truly original view that treaties are not really law, was made Bush's point-man to keep the ICC at bay.[22] On the basis partly of exceptionalism and partly of realism, the administration, with strong bipartisan support in Congress, is not prepared to have its decisions on targets and choice of weapons in armed conflict subjected to authoritative international legal review. Such matters as the bombing of dual-use targets (for example, TV facilities in Belgrade and Baghdad), or the use of depleted uranium shells to pierce enemy armor (alleged to still be causing health hazards in Kosovo and southern Iraq, among other places), and the use of cluster bombs in civilian areas (at issue in both Afghanistan and Iraq) raise serious legal issues about war crimes.

Given that neither Congress nor the courts are likely to conduct a proper review of such matters, it is possible that a responsible prosecutor of the ICC might wish to question such policy by way of an indictment—not of lower-ranking military personnel but of high policy-makers.[23] Whether the first prosecutor of the ICC, a distinguished Argentine lawyer who was involved in criminal proceedings against former military leaders in that country, and who has taught at the Harvard and Stanford law schools, would be inclined to pursue such matters is a good question.

Rather than seriously review controversial policies about targeting and weaponry, the Bush administration prefers to undercut the ICC at the cost of increased friction with its NATO allies and others. And at the end of the war in Iraq, the Bush team moved toward creation of national military courts to pursue various legal charges against both Iraqis and those detained in the preceding armed conflict in Afghanistan. Predictably, the administration was widely criticized for not utilizing the ICC or some other multilateral arrangement. The administration could have turned over top Iraqi officials for trials that would have broad international support. U.S. legal proceedings against those captured in relation to Afghanistan and Iraq inherently raise questions about fair trials, victor's justice, and whether Washington is going to repeat the procedures used in the Nuremberg and Tokyo tribunals, which are often viewed as poor legal precedents.

The basic rationale for the ICC is that it serves as an inducement to states to exercise primary responsibility to enforce the law regarding war crimes, crimes against humanity, and genocide. As was true of the Clinton administration in Rwanda during 1994, the Bush administration finds that taking the law seriously can sometimes complicate its independence and desire to avoid certain issues. The current administration resembles earlier ones in that it is more interested in national independence than in giving serious attention to international criminal law. Most members of Congress, including most Democrats, support this orientation.[24] U.S. nationalism has trumped reasonable concern for more effective international law on genocide, war crimes, and other gross violations of human rights.

One sees this ultra-nationalist and unilateralist orientation by the Bush administration not only on international criminal justice, but also on the closely related subject of applying international humanitarian law to the detainees held at Guantánamo.[25] Despite the evident armed conflict in which it was participating in Afghanistan, the administration initially argued that the 1949 Geneva Conventions did not apply to any of the detainees. This obviously was at odds with reality, and the administration then contended that while Taliban fighters might fall under the Geneva law, they would not benefit from prisoner of war (POW) status. Article 5 of the Third Geneva Convention of 1949 requires that an independent tribunal decide the status of detainees in contested cases, and that until that judgment is rendered the detainee should be treated as if he or she were a POW.

Further, the administration refused to accord any status under the 1949 Geneva Conventions to Al Qaeda detainees. If such detainees are not covered by the Third Geneva Convention pertaining to irregular forces, they are almost certainly covered by the Fourth, pertaining to civilians who fall into the hands of an adversary during international armed conflict as long as their state is a party to the conventions. This the Bush administration flatly refuses to accept.

Although the Bush team does allow the International Committee of the Red Cross (ICRC) to regularly visit the detainees at Guantánamo, which has largely satisfied Congress, other parties continue to raise questions about whether the U.S. is violating international humanitarian law. A British court did so in the fall of 2002.[26] These critics sometimes point out, moreover, that the U.S. has special forces abroad out of uniform, and thus has an interest in careful attention to the terms of that law. The Bush administration seems to prefer as free a hand as possible with regard to the long detention and prolonged interrogation of detainees who are held without access to legal counsel. It should be noted that not every violation of the Geneva Conventions is a war crime that leads to individual prosecution, and it is unlikely that any U.S. official would ever have to answer for these detention policies at the ICC. These potential U.S. violations of the Third and Fourth Geneva Conventions of 1949 would not be defined as grave breaches and thus do not constitute war crimes in terms of the Rome Statute; moreover, the prosecutor can only pursue indictments for acts occurring after July 1, 2002. But they still indicate a self-serving unilateralism that rankles others, particularly states whose nationals are detained. They also suggest that playing fast and loose with treaty law is an approach to multilateral arrangements that is not in the U.S.'s long-term self-interest.

As expected, in the war in Iraq of 2003, the U.S. demanded proper attention to the Third Geneva Convention of 1949 when its military personnel were missing or were confirmed as captured by the Iraqi side. As in the 1991 Gulf war, in the hope of reciprocity, the U.S. gave considerable attention to that law with regard to the thousands of Iraqi combatants detained by U.S. and U.K. forces. All of this had no effect on Washington's views toward detainees at Guantánamo. Thus, when there was countervailing power bringing into play considerable self-interest, the U.S. was more careful with legal argument. When there was no effective countervailing power, the U.S. manipulated the legal argument as it liked. In either case, however, Washington was unwilling for the ICC to have any say even as a back-up safeguard operating on the principle of complementarity.

It is true that the two U.N. ad hoc tribunals, one for the former Yugoslavia and one for Rwanda, did not function expeditiously and perfectly from their respective origins in 1993 and 1994. But both courts have evolved over time and produced an important record of holding high officials responsible for heinous acts. Both have contributed to the refinement of international law on genocide, war crimes, and crimes against humanity, and to standards of universal due process. Both have made positive contributions to other courts such as the ICC and to the other two transnational courts for Sierra Leone and Cambodia. There is nothing in the record of the two U.N. ad hoc courts and certainly not anything reflected in the actions of the international prosecutor that should give the U.S. pause about the ICC.

It is also true that there are roads to social justice beyond juridical proceedings. Of late there has been much debate about truth commissions, apologies, reparations, and other non-judicial reactions to gross violations of human rights and humanitarian law.[27] Even if it is agreed that it was wise in places such as South Africa and El Salvador to forgo trials of national leaders for the atrocities of the past in favor of looking forward to the construction of a stable liberal democracy, such agreement does not undercut the value of the ICC. Under the Rome Statute, the Security Council can suspend ICC action for one year, renewable. Thus provision is made for the possible judgment that in some situations one might want to bypass international criminal justice for other conceptions of justice.

Democracy promotion after September 11

President Bush's National Security Strategy of September 2002 is as much about democracy and freedom and human dignity as about fighting terrorism, and claims to pre-emptive self-defense.[28] Consistent with exceptionalism, the administration has always stressed its historic role to lead the global struggle for democracy. On the basis of executive discretion as well as bipartisan Congressional support, the U.S. in recent years has spent some $500 million per annum on democracy promotion programs.[29] Early efforts were directed to organizing and supervising elections, then to state-building via reform of governing agencies. Now the emphasis is on building civil society—creating the nonprofit private sector organizations that can exercise a vertical check on state institutions from below, while deepening citizen participation in public affairs.

Bush administration rhetoric fits nicely with Congressionally mandated and funded programs. It is highly difficult to evaluate such programs, given that no one knows exactly what produces stable liberal democracy in a given country, and that the U.S. official role is but one factor out of many.[30] Most Western states, and international organizations like the Council of Europe, the European Union (E.U.), the Organization of American States (OAS), the Organization for Security and Cooperation in Europe (OSCE), and the U.N., have democracy promotion programs. Thomas Carothers suggests that the U.S. focus should be supporting local volunteer service organizations dedicated to solving practical problems like adequate housing rather than Western-style professional advocacy groups.[31]

Perhaps the most important problem for the Bush team on this subject lies not in good intentions or grass roots efforts but in the consequences of defining the war against terrorism everywhere as the be-all and end-all of the administration. According to press reports, the President has determined that anti-terrorism will be the focus of his administration, that his is a wartime presidency, and that most other issues will just have to receive less of his time.[32] Such an articulated position necessarily reduces U.S. pressure on authoritarian or transition governments to move seriously to respect civil and political rights and genuinely implement liberal democracy. Foreign leaders know that if they cooperate with Washington on anti-terrorism measures, for example on voting in the U.N. Security Council or on participating in military coalitions, they will not be seriously sanctioned for dragging their feet on political reform.

If the Bush team gets China to acquiesce in moves against terrorists, and reaches agreement with Beijing that certain groups in China's northwest Xinjiang Province are terrorists, then the administration is certainly not going to sanction China for lack of serious political reform.[33] High-level pressure from Washington, if it ever existed, is thus alleviated in exchange for support on anti-terrorism measures. Of course the Bush team can adopt the Clinton approach to political reform in China: by pushing for economic freedom and the rule of law, one eventually will advance political freedom and individual rights.

If one takes Uzbekistan and Egypt as examples, one can demonstrate the dynamic at work. Despite administration rhetoric stressing continuing interest in democracy, human rights, and political reform, the U.S. does not seriously press regimes on these "liberal" issues when they are deemed crucial for U.S. military and paramilitary operations in places like Afghanistan and Iraq.[34] Uzbekistan was and is useful to the U.S. for its military operations in Afghanistan and neighboring areas after September 11. At first the administration was quiet about that country's human rights record. But after certain members of Congress began to raise questions about the U.S. "dance with dictators," the administration shifted ground.[35] U.S. Assistant Secretary of State for Democracy, Human Rights, and Labor (DRL) Lorne W. Craner began to say all of the right things—namely that a lasting relationship between the two states had to be built on more than military cooperation, that it had to be based also on shared values pertaining to "hunger and poverty and political freedom."[36] The DRL used its discretionary authority to make several grants to human rights groups in Uzbekistan: nongovernmental organization (NGO) capacity-building got $795,000, efforts to advance the rule of law got $500,000, political party development got $300,000.[37] But things did not significantly change in the short run. The ICRC suspended its prison visits during April 2002, given that the regime of President Karimov did not agree to unfettered visits. Freedom House, which measures civil and political freedoms around the world, continued to give the Karimov government the worst possible score on political freedom and the next to worst possible score on civil freedom. The U.N. Special Rapporteur on Torture found that practice to be systematic in Uzbekistan.[38] Uzbekistan's leadership saw no need to make changes that would jeopardize its iron grip on power given the regime's value to the U.S. in the war on terrorism. Unlike the European Bank for Reconstruction and Development (EBRD), which insisted on changes in civil and political rights in exchange for its loans,[39] the Bush administration did not try to use economic leverage to get the Karimov regime to liberalize.

As for Egypt, the U.S. war on terrorism and the war in Iraq accentuated Cairo's strategic value. It has been the case for some time that the Hosni Mubarak regime is key to the U.S. on the Israeli–Palestinian dispute and other political disputes in the region. Thus the U.S. mostly ignores the lack of democracy, systematic torture, persistent repression, and other violations of human rights in Egypt. The U.S. occasionally uses quiet diplomacy to tell the Mubarak regime when Egyptian repression may be creating political problems. The Bush administration did quietly protest the initial conviction of the well-known and well-connected Saadeddin Ibrahim and several associates on trumped-up charges and applauded the reversal of that conviction in early 2003.[40] But when the Mubarak regime renewed the emergency decrees that, recalling the Ferdinand Marcos era in the Philippines, allowed the government to continue authoritarian rule despite occasional elections, the Bush administration was silent.

The Bush team now had additional reasons not to press Mubarak on such issues as authoritarianism, torture, gay rights, and lack of judicial due process. Amnesty International has consistently raised concern about these and other issues.[41] Freedom House for some time has given Egypt the next to worst possible scores on both civil and political freedoms. If anything, Mubarak after September 2001 must feel more immune from foreign pressure. There were press reports that suspected terrorists were flown to Egypt to undergo harsh interrogation beyond the reach of both U.S. courts and the ICRC (which at the time of writing does not make prison visits there, since there is no armed conflict, civil war, or pronounced domestic instability).[42]

U.S. democracy promotion is nonexistent in Egypt. There is no indication that Washington has pressed for democratic reforms under the logic that repression and frustration breed terrorism against the West in countries such as Egypt, Saudi Arabia, and Algeria. Whether the trigger was repression condoned by the U.S., support for controversial Israeli policies, talk of invading Iraq, or some other reason, anti-American feeling was rampant in Egypt.[43] Mubarak, however, advised against the U.S. invasion of Iraq on the grounds that such an attack would increase Arab and Islamic terrorism.

It is certainly paradoxical at best that the Bush administration undertook war in Iraq in 2003 not only for alleged reasons of pre-emptive self-defense, but to liberate the Iraqi people from tyranny and to create a model democracy that will transform the Arab world. But to pursue that invasion, partly in the name of human rights and democracy, the Bush team has chosen to turn a blind eye to human rights and democracy in places like Uzbekistan and Egypt.

The future is unpredictable, but it is likely that a group of scholars at the Brookings Institution is right: such a scenario for militant democracy promotion in Iraq is "a dangerous fantasy."[44] Iraq is deeply divided between Arabs and Kurds, Shi'sa and Sunni, and between supporters and opponents of the Saddam Hussein regime. The opposition in exile is badly fractured, as are the Iraqi Kurds in the north. Divided societies can arrive at some type of democracy, witness Belgium or Lebanon in the past. But Iraq is a difficult case. Many Iraqis do not want the U.S. to linger and influence their political evolution after the Saddam Hussein regime. Moreover, Iran will clearly try to influence the course of political events in Iraq, where a pro-American government allowing U.S. military access can hardly be applauded by the clerics in power in Tehran. To the extent that there is a movement toward democracy in the Middle East, it is more likely to come in slow and incremental steps in places like Iran, where it is already under way, and not from U.S. occupation of divided Iraq. The U.S. has had troops in Bosnia since 1995, and, despite considerable multilateral help, movement toward liberal democracy is still quite fragile.

The Bush administration continues to present itself as the leader for democracy promotion around the world. The war on terrorism supposedly accentuates the need for democracy, which presumably does not produce terrorists.[45] Yet the emphasis on the "war" against terrorism in fact reduces the prospect of actual high-level U.S. pressure for political reform in countries seen as crucial for success in that "war." The Bush team fought a war partly for democracy in Iraq, but at the same time the administration is a willing accessory to authoritarianism in many neighboring and other countries. Uzbekistan and especially Egypt are classic examples.

Welfare rights after September 11

The Bush administration inherited strong opposition to the International Criminal Court, as well as strong opposition to internationally recognized human rights pertaining to adequate food, clothing, shelter, and health care. I refer to these as "welfare rights," as distinct from other internationally recognized socioeconomic rights pertaining to labor and education. The latter are not opposed by Washington in principle, although they may not always receive as much attention as welfare rights in U.S. foreign policy.[46]

While Franklin D. Roosevelt spoke about the importance of "freedom from want," and while the Nobel Laureate Amartya Sen has argued that a person who lacks adequate medical care is not really a free person,[47] the U.S. has never been comfortable with that part of the 1948 Universal Declaration of Human Rights that addresses welfare rights—the right to adequate food, clothing, shelter, and health care. When the U.S. endorses international human rights in the abstract, and when it presses other countries like China to take the Universal Declaration seriously, the U.S. simply glosses over international welfare rights as if they did not exist. While in 1977 Carter signed the 1966 International Covenant of Economic, Social, and Cultural Rights, neither he nor any other president ever submitted it to the Senate for advice and consent.

There is a broad consensus in the U.S. that food, clothing, shelter, and health care have nothing to do with fundamental human rights, but rather that they are desirable goods in private markets. To the extent that state involvement is necessary to help the less fortunate acquire adequate provisions, these are voluntary, non-obligatory governmental programs. Individuals have no entitlements. If provided, the state must meet civil rights provisions pertaining to equality of access and treatment. But the state is not obligated to start or continue such programs. In November 2002 Oregon defeated a ballot proposal to provide "universal health care" for its citizens. Health care is treated as a human right in Canada and most other Western-style democracies. It has never been in the U.S. The emphasis in this area, as in most others, is on individual responsibility, market solutions, and small government.

The Bush administration thus has manifested no interest in internationally recognized welfare rights. The tragic events of September 2001 made no difference in this regard. The Bush administration, however, to the surprise of many observers, did announce a plan to double U.S. foreign assistance to certain countries of the global South. In part as a complement to the war on terrorism, the Bush team announced plans for a Millennium Challenge Account, which over several years was designed to increase U.S. foreign development assistance by five billion dollars. This fund was intended to help countries that engaged in several reforms, including movement toward "good governance." Debate has continued about refinement of the proposal.[48]

Much of the U.S. emphasis was clearly on getting countries to accept the neo-liberal model of economic growth that stressed more capitalism and free trade and less governmental involvement in the economy. It is relevant to recall that despite talk of U.S. support for democracy and humanitarian objectives in Russia and the Newly Independent States (NIS) formerly part of the Soviet empire, most of that foreign aid has gone for support for business and strictly market reform.[49]

But some of the rhetoric about the Millennium Challenge Account was on development through human rights and with attention to human dignity. There was thus some overlap with democracy promotion. There was also some increased attention in Washington to the problem of HIV/AIDS in such places as sub-Saharan Africa. The President promised a U.S. contribution to fighting this health crisis on humanitarian grounds. The administration was active in trying to get lower prices in developing countries for drugs needed in the treatment of HIV/AIDS, despite the World Trade Organization's Trade-Related Intellectual Property Rights agreement protecting patent rights of pharmaceutical companies for 20 years.

Thus, if the issue was not framed in terms of a human right to adequate food or health care, but was presented as a matter of voluntary foreign assistance to help the less fortunate, the Bush administration showed increased interest in the issue. Given that antecedent Republican administrations had minimized the role of foreign assistance for development, preferring the neo-liberal model with an emphasis on the role of direct foreign investment from the private sector, this considerable "bump" in U.S. development assistance, if Congress followed through on appropriation, was noteworthy. At an international meeting in Monterrey, Mexico, in 2002, the Bush administration was part of a North–South consensus that the developed countries should help in the advance of the developing counties.

Heretofore, most developed states projected their domestic models abroad on these issues.[50] States that had large welfare programs at home tended to provide relatively high levels of developmental assistance (as a percentage of their gross domestic product). States, especially the U.S., that had small welfare states at home tended to have small levels of foreign assistance (again as a percentage of the GDP). The Bush administration promised to break with this pattern at least somewhat, undoubtedly stirred by the war against terrorism.

It still remained true that the Bush team rejected welfare rights as human rights, which reflected a societal consensus. Since the Great Depression, social democracy has been weak in the U.S. Carter and Clinton were not able to re-establish the Roosevelt tradition of viewing welfare rights as human rights. Carter tried, up to a point, whereas Clinton—being a "New Democrat" and presenting a "third way" that featured close ties to business—did not.

Conclusion

In some ways the events of September 11 have not changed the U.S. approach to internationally recognized human rights very much, if at all. Washington continues to view human rights as "international" mostly as a direct application of the U.S. domestic experience abroad.[51] It is very difficult to document a situation in which the U.S. has changed its stance on a human rights issue because of international pressure.[52] Thus, when in 1992 the U.S. ratified the International Covenant on Civil and Political Rights, which contains some provisions different from the U.S. Constitution concerning free speech, war propaganda, and the like, the Senate insisted on reservations, declarations, and understandings that amounted to a statement that the U.S. would not change any of its existing practices. That is precisely why the Netherlands challenged these statements as inconsistent with the purpose of the treaty, and thus not allowed under international law. The U.S. endorses international human rights in the abstract, but practices a human rights policy that reflects cultural relativism and national particularity. This is very clear on welfare rights and on the rights of the child.[53]

Is it difficult to understand why most countries resent the U.S.'s lecturing them on their human rights record? For example, the rest of the world at least formally agrees that children deserve special protection. But the U.S. is alone among states and continues to chart its own unilateral course on this matter, rejecting the treaty on the rights of the child. This situation undermines the "soft power" of the U.S. when it approaches other states on such matters as religious freedom. Other countries have no obligation to implement the U.S. Bill of Rights, so when Washington is lax with international human rights standards, it undercuts U.S. leadership for human rights.

Of course U.S. power still may come into play, and other countries may find it necessary to bend to Washington's desires. Belgrade finally decided to hand Slobodan Milošević over to the U N. ad hoc court at The Hague, lest Washington continue to hold up important foreign assistance.

But Washington's orientations certainly create frictions and resentments. Growing anti-U.S. fervor in the world is not just the product of foreign jealously of U.S. wealth and power, but more rationally results from a series of unilateral policies at variance with the considered judgment of many governments. We have already reviewed issues like global warming, trade in light arms, and the ban of anti-personnel landmines. The end result is that the objectives of U.S. foreign policy meet determined resistance and thus are achieved only with difficulty. Also, U.S. power ceases to be hegemonic, based on persuasion and "voluntary" cooperation. It becomes dominant power, imposed by coercion, which is more difficult and costly and in the long run more counterproductive to a peaceful world built on agreement.

As already noted, the U.S. has never been very keen on the ICC as it took final shape at Rome in 1998. The U.S. was one of only seven states (and one of only two liberal democracies, Israel being the other) to vote against the Rome Statute. And Clinton never submitted it to the Senate for approval. But with U.S. use of force in Afghanistan and Iraq, the Bush administration is even more determined not to allow, if at all possible, the ICC to have the opportunity to review U.S. policy-makers' decisions about weapons and targets in armed conflict. Rather than review policies that might reasonably lead to charges of war crimes, the Bush team prefers to undercut the ICC by seeking a special exemption for all U.S. citizens—even at the cost of friction with allies, impediments to

U.N. peacekeeping, and an imperiled court for the prosecution of those like Saddam Hussein who are truly a menace to both human rights and international peace and security. The current administration's handling of this issue, with its bipartisan support, suggests more an ideological crusade on behalf of national authority and freedom of policy-making than a reasoned evaluation of the costs and benefits of effective international criminal justice.

Given that U.S. citizens may still be subject to the jurisdiction of the ICC under present rules, U.S. opposition has created great friction with many states without making any fundamental change. A prosecutor can still bring charges against U.S. citizens. While this is unlikely, all of Washington's maneuvers have failed to alter legal facts. One does wonder whether long-term U.S. interests would not be better served by accepting the court, and at the same time undertaking a serious national review of policies that might turn out to be on the wrong side of international law. If the ICC is acceptable to Tony Blair and the United Kingdom, it is difficult to understand how it can be so deleterious for the United States. But here once again we have to take into account an emotive nationalism in the form of exceptionalism.

Likewise, on international welfare rights, the Bush administration reflects little difference from previous Republican and Democratic administrations. There is a strong societal consensus against welfare rights as human rights, although that consensus does allow space for relatively small welfare programs. What is new in this domain is a Republican administration's promise of increased foreign assistance to deal with the less fortunate in the global South, which runs counter to the hegemonic neo-liberal model of economic growth featuring private-sector solutions to most problems. If we take the situation in sub-Saharan Africa as an example, however, no doubt one is on safe ground in surmising that the Bush administration is driven more by the desire to appear responsive to a human problem than by the argument that persons with HIV/AIDS have an internationally recognized right to adequate health care. Given the declared war on terrorism, the Bush team no doubt is more interested in projecting itself as a sensitive and constructive international partner than as one that is obligated to help respond to the welfare rights of foreigners.

There is a growing concern for international welfare rights in Western academic circles.[54] There may also be some increased attention to these rights by certain NGOs like Amnesty International and Human Rights Watch, which now recognize how much poverty and its related ills contribute to denial of civil and political rights. Still, international welfare rights remain the stepchild of the global human rights movement. These rights even have secondary status in Europe where from time to time social democratic governments take them seriously. Thus it is doubtful that there will be a negative impact on U.S. foreign policy in the short term resulting from its disregard for socioeconomic rights. Other governments mostly do not care. Clearly the U.S. public is either apathetic, or supportive of the status quo.

It is on the subject of democracy promotion that one sees the greatest change affecting the current administration's approach to a general human rights issue.

The rhetoric from Washington has not changed, and the administration still sees itself as the global leader for enlarging the democratic community. But in reality, the emphasis on a war against all terrorism as the defining characteristic of the administration means that U.S. officials cannot help but be ineffective in influencing political reform in allies and would-be partners in the short term. Foreign leaders know very well that the real Bush emphasis is on cooperation in the war on terrorism, not on democratic change that might undermine the power of the very leaders that are offering various types of concrete support to the U.S. The 2003 annual report of Amnesty International documents the decline of attention around the world to democracy and human rights because of U.S. foreign policy after September 11.[55]

It remains supremely ironic that in order to pursue a war allegedly in part for democracy in Iraq, Washington finds it useful to turn a blind eye to lack of democracy and related human rights violations in key supporting states such as Egypt or Pakistan. One wonders how long it will take for the evident contradictions in U.S. foreign policy on democracy promotion to make themselves felt in official circles in Washington and in the country. Perhaps continued resistance to political repression in states like Egypt and Pakistan will come to endanger the American connection as happened in Iran in the late 1970s. At the same time, as long as Pakistan makes an effective contribution to the arrest of Islamic terrorists, and as long as Egypt supports U.S. policy in the Israeli–Palestinian conflict, it is highly unlikely that Washington will bring effective pressure to bear on Islamabad and Cairo in the name of democracy and human rights.

Contemporary U.S. foreign policy on human rights is greatly affected by the ideas of exceptionalism, unilateralism, and realism. Exceptionalism remains strong, as the President sees the country as reflecting a divinely blessed greatness. Unilateralism is under attack but remains strong.[56] American unilateral exceptionalism flourishes when backed by clear primacy of hard, coercive power.[57] Liberalism and human rights have reduced importance. A threatening international setting normally leads to the predominance of realism over liberalism. The normal process of making foreign policy has been tilted toward presidential power, as it always is in times of national insecurity. This primacy for security managers reduces the attention to many human rights issues that Congress normally pursues in its fragmented way.

The decline in importance of most human rights issues in U.S. foreign policy can be anticipated when one finds a Republican administration perceiving a clear and present danger to national security. The inherent tension, however, between international human rights and national security could have been managed better by the Bush team. The war against terrorism could have been defined in less sweeping terms. The President could have made it clearer that protecting various human rights at home and abroad was just as important in undermining terrorism.

In the last analysis, George W. Bush, who believes strongly in exceptionalism, cannot provide strong leadership for truly international human rights. No president who believes that the U.S is divinely blessed and stands above human rights standards that hold for other states can exercise leadership on issues like the International Criminal Court. Such presidents will always oppose an equitable international law in favor of absolute national sovereignty. Such presidents will always seek double standards that benefit the U.S. and deeply irritate other governments and citizens of other countries. Moreover, given the great military power of the U.S., it is difficult for Washington to accept muscular international law and organization. States with great power do not normally make great multilateralists.[58]

What is really needed in the twenty-first century is presidential leadership that can reorient U.S. society to accept limits on state sovereignty and unilateral action, which are necessary for an equitably managed interdependent world. Recent presidents have been sorely lacking in this regard. The lack of effective attention to various human rights by the Bush team is but part of this larger question.

Notes

1 The present analysis draws on two publications by the author: "The United States and International Criminal Justice," *Human Rights Quarterly* 24, no. 4 (November, 2002), pp. 974–91; and "Human Rights and U.S. Foreign Policy," *Journal of Human Rights* 1, no. 4 (December 2002), pp. 501–21. The first part of the present analysis is cursory with the emphasis on what is distinctive about human rights in U.S. foreign policy since September 11.
2 For a modern defense of this latter position see Michael H. Hunt, *Ideology and U.S. Foreign Policy* (New Haven, CT: Yale University Press, 1987).
3 See further Michael O'Hanlon, "Why Rumsfeld Should Lay off the French," *International Herald Tribune*, May 28, 2003, http://www.iht.com/articles/97733.html. But even this critique of U.S. policy fails to note that the French position opposing U.S. use of force was quite reasonable given widespread interpretations of international law.
4 See, for example, Richard N. Haass, *Intervention: The Use of American Military Force in the Post-Cold War World* (Washington: Brookings, 1999).
5 Lloyd E. Ambrosius, *Wilsonianism: Woodrow Wilson and His Legacy in American Foreign Relations* (New York: Palgrave, 2002).
6 Henry Kissinger regards Teddy Roosevelt as a realist; see his *Diplomacy* (New York: Simon and Schuster, 1994). William Pfaff regards him as a romantic nationalist; see his *Barbarian Sentiments* (New York: Hill and Wang, 2000).
7 See further, for example, Ole Holsti, "Public opinion on human rights in American foreign policy," in David P. Forsythe, ed., *The United States and Human Rights: Looking Inward and Outward* (Lincoln, NE: University of Nebraska Press, 2000), pp. 131–74.
8 The literature is reviewed in David P. Forsythe and Patrice C. McMahon, *Human Rights and Diversity: Area Studies Revisited* (Lincoln, NE: University of Nebraska Press, 2003, forthcoming).
9 See especially Ryan Hendrickson, *The Clinton Wars* (Nashville: Vanderbilt University Press, 2002).
10 http://www.odur.let.rug.nl/~usa.P/gwb43/speeches/gwbush1.htm.
11 http://www.whitehouse.gov/news/releases/2002/09/print/20020911-3html.
12 http://www.whitehouse.gov.news/releases/2002/06/20020601-3.html.
13 *New York Times*, April 23, 2002, p. A4.
14 Ibid., September 5, 2002, p. A1.

15 See Michael Hirsh, "Bush and the World," John Ikenberry, "The Lures of Preemption," and Michael Mandelbaum, "The Limits of Power," all in *Foreign Affairs* 81, no. 5 (September–October 2002), pp. 18–95. Among various critiques by the *New York Times* journalist Thomas L. Friedman see "Noah and 9-11," September 11, 2002, p. A35, noting U.S. efforts to exempt itself from rules applicable to others. See also the commentary by the two top leaders of the U.N. University, Hans van Ginkel and Ramesh Thakur, in the *United Nations Chronicle*, XXXDVIII, no. 3 (2001), pp. 9f.

16 William Pfaff, "America and Europe: A New World Order Will Have to Wait," *International Herald Tribune*, May 17, 2001, p. 10.

17 Ramesh Thakur, "Diplomacy's Odd Couple: The U.S. and the U.N.," *International Herald Tribune*, June 27, 2002, p. 11.

18 David Broder wrote a column lambasting the Security Council when it proved reluctant to endorse all U.S. policies; no such attack was made earlier when the Council approved the U.S. exercise of self-defense in Afghanistan and voted to try to curtail funding for terrorism as desired by the United States. *Lincoln Journal Star*, September 18, 2002, p. 7B. In general, the *Washington Post* published a number of columns and editorials that were highly nationalistic. See, for example, Robert Kagan, "Europeans Courting International Disaster," June 30, 2002, p. B7. And see below note 24 regarding James Hoagland.

19 See further "U.S. Fails to Polish Image Abroad," *International Herald Tribune*, July 30, 2002, p. 7. And Peter Peterson, "The Need for Public Diplomacy," *Foreign Affairs* 81, no. 5 (September–October 2002), pp. 74–95.

20 Jessica T. Mathews, "September 11, One Year Later," *Policy Brief*, Special edition 18 (2002), pp. 1–10, quote at p. 10.

21 *International Herald Tribune*, August 14, 2002, p. 4.

22 It is patently wrong to say that treaties are not part of the law of the U.S. as a general rule, given the wording of the Constitution and the large number of federal and state judicial pronouncements that turn on a question of treaty law. For a classic case see *Missouri v. Holland*. But see John Bolton, "The Global Prosecutors: Hunting War Criminals in the Name of Utopia," *Foreign Affairs* 78, no. 1 (January–February 1999), pp. 158–64.

23 The Bush administration apparently now acknowledges that a focus on lower-ranking service personnel, and the American Service Members Protection Act, are diversions from the more serious problem. See Elizabeth Becker, "On World Court, U.S. Focus Shifts to Shielding Officials," *New York Times*, September 7, 2002, p. A4.

24 One of the few Democrats to openly challenge the Bush team regarding the ICC is Christopher Dodd. Most other Democrats seem to fear being labeled unpatriotic on the issue of an international court theoretically being able to try Americans. Forgotten is the statement by none other than Republican (and isolationist) Robert A. Taft, who said that international peace depended on "international courts to determine whether nations are abiding by that law," quoted in Pfaff, *Barbarian Sentiments*, p. 11; and the statement by Dwight D. Eisenhower, who said, "It is better to lose a point now and then in an international tribunal and gain a world in which everyone lives at peace under the rule of law," quoted in David P. Forsythe, *The Politics of International Law* (Boulder, CO: Lynne Rienner, 1990), p. 51. James Hoagland, the foreign correspondent of the *Washington Post*, wrote a column quoting Camus to the effect that defending his mother came before defending justice. In context, the argument seemed to be that nationalism was more important than justice. John Hoagland, "Liberals Ought to Join the Real World," *International Herald Tribune*, December 6, 2002, www.iht.com/articles/79305.html.

25 See further Erin Chlopak, "Dealing with the Detainees at Guantánamo Bay: Humanitarian and Human Rights Obligations under the Geneva Conventions," *Human Rights Brief* 9, no. 1 (Spring 2002), American University Center for Human

Rights and Humanitarian Law, pp. 6f.; and David Luban, "The War on Terrorism and the End of Human Rights," *Philosophy and Public Policy Quarterly* 22, no. 3 (Summer 2002), pp. 9f. The latter author suggests that the Bush administration has even misrepresented the notion of "enemy combatant" in order to skirt not only international but also national law.

26   *New York Times*, November 9, 2002, p. A11.

27   A useful short overview is Martha Minow, *Between Vengeance and Forgiveness: Facing History after Genocide and Mass Violence* (Boston, MA: Beacon, 1998).

28   http://www.nytimes.com/2002/09/20/politics/20STEXT_FULL.html. This document is a blend of U.S. exceptionalism, realism, and liberalism suggesting that the U.S. will lead in the creation of a balance of power that favors freedom.

29   Marina Ottaway and Thomas Carothers, eds., *Funding Virtue: Civil Society Aid and Democracy Promotion* (Washington, D.C.: Carnegie Endowment, 2000).

30   From a vast literature see further David P. Forsythe and Barbara Ann J. Rieffer, "U.S. Foreign Policy and Enlarging the Democratic Community," *Human Rights Quarterly* 22, no. 4 (November 2000), pp. 988–1,010. And Michael Cox, G. John Ikenberry, and Takashi Inoguchi, eds., *American Democracy Promotion: Impulses, Strategies, and Impacts* (Oxford: Oxford University Press, 2000).

31   Ottaway and Carothers, *Funding Virtue*.

32   *New York Times*, September 11, 2002, p. A1.

33   Erick Eckholm, "Chinese Muslim Group Planned Terror, U.S. Says," *New York Times*, August 31, 2002, p. A5. Debate ensued about this U.S. decision. Some said that Muslim Uighur groups were resisting Chinese repression through mostly peaceful means, and that the particular group in question had not clearly used or planned violence.

34   See the exchange between Paula Dobriansky of the Bush State Department and Thomas Carothers in *Foreign Affairs* 82, no. 3 (May–June, 2003), pp. 141–5.

35   Human Rights Watch, "U.S. Strengthens Human Rights Effort on Uzbekistan," http://hrw.org/press/2002/08/uzbek080202.htm.

36   U.S. Department of State, "Democracy and Human Rights in Uzbekistan," http://www.state.gov/g/drl/ris/rm/11112.htm.

37   U.S. Department of State, FY 2000–1 HRDF Funds, http://www.state.gov.drl/13665.htm.

38   Human Rights Watch, *Annual Report 2002*, www.hrw.org.

39   Human Rights Watch, "Uzbekistan: New Strategy from EBRD," electronic press release, March 18, 2003.

40   Human Rights Watch, "Egypt High Court Overturns Conviction of Rights Activists," electronic press release, March 18, 2003.

41   http://web.amnesty.org/library/eng-egy/index.

42   Dana Priest and Barton Gellman, "For CIA Suspects Abroad, Brass-Knuckle Treatment," *Washington Post*, December 27, 2002, http://www.iht.com/articles/81546.html. This article produced virtually no concern within official Washington. It did lead to a cover story for *The Economist*, January 11, 2003. Likewise, the deaths of two detainees under U.S. control in Afghanistan, and as many as 20 suicide attempts among detainees at Guantánamo did not lead to a broad national debate about U.S. violations of civil rights pertaining to prisoners.

43   Brian Knowlton reports that Egyptian mass opinion was unfavorable to the U.S. by an 11–1 margin in "A Global Image on the Way Down," *International Herald Tribune*, December 5, 2002, http://www.iht.com/ihtsearch.php?id=79425&owner=(International%20Herald%20Tribune)&date=20021208122757.

44   Marina Ottaway *et al.*, "Democratic Mirage in the Middle East," *Policy Brief*, 20, Brookings, October 7, 2002, p. 1.

45   When the Reagan administration organized the "Contras" against Nicaragua in the 1980s, was this an example of state-supported terrorism?

46 According to Human Rights Watch, the Bush team granted Ecuador enhanced trade benefits despite that country's failure to implement certain labor rights required by U.S. law. http://www.http://hrw.org/reports/2002/ecuador. As a general rule, while the Congress can put human rights standards in its legislation, it lacks the ability to exercise effective oversight. See further David P. Forsythe, *Human Rights and U.S. Foreign Policy: Congress Reconsidered* (Gainesville: University Presses of Florida, 1988).

47 Amartya Sen, *Development as Freedom* (Oxford: Oxford University Press, 2001).

48 *New York Times*, February 3, 2003, p. A6.

49 Gail W. Lapidus, "Transforming Russia: American policy in the 1990s," in Robert J. Lieber, ed., *Eagle Rules? Foreign Policy and American Primacy in the Twenty-first Century* (Upper Saddle River, N.J.: Prentice-Hall, 2002), pp. 97–132.

50 Alain Noel and Jean-Phillippe Therien, "From Domestic to International Justice," *International Organization* 49, no. 3 (Summer 1995), pp. 523–53.

51 See further, for example, Stefanie Grant, "The United States and the international human rights treaty system: for export only?" in Philip Alston and James Crawford, eds., *The Future of U.N. Human Rights Treaty Monitoring* (Cambridge: Cambridge University Press, 2000), pp. 317–32.

52 It is possible that the U.S. position on the death penalty is beginning to change, and that this change has been stimulated by foreign criticism and pressure. Thus far, however, while the death penalty per se is not prohibited by the International Covenant on Civil and Political Rights, and while European democracies in particular object to the use of the death penalty as practiced by federal and most state authorities, the U.S. continues to look to its own laws and to domestic public opinion as the determinants of policy on this issue. See Mary L. Dudziak, *Cold War Civil Rights: Race and the Image of American Democracy* (Princeton, N.J.: Princeton University Press, 2000). U.S. leaders during the Cold War were aware of foreign criticism of American racism and segregation, but they opted for slow change through U.S. democracy rather than emphasize international norms and procedures.

53 On the issue of women's rights, the Bush administration has avoided taking a stand on CEDAW—the Convention on the Elimination of Discrimination against Women. When the Senate Foreign Relations Committee in 2002 moved the treaty to the Senate floor with a vote of approval, most Republican senators voted against it. Bush's State Department seemed to favor, but the Justice Department seemed opposed. See further Nicholas D. Kristof, "Women's Rights: Why Not?" *New York Times*, June 18, 2002, p. A23.

54 See for example William Felice, *The Global New Deal: Economic and Social Rights in World Politics* (Lanham: Rowman and Littlefield, 2002).

55 Amnesty International, *Amnesty International Report 2003*, http://web.amnesty.org/aidoc/aidoc_pdf.nsf/Index/POL100032003ENGLISH/$File/POL1000303.pdf.

56 In general see Joseph S. Nye Jr., *The Paradox of American Power: Why the World's Only Superpower Can't Go It Alone* (Oxford: Oxford University Press, 2002).

57 One take on the Bush administration sees the President and his Deputy Secretary of Defense Paul Wolfowitz as militant exceptionalists and crusaders, and Secretary of Defense Donald Rumsfeld and Vice-President Dick Cheney as realists.

58 Steven Holloway, "U.S. Unilateralism at the U.N.: Why Great Powers Do Not Make Great Multilateralists," *Global Governance* 6, no. 3 (July–September 2000), pp. 361–82. See further Michael Glennon, "The U.N. vs. U.S. Power," *Foreign Affairs* 82, no. 3 (May–June, 2000), pp. 16–35 regarding the damage that Bush's invasion of Iraq has done to the effort since 1920 to restrain first use of force by international law and organization.

4 International human rights

Unintended consequences of the war on terrorism

Jack Donnelly

The tragedy of September 11, 2001 has led to a substantial redirection of U.S. foreign policy. This chapter explores the consequences of these changes for U.S. international human rights and democratization policies. Anti-terrorism has provoked a one-dimensional ideological campaign that has marginalized human rights in much the same way as, although somewhat less intensely than, the crusade against communism did during the Cold War.

The chapter begins by charting the gradual emergence of human rights as an interest of American foreign policy during the second half of the Cold War—at first as a matter of considerable controversy, but by the late 1980s as a concern with widespread bipartisan support. The decline of serious security threats that accompanied the end of the Cold War led to the growing prominence of international human rights in U.S. foreign policy in the 1990s. Against this baseline, and a long-established pattern of growing attention to human rights, this chapter explores the substantial retrenchment that has occurred as a result of the American reaction to September 11.

There has been no conscious and overt decision to downgrade the place of human rights in U.S. foreign policy. If anything, the Bush administration now talks more of human rights and democracy as foreign policy objectives than it did prior to September 11. Nonetheless, the overriding emphasis on combating terrorism has shifted (always limited) attention and resources away from human rights. It has also enabled deeply rooted tendencies toward unilateralism and the demonization of enemies. As a result, the space in U.S. foreign policy for human rights and democracy has been significantly reduced—not by design, but no less surely, and with quite unfortunate consequences for the international struggle to realize human rights.

Human rights in post-Cold War American foreign policy

Assessing the impact of September 11 requires a baseline of comparison. The preceding dozen years witnessed a significant increase in the prioritization of democracy and human rights objectives. In addition, the 1990s saw the development of a stream of unilateral and multilateral practices that established an international right to humanitarian intervention against genocide.[1]

Although there is little controversy about the existence of these changes, their cause is a matter of contention. How much was due to their rise in the hierarchy of U.S. foreign policy interests? How much was due instead to the spaces that the demise of anti-communism opened for the pursuit of other objectives? The evidence since September 11 suggests that it was much more the latter.

Perhaps the easiest way to present the case is in terms of a simple three-interest model of foreign policy. If foreign policy is constructed out of security, economic, and "other" interests then, in general, security trumps everything else. Economic interests usually (although not always) take priority over "other" interests. Occasionally economic interests may even compete with (secondary) security concerns. "Other" interests generally come last. This model is a pretty good first approximation of the foreign policy priorities of the United States, and most other countries as well.

The place of an interest within this hierarchy (and within the hierarchy of "other" interests) may change either absolutely or relatively; that is, the absolute value attributed to it may change or the absolute value of another interest above or below it may change. The increased attention to human rights and democracy in post-Cold War U.S. foreign policy was largely relative rather than absolute. It did not rest on altered priorities among these three classes of interest. There may have been a modest absolute increase in the value attributed to human rights. But the most important change was a dramatic contraction in the scope of security concerns that opened space for increased attention to human rights.

How does this compare to the absolute change in the place of human rights in U.S. foreign policy that took place a decade earlier? The introduction of human rights on the agenda in the 1970s—beginning with Congressional mandates linking human rights and foreign aid and the linkage between human rights and broader foreign policy concerns reflected in the Helsinki Final Act—is well documented.[2] But throughout the presidency of Jimmy Carter, considerable (and often intense) debate raged over whether human rights were even an appropriate foreign policy concern.[3]

A decade later, however, debate focused not on whether the United States should be pursuing international human rights objectives, but on what place human rights should be given in particular cases and relative to other foreign policy interests. By the late 1980s, human rights had become entrenched on the U.S. foreign policy agenda as a largely nonpartisan objective. Across the entire mainstream of the political spectrum, which had shifted to the right throughout the decade, human rights had become an accepted, and valued, objective of American foreign policy.

Ironically, this change took place during Ronald Reagan's presidency. During his early years in office, Reagan worked aggressively to turn his campaign criticisms of Carter's human rights policies into action. Where human rights could not be eliminated altogether from foreign policy (usually because of Congressional and popular political pressure), they were either marginalized or cynically manipulated.[4] Furthermore, the Reagan administration conceptualized democracy in largely geopolitical terms: anti-communism plus elections, with elections not even necessary for friendly regimes with strong anti-communist credentials.

These efforts, however, largely failed. Although the advocates of human rights lost most of the individual battles (most notably over Central America), ultimately they prevailed. In its second term, the Reagan administration largely adopted the language of human rights, especially when anti-communism did not get in the way. And when Reagan's Vice-President, George H.W. Bush, ran successfully for the presidency in 1988, he regularly and freely used the language of human rights, with apparent sincerity.

The changes in U.S. international human rights policy after the end of the Cold War built on this entrenchment of human rights on the foreign policy agenda. The geopolitical impediments to the pursuit of human rights objectives dramatically receded. In what has often been referred to as a "unipolar world,"[5] there were fewer security concerns to interfere with the pursuit of human rights objectives.

The U.S. and international reaction against the Tiananmen massacre in June 1989 is perhaps the clearest indication of the new geopolitical space for international human rights.[6] China, which previously had been largely exempted from U.S. human rights criticism because of its shared enmity toward the Soviet Union,[7] not only came under harsh verbal attack but found itself the subject of significant international sanctions. And the United States continued to press human rights as a major issue in Sino-American relations through the mid-1990s. In other words, in the case of relations with a major world power, Washington was willing to make modest but real sacrifices of economic interests, and even accept minor security costs, in order to pursue human rights objectives.

No less important than the changes in the international agenda was the ideological space opened by the demise of communism. During the Cold War, protecting "democracy" and "the free world" was often deemed to require tolerating or even actively supporting human rights violations directed against the "enemies of freedom." With the end of ideological rivalry, which had been at the heart of U.S. support for repressive regimes on the right, the "threat" posed to "friendly" dictators largely evaporated.

With the definition of democracy liberated from the tyranny of anti-communism, the United States not only developed a renewed emphasis on elections but increasingly came to see that "real" democracy required an active and effective independent civil society. As civil society promotion programs expanded, important conceptual and practical linkages were forged between human rights and democratization agendas. Whatever the shortcomings in program design, and for all the restrictions imposed by competing interests, this was a major advance in the sophistication and potential impact of U.S. human rights diplomacy.[8]

During the Cold War, international human rights policies were preoccupied by a largely reactive and remedial emphasis on stopping, and aiding victims of, systematic and often brutal repression. With the demise of numerous dictatorships of the left and right alike, new opportunities developed for a more positive emphasis on helping to build a human rights culture. Once the old authoritarian regimes were gone, it became increasingly clear that the work of building rights-respecting societies and rights-protective regimes had only begun. This new attitude tended to be expressed primarily in the growing use of the language of democracy and democratization. Bureaucratically, it was reflected in the change from the Bureau of Human Rights and Humanitarian Affairs to the Bureau of Democracy, Human Rights, and Labor.

In its least attractive dimensions, this new orientation sometimes led to a fetishistic pursuit of elections.[9] U.S. policy has also often confused political liberalization (that is, reductions in or even elimination of old forms of repression) with democratization, in a naive belief that all progressive political change lies on a path that leads to democracy.[10] But in its more attractive dimensions— which were not entirely lacking during the administration of Bill Clinton, and even that of his predecessor—it involved a vision of human rights that went well beyond the Cold War era's simplistic vision of stopping torture, freeing political prisoners, and "throwing the rascals out."

As these last paragraphs have suggested, in the 1990s there was genuine rethinking and learning that contributed to redesigned international human rights policies—not just in the U.S. but in many other countries as well. One might also argue that there was a modest absolute increase (especially outside the United States) in attention and commitment to international human rights issues. The crucial change, however, was less in the substance or absolute intensity of U.S. human rights and democracy promotion interests than in the space opened for such initiatives by the end of geopolitical and ideological rivalry with the Soviet Union. Since September 11, human rights have not so much retreated from American foreign policy as they have been eclipsed by a focus on terrorism.

The eclipse of human rights

Some of the changes discussed in the preceding section have become deeply entrenched, most notably the acceptance throughout the political mainstream of human rights as a legitimate foreign policy concern. But the relative priority attached to international human rights objectives remains a matter of controversy. The previous argument suggests that the post-Cold War upsurge of human rights and democracy as objectives of U.S. foreign policy was vulnerable to a reinflation of security concerns. Since September 11 we have indeed witnessed democracy and human rights being obscured, and thus effectively pushed back toward the margins of U.S. foreign policy, by a new geopolitical vision and a new ideological crusade. Both have striking analogies to their Cold War predecessors.

Most notable, perhaps, was the transformation, almost overnight, of Pakistan, in the official U.S. representation, from a retrograde military dictatorship —and one that, in addition, was a major supporter of international terrorism, the preceding decade's most flagrant violator of the non-proliferation regime, and a bellicose threat to regional security in south Asia—into a leading U.S. ally. And despite the lack of any substantial human rights improvements or progress toward democracy in Pakistan, the U.S. embrace has continued long after the war in Afghanistan. For example, on his visit to the United States in the summer of 2003, Pakistani strongman Pervez Musharraf was lavishly praised by the administration.

Much more generally, governments have taken advantage of the rhetoric of anti-terrorism to intensify their attacks on domestic and international enemies. As Human Rights Watch has put it, "Particularly troubling, and common, have been the pretextual use of counter-terrorism laws as new weapons against old political foes."[11] Russia and Israel provide perhaps the most tragic examples of the war on terrorism run amok.

In Chechnya,[12] intensified Russian military action certainly owed much to the natural ebb and flow of that terrible conflict. Russia, however, has been emboldened by the language and logic of a global war on terrorism, calculating, correctly, that appeals to anti-terrorism provide partial insulation from international criticism.[13] The muting and partial disabling of humanitarian criticism has certainly not caused Russian brutality, but it has facilitated it.

In Israel, the government of Ariel Sharon has responded to the upsurge of terror bombings with a vengeance that reflects not only its own inclinations but also Washington's tolerance for a brutal war on terrorism.[14] Assassination and collective punishment have become standard operating procedures. The indignities and human rights violations that have long characterized military occupation have intensified in number and severity. Perhaps most brutal have been policies consciously aimed at destroying the Palestinian economy and making every Palestinian civilian suffer, both economically and through the denial of personal liberties,[15] for the actions of a tiny group of extremists and the unwillingness or inability of the Palestinian Authority to control them.

The terrorist threats faced by Russia and Israel—and the difficulties of responding to them—are real. Unfortunately, however, responses have themselves relied on systematic human rights violations and terrorist tactics.[16] But the United States and its allies have backed off from their criticism of Russia.[17] And the U.S. has done little to impede the slide of Israel into policies that can only accurately be described as state terrorism. Even the new "Road Map" for peace places virtually all the blame on Palestinian terrorists, and the administration continues to treat Israeli state terrorism less critically.

Suffering by innocent civilians has perhaps brought some of the satisfactions of retribution. But as the continuing suicide bombings in Israel and the theater hostages and ongoing bombings in Moscow indicate, it has not made its perpetrators more secure. Quite the contrary, it has plunged them even deeper into a cycle of violence and despair.[18]

Washington's tolerance for systematic human rights violations, and even state terrorism, when responding to terrorism, has been facilitated by the tendency to see anti-terrorism less as a material interest of U.S. foreign policy than as a crusade against evil. In a struggle against evil, in contrast to the pursuit of material interests, victory is all that matters. As the struggle progresses, the end comes to be seen as justifying a growing range of morally and legally problematic means.

The ordinary restraints of law and the conventional limits on the use of force regularly lose out to the imperatives of the crusade. Where the conflict is militarized, the classic just-war restrictions increasingly are eroded or ignored; noncombatants are directly targeted, proportionality is disregarded, and the very idea of innocent civilians is undermined by direct and indirect attributions of collective responsibility and guilt. Where the struggle is carried out through the institutions of "law and order" and the internal security forces, human rights are the price exacted not just from terrorists but from peaceful political opponents, members of groups that are feared or despised, and ordinary individuals accidentally or arbitrarily caught up in the security apparatus.[19]

These relatively dramatic examples, which enable rights-abusive policies, are matched by a general decline in Washington's official attention to human rights and democracy promotion. The United States remains committed rhetorically to human rights and democracy. But in practice these objectives have been overshadowed, and thus moved to the background, in a growing number of cases. Although the decline has been substantially less dramatic in the two years since September 11 than during the Cold War—an analogy with the impact of the war on drugs on American policy in the Andean region is closer to the mark—U.S. support for human rights and democracy has been among the more prominent casualties of the war on terrorism.

Some have suggested that this is, at the very least, not incompatible with the preferences of the current Bush administration.[20] But these changes are by no means restricted to the political right. In fact, the most striking fact has been the participation in or tolerance of this shift in policy by moderates and liberals, who have more of an inclination to pursue international human rights objectives. The Bush administration's anti-terrorism policy has strong bipartisan support. Although its domestic dimensions have provoked sustained (although rarely harsh) criticism from prominent mainstream political figures, criticism of its international dimensions has been restricted primarily to human rights NGOs and figures on the fringes of the political mainstream.

In any case, even within the administration and among its allies, there has been no attack on human rights and democracy objectives. They remain rhetorically important goals of U.S. foreign policy.[21] One need not be overly charitable to suggest that this reflects a genuine commitment to these values. At the very least, it indicates that other important internal and international constituencies continue to take them seriously. Hypocrisy is effective only to the extent that it taps into widely and genuinely held values.

In an important sense, then, the relative decline of human rights in U.S.

foreign policy has been largely unintended. The explicit aim has been not to harm or even slight human rights but rather to pursue security objectives that are deemed to be more important.

This does not in any way lessen American responsibility. Although "unintended," the negative human rights consequences have been very real, were easily anticipated, and are now well known. The lack of intent, however, is important for thinking about the prospects for reversing these trends.

If the decline in the position of human rights in U.S. foreign policy has been largely relative, then any revival—much like the initial post-Cold War increase in the prominence of international human rights concerns—will depend on space being opened by the retreat of competing security objectives. A return to a more active, aggressive, and consistent international human rights policy must await the reopening of the political space currently pre-empted by the war on terrorism. We can perhaps hope for such a change in a couple of years, especially if George W. Bush is not re-elected. But in the short term, human rights are almost certain to remain eclipsed by anti-terrorism in American foreign policy.

Human rights, security, and foreign policy

A defender of the war on terrorism might argue that the account so far is a simple one of competing foreign policy objectives: major security interests have appropriately pushed human rights and democracy promotion to the sidelines. However, the actual dynamic has been rather different. This section focuses on qualitative substantive changes in the understanding of security. The following section examines the tendency to conceive new threats in moralized terms and to respond with an irrational exuberance for a militarized crusade.

Up to this point, "security" has been treated as if its meaning was obvious and constant. Protecting the national territory from invasion may fit this description. Most other "security" interests, however, are more thoroughly constructed and variable. It is instructive to consider a simple three-variable model, each with two possible values. What is to be secured—the state (national security) or citizens (personal security)? Where does the threat lie—externally or internally? And what is the nature of the threat—material or moral (ideological)?

The relatively constant and uncontroversial dimensions of "security" address external material threats to the state. Security thus understood is indeed plausibly seen as an appropriately overriding concern of foreign policy: without national security from external material threats, all other interests and values are at risk. The tradition of realpolitik understands the national interest, and thus national security, as largely restricted to such external material interests.[22] As we move away from this relatively simple case, however, "security" becomes more obscure, its priority becomes more contentious, and its conceptual and normative relationships to human rights may vary considerably.

A focus on the security of individual citizens has strong positive connections with human rights. In fact, internationally recognized human rights can be seen as measures to secure individuals from the threats to their dignity and security posed by modern states and markets. A focus on state security, however, has no necessary connection to individual human rights; it depends on the character of the state being protected and the means used to secure it.

To oversimplify, human rights are about protecting citizens from the state. More precisely, the state, in contemporary international human rights law, has the principal obligation of implementing internationally recognized human rights. Violations thus usually involve either direct action by the state or the failure of states to take action that implements or enforces human rights.

National security, by contrast, is about protecting the state from its (perceived) enemies. Those enemies may themselves be citizens. And even when the enemies are external, the rights of citizens may need to be sacrificed in order to carry out defensive measures.

An antagonistic relationship between national security and human rights is especially likely when security is seen in moral rather than material terms and to the extent that the causes of insecurity are seen as internal. This was common during the Cold War. With "security" understood almost exclusively as a matter of *national* security (which was understood to have a substantial ideological dimension), U.S. foreign policy was extremely tolerant of regimes that systematically sacrificed the human rights of their citizens to the alleged imperatives of protecting the nation from communist attack and subversion. Latin America provides perhaps the most striking examples—Guatemala in the 1950s, the southern cone of South America during the 1970s, El Salvador during the 1980s—but there were many instances in Asia (for example, South Korea and Vietnam) and Africa (for example, South Africa and Zaire) as well.

The end of the Cold War led to a redefinition of U.S. security interests in less ideological terms. This eliminated incentives for the United States to court repressive regimes in order to keep them out of the communist camp. At the same time, it undermined the principal rationale for repression by rightist dictatorships. Taken together, these changes greatly reduced the antagonism between human rights and national security in U.S. foreign policy.

In other words, after the end of the Cold War not only were security concerns reduced in number but the concept of "security" was rethought. Consider, for example, the Soviet/Russian threat. Russia still posed most of the same material threats in 1995 that it did in 1985; the end of the Cold War simply did not coincide with a substantial reduction in Soviet military power. Rather, the ideological threat posed by communism disappeared, beginning with liberalization at home and "new thinking" in Soviet foreign policy, accelerating the processes that ultimately led to the collapse of the Soviet bloc and the dissolution of the Soviet Union.

In addition, there was a partial move toward a conception of security with more of a personal dimension or, in the language that became popular in the 1990s,[23] "human security."[24] The roots of this change can be traced to the Conference on Security and Cooperation in Europe. The 1975 Helsinki Final Act, and especially Principle VII ("Respect for Human Rights and Fundamental Freedoms") and Basket III ("Cooperation in Humanitarian and Other Fields"), introduced human rights explicitly into the mainstream of international security discussions. And in follow-up meetings in Belgrade (1977–8), Madrid (1980–3), and Vienna (1986–9), human rights were central.

Certainly human security never displaced national security on the U.S. foreign policy agenda. But in the 1990s it did come to occupy a significant space. This is perhaps most evident in a series of armed humanitarian operations that received strong U.S. support, running from Somalia and Bosnia through Kosovo and East Timor.[25] More broadly, the concept of "peace-building" was added to the international security lexicon[26] and a human rights dimension was incorporated into a number of post-conflict peacekeeping operations.[27]

As many of the examples presented above suggest, the trend since September 2001 has been in the opposite direction. National security trumps all. And the appeal to homeland security, which to my ears sounds like the languages of fascism and Stalinism, makes it clear that it is the security of the country, not the rights of U.S. citizens (let alone the human rights of foreigners) that is to be protected.

It is certainly true that recent terrorist acts have modestly increased the material threat to the United States. The most important changes since September 11, however, have involved the expansion of the other dimensions of security.

The war on terrorism has led to a significantly more ideological vision of security. This theme is pursued in greater detail below. The internal dimensions of security, as expressed in the language of homeland security, have moved to the forefront. And the focus on personal security has receded in favor of a renewed emphasis on national security.

Taken together, the result has been an increasing tendency to see security and human rights as competing rather than reinforcing concerns. Part of the change has been the rise of new threats to the material interests of the United States. But no less important has been a reconceptualization of the very meaning of security.

Irrational exuberance: the case of axis of evil

The implication of the preceding section is that human rights and democracy promotion have lost out less as a result of carefully considered trade-offs of competing interests and more due to a decision to reorient U.S. policy around an ideological crusade, which has introduced a substantially irrational element into Washington's policy. Moreover, the new crusade against terrorism has facilitated the expression of dangerous tendencies in U.S. foreign policy, particularly to demonize enemies and to act unilaterally.

One striking consequence of the post-September 11 environment has been the rhetorical creation of, and reorientation of U.S. foreign policy toward opposing, the "axis of evil," which was introduced into public discourse by President Bush in his State of the Union Address on January 29, 2002.[28] In fact, there are not the actual connections between these three countries that would plausibly make them an axis. Quite the contrary, Iran and Iraq have been bitter enemies and North Korea is not closely linked to either of the other two regimes. This new enemy has been constructed out of a hodgepodge of very different (and largely unrelated) concerns—most notably terrorism, proliferation, regional security, and general anti-U.S. sentiment.

The glue that holds together this disparate set of issues and countries is the general anti-terrorist hysteria. No rational assessment of U.S. interests would suggest that its policy ought to focus on these three regimes. This is true even in the narrow case of a well-designed war on terrorism.

Terrorists sponsored by these three regimes have not directed their activities against the territory or military of the United States. In fact, nationals of these countries—in sharp contrast to, most notably, those of Saudi Arabia—have not even been centrally involved in the widely publicized terrorist attacks on U.S. citizens. The global role of these three countries makes them no more deserving of special attention than any other nations. Other states, including U.S. allies, are equally culpable. Syria, for example, has been as active in the Middle East as Iran. The devastation wreaked by Pakistani-supported Kashmiri terrorists has been at least as significant as anything caused by terrorists supported by the axis of evil—not to mention the long-standing Pakistani support for the Taliban, prior to its post-September 11 about-face.

Much the same is true of the other "crimes" of these regimes. North Korea has indeed been guilty of breaching general international non-proliferation norms, as well as particular agreements with the United States. But Pakistan, a U.S. "ally," is the most flagrant proliferator of the past decade in a regional security context that is at least as unstable as that of the Korean peninsula. Furthermore, evidence also suggests that Pakistan has contributed to North Korea's nuclear program. Iraq's nuclear ambitions seem, by the evidence of the recent war, to have been thwarted by international sanctions and monitoring. And Iran, although a legitimate proliferation concern, does not appear to be an imminent threat.

From a human rights perspective, these problems might be forgivable if these "evil" states were not the world's leading human rights violators. A strong case can be made that North Korea and Saddam Hussein's Iraq belonged on any "top ten" list. But the inclusion of Iran in such company is far-fetched, which can only be explained by the tendency to demonize enemies that has arisen since September 2001.

Revolutionary Iran is in many regards an extremely unappealing regime. But respect for human rights and democracy are far more advanced in Iran than in the U.S.'s leading ally in the region, Saudi Arabia. Iran is the only country in the region with a vibrant opposition and immediate possibilities for reform. Relatively free elections are held regularly for a legislature and government that have considerable influence over policy. Despite substantial censorship and a serious problem of legal and political attacks on opposition journalists, Iran is one of the few countries in the region with a substantial cadre of opposition journalists. State-supported vigilante violence is a recurrent problem, but opposition political figures face far fewer threats to their personal security than in the rest of the region. And women's rights are further advanced in Iran than in all but one or two Arab countries; certainly compared to Saudi Arabia, Iran, especially Tehran, allows more women's rights.

U.S. policy, however, has largely sacrificed the chance to facilitate the ongoing process of reform in Iran. Indeed, Washington's bellicosity has made life more difficult for reformers. Rather than recognize the positive, if limited, changes in Iran over the past decade, Washington has chosen to single out Iran for special attack. It has even sacrificed opportunities to pursue convergent interests cooperatively, most notably in Afghanistan and Iraq.

There has been, in effect, a choice to keep Iran as an enemy rather than either help to reform it or try to settle outstanding issues, which at this point are largely symbolic on both sides. Hence Iran is not just an ordinary enemy, but a demonized one, particularly since the hostage crisis in 1979–81. The re-demonization of Iran, as part of the axis of evil, has been largely driven by the hysteria of the war on terror.

The idea that these three second- or third-rate powers are the appropriate focal point for the foreign policy of the world's only superpower is ludicrous. But this approach has had serious negative consequences, most directly for reformers and human rights in Iran, and more generally in the turn of U.S. attention away from human rights and other concerns. But the consequences pale before those associated with the war on Iraq.

As in the creation of the axis of evil, the justification for the war in Iraq was cobbled together out of a variety of disparate concerns: weapons of mass destruction (WMD), terrorism, regime change, a history of animosity, and regional security. As in the general axis-of-evil charge, the particular elements of the charge are problematic. And the combination was held together mainly with the glue of post-September 11 hysteria.

The threat of WMD seems, by the current evidence, to have been overstated. As noted, Iraq's contribution to international terrorism has been real but certainly not especially notable. There is no hint elsewhere in U.S. foreign policy that it considers even the most vicious behavior to be legitimate grounds for an invasion to overthrow a regime. And Iraq was no serious threat to its neighbors, having been effectively hobbled by the Gulf war and a decade of international sanctions and monitoring.[29]

As in the previous examples, there is no simple story of direct causation. The war against terrorism exacerbated existing tendencies, most notably toward unilateralism and the demonization of enemies, and also helped to hold together the various justifications that were used to build the political coalitions that backed the war in Iraq. But without the paranoia over terrorism, it is hard to imagine the Bush administration's marshaling the national and international support needed to launch the war against Iraq.

Conclusion

The world has become a worse place since September 11, and the United States bears some responsibility for the deterioration. In the 1990s and with surprising frequency, the U.S. used its immense power on behalf of humanitarian concerns. Security and economic interests remained at the core of foreign policy, but power was used, repeatedly and very prominently, on behalf of the victims of repression, thereby adding moral and legal legitimacy to its superpower status. No less importantly, the number of reprehensible countries treated as "friends" declined dramatically.

The war on terrorism has not produced a dramatic and complete reversal. But the United States today embraces repression more frequently than at any time since the end of the Cold War. It seems less willing to expend its resources on behalf of human rights and humanitarian concerns. When Washington asserts itself—increasingly more unilaterally—it is on behalf of a vision of security that has little human dimension. And interests evoke much less international support as a result. Ironically, not only do human rights suffer but, by pushing human rights back into the shadows, the United States—for example, in postwar Iraq—finds itself less able to achieve its other foreign policy interests.

Notes

1 See Jack Donnelly, *Universal Human Rights in Theory and Practice*, 2nd edition (Ithaca, N.Y.. Cornell University Press, 2003), Chapter 14. For an excellent assessment of the status of the right of humanitarian intervention, see J.L. Holzgref and Robert O. Keohane, eds., *Humanitarian Intervention. Ethical, Legal and Political Dilemmas* (Cambridge: Cambridge University Press, 2003). See also International Commission on Intervention and State Sovereignty, *The Responsibility to Protect* (Ottawa: ICISS, 2001).

2 See David P. Forsythe, *Human Rights and U.S. Foreign Policy: Congress Reconsidered* (Gainesville: University of Florida Press, 1988); Donald M. Fraser, "Congress's role in the making of international human rights policy," in Donald P. Kommers and Gilburt D. Loescher, eds., *Human Rights and American Foreign Policy* (Notre Dame: University of Notre Dame Press, 1979), pp. 247–54; and William Korey, *The Promises We Keep: Human Rights, the Helsinki Process, and American Foreign Policy* (New York: St. Martin's Press, 1993).

3 For classic arguments against including human rights in U.S. foreign policy, see William F. Buckley Jr., "Human Rights and Foreign Policy: A Proposal," *Foreign Affairs* 58 (Spring 1980), pp. 775–96; Jeane J. Kirkpatrick, "Dictatorships and Double Standards," *Commentary* 68 (November 1979), pp. 34–45; and Hans J. Morgenthau, *Human Rights and Foreign Policy* (New York: Council on Religion and International Affairs, 1979).

4 Central America was the most important focus of debate, with the United States embracing El Salvador despite its poor record on human rights and democracy while opposing and seeking to undermine by force a democratically elected government in Nicaragua that had a much better human rights record. See Cynthia J. Arnson, *Crossroads: Congress, the Reagan Administration, and Central America* (New York: Pantheon Books, 1989); and Noam Chomsky, "U.S. polity and society: the lessons of Nicaragua," in Thomas W. Walker, ed., *Reagan versus the Sandinistas: The Undeclared War on Nicaragua* (Boulder, CO: Westview Press, 1987), pp. 285–310. On the political

manipulation of the human rights of El Salvador and Nicaragua by the Reagan administration, see Daniel C. Kramer, "International human rights," in Tinsley E. Yarbrough, ed., *The Reagan Administration and Human Rights* (New York: Praeger, 1985), pp. 230–54.

5 Charles Krauthammer, "The Unipolar Moment," *Foreign Affairs* 70 (Winter 1991), pp. 23–33.

6 Rosemary Foot, *Rights Beyond Borders: The Global Community and the Struggle Over Human Rights in China* (Oxford: Oxford University Press, 2000) provides a superb overview of the decade following Tiananmen, with attention to bilateral, multilateral, and non-governmental responses as well as changes in Chinese international behavior. See also Ann Kent, *China, the United Nations, and Human Rights* (Philadelphia: University of Pennsylvania Press, 1999), which stresses the multilateral dimension, and Elizabeth Economy and Michael Oksenberg, eds., *China Joins the World: Progress and Prospects* (New York: Council on Foreign Relations Press, 1999), which looks at the later 1990s in a broader foreign policy and international context.

7 The classic discussion is Roberta Cohen, "People's Republic of China: The Human Rights Exception," *Human Rights Quarterly* 9 (November 1987), pp. 447–549.

8 For a good general overview of the work of the 1990s, see Marina Ottaway and Thomas Carothers, eds., *Funding Virtue: Civil Society Aid and Democracy Promotion* (Washington, D.C.: Carnegie Endowment for International Peace, 2000).

9 See Terry Lynn Karl's widely cited discussion of the "fallacy of electoralism," or "the faith that the mere holding of elections will channel political action into peaceful contests among elites, the winners of which are accorded public legitimacy," in "The Hybrid Regimes of Central America," *Journal of Democracy* 6, no. 3 (1995), p. 73. For Karl's original discussion of electoralism, see "Imposing consent? Electoralism v. democratization in El Salvador," in Paul Drake and Eduardo Silva, eds., *Elections in Latin America* (San Diego: University of California, 1986), pp. 9–36.

10 See Thomas Carothers, "The End of the Transition Paradigm," *Journal of Democracy* 13, no. 1 (2002), pp. 5–21. Carothers points to USAID's depiction of the Democratic Republic of Congo as a country transitioning to "a democratic, free market society" to illustrate the common assumption that any movement away from authoritarianism is movement toward democracy (p. 6). USAID's report, "Building Democracy in the Democratic Republic of Congo," can be found at http://www.usaid.gov/democracy/afr/congo.html.

11 Human Rights Watch, *In the Name of Counter-Terrorism: Human Rights Abuses Worldwide*, http://hrw.org/un/chr59/counter-terrorism-bck4.htm#P286_64797.

12 For an overview of the human rights situation in Chechnya, see Human Rights Watch, "Russia: Abuses in Chechnya Continue to Cause Human Suffering" (January 29, 2003), http://www.hrw.org/press/2003/01/russia012903.htm and "Human Rights Situation in Chechnya" (April 2003), http://www.hrw.org/backgrounder/eca/chechnya/index.htm. For current (although in some cases not entirely nonpartisan) information, see http://www.watchdog.cz/.

13 "Since it launched a military operation in Chechnya in 1999, Russia's leaders have described the armed conflict there as a counter-terrorism operation and have attempted to fend off international scrutiny of Russian forces' abusive conduct by invoking the imperative of fighting terrorism. This pattern has become more pronounced since the September 11 attacks, as Russia sought to convince the international community that its operation in Chechnya was its contribution to the international campaign against terrorism . . . World leaders, until then critical of Russia's conduct in Chechnya, did little to challenge these claims." Ibid.

14 Information on Israeli human rights violations is highly politicized. B'Tselem, the Israeli Information Center for Human Rights in the Occupied Territories, is perhaps the best neutral source. See http://www.betselem.org.

15 For a powerful illustration of this phenomenon in microcosm, see B'Tselem, *Al-*

Mawazi, Gaza Strip: Intolerable Life in an Isolated Enclave (March 2003), http://www.betselem.org/Download/2003_Al_Mwassy_Eng.pdf.

16 Political assassinations—if not terrorism, then extrajudicial executions—have become a regular part of the Israeli response to terrorism. In Chechnya, torture has become so pervasive that in the summer of 2003 the European Committee for the Prevention of Torture issued a rare public statement (http://www.cpt.coe.int/documents/rus/2003-33-inf-eng.htm), following strongly worded criticism by the Parliamentary Assembly of the Council of Europe in the spring.

17 For appeals by human rights NGOs calling on Western states to be more vocal on the issue of Chechnya, see http://www.hrw.org/press/2003/06/russia062003.htm, http://www.hrw.org/press/2003/05/russia053003.htm, and http://www.reliefweb.int/w/rwb.nsf/0/5404f2f0528bc31949256cb6000da38f?OpenDocument.

18 On the spread of Russian brutality into neighboring Ingushetia, see Human Rights Watch, "Russia: Abuses Spread Beyond Chechnya," http://www.hrw.org/press/2003/07/russia071603.htm.

19 Restrictions on civil liberties in the United States represent a similar dynamic, although on a much smaller scale.

20 See, for example, Lawyers Committee for Human Rights, "A Year of Loss: Reexamining Civil Liberties since September 11," http://www.lchr.org/pubs/descriptions/loss_report.pdf, where it is noted (on p. 1) that the administration's inclination to use national security arguments to undermine civil liberties predates September 11.

21 For example, in the 2003 State of the Union Address, President George W. Bush noted that: "The American flag stands for more than our power and our interests. Our founders dedicated this country to the cause of human dignity, the rights of every person, and the possibilities of every life. This conviction leads us into the world to help the afflicted, and defend the peace, and confound the designs of evil men." http://www.whitehouse.gov/news/release/2003/01/20030128-19.html. See also the U.S. State Department "Human Rights" website at http://www.state.gov/g/drl/hr/ where it is claimed that "a central goal of U.S. foreign policy has been the promotion of respect for human rights, as embodied in the Universal Declaration of Human Rights. The United States understands that the existence of human rights helps secure the peace, deter aggression, promote the rule of law, combat crime and corruption, strengthen democracies, and prevent humanitarian crises."

22 Hans Morgenthau's national interest defined in terms of power provides a classic statement. See, for example, his *In Defense of the National Interest: A Critical Examination of American Foreign Policy* (New York: Alfred A. Knopf, 1951).

23 See, for example, *Human Development Report 1994: New Dimensions of Human Security* (New York: United Nations Development Programme, 1994), http://hdr.undp.org/reports/global/1994/en/. See also Laura Reed and Majid Tehranian, "Evolving security regimes," in Majid Tehranian, ed., *Worlds Apart: Human Security and Global Governance* (New York: I.B. Tauris, 1999), pp. 23–53.

24 For a recent expression by a high-level international commission, see Commission on Human Security, *Human Security Now* (New York: Commission on Human Security, 2003).

25 See, for example, Thomas G. Weiss, *Military–Civilian Interactions: Intervening in Humanitarian Crises*, 2nd edition (Lanham, MD: Rowman and Littlefield, forthcoming).

26 The term "peace-building" became widely used after the publication of Boutros Boutros-Ghali, *An Agenda for Peace: Preventive Diplomacy, Peacemaking and Peacekeeping* (New York: Department of Public Information, United Nations, 1992). Document A/47/277–S/241111, 17 June 1992, http://www.un.org/Docs/SG/agpeace.html. See also Elizabeth M. Cousens and Chetan Kumar, eds., *Peacebuilding as Politics: Cultivating Peace in Fragile Societies* (Boulder, CO: Lynne Rienner, 2001); and A.B. Fetherston, *Towards a Theory of United Nations Peacekeeping* (New York: St. Martin's Press, 1994).

27 The changes in peacekeeping began in the last years of the Cold War but really took off only in the early 1990s. See Tamara Duffey, "United Nations peace-keeping in the post-Cold War era," in Clive Jones and Caroline Kennedy-Pipe, eds., *International Security in a Global Age: Securing the Twenty-first Century* (Portland, OR: Frank Cass, 2000), pp. 116–37; and David M. Malone and Karin Wermester, "Boom and Bust? The Changing Nature of U.N. Peacekeeping," *International Peacekeeping* 7, no. 4 (Winter 2000), pp. 37–54.

28 George W. Bush, The President's State of the Union Address, January 29, 2002, http://www.whitehouse.gov/news/releases/2002/01/20020129-11.html.

29 See Jean E. Krasno and James S. Sutterlin, *The United Nations and Iraq: Defanging the Viper* (Westport, CT: Praeger, 2003).

5   The fight against terrorism

The Bush administration's dangerous neglect of human rights

Kenneth Roth

Leadership requires a positive vision shared by others and conduct consistent with that vision. The campaign against terrorism is no exception. The United States, as a major target, took the lead in combating terrorism. But the global outpouring of sympathy that followed the attacks of September 11, 2001 soon gave way to a growing reluctance to join the fight and even resentment toward the government leading it.[1]

How has this goodwill been depleted so quickly? In part the cause is traditional resentment of the U.S. and its role in the world—resentment which was softened only temporarily by the tragedy of September 11. In part it is opposition to U.S. policy in the Middle East—in Israel, Palestine, and Iraq. And in part it is growing disquiet that the means used to fight terrorism often conflict with the values of freedom and law that most people embrace and that President George W. Bush says the United States is defending.

Despite its declared policy of supporting human rights, the Bush administration in fighting terrorism refuses to be bound by human rights standards. Despite a U.S. tradition at home of government under law, the administration rejects legal constraints, especially when acting abroad. Despite a constitutional order that is premised on the need to impose checks and balances, the U.S. government seems to want an international order that places no limits on its own actions. These attitudes are jeopardizing the campaign against terrorism. They are also putting at risk the human rights ideal.

This is not to say that the United States is among the worst human rights offenders. But because of America's extraordinary influence, the Bush administration's willingness to compromise human rights to fight terrorism sets a dangerous precedent. Because of the leadership role that the U.S. government so often has played in promoting human rights, the weakening of its voice weighs heavily, particularly in some of the frontline countries in the war against terrorism, where the need for a vigorous defense of human rights is great. This degrading of international standards threatens to come back to haunt the United States.

Human rights and the challenge of terrorism

Terrorism is antithetical to human rights. Since targeting civilians for violent attack is repugnant to human rights norms, those who believe in human rights have a direct interest in the success of the anti-terrorism effort. Yet the Bush administration's tendency to ignore human rights in fighting terrorism is not only disturbing in its own right, it is dangerously counterproductive. The smoldering resentment that it breeds risks generating terrorist recruits, puts off potential anti-terrorism allies, and weakens efforts to curb terrorist atrocities. The perceived short-term need to compromise human rights in fighting terrorism thus can have a dangerous boomerang effect.

Terrorism cannot be defeated from afar. Curbing terrorism requires the support of people in the countries where terrorists reside. They are the people who must cooperate with police inquiries rather than shield terrorist activity. They are the people who must take the lead in dissuading would-be terrorists—not the Osama bin Ladens of the world, but their potential recruits. But people will hardly be inclined to help the anti-terror cause if they see Washington embracing the governments that repress their human rights. Their reluctance only increases if their entire community is viewed as suspect, as many young male Middle Easterners and North Africans feel since September 11.

Clearly the United States needs to take extra security measures. But the U.S. government must also pay attention to the pathology of terrorism—the set of beliefs that leads some people to join in attacking civilians, to claim that the ends justify the means. A strong human rights culture is an antidote to this pathology. Human rights and security are mutually reinforcing, yet too often the administration treats them as a zero-sum game.

President Ronald Reagan at the height of the Cold War understood the need for a positive vision. He understood that the United States could not afford to be only *against* communism. It had to stand *for* democracy, even if at times his support was no more than rhetorical. Similarly, it will not work for the Bush administration today to be only against terrorism. The administration will have to stand for the values that explain what is wrong with attacking civilians—namely, the values of human rights.

At times there have been hints of such a positive vision: in prominent parts of a speech that President Bush gave at West Point in June 2002; in part of his administration's National Security Strategy released in September 2002; and in the conditions for disbursing increased international assistance (the Millennium Challenge Account), announced in November 2002.[2] But this rhetorical embrace of human rights has translated only inconsistently into U.S. conduct and foreign policy.

For much of the past half-century, the United States was often a driving force for strengthening the human rights ideal. It took the lead in drafting the Universal Declaration of Human Rights, building the international human rights system, and lending its voice and influence on behalf of human rights in many parts of the world. Often this support for human rights was inconsistent—tempered by strategic concerns and a deep resistance to applying international law at home. Yet the U.S. government could still be found at the forefront of many human rights battles, and it contributed significantly to building a global consensus about the importance of human rights as a restraint on legitimate governmental conduct.

The Bush administration, too, has tried to advance human rights in places where the war on terrorism was not implicated, such as Burma, Belarus, and Zimbabwe. The administration has publicly recognized the connection between repression and terrorism, and to a limited extent has tried to promote human rights in some places that are more directly involved in the fight against terrorism, such as Egypt and Uzbekistan. Yet the administration has compromised the long U.S. engagement on human rights in three important respects.

First, in several key countries involved in the campaign against terrorism, such as Pakistan and Saudi Arabia, even rhetorical U.S. support for human rights has been sparing—often nothing more than the State Department's once-a-year pronouncements in its global human rights report. The administration also has shown little inclination to confront such influential governments as Russia, China, and Israel that have used the fight against terrorism to cloak or intensify repression aimed at separatist, dissident, or nationalist movements that are themselves often abusive.

Second, even when the Bush administration has tried to promote human rights, its authority has been undermined by its refusal to be bound by the standards that it insists others abide by. From its rejection of the Geneva Conventions for prisoners from the war in Afghanistan to its misuse of the "enemy combatant" designation for criminal suspects at home, from its threatened use of substandard military commissions to its reported use of "stress and duress" interrogation techniques and its abuse of immigration laws to deny criminal suspects their rights, the administration has fought terrorism as if human rights were not a constraint.

Third, the Bush administration has intensely opposed the enforcement of international human rights law, from the International Criminal Court (ICC) to more modest efforts to affirm or reinforce human rights norms. Similar exceptionalism could be seen in such actions as the administration's rejection of the Kyoto Protocol on global warming, its blocking of efforts to strengthen the Biological Weapons Convention, and its determination to go to war in Iraq without Security Council approval. This opposition suggests a radical vision of world order, a view of the superpower unconstrained by international law. Certain influential elements in the administration seem to view international law as an unnecessary encroachment on U.S. action—a set of rules to be avoided because they might restrict future U.S. latitude in unforeseeable and inconvenient ways. Instead, they advocate determining the proper scope of governmental conduct, if not through unilateral assertions of power, then at least through case-by-case negotiations, in which the U.S.'s overwhelming economic and military strength is more likely to prevail.

But even might has limits. Shared norms—of commerce, peace, or human rights—are needed so that most governments voluntarily abide by them. Pressure may still be necessary to rein in recalcitrant governments, but an effective global order depends on most governments' living voluntarily by agreed-upon rules. Even if the result is disappointing in a particular case, most governments recognize that a system of law is in their interest over the long run. But that logic breaks down if the sole superpower routinely exempts itself from shared rules. If these common norms give way to relations built on power alone, the world will revert to a premodern, Hobbesian order. That can hardly be in the long-term interest of the United States or anyone else.

The Bush administration's neglect of human rights in fighting terrorism has been visible in its own treatment of terrorist suspects, its bilateral relations with other governments, its behavior in international forums, and in elements of its war in Iraq.

Treatment of terrorist suspects

Much of the criticism of the Bush administration's human rights record since September 11 has focused on the U.S.A. Patriot Act. This act—a law passed by Congress and signed by President Bush—contains many troubling provisions, such as those allowing enhanced official scrutiny of medical, library, and student records. But many of the administration's most flagrant abuses toward terrorist suspects have had nothing to do with the Patriot Act. As the following examples illustrate, much of the administration's most troubling conduct reflects unilateral executive action unconnected to any Congressional grant of authority.

A good example is the Bush administration's disregard of the 1949 Geneva Conventions in its treatment of prisoners of war (POWs). Historically, the United States has been expansive in its compliance with the requirements of international humanitarian law (or the laws of war) with regard to belligerents captured in the course of an armed conflict. For example, the U.S. afforded POW status to Chinese soldiers captured during the Korean War even though the People's Republic of China was not a party to the Geneva Conventions. It provided POW status to many captured guerrillas during the Vietnam War. During the 1991 Gulf war, the U.S. military convened special tribunals to determine the legal status of more than one thousand captured Iraqis, as the Geneva Conventions require.

The United States upheld international standards in part out of recognition that they ultimately benefit U.S. soldiers. Needless to say, the reverse is also true: failure to comply with the Geneva Conventions encourages noncompliance by others when U.S. service members must depend on the Conventions for their protection. Unfortunately, the Bush administration broke with this long U.S. tradition in its treatment of terrorist suspects and others detained in the war on terrorism. Ironically, it then found itself in the awkward position of having to rely on the Geneva Conventions to try to protect its captured troops in Iraq.

In its treatment of the people detained at Guantánamo Bay, the administration has adopted an unjustifiably narrow reading of the Geneva Conventions, which effectively places these detainees in a legal black hole, allowing them to be kept in long-term arbitrary detention despite international prohibitions. For instance, the Third Geneva Convention provides that captured combatants are to be treated as prisoners of war until a "competent tribunal" determines otherwise.[3] Under the standards set out in the convention, the detainees who were former Taliban soldiers almost certainly qualify as POWs, while many of the detainees who were members of Al Qaeda probably do not.[4] But the administration has refused to bring any of the detainees before a tribunal and has unilaterally asserted that none qualifies as a POW.[5]

This flouting of international humanitarian law cannot be explained by the exigencies of fighting terrorism. Treating the detainees as POWs would not preclude the United States from interrogating them or prosecuting them for committing terrorist acts or other atrocities. And POWs, like other detained combatants, can be held without charge or trial until the end of the relevant armed conflict.

The administration's refusal to apply the Geneva Conventions seems to stem in part from its desire to minimize public scrutiny of its conduct. For instance, in the absence of criminal prosecutions, the Geneva Conventions require that all detainees, regardless of their status, be repatriated once "active hostilities" have ended.[6] In the case of at least the Taliban detainees, that would seem to have required repatriation as soon as the war with the Afghan government was over—that is, presumably, after a *Loya Jirga* ("Grand Assembly") elected Hamid Karzai President of Afghanistan in June 2002.

The Bush administration also breached the rule of law to take custody of some detainees. In October 2001 it sought the surrender in Bosnia of six Algerian men who were suspected of planning attacks on Americans. After a three-month investigation, Bosnia's Supreme Court ordered the men's release from custody for lack of evidence. When rumors spread of U.S. efforts to seize the suspects anyway and spirit them out of the country, Bosnia's Human Rights Chamber—which in fact was established under the U.S.-sponsored Dayton Peace Accord and includes six local and eight international members—issued an injunction against their removal. Yet in January 2002, under pressure from Washington, the Bosnian government ignored this legal ruling and delivered the men to U.S. forces, who whisked them away, reportedly to Guantánamo. The U.S. government showed similar contempt for national justice systems when in June 2003 it quickly removed five terrorist suspects from Malawi in violation of a court order.[7]

Similarly, the administration has crossed the appropriate line between war and law enforcement in the cases of: José Padilla, a U.S. citizen arrested in May 2002 as he arrived from Pakistan at Chicago's O'Hare International Airport, allegedly to explore creating a radiological bomb; and Ali Saleh Kahlah al-Marri, a Qatari student arrested in December 2001 at his home in Peoria, Illinois, where he was said to have been a "sleeper" available to help others launch terrorist attacks. Padilla was briefly held as a material witness and Marri even had minor criminal charges filed against him. Then, in each case, rather than pursuing criminal prosecution, the Bush administration declared the men "enemy combatants." That designation, the administration claims, permits it to hold them without access to counsel and without charge or trial until the end of the war against terrorism, which may never come.

If Padilla's and Marri's alleged offenses are rightfully viewed as acts of war, the administration would be within its rights to hold them as enemy combatants. But if they are more appropriately seen as crimes, the men should be prosecuted with full due-process rights. International law is weak in explaining whether war rules or law-enforcement rules should apply, but our moral judgments can provide guidance. If Padilla and Marri were really "enemy combatants," U.S. security forces would have been entitled to summarily shoot them rather than take them into custody. In war there is no obligation to take custody of, rather than kill, an enemy soldier who has not offered to surrender. Padilla could have been gunned down as he stepped off his plane at O'Hare, Marri as he left his home in Peoria. Most people, though, would have been deeply troubled by such summary killing. But if Padilla and Marri are not properly treated as enemy combatants for the purpose of killing them, they should also not be treated as enemy combatants for the purpose of detaining them.[8]

The administration's expansive use of the "enemy combatant" designation threatens to create a giant exception to the most basic guarantees of criminal justice. Anyone could be picked up and detained forever as an "enemy combatant," even someone far from any recognizable battlefield, upon the unverified assertion of the Bush administration or any other government. The administration's radical claim in the Padilla case is being litigated before U.S. District Judge Michael Mukasey in the Southern District of New York.

Due-process shortcuts also plagued the Bush administration's detention of some 1,200 non-U.S. citizens whom the government sought to question regarding their links to or knowledge of the September 11 attacks. Of this group, whose number has never been fully disclosed, 752 were detained on immigration charges but treated like criminals. Rather than grant them the rights of criminal suspects, the administration used immigration law to detain and interrogate them secretly, without their usual right to be charged promptly with a criminal offense and (in case of economic need) to government-appointed counsel. Immigration detainees would ordinarily be deported, allowed to leave the country voluntarily, or released on bond pending a hearing on their case. But these "special interest" detainees were kept in jail until "cleared"—that is, until proven innocent of terrorist connections—often for many months. None to date has been charged with a crime related to September 11.[9]

President Bush's November 2001 order authorizing the creation of military commissions to try non-U.S. suspects lacked the most basic due-process guarantees and raised the prospect of trials that would have been a travesty of justice. In March 2002 the Defense Department issued regulations for the commissions that corrected many of the due-process problems of the original order. However, the regulations still allow the commissions to operate without even the fair-trial standards applicable in U.S. courts-martial in which defendants are entitled to appeal to the U.S. Court of Appeal for the Armed Forces (a civilian court outside the control of the executive branch) and ultimately to petition the U.S. Supreme Court. The commission regulations permit appeal only to another military panel of people who must answer to the President. Through his surrogates, the President becomes prosecutor, trial judge, and appellate judge. Especially as applied away from the exigencies of the battlefield, these compromised commissions violate the minimum legal requirement of "an impartial and regularly constituted court respecting the generally recognized principles of regular judicial procedure."[10] If these commissions are used to try detainees who should be considered prisoners of war, and thus are entitled to the more protective procedures of a court-martial,[11] the Bush administration will open itself to war-crimes charges.[12]

Perhaps the most disturbing example of the administration's attitude toward human rights was the Central Intelligence Agency's (CIA) reported use of "stress and duress" interrogation techniques at a U.S. air force base in Bagram, Afghanistan. Detailed and carefully researched press accounts described the use of such interrogation techniques as prolonged hooding, standing while hand-cuffed to the ceiling, sleep deprivation, and confinement in painful positions.[13] Individually these techniques probably stop short of torture. Taken together, however, they almost certainly constitute "cruel, inhuman and degrading treatment" which is prohibited by the U.S.-ratified Convention Against Torture.[14]

The administration's response to this evidence has been extraordinarily damaging. It has refused to discuss the evidence, thus leaving the impression that the press reports are accurate. It initially stated that it rejected the use of torture,[15] but that was largely beside the point; the issue was mainly cruel, inhuman, and degrading treatment, not torture. It then went on to claim that its interrogators were acting "in full compliance with domestic and international law."[16] That had the effect of suggesting that, in the administration's view, it does not violate the prohibition on cruel, inhuman, and degrading treatment to use these "stress and duress" interrogation techniques.

As noted above, this is almost certainly inaccurate as a matter of law. Moreover, in ratifying the Convention Against Torture, the administration effectively equated the prohibition on cruel, inhuman, and degrading treatment with the Eighth Amendment to the U.S. Constitution's ban on cruel and unusual punishment.[17] But no U.S. judge today would ever permit a detainee to be subjected to similar "third degree" techniques. The administration's insistence that these interrogation techniques are nonetheless lawful thus has the effect of legitimizing similar techniques being used by unsavory regimes around the world, potentially even against U.S. detainees.

In June 2003, at the urging of human rights groups, the Bush administration affirmed that it would conduct worldwide investigations consistent with the U.S. Constitution's prohibition of "cruel, unusual, and inhumane treatment and punishment." "United States policy is to treat all detainees and conduct all interrogations, wherever they may occur, in a manner consistent with this commitment," announced William J. Haynes II, General Counsel of the Department of Defense. He promised that "credible allegations of illegal conduct by U.S. personnel will be investigated and, as appropriate, reported to proper authorities," noting that two deaths in U.S. custody at Bagram were still under investigation by the Defense Department.[18] This was an important step forward. Nonetheless, the administration has not made clear whether it has issued orders prohibiting any of the "stress and duress" interrogation techniques reportedly practiced at Bagram or whether, except in the two death cases, any interrogators are under investigation.

This overall pattern of abuse in the Bush administration's own treatment of terrorist suspects sends a signal of contempt for basic human rights standards. It suggests that the administration sees international human rights standards as an inconvenient obstacle to fighting terrorism that is readily sidestepped rather than as an integral part of the anti-terrorism effort.

Bilateral relations

A similar disregard for human rights can be found in U.S. bilateral relations with many countries that are critical to the fight against terrorism. Afghanistan, the primary focus of anti-terrorism efforts immediately after September 11, illustrates the problem. The military overthrow of the highly abusive Taliban raised the prospect of greater freedom for the Afghan people. And if one judged by Kabul, where international peacekeepers patrol, life has improved dramatically. But the Bush administration has offered lukewarm support for the deployment of international troops outside of the capital (European governments have been equally reluctant) and has taken few meaningful steps to demobilize factional forces or establish a professional Afghan army. Instead, it has delegated security to resurgent warlords and provided them with money and arms.

In some parts of the country, the consequences look much like life under the Taliban, a far cry from President Bush's vow to help Afghanistan "claim its democratic future."[19] For example, Ismail Khan, the Herat-based warlord in western Afghanistan, has stamped out all dissent, muzzled the press, and bundled women back into their burqas. Those who resist face death threats, detention, and sometimes even torture.[20] Afghans who had taken refuge in Iran during Taliban rule complained to Human Rights Watch that they had been freer under the Iranian clerics than they are under Khan. Yet U.S. Defense Secretary Donald Rumsfeld, after a visit to Herat in April 2002, called Khan an "appealing person."[21] Under growing pressure to address the violence and insecurity outside of Kabul, the Bush administration has sent small teams of soldiers and civil affairs officers to various Afghan provincial cities, mainly for development work. Their presence offers some modestly enhanced security, but it is far from the focused security effort needed to end the reigns of the warlords. In May 2003 the Bush administration rejected Afghan President Hamid Karzai's request for military assistance to remove some of the more abusive warlords.[22]

In Pakistan, some form of military alliance with General Pervez Musharraf, who overthrew an elected government in 1999 was probably unavoidable. In the process, however, the Bush administration has virtually abandoned the promotion of human rights and democracy in that country. In 2002 Musharraf pushed through constitutional amendments that extended his presidential term by five years, arrogated to himself the power to dissolve the elected parliament, and created a military-dominated National Security Council to oversee civilian government. When asked about this disturbing trend, President Bush said, "My reaction about President Musharraf, he's still tight with us on the war against terror, and that's what I appreciate."[23] Only as an afterthought did Bush also mention the importance of democracy.[24] With Washington supporting Pakistan's military ruler and the repressive warlords next door in Afghanistan, it should have been no surprise that anti-U.S. political parties in Pakistan were the big winners in the parliamentary elections of October 2002. Their victory as well in simultaneous local elections in the two provinces bordering Afghanistan has complicated U.S. efforts to apprehend residual Taliban and Al Qaeda forces in the area.

In Indonesia an abusive military and allied militia have been major factors in separatist and communal strife in places such as the western province of Aceh. The government's inability to hold abusive military figures accountable has been a major cause of popular discontent. Military-sponsored atrocities in East Timor in 1999 led the United States to cut off some military assistance. But with Indonesia seen as a major front in the battle against terrorism, the Bush administration has tried to resume military training, even though little if any progress has been made in subjecting the military to the rule of law.

The administration also sought dismissal of a lawsuit brought in a U.S. court by victims of military atrocities in Indonesia who sought compensation from Exxon Mobil for its alleged complicity in the abuse. The suit, filed in June 2001 in Washington, alleged that the Indonesian military had provided "security services" for Exxon Mobil's joint venture in Indonesia's conflict-ridden Aceh province, and that the Indonesian military had committed "genocide, murder, torture, crimes against humanity, sexual violence and kidnapping" while providing security for the company from 1999 to 2001. The plaintiffs claimed that Exxon Mobil had been aware of widespread abuses committed by the military but had failed to take preventive action. In a July 2002 letter from State Department Legal Adviser William H. Taft IV, the administration justified its opposition to this effort to enforce human rights standards in part out of its stated fear that Indonesia would retaliate by stopping its cooperation in the war on terrorism.[25]

A broad range of other U.S. allies in the war on terrorism have received similarly soft treatment for their human rights abuses. For example, Russian President Vladimir Putin has faced only mild criticism of his troops' continuing brutal behavior in Chechnya; their atrocities have only intensified after Chechen militants took some 700 people hostage in a Moscow theater in October 2002. In China's western Xinjiang province, Beijing has long repressed the

Turkic-speaking Uighur majority, China's largest Muslim population. Despite the administration's occasional criticism of Chinese conduct in Xinjiang, the decision to designate as a terrorist organization the small Eastern Turkistan Islamic Movement, which was said to be a Uighur movement from Xinjiang, provides added cover for Chinese repression of the Uighurs. In a break with past U.S. practice, the current Bush administration announced in April 2003 that, in light of supposed "progress," it would not sponsor critical resolutions against either Russia or China at the March–April 2003 session of the Commission on Human Rights (CHR), the U.N.'s leading human rights body.[26]

The overriding message sent by these U.S. bilateral actions was that human rights are dispensable in the name of fighting terrorism. That policy may provide greater leeway for short-term security measures. But if an important aim is to build a culture of human rights in place of the pathology of terrorism, it sends a dangerous and counterproductive signal, that it is acceptable to replace respect for the life of every person with the view that the ends justify the means.

International forums

At the multilateral level, the Bush administration has consistently opposed any effort to enforce human rights standards. This posture is not entirely new. Both Democratic and Republican administrations have always kept human rights treaties at arm's length. The U.S. government has never ratified three of the seven leading human rights treaties[27] or the leading treaty governing modern armed conflict.[28] Even when it ratifies a human rights treaty, it does so in a way that denies Americans the ability to enforce the treaty in any court, whether international or domestic.[29] This resistance to enforceable human rights standards has only intensified since September 11.

The resistance was on display at the March–April 2002 session of the Commission on Human Rights in Geneva. Mexico proposed a resolution that stressed the importance of fighting terrorism consistent with human rights. The resolution did not condemn any state; it simply reaffirmed an essential principle. Yet the Bush administration opposed it. It was joined by Algeria, India, Pakistan, and Saudi Arabia—hardly committed supporters of the international enforcement of human rights. Mexico ultimately withdrew the resolution. Not until eight months later, in December 2002, did the General Assembly eventually adopt a similar resolution, when the administration's opposition failed to derail it. The CHR then reaffirmed that resolution in its March–April 2003 session.

The administration also opposed efforts at the United Nations to strengthen the prohibition against torture. It objected to a proposed new Optional Protocol to the Convention Against Torture, which establishes a system for inspecting detention facilities where torture is suspected, an important preventive measure. The administration's position was at first puzzling, because the United States opposes torture as a matter of policy and has ratified the Torture Convention. If

Washington wanted to avoid scrutiny under this new inspection procedure, it could simply not ratify the protocol, which, as its name suggests, is optional. The administration's decision, instead, to try to deprive other states of this added human rights protection stems from an evident desire to avoid strengthening any international human rights law that might even remotely be used to criticize its own conduct—especially, one must assume, its interrogation of security suspects at Bagram air base in Afghanistan.[30] The Optional Protocol came to a vote before the General Assembly in December 2002; the United States was one of only four governments to oppose it, against 127 supporters.

The administration's opposition to the enforcement of human rights standards has been most extreme in the case of the International Criminal Court. The court has numerous safeguards to address legitimate U.S. concerns about politicized prosecutions. Crimes are defined narrowly—in fact, more narrowly than even U.S. military manuals define them. Several independent panels of judges oversee prosecutorial decisions. A mere majority of the states party can impeach an abusive prosecutor (and most of the states party are democracies, given that ratification subjects a government's own conduct to the court's jurisdiction). Governments can avoid ICC prosecution altogether by conducting their own good-faith investigations and, if appropriate, prosecutions. Moreover, the ICC does not purport to exert jurisdiction over a suspect unless the suspect's government has ratified the Court's treaty or the suspect is alleged to have committed a crime on the territory of a government that has ratified the treaty—both long-accepted bases of jurisdiction.

Yet the Bush administration has declared a virtual war on the Court. It took the unprecedented step of repudiating former President Bill Clinton's signature on the ICC treaty. It threatened to shut down U.N. peacekeeping unless U.S. participants in operations authorized by the world organization were exempted from ICC jurisdiction. Washington has threatened to cut off military aid to governments unless they agree never to deliver to the court a suspect who is a U.S. citizen. And President Bush signed legislation authorizing military intervention to free any U.S. suspect held by the ICC, dubbed the "Hague Invasion Act." With occasional exceptions, the administration did not discourage governments from ratifying the ICC treaty for the sole purpose of addressing conduct by others, and by mid-2003 some 90 governments had joined the Court—well above the 60 needed for the treaty to take effect. But the Bush administration's efforts to exempt U.S. nationals from the Court's investigations and prosecutions advance a double standard that threatens to undermine its legitimacy. Indeed, that may well be the administration's goal. Its posture is particularly disappointing because the states party to the ICC treaty have selected a top-notch prosecutor and a highly professional group of judges.[31]

By these multilateral interventions, across a wide range of issues, the Bush administration signals that human rights standards are at best window dressing. They are fine grand pronouncements, but their universal enforcement, which might affect the United States even indirectly, is to be avoided. This undermines these norms. It also undermines the credibility of the United States as a proponent of human rights, whether in fighting terrorism or in combating more traditional affronts to human rights.

Consequences for the campaign against terrorism

The Bush administration's willingness to sidestep human rights as it fights terrorism has potentially profound and dangerous consequences. At the very least, it means that the United States is a party to serious abuse. If Washington provides assistance to abusive warlords in Afghanistan or a military dictatorship such as Pakistan's, it becomes complicit in the abuses that they foreseeably commit. And senior officials in Washington seem to be covering up for the use of abusive techniques by CIA interrogators at Bagram air base.

In addition, Washington's neglect of human rights threatens to impede its campaign against terrorism. As President Bush himself has observed, repression fuels terrorism by closing off avenues for peaceful dissent. Yet if the U.S. campaign against terrorism reinforces that repression, it risks breeding more terrorists as it alienates would-be allies in the fight against terrorism.

The administration's subordination of human rights to the campaign against terrorism also has bred a "copycat phenomenon." By waving the anti-terrorism banner, governments such as Uzbekistan's seem to act as if they have greater license to persecute religious dissenters, while governments such as Russia's, Israel's, and China's seem to act with greater freedom as they intensify repression in Chechnya, the West Bank, and Xinjiang.[32] Similarly, Tunisia has stepped up trying civilians on terrorism charges before military courts that flagrantly disregard due-process rights.[33] Claiming that asylum-seekers can be a "pipeline for terrorists" entering the country, Australia has imposed some of the tightest restrictions on asylum in the industrialized world.[34] Facing forces on the right and left that had been designated terrorists, Colombia's President Álvaro Uribe tried to permit warrantless searches and wiretaps and to restrict the movement of journalists (until the country's highest court ruled these measures unconstitutional).[35]

In sub-Saharan Africa, Ugandan President Yoweri Museveni shut down the leading independent newspaper for a week in October 2002 because it was allegedly promoting terrorism. It had reported a military defeat for the government in its battle against the Lord's Resistance Army rebel group.[36] In June 2002 Liberia's President Charles Taylor declared three of his critics—the editor of a local newspaper and two others—to be "illegal combatants" who would be tried for terrorism in a military court.[37] Eritrea justified its lengthy detention of the founder of the country's leading newspaper by citing the widespread U.S. detentions.[38] Zimbabwean President Robert Mugabe justified the November 2001 arrest of six journalists as terrorists because they wrote stories about political violence in the country.[39] Elsewhere, even former Yugoslav President Slobodan Milošević defended himself against war-crimes charges by contending that abusive troops under his command had merely been combating terrorism.[40]

The inconsistency of the Bush administration's attention to human rights abroad also weakens an important voice for human rights when the United States does speak out. The most dramatic example was the case of Saadeddin Ibrahim, the Egyptian democracy activist who was sentenced in July 2002 to seven years in prison for his peaceful political activities. To its credit, the administration not only protested but also said it would withhold an incremental increase in aid that might have gone to Egypt. That was a dramatic step—the first time that the United States had conditioned aid on the positive resolution of a human rights case in the Middle East. But in light of Washington's long history of closing its eyes to human rights abuses in the region, and its failure to protest Egypt's similar persecution of Islamists for nonviolent political activity, many Egyptians distrusted the administration's motives. Even some Egyptian human rights groups denounced the action. In December, Egypt's highest appeals court—with a long tradition of independence of the government—reversed Ibrahim's conviction and ordered a new trial. But the effectiveness of Washington's voice as a means to build broad public support for human rights was shown to have been compromised.

The war in Iraq

The Bush administration sought to justify the military overthrow of Saddam Hussein as part of the war against terrorism. The war's origins were clearly more complex than that, but this rationale nonetheless bears discussion in light of the administration's broader disinclination to recognize human rights as a constraint on the fight against terrorism. Because the invasion was so controversial, risking long-term damage to the U.S.'s reputation in the Middle East and around the world, the Bush administration had an especially strong incentive to fight the war consistently with international humanitarian law. In many respects it did, but even in Iraq it fell short of these requirements in several important respects.

Saddam Hussein's human rights record is as bad as they come, lending some credibility to the claim that human rights in part motivated the war, even though he was a U.S. ally at the time of some of his gravest crimes. In 1988, in the notorious *Anfal* campaign, he committed genocide against the Kurds. After using chemical weapons on at least 40 occasions to drive Kurds from their highland villages, his forces rounded up and executed some 100,000, mostly men and boys. In suppressing the 1991 uprisings, his forces killed an estimated 30,000 Iraqis, mostly Kurds in the north and Shi'a in the south. In the following years, untold atrocities were committed against the so-called Marsh Arabs. On a daily basis, the Iraqi government used arbitrary detention, torture, and execution to maintain power. A conservative estimate would be that under Saddam Hussein's rule the Iraqi government killed some quarter of a million Iraqis—an average of 10,000 a year.

But the war on Iraq was never a humanitarian intervention in the sense that it was waged primarily for the benefit of the Iraqi people. If Saddam Hussein had been overthrown in a palace coup and replaced by an equally repressive dictator who nonetheless was willing to cooperate in ridding the country of alleged weapons of mass destruction (WMD), there clearly would have been no invasion. It is, of course, important from a human rights perspective to stop the possible use of WMD, but the Bush administration never provided credible evidence of such a current (as opposed to a historical) threat.

In part because of the questionable justification for the war, the Bush administration's conduct of the war was closely scrutinized for its compliance with international humanitarian law. Preliminary investigation suggests that several troubling practices were discernible.

First, despite the duty to refrain from indiscriminate warfare and to take all feasible precautions to avoid civilian casualties, the Pentagon continued to use cluster munitions near populated areas. These weapons are particularly deadly when used near civilians because they disperse over a wide area and are difficult to target precisely. In the Yugoslav war of 1999 the use of cluster munitions in populated areas was responsible for some quarter of the civilian deaths caused directly by the North Atlantic Treaty Organization's bombing. Apparently because of this death toll, the U.S. Air Force made little use of cluster bombs near populated areas in Afghanistan,[41] and it seemed largely to refrain from such use in Iraq as well. However, available evidence suggests that the U.S. Army did use cluster munitions in Iraqi population centers, including Baghdad, Basra, Hilla, and Nasiriya. This represents a disturbing regression in Pentagon practice. It is too early to tell why this occurred, but one working hypothesis is that while U.S. air forces learned the dangers of cluster bomb use in populated areas, U.S. ground forces had not integrated that lesson because they had not taken part in the Yugoslav and Afghan wars in large numbers. The Pentagon's leadership can be faulted for apparently failing to bring ground forces up to the level of practice of air forces.[42]

A second test for U.S. forces in Iraq is whether they did everything feasible to prevent Iraqis from killing other Iraqis during the war—a genuine fear in light of Iraq's recent history. In one respect, the Bush administration did well in meeting this challenge, but in another respect it was disappointing. One of the greatest fears before the war was that Saddam Hussein, as a last resort in the face of his imminent overthrow, would take to massacring Iraqi civilians, especially groups seen as historically opposed to his rule, such as the Kurds and the Shi'a. In an effort to dissuade his lieutenants from carrying out any such orders, President Bush personally vowed on several occasions that any Iraqi who committed atrocities during the war would be prosecuted.[43] It is difficult to know how decisive his warning was—the bombing of communications facilities was undoubtedly also important—but once the war began Iraqi government forces did not apparently commit any further large-scale massacres.

The Bush administration was less effective in preventing private Iraqis from seeking summary vengeance against other Iraqis. During the 1991 uprising, Iraqi rebel forces, both Kurdish and Shi'a, summarily executed government officials, Baath Party members, and other perceived supporters of Saddam

Hussein. To prevent a recurrence of this slaughter, Human Rights Watch and others argued that it was essential, as U.S. troops gradually toppled Saddam Hussein's government, not to leave a security vacuum. Instead, the Pentagon was urged to ensure that fighting troops were followed closely by military police who would be capable of vigorously patrolling and keeping the peace. However, the Bush administration was anxious to begin the war before summer's heat arrived—not to mention before the growing political heat of anti-war demonstrations around the world intensified. Hence the U.S. launched the invasion before sufficient troops were in place to maintain security after predictable victory. As a result, widespread looting and general lawlessness occurred.[44] U.S. troops, apparently lacking adequate training in policing, have also left a significant death toll as they attempt to maintain order.[45]

Future tests of the Bush administration's commitment to human rights in Iraq remain. Does the administration have the long-term commitment needed to build a stable, secure, and democratic environment, or will it resort to short-cuts similar to its "warlord strategy" in Afghanistan? Will the administration ensure that Iraq's oil riches do not become an incentive for renewed dictatorship and corruption?[46] Will the administration endorse a fair and legitimate process to bring to justice those who have been responsible for the worst atrocities of the past two-and-a-half decades?

So far, on the issue of justice, the administration has been particularly disappointing in proposing "Iraqi-led" tribunals. That sounds fine in theory—why not let Iraqis build the rule of law themselves? But in practice it shows little regard for the rule of law. It will be difficult to find Iraqi jurists who have the expertise needed to conduct a complex trial of genocide or crimes against humanity. Moreover, whether they served under Saddam Hussein's government or fled into exile, many Iraqi jurists will be seen as biased—and particularly if they are handpicked by Washington rather than selected by the United Nations or some other international body. Tribunals are likely to have much more capability and credibility if they have a significant international component—either an entirely international tribunal such as those established for Rwanda and the former Yugoslavia, or an internationally led tribunal with local participation, such as the special court established for Sierra Leone.

However, the Bush administration is adamantly opposed to an international tribunal. Three reasons seem to lie behind this opposition. First, the administration seems to fear that an international tribunal might scrutinize the conduct of allies or even of the United States itself, whereas a tribunal made up of handpicked Iraqis would be more pliable. Second, international tribunals traditionally do not impose the death penalty, which the administration hopes to apply. Third, the administration opposes any international tribunal for fear that it would lend credibility to the entire project of international justice, including the ICC. The resolution of this issue will play an important part in determining whether Saddam Hussein's overthrow will lead the way to a government bound by the rule of law.[47]

Conclusion

The security threat posed by terrorism should not obscure the importance of human rights. Military or police action can be seductive. It leaves the impression that the problem is being addressed head-on. Concern with human rights, by contrast, may seem peripheral—of long-term utility, undoubtedly, but not an immediate priority.

That view is profoundly mistaken. An anti-terrorism policy that ignores human rights is a gift to terrorists. It reaffirms the violent instrumentalism that breeds terrorism and undermines the public support needed to defeat it. This approach is likely to make the United States less secure, not more. A strong human rights policy cannot replace the actions of security forces, but it is an essential complement. A successful anti-terrorism policy must endeavor to build strong international norms and institutions on human rights, not provide a new rationale for avoiding and undermining them.

Notes

1 Adam Clymer, "World Survey Says Negative Views of U.S. Are Rising," *New York Times*, December 5, 2002, p. A22; The Pew Research Center for the People and the Press, "What the World Thinks in 2002: How Global Publics View: Their Lives, Their Countries, The World, America," December 4, 2002, http://people-press.org/reports/display.php3?ReportID=165.
2 "President Bush Delivers Graduation Speech at West Point," http://www.whitehouse.gov/news/releases/2002/06/20020601-3.html; "The National Security Strategy of the United States of America," http://www.whitehouse.gov/nsc/nss.html; "The Millenium Challenge Account," http://www.whitehouse.gov/infocus/developingnations/millennium.html.
3 Geneva Convention Relative to the Treatment of Prisoners of War of August 12, 1949 (Third Geneva Convention), Article 5. The United States ratified the convention in 1955.
4 Taliban detainees should have been eligible for POW status under Article 4 (A) (1) of the Third Geneva Convention, which grants such status unconditionally to "members of the armed forces of a Party to the conflict." The same should have been true for Al Qaeda detainees who had belonged to a militia "forming part of" the Taliban forces. However, Al Qaeda members operating outside of Taliban structures would have to meet a separate four-part test under Article 4 (A) (2) of the Convention—having a responsible chain of command, wearing a distinctive sign, carrying arms openly, and respecting the laws and customs of war. Because these Al Qaeda members would likely fail one or more of these requirements, they would probably be ineligible for POW status.
5 The administration justified its position by merging two distinct provisions of the Third Geneva Convention with regard to prisoners of war. One section provides that the regular armed forces of a state party to a conflict are entitled to automatic POW status. The second section provides that certain irregular militia are entitled to POW status only if they meet a four-part test, involving having a responsible chain of command, wearing a distinctive uniform, bearing arms openly, and generally respecting international humanitarian law. The first section likely would embrace the Taliban detainees, but the Bush administration refused in light of a Red Cross commentary suggesting that "regular armed forces" are presumed to meet the four-part test. The Taliban, the administration claimed, did not meet that test. However, the

administration's interpretation of the law would invite unscrupulous governments to ignore POW rules on the grounds that an enemy government's regular armed forces did not meet the four-part test—a loophole that the plain language of the Third Geneva Convention avoids.

6 Third Geneva Convention, Article 118.

7 See, for example, "Families speak of terror in Malawi al Qaeda raids," Reuters, June 25, 2003; "Emeutes au Malawi après le transfert de suspects vers Guantánamo," *Le Monde*, July 1, 2003.

8 For an elaboration of this argument in the Padilla case, see Kenneth Roth, "Foreign Enemies and Constitutional Rights," *Chicago Tribune*, November 10, 2002, p. 6.

9 For more on the Bush administration's abuse of immigration laws to conduct criminal investigations, see Human Rights Watch, "Presumption of Guilt: Human Rights Abuses of Post-September 11 Detainees," August, 2002, http://www.hrw.org/reports/2002/us911/Index.htm#TopOfPage; see also "The September 11 Detainees: A Review of the Treatment of Aliens Held on Immigration Charges in Connection with the Investigation of the September 11 Attacks," U.S. Department of Justice, Office of Inspector General, April 2003, http://www.usdoj.gov/oig/special/0603/full.pdf.

10 Protocol Additional to the Geneva Conventions of 12 August 1949, and Relating to the Protection of Victims of International Armed Conflict (Protocol I), Article 75. Although the United States has not ratified Protocol I, the requirements of Article 75 nonetheless bind the United States because they reflect customary international law.

11 Third Geneva Convention, Article 102. POWs can be "validly sentenced only if the sentence has been pronounced by the same courts according to the same procedure as in the case of members or the armed forces of the Detaining Power."

12 Third Geneva Convention, Article 130, defining "grave breaches," or war crimes, to include "willfully depriving a prisoner of war of the rights of fair and regular trial prescribed by this Convention."

13 Dana Priest and Barton Gellman, "U.S. Decries Abuse but Defends Interrogations; 'Stress and Duress' Tactics Used on Terrorism Suspects Held in Secret Overseas Facilities," *Washington Post*, December 26, 2003, p. A1; see also Carlotta Gall, "U.S. Military Investigating Death of Afghan in Custody," *New York Times*, March 4, 2003, p. A14.

14 See, for example, the European Court of Human Rights's decision in *Ireland v. the United Kingdom* (1978) or the Israeli Supreme Court's decision on the interrogation methods of the General Security Service (1999).

15 Reuters, "Bush Assures U.N. Rights Boss U.S. not Using Torture," March 7, 2003.

16 Alan Cooperman, "CIA Interrogation Under Fire; Human Rights Groups Say Techniques Could Be Torture," *Washington Post*, December 28, 2002, p. A9.

17 U.S. reservations, declarations, and understandings, Convention Against Torture and Other Cruel, Inhuman or Degrading Treatment or Punishment, Congressional Record S17486–01, daily edition, October 27, 1990, http://www1.umn.edu/humanrts/usdocs/tortres.html.

18 Letter from William J. Haynes II, General Counsel of the Department of Defense, to Senator Patrick J. Leahy, June 25, 2003, http://hrw.org/press/2003/06/letter-to-leahy.pdf. See also Peter Slevin, "U.S. Pledges Not to Torture Terror Suspects," *Washington Post*, June 27, 2003, p. A1.

19 Remarks by the President on U.S. Humanitarian Aid to Afghanistan, The White House, October 11, 2002, http://www.whitehouse.gov/news/releases/2002/10/20021011-3.html.

20 Human Rights Watch, "We Want to Live As Humans: Repression of Women and Girls in Western Afghanistan," December 2002, http://www.hrw.org/reports/2002/afghnwmn1202/; Human Rights Watch, "All Our Hopes Are Crushed: Violence and Repression in Western Afghanistan," October 2002, http://hrw.org/reports/2002/afghan3/.

21 Linda D. Kozaryn, "'On the Edge' with Rumsfeld in Afghanistan," *American Forces Press Service*, May 3, 2002, http://www.vnis.com/vetnews/usdefense/usdefense2002/usdefense2002-018.htm#7; see also Glenn Kessler, "Study Cites Repression by Afghan Governor," *Washington Post*, November 5, 2002, p. A22.

22 See Sarah Chayes, "Afghanistan's Future Lost in the Shuffle," *New York Times*, July 1, 2003.

23 "President Tours Area Damage by Squires Fire, Ruch, Oregon," August 22, 2002, http://www.whitehouse.gov/news/releases/2002/08/20020822-1.html.

24 Bush was equally fulsome in his praise of Musharraf's cooperation in fighting terrorism and not much more outspoken in pressing for democracy during Musharraf's visit to Washington in June 2003. See White House transcript of remarks, June 24, 2003, http://www.whitehouse.gov/news/releases/2003/06/20030624-3.html.

25 For a copy of the Taft letter, see http://www.hrw.org/press/2002/08/exxon072902.pdf. For a discussion of the lawsuit, see Human Rights Watch, "U.S./Indonesia: Bush Backtracks on Corporate Responsibility," August 7, 2002, http://www.hrw.org/press/2002/08/exxon080702.htm. On May 8, 2003, in a separate suit against Unocal, U.S. Attorney General John Ashcroft filed an amicus brief opposing any use of the Alien Tort Claims Act to bring civil suit against human rights abusers. See Human Rights Watch, "U.S.: Ashcroft Attacks Human Rights Law," May 15, 2003, http://www.hrw.org/press/2003/05/us051503.htm.

26 Edward Alden, "US Drops Censure of China on Human Rights," *Financial Times Online*, April 11, 2003, http://www.ft.com.

27 The United States has ratified the International Covenant on Civil and Political Rights; the Convention Against Torture and Other Cruel, Inhuman or Degrading Treatment or Punishment; the International Convention on the Elimination of All Forms of Racial Discrimination; and the Convention on the Prevention and Punishment of the Crime of Genocide. It has not ratified the International Covenant on Economic, Social and Cultural Rights; the Convention on the Elimination of All Forms of Discrimination Against Women; or the Convention on the Rights of the Child.

28 Protocol I of the Geneva Convention.

29 For a discussion of the methods that the U.S. government has used to prevent judicial enforcement of human rights treaties, see Kenneth Roth, "An Empire Above the Law," *Bard Journal of Global Affairs* 2 (Fall 2002), pp. 32–6; Kenneth Roth, "The Charade of U.S. Ratification of International Human Rights Treaties," *Chicago Journal of International Law* 1, no. 2 (Fall 2000), pp. 347–53.

30 See, for example, Dana Priest and Barton Gellman, "U.S. Decries Abuse but Defends Interrogations: 'Stress and Duress' Tactics Used on Terrorism Suspects Held in Secret Overseas Facilities," *Washington Post*, December 26, 2002, p. A01.

31 See, for example, "The International Criminal Court," *New York Times* (National edition), March 29, 2003.

32 For more on the human rights record of these countries in 2002, see Human Rights Watch, *World Report 2003* (New York: Human Rights Watch, 2003), pp. 216–29 (China), 350–9 (Russia), 382–90 (Uzbekistan), 459–72 (Israel). See also Human Rights Watch, "Russia: Clock Running Out for Displaced Chechens in Ingushetia," December 26, 2002, http://www.hrw.org/press/2002/12/russia1226.htm; Mike Jen drzejczyk, "Condemning the Crackdown in Western China," *Asian Wall Street Journal*, December 16, 2002, p. A16; Reuters, "China steps up call to fight Muslim separatists," December 23, 2002.

33 Human Rights Watch, *World Report 2003*, pp. 488–96.

34 Human Rights Watch, *By Invitation Only: Australian Asylum Policy* (New York: Human Rights Watch, 2002).

35 Human Rights Watch, *World Report 2003*, p. 127.

36 Human Rights Watch, "Uganda Attacks Freedom of the Press: Closes Main In-

dependent Newspaper," October 11, 2002, http://www.hrw.org/press/2002/10/uganda1011.htm.

37 Human Rights Watch, "Leading Liberian Journalist Re-Arrested: Facing Possible 'Terrorist' Charges," July 4, 2002, http://hrw.org/press/2002/07/liberia0704.htm.

38 Fred Hiatt, "Truth-Tellers in a Time of Terror," *Washington Post*, November 25, 2002, p. A15. See also Human Rights Watch, "Opportunism in the Face of Tragedy: Repression in the Name of Anti-Terrorism," http://www.hrw.org/campaigns/september11/opportunismwatch.htm#Eritrea; Human Rights Watch, "Eritrea: Cease Persecution of Journalists and Dissidents," May 16, 2002, http://hrw.org/press/2002/05/eritrea0516.htm; Human Rights Watch, "Escalating Crackdown in Eritrea: Reformists, Journalists, Students At Risk," September 21, 2001, http://www.hrw.org/press/2001/09/eritrea0921.htm.

39 Human Rights Watch, "Opportunism in the Face of Tragedy: Repression in the Name of Anti-terrorism," http://www.hrw.org/campaigns/september11/opportunismwatch.htm#Zimbabwe.

40 On February 14, 2002, Milošević delivered his opening defense at the International Criminal Tribunal for the Former Yugoslavia, in The Hague: "The Americans go right the other side of the globe to fight against terrorism—in Afghanistan, a case in point, right the other side of the world, and that is considered to be logical and normal. Whereas here the struggle against terrorism in the heart of one's own country, in one's own home, is considered to be a crime," http://www.un.org/icty/transe54/020214IT.htm, pp. 248–9.

41 Human Rights Watch, *Fatally Flawed: Cluster Bombs and their Use by the United States in Afghanistan* (New York: Human Rights Watch, 2002).

42 Human Rights Watch, "U.S. Misleading on Cluster Munitions," April 25, 2003, http://www.hrw.org/press/2003/04/us042503.htm; Human Rights Watch, "U.S. Use of Clusters in Baghdad Condemned," April 16, 2003, http://www.hrw.org/press/2003/04/iraqclusterbombs.htm.

43 See, for example, "Bush's Speech on Iraq: 'Saddam Hussein and His Sons Must Leave'," *New York Times*, March 18, 2003, p. A14.

44 Human Rights Watch, "Iraq: Killings, Expulsions on the Rise in Kirkuk: U.S. Not Fulfilling Duties of 'Occupying Power'," April 15, 2003, http://www.hrw.org/press/2003/04/iraq041503.htm.

45 See, for example, Ian Fisher, "U.S. Troops Fire on Iraqi Protesters, Leaving 15 Dead," *New York Times*, April 30, 2002.

46 See Human Rights Watch, "Post-War Oil Management Should Bolster Rights, Benefit Iraqis," April 18, 2003, http://www.hrw.org/press/2003/04/iraqoil041803.htm.

47 For more on this, see Kenneth Roth, "Give Iraqis Real Justice—Not a U.S. Puppet Show," *Globe and Mail (Toronto)*, April 10, 2003, p. A21.

Part 3

U.S. unilateralism in the wake of Iraq

6 Bush, Iraq, and the U.N.

Whose idea was this anyway?

Edward C. Luck

Who or what convinced President George W. Bush in August 2002 to make the United Nations the centerpiece of his campaign to build domestic and international support for using force in Iraq? And why did he persist in that effort for so many months despite substantial frustrations along the way? To some the answer may seem obvious: the U.N. is the world's premier political body, its Charter requires Security Council authorization for the use of force, and the Council has been seized of various aspects of the Iraqi challenge to global order for a dozen years. Yet the world body had failed in all those years to attain the goals that the President was seeking, in large part because the Council was bitterly and chronically divided on the critical question of how—sometimes even on whether—to enforce its numerous resolutions on Iraq. The President's enthusiasm for international law and multilateralism, moreover, had been episodic at best. To many, he would have seemed an unlikely candidate and this would have appeared an unpropitious moment to try to stiffen the Security Council's resolve in dealing with Saddam Hussein and to rescue its lagging credibility in the process. That would have been a tall order even for a Texan with the potential to be the world's last idealist or its newest imperialist.

This chapter weighs against the available evidence the four factors most often cited for the President's decision: U.S. public opposition to a war with Iraq and its preference for a more multilateral approach; Congressional pressure; the insistence of British Prime Minister Tony Blair and other foreign leaders; and the persuasiveness of Secretary of State Colin Powell, backed by many of the U.S. foreign policy elite. These findings should be tested against additional information on the inner workings of the Bush White House as it becomes available. While each of these dimensions has its place as part of the explanation, this chapter finds that a largely overlooked fifth factor—the President's own views, values, and priorities—appears to have been the decisive link and glue among them.[1] Once he decided to engage the U.N., he did manage to have some success not only in framing the issues to be addressed and defining the political context in which they were to be considered, but also in influencing the positions of other actors. To a certain extent, the successes and failures of the prewar political-diplomatic campaign, and it had plenty of both, were attributable to the strengths and weaknesses of the President's understanding of the world and of his office. Key in this case was his abiding confidence that he could persuade the world and employ the Security Council to advance his vision of a transformed and disarmed Iraq and of a reinvigorated and more muscular United Nations.

The chapter focuses on the critical six weeks preceding the President's watershed speech to the General Assembly on September 12, 2002, when he challenged the member states to enforce more than a decade of Security Council resolutions demanding that Iraq give up its weapons of mass destruction and related surface-to-surface missiles. Two decisions were critical during this period: to attempt to arouse and engage the world body on this matter; and to call for specific U.N. action, in particular for yet another resolution that could be interpreted as an authorization to use force to disarm Iraq. This chapter lacks room to consider the ill-fated third decision, in February 2003, to seek a second resolution on Iraq's non-compliance given growing international opposition to the use of force to disarm the Baghdad regime. While that decision in some ways seems even more problematic than the first, the die was cast, in large measure, in August 2002 in choosing to go the U.N. route in the first place. In some ways, the decision to return to the Security Council following the war for the negotiation of Resolution 1483 on the legal and institutional framework for postwar reconstruction represented an important step toward the reconciliation of national and international goals. Though the chapter cannot address in any detail the dynamics of the Bush administration's postwar decision-making, the decision to pursue 1483 would seem consistent with the principal conclusions.

The analysis and conclusions should be considered to be more suggestive than definitive given the nature of the evidence that has been made available to date. The chapter relies heavily on Bob Woodward's book, *Bush at War*, and on press accounts of political and diplomatic developments during those crucial weeks. It is possible that Woodward's account of decision-making within the Bush White House is cast in a way to emphasize George W. Bush's leadership qualities and stewardship of the war on terrorism because that may be the impression that administration figures wanted to convey in the interviews on which the book is based. However, it would be highly unusual either for cabinet-level figures in Washington to downplay their own roles or for a president to be able to impose such discipline on his inner circle. Either explanation, in any case, would seem to confirm that the President is very much in charge of policy-making. It is striking, moreover, that no one has come forward to contradict Woodward's account, which seems consistent with the other evidence cited here.

Wrong place, wrong time?

Before turning to the four factors most widely seen as influential in steering the administration in the U.N.'s direction, it would be useful to consider the extent to which Washington's and Turtle Bay's agendas vis-à-vis Iraq appeared to overlap or diverge before the President's September 2002 address to the General Assembly. If there was a substantial convergence of views, then the choice would have been a relatively simple one: Washington could have expected a fairly quick and painless endorsement of its conviction that it was high time to get tough with Saddam Hussein. But this obviously was not the case in terms of the goal of regime change in Baghdad. While this objective had been in the forefront of the Bush administration's arguments prior to September, it had never been accepted by the Security Council or most member states as an appropriate target. The U.N., after all, is a sovereignty-conscious inter-governmental organization whose decisions are supposed to further and to be based on international law. Indeed, for several months after his speech, the President appeared to downplay this rationale in favor of the disarmament and compliance concerns shared more widely among the U.N. membership. It should be recalled in this regard that one of the reasons that President Bush's father decided not to pursue Saddam Hussein's retreating forces far into Iraq in 1991, following Operation Desert Storm, was the lack of Security Council authorization for regime change.

The Bush team in 2002 should have been well aware both of the constraints that would come with operating under a U.N. mandate and of how different the 1990–1 and 2002 situations were. Most of President Bush's key advisers in the 2002 decision—including Vice-President Dick Cheney, Secretary of State Colin Powell, and Secretary of Defense Donald Rumsfeld—had been among the chief architects of his father's strategy for dealing with the Iraqi invasion of Kuwait a dozen years before. A great deal had changed over those years and the two scenarios had little in common other than the same villain, Saddam Hussein. President Bush, in fact, has made scant effort to link the two cases of Baghdad's intransigence, other than to list the invasion of Kuwait as one of a long series of Iraqi transgressions. Perversely, it seems that rousing publics and other capitals to react to a pattern of flouting the rules may be considerably harder than getting them to respond to a single transgression that is particularly egregious. People had tended to get inured to the fact that Baghdad habitually ignored Security Council resolutions about its weapons of mass destruction, while the media asked: "what is new?"

Two elements lacking in the 2002 scenario had been essential to rallying a broad coalition in 1990–1. First, the disarmament norm was not nearly as well established or widely accepted as that forbidding the conquest and absorption of a smaller neighboring country. Some member states continue to express ambivalence about the former, while the latter remains fundamental to the functioning of the nation-state system. The vast majority of member states, of course, are relatively small and potentially vulnerable to larger aggressors. In 1990–1, many of the newer member states were particularly wary of Iraq's claim that Kuwait's borders and even identity were artificial. Second, the more recent crisis lacked a clear precipitating event. The U.N. arms inspectors had been expelled from Iraq almost four years before and there was no internationally sponsored source of information on current Iraqi weapons developments.

These factors led to a questioning of British and American intelligence evalua-
tions of the situation on the ground, as well as of the timing and urgency of the
need to respond. One of the most frequently posed questions, even in the
United States, was "why now?"

Over the course of the 1990s, the mosaic of relationships among the U.N.,
the U.S., and the other member states had evolved in unexpected ways, and
none of them propitious for building the kind of broad-based coalition that
Bush had in mind. As the first post-Cold War effort to build such support
across east–west lines, his father's attempt to pull the Security Council together
involved considerable political risk, but it also generated a contagious sense of
excitement and optimism. Talk of a "new world order," however, could not
long be maintained in the face of a series of peacekeeping debacles over the
first half of the decade. Rocky relations between Washington and the world
organization were eased temporarily by the achievement of a package of
administrative reforms in the late 1990s and by agreement on a new assessment
scale with lowered U.S. obligations in 2000, but these episodes left a bitter taste
among the other member states. They complained about Washington's strong-
armed tactics, lukewarm support for others' agendas and for the institution
itself, and a highly selective approach to international organization and multilateral cooperation.[2]

Although many of these frustrations with the U.S. stance in the U.N. had
accumulated during the two Clinton administrations, they boiled over during
the first eight months of the Bush administration. The latter's distinct lack of
enthusiasm for a variety of international norm-building exercises—prominently
including the International Criminal Court (ICC), the Kyoto Protocol on global
warming, and a range of arms control and disarmament accords—angered officials and alienated public constituencies in those countries historically allied
most closely with the United States. The administration's blunt style and "us-or-
them" rhetoric soon squandered much of the empathy generated by the
September 11 terrorist attacks. Striking, in this regard, was that more than
three-quarters of the respondents to a Pew Research Center survey in the four
largest countries of Western Europe agreed in April 2002 that President Bush
"makes decisions based entirely on U.S. interests," duplicating the results of a
similar poll one month prior to September 11.[3]

It would appear that, in the U.N. and in the court of public opinion at least,
reputation does matter. The Bush administration had, by the critical month of
August 2002, gained a widespread reputation for having a distinct preference
for acting unilaterally. As this author has argued elsewhere, it has been difficult
for the current administration to shake this perception even on issues, such as
building an international counter-terrorist coalition, on which it has worked
very hard to make multilateral cooperation work.[4] Yet the President nevertheless decided to enter the diplomatic lion's den on the high-priority issue of Iraq
and did so, appearances suggest, with a good deal of confidence. It is worth
noting, in that regard, that while his father has gained a reputation as the internationalist in the family, the latter stresses in his foreign policy memoirs that he

would have abandoned the Security Council process at any point that it looked like it would not succeed in producing an authorization for Operation Desert Storm.[5] He was determined to push the Iraqi forces out of Kuwait, with or without the prior approval of the Security Council.

In August 2002, unlike August 1990, Washington faced three additional factors that made the politics of the Security Council decidedly bearish in terms of lining up support for a U.S.-led military campaign against Iraq. First, given the uneven results of efforts in the 1990s to enforce Security Council resolutions, whether by military or economic means, the U.N.'s membership appeared to be increasingly uncomfortable with the employment of Chapter VII enforcement measures to address any but the most discrete and localized threats to international peace and security. Economic sanctions, it was widely believed, tended to be both ineffective and cruel, with large-scale humanitarian consequences and little effect on critical elites. By the end of the decade, intensive efforts were under way to identify more finely tuned and carefully targeted sanctions.[6] If the consequences of sanctions were deemed to be bad, the use of military force was seen as worse. Ignoring the history of the Charter and its Chapter VII provisions, the collective use of force was commonly labeled the last resort and an admission that the U.N. had failed in its mission of peace. Secretaries-General Boutros Boutros-Ghali and Kofi Annan, among others, solemnly declared that the U.N.—despite its Charter—no longer was in the business of military enforcement. That task must be delegated to ad hoc groupings of willing and able member states. The loss of control that accompanied this novel doctrine, of course, served to make Council members that much more uncomfortable with authorizing acts that could not be monitored and that could easily have unforeseen and unwelcome effects.

Second, as the end of the Cold War rivalry was followed by the prospect of growing U.S. dominance of world affairs, other member states began to demonstrate increasing ambivalence toward the expression of American power, whether exercised inside or outside of the U.N. The temptation was great to use the world body as a means to counterbalance, at least politically, U.S. power and to constrain its policy options. In no realm, of course, did the primacy of U.S. capacities stand out as decisively as in military affairs, particularly in terms of force projection capabilities. Potential coalition partners were bound to be concerned that the United States had to carry the brunt of the fighting in Desert Storm, Kosovo, and Afghanistan and that its margin of superiority in conventional military technology was growing, not shrinking. Surely the political implications that such an asymmetrical arrangement was likely to have for postwar Iraq, as well as for the future architecture of the Gulf region and even of the Middle East, were obvious to friend and foe alike. While many in the U.N. and academic communities were consumed with the question of whether the existing decision-making structure in the Security Council could cope with such enormous disparities in capacity and power outside of its walls, the Bush administration seemed undeterred and proceeded with remarkable confidence to seek to enlist junior partners in its diplomatic and military coalitions.

Third, even a cursory review of the Security Council's track record in dealing with Iraq over the course of the 1990s would have underlined the likelihood of trouble ahead. There had been persistent and deep divisions on how to address Iraqi intransigence, with London and Washington generally on the tougher side of the equation and Russia, France, and China taking a much softer line. Differences arose over how intrusive the inspections should be, over whether Iraq should have any say on the composition of the U.N. monitoring teams, over how stringent compliance standards should be, over whether Iraq was making sufficient effort to comply, and, repeatedly, over the shape, rigor, and longevity of the sanctions regime.[7] France, Russia, and China, for example, abstained both on the 1997 resolution (1134) criticizing Iraqi non-compliance and raising the possibility of a travel ban on key Baghdad officials and on the 1999 resolution (1284) that set up the current arms monitoring regime, the United Nations Monitoring, Verification and Inspection Commission (UNMOVIC). Though the ferocious debate President Bush triggered in the Council in late 2002 and early 2003 was couched in terms of war, peace, and legality and of preserving an inspections arrangement that its current defenders had not even voted for, the fissures in the Council had much deeper geopolitical roots.[8] These were just as visible in August 2002 as they were on the eve of the war, seven months and much obfuscation later. Nevertheless, the President, shrugging off the diplomatic torpedoes, decided at that point to plunge straight into the U.N.'s icy waters.

A doveish public?

Did declining public support for a war on Iraq or increasing public demands for getting U.N. authorization for such an action lead President Bush to decide in August 2002 to take this question to the General Assembly? While this author does not have access to any private polling or focus group activities sponsored by the Republican Party or other groups close to the White House, there is little evidence of either of these trends in national opinion surveys. In fact, the polls suggest that public support for military action in Iraq had been remarkably consistent in the months leading up to the President's decision.

Among the dozens of organizations conducting and publishing surveys on attitudes toward conflict with Iraq, the following three are most useful for tracking purposes since they repeated the same questions at intervals over 2002–3. ABC News obtained the following margins in favor when asking "would you favor or oppose having U.S. forces take military action against Iraq to force Saddam Hussein from power?":[9]

January 2002	71 to 24
March 2002	72 to 24
August 2002	63 to 28
September 2002	65 to 32
November 2002	64 to 29
December 2002	61 to 35

January 2003	63 to 34
February 2003	67 to 30

CBS News and the *New York Times* received the following favorable responses when querying "do you approve or disapprove of the United States taking military action against Iraq to try to remove Saddam Hussein from power?":[10]

February 2002	74 to 18
June 2002	70 to 20
July 2002	73 to 21
August 2002	66 to 26
September 2002	68 to 26
October 2002	66 to 26
November 2002	70 to 23
January 2003	64 to 30
February 2003	68 to 25

The story looks much the same for the Princeton survey/*Newsweek* polls, which asked, "in the fight against terrorism, the Bush Administration has talked about using military force against Saddam Hussein and his military in Iraq. Would you support using military force against Iraq, or not?"[11] The favorable responses were.

April 2002	68 to 24
August 2002	62 to 31
September 2002	63 to 29
October 2002	65 to 28
January 2003	62 to 33
February 2003	70 to 25

For our analysis, several conclusions can be drawn from these three sets of surveys: by a fairly steady 2-to-1 margin, for the year prior to the war the public expressed support for U.S. military action in Iraq; these results neither sagged markedly before the President decided to go to the U.N., nor rose after he addressed the General Assembly or after the unanimous Security Council Resolution 1441 in early November. And the rationale for using U.S. force in these questions was regime change in Baghdad, not disarmament or complying with U.N. resolutions.[12]

While these surveys did not factor in the prospect of allied participation or U.N. authorization, traditionally the public has been markedly more comfortable with such international support for the use of force than without it. This has been particularly true for women, minorities, and Democrats—that is, for those constituencies least likely to vote for a Republican president in any case.[13] A February 2003 survey conducted by the Pew Research Center for the People and the Press and the Council on Foreign Relations concluded that:

Americans continue to express the need for securing international backing for military action against Iraq, but they appear to make a distinction between formal authorization for force by the United Nations and support from U.S. allies. The former is seen as desirable, while the latter is viewed as essential.

A majority of those favoring the attempt to secure a U.N. resolution, they continued, "are willing to use force even if such a veto occurs."[14]

What is most striking, however, is the extent to which public support for going to the U.N. on Iraq seems to have been latent in the months leading to the President's decision. A search of the voluminous records of the Public Opinion Online service of the Roper Center at the University of Connecticut uncovered only two questions on getting U.N. support for an attack on Iraq over the first eight months of 2002.[15] So if President Bush was moved by poll results, it must have been by private ones that have not yet been made public. Ironically, it appears to have been his decision to go to the U.N. that spurred heavy polling on America's preferences for multilateral backing, not the other way around. In marked contrast to the period prior to the General Assembly speech, the issue of gaining U.N. support became the centerpiece of polling questions, as well as of much of the public debate, after his September 12 address. In November, after the Council agreed on Resolution 1441, Secretary Powell did acknowledge, in response to a question on *Face the Nation* about the public's readiness to go to war, the following:

> The polls last week were very instructive on this question. If you had U.N. support for it, if it was the international community speaking, then the American people are solidly in support of such action. If it was just us acting unilaterally, then the support dropped considerably. And I hope that with the vote on Friday, this made it clear to the people of the world and to the people of the United States that we are not alone in this.[16]

At this point, however, there is no public evidence that he used those public-opinion arguments in his efforts in August to convince the President to take the U.N. route. Bob Woodward's detailed and apparently authoritative account of the deliberations of the Bush team vis-à-vis terrorism and Iraq does not mention these as among Powell's points, which focused instead on international implications.[17]

At the same time, the decision to focus on Iraq in the General Assembly speech apparently compelled the administration to develop a fuller, more coherent, and more widely persuasive rationale for using force against Iraq. According to the Pew Center, the President's "well-received speeches at the United Nations and for the commemoration of the 9/11 anniversary" helped to convince the public that he had a strong case for employing force. In late August Pew found, by a 52 to 37 percent margin, that respondents believed that Bush had not "explained the reasons clearly enough." By mid-September, however, by the same 52 to 37 percent edge (a 30 percent swing), they affirmed that he had made a sufficiently clear case.[18] By going to the U.N., in other words, it appears as if the President bolstered the credibility of his argument, but he also seems to have reinforced the notion that multilateral approval was important for moving ahead and therefore that compliance and disarmament, not regime change, would become his key objective. By deciding to seek broad multilateral cooperation, in part through the U.N., for his post-September 11 counter-terrorism campaign and for the efforts to disarm Saddam Hussein, George W. Bush apparently encouraged Republicans, at least temporarily, to become more internationalist and multilateralist. According to the Pew Center, the shift in public attitudes in that direction between September 2001 and December 2002 had been largely on the Republican side, as the go-it-alone tendencies among Republicans had ebbed under the global war on terrorism.[19] Subsequently, however, the Security Council's bitter divisions over the use of force in Iraq during the early months of 2003 soured American public support for the United Nations.[20]

A controlling Congress?

Members of Congress, like the public, generally prefer to have allies at our side and U.N. authorization for the use of force at our back. Again, this predilection is strongest among Democrats. In 1990–1, President George H.W. Bush therefore worked first to get the Security Council on board and then used this international support to help build Congressional backing for the use of force. But partly because of this experience, the equation was largely reversed in 2002. In 1990–1 Democrats controlled both Houses of Congress, and the House and Senate leadership adamantly opposed legislation authorizing the President to undertake hostilities in the Persian Gulf. Those Democratic legislators sympathizing with the President's position needed the political cover of allied and Security Council support to justify their stance before doveish, hard-core Democratic voters. In 2002, on the other hand, the Republicans enjoyed a majority in the House and were just one seat shy in the Senate. A number of senior Democrats, including some with presidential ambitions, regretted having voted against what turned out to have been a popular war in 1991 and vowed not to repeat the error.[21] The terrorist attacks of September 2001 served to reinforce that lesson.

This time, the Democratic leaders in the House and Senate rallied to the President's side. When the House voted on October 10 on a bill giving the President broad authority to act, the Democrats split 81 in favor to 126 opposed (far better than the 86 to 179 Democratic vote in January 1991 with the Security Council's authorizing resolution in hand). The more lopsided vote the following day in the Senate included a majority of Democrats, 29 to 21, in favor.[22] Some Democratic legislators have since come to regret that they failed to offer a more viable and stubborn alternative to the President's initiative, for in fact their resistance to the war resolution of 2002 was feeble compared to their opposition in

1991. Congressional and international attitudes, in fact, were out of sync in both cases: Congress was cool when other countries were warm, and vice versa.

There is little doubt that the strong majorities for the October 2002 legislation were facilitated by the content and timing of the President's speech to the General Assembly in the previous month. Framing the issue as one of boosting the credibility of the Security Council and of the non-proliferation regime had great appeal for what became known as "liberal hawks." Among Senate Democrats voting for the measure, the value of demonstrating bipartisanship in facing the twin challenges of taming Saddam Hussein and of building an international coalition was frequently voiced. According to the Senate Majority Leader, Tom Daschle of South Dakota, "it is important for America to speak with one voice at this critical moment." Hillary Rodham Clinton, the junior Senator from New York, argued that such bipartisan support would make the chances of success at the U.N. "more likely and, therefore, war less likely."[23] In this round, unlike the first, unity at home was to be used as a card in seeking unity abroad.

To conclude that the choice of taking the U.N. route would be helpful on the Hill, however, does not necessarily suggest that pressures from Congress prompted the President's decision. In fact, it appears that Congressional Democrats were anything but eager to draw attention to the simmering Iraq crisis in the months leading up to the November mid-term elections. They much preferred to turn the public's attention to domestic economic and social issues, which, they believed, played to their advantages and the President's liabilities. As Jim Jordan, director of the Democratic Senate Campaign Committee, put it: "it's absolutely clear that the administration has timed the Iraq public relations campaign to influence the midterm elections . . . and to distance the voting public from a failing economy and an unpopular Republican domestic agenda."[24] Indeed, Bush found that challenging the U.N. to enforce its resolutions or risk fading into irrelevance was well received on the campaign trail. In the weeks before that electoral victory, the President campaigned hard, frequently asserting that the world body has a choice: "you can show the world whether you've got the backbone necessary to enforce your edicts or whether you're going to turn out to be just like the League of Nations."[25]

Once he had seized the make-the-U.N.-work theme and made it his own, Democratic strategists started asking why they had not taken the initiative in pushing a U.N.-based strategy for dealing with Iraq—an approach that should have been natural. As Heather Hurlburt, a former speechwriter for President Clinton, complained: "Democrats didn't lead Bush to that position. They were instead dragged to it, and looked weak and craven as a result."[26] While she, E.J. Dionne Jr. and others have been seeking answers to the Democratic Party's perennial weakness on issues of peace and security,[27] former Permanent Representative to the U.N. Richard C. Holbrooke was one of the few party leaders to call on President Bush to take the Iraq issue to the world body during those pivotal weeks.[28] So neither Congress nor the loyal opposition can claim much credit for turning the ship of state in this case.

Persuasive allies?

It has been widely speculated that British Prime Minister Tony Blair, and to a lesser extent other foreign leaders, convinced a reluctant President George W. Bush to take the U.N. route. Undoubtedly Blair favored this option for both strategic and domestic political reasons. In a late summer 2002 British survey by ICM Research, 71 percent of the respondents opposed U.K. "involvement in an invasion of Iraq" and 38 percent agreed that the Prime Minister "is Bush's poodle."[29] Given the latter caricature, Blair's supporters have been at pains to stress the extent to which he has influenced Bush, rather than vice versa. Given the similarity in their positions, as well as the frequency of their off-the-record conversations, it is not possible to make a definitive judgment about who was influencing whom at any given point. But there is no reason to assume that this was a one-way street.

At the same time, it was in London's strategic interest to articulate a position that allowed it both to maintain its special relationship with Washington and to retain its utility as a bridge between the U.S. and its continental allies. On handling Saddam Hussein, the U.K. had long identified more closely with the tougher U.S. stance, even while stressing the need for a united, multilateral front in dealing with the dictator. Over the summer of 2002 it was becoming increasingly difficult for Blair to reconcile all of these competing pressures, especially as the British public began to sound increasingly continental in its doubts about President Bush's leadership qualities and world view. This reconciliation would be aided, of course, if Bush decided to take his case to the U.N.

However, as with public opinion and Congress, the fact that the President decided to move in the direction that Tony Blair favored did not necessarily mean that the latter's voice was decisive. Two other possibilities should also be considered: that Blair and Bush shared similar and quite deeply held convictions; and that the President's hard line on Baghdad tended to pull the Prime Minister in the direction of war even as the latter reinforced the former's willingness to give the Security Council the chance to support coercion. As practical politicians with a shared objective, it would be reasonable to assume that both saw the potential benefits of building a broad coalition on Iraq, in part through the U.N., just as they had done on counter-terrorism the previous year. If that could be done without significantly watering down their insistence on compelling Iraqi disarmament, why not give the U.N. option a chance?

One of the shortcomings of the "Blair-did-it" thesis is timing. When during the critical weeks in August, as Bush and his chief advisers were struggling to and then arriving at the decision to make Iraq the centerpiece of the President's upcoming General Assembly speech, did the Prime Minister make his decisive intervention? In a telephone conversation in the last week of August, Blair reportedly urged President Bush to "re-engage" with the United Nations.[30] Then, on September 7, they met for more than four hours of talks at Camp David. Press accounts in both countries described the summit as an effort to develop a coordinated strategy for dealing with Iraq and to build international support for their position.[31] According to Bob Woodward, "Tony Blair told Bush privately that he had to go the U.N.-resolution route. David Manning, the British national security adviser, told [Condoleezza] Rice the same."[32] It appears, however, that they were largely pushing on an open door. The "principals" on the Bush team had agreed on August 14 that the President's speech should be on Iraq and on what needed to be done to enforce the relevant Council resolutions, and the President signed off on this two days later.[33] As a senior Downing Street official later told the *Financial Times*, "by the time we got there, Mr. Bush was predisposed to go the U.N. route."[34]

There is some evidence, as well, that Bush had at least as much influence on Blair as the latter did on him.[35] A few days before heading for Camp David, the British Prime Minister appeared to endorse the President's call for regime change in Baghdad, telling a press conference that "either the regime starts to function in a completely different way—and there's not much sign of that—or the regime has to change." He went on to insist that, while the U.N. had to be "a way of dealing with it, not a way of avoiding dealing with it," if the world body could not agree, then action to deal with Iraq should go ahead anyway.[36] On the trip to Camp David, Blair intimated to reporters that inspections might not be the most effective way to disarm Saddam Hussein and that a further resolution authorizing the use of force might not be needed.[37] On his return, he articulated several of these themes in a speech to the decidedly doveish Trades Union Congress in Blackpool.[38] Following the talks at Camp David, the Prime Minister began to sound positively Bushian in his passion for dealing forcefully with Saddam Hussein.

Tony Blair, of course, was hardly the only international leader both to have strong views on Iraq and the U.N. and to be in contact with the President during these critical weeks. Indeed, Chancellor Gerhard Schroeder of Germany and President Jacques Chirac of France called for a cohesive European front against unilateral U.S. military action against Baghdad at that point.[39] Similar calls for using the U.N. and shunning unilateral action continued to be heard from Moscow and Beijing as well. The three permanent members that had taken a soft stance all along toward Baghdad, in other words, were underlining their continued doubts about the use of force and their insistence that any action be authorized by the Security Council. Given the President's views and goals on Iraq, however, one would surmise that the likely effect of their appeals would have been to reinforce whatever trepidations he might have had about going to the U.N. to fulfill his objectives. Unless they were giving the President a more nuanced and encouraging message privately, it would have seemed that the louder their public demands about the centrality of the U.N., the riskier and more inhospitable it would have appeared as a place to pursue his policies.

The intrepid General Powell?

If any individual were to be credited with coaxing George W. Bush to embrace the U.N. option, it would have to be Secretary of State Colin Powell. It is no secret that the President's team was deeply divided in the summer of 2002 over tactical questions on how to handle Iraq, including whether to pursue their dual Iraq agenda of disarmament and regime change through the United Nations. These debates generally pitted Powell against the more unilateralist Vice-President Cheney and Secretary of Defense Rumsfeld. All agreed on the ultimate objectives, but the latter two, along with Rumsfeld's deputy, Paul Wolfowitz, had embraced this cause with greater passion and much earlier, well before the 2000 election.[40] According to the *Washington Post*, "people close to Powell suggest that he understood that Iraq would be an issue when he agreed to become Secretary of State, and so he had reconciled himself to supporting a policy of toppling Saddam Hussein even before he took office."[41] Powell's deputy and close friend, Richard Armitage, suggested to an Australian journalist over the summer that if he and Powell appeared to be "the two relative doves," it may be because they "are the two that have seen combat."[42] It was widely noted in the press over the summer of 2002 that the Secretary of State had little to say publicly about Iraq, while the more unilateralist and hawkish figures in the President's inner circle made a vivid public case for military action to topple Saddam Hussein.[43]

Unlike Cheney and Rumsfeld, Powell did not have a strong pedigree as a partisan Republican politician and was not thought to have as close and easy a personal relationship with the President as the other two. Some prominent conservative commentators, such as William Kristol, openly questioned whether Powell shared the President's agenda sufficiently and suggested that it would be no great loss for him to resign.[44] A year earlier, Kristol had noted, "Eleven years ago, then-President Bush overrode Powell's resistance to fighting Saddam. Bush was vindicated in doing so. Will the current President Bush follow Powell's lead? Or will Bush lead and demand that Powell follow?"[45] Less is known about the personal preferences of national security adviser Condoleezza Rice in these internal debates, though she appears to have sought to ensure that the President heard the range of views represented in his administration. Yet she did speak out strongly for the regime-change agenda at points that summer, reflecting something she had publicly advocated prior to the election.[46]

According to Bob Woodward's account, Powell realized over the course of the summer that he needed more private time with Bush to present an alternative view to that which he had been hearing from Cheney and Rumsfeld regularly. On August 5, the President agreed to what turned into a two-hour meeting, partly over dinner, with Powell and Rice. This was the Secretary of State's first opportunity to lay out in detail the arrangements for building as broad a coalition as possible for any military action in Iraq. He reportedly contended that "the U.N. was only one way. But some way had to be found to recruit allies."[47] On August 14, at a principals' meeting without the President, Powell suggested that Bush make Iraq the focus of his upcoming General Assembly speech. Rice and Cheney agreed, although the group discussed how to avoid endless debate, compromise, and delay "once they started down the U.N. road—words not action." Cheney reportedly urged that a failure of the

U.N. to enforce its resolutions should be made the central theme, and Rice agreed.[48]

Two days later, Woodward reports, this notion was put before the President, with the support of all of the principals, including Cheney and Rumsfeld. Bush readily agreed, cautioning that the speech "couldn't be too shrill . . . or put too high a standard so that it was obvious to all that they weren't serious. He wanted to give the U.N. a chance."[49] Starting on the U.N. route, apparently, was not so controversial within the administration, but the implications of the choice certainly did prove to be. On August 26, ten days after the President signed off on making the U.N. speech, Vice-President Cheney gave a very tough speech to the Veterans of Foreign Wars in Nashville, denigrating the value of sending U.N. weapons inspectors back to Iraq.[50] The BBC followed with the release of excerpts from an earlier interview in which Powell had said that Bush favored the return of inspectors as a "first step" toward dealing with the Iraqi threat.[51] Amid press charges of disarray, the Secretary of State met with the President on September 2 to receive his assurance that indeed it was his policy to try to send the inspectors back, even "though he was skeptical that it would work." The President also confirmed that going to the U.N. to ask for support on Iraq "meant asking for a new resolution."[52] Even as Powell was meeting with Bush, press reports began to appear that administration sources had let it be known that the White House had not cleared key points of Cheney's speech.[53]

Though the policy had been set, the debate at the principals' level got more pointed, again according to Bob Woodward. At two more meetings in the ten days before the President's speech—neither of which he attended—Powell and Cheney, the latter sometimes supported by Rumsfeld, fought about whether Bush should call for a new U.N. resolution. The phrasing calling for that step moved in and out of subsequent drafts of the speech as the battle raged. Finally, the night before his appearance in the General Assembly Hall, Bush informed Powell and Rice that "he had decided he was going to ask for new resolutions." Somehow the version of the speech fed into the U.N.'s teleprompter omitted that line, so the President improvised, adding that "we will work with the U.N. Security Council for the necessary resolutions."[54]

This round of the bureaucratic battle indeed could be said to have been won by the former general. Even Vice-President Cheney "struck a newly measured tone" on Iraq.[55] Two months later, when the Security Council unanimously passed Resolution 1441, Powell's triumph seemed to be confirmed. As Senator Chuck Hagel, the moderate Nebraskan Republican, put it, the U.N. action was "a significant win for Powell" because "he was able to redirect the administration's efforts into a responsible, international channel."[56] Yet, it could be asked—as the concluding section of this chapter does—whether there is convincing evidence that Secretary Powell actually had to persuade the President to take this course. As James Mann cogently argues, "it is hard to find daylight between the words of Powell and those of Bush." Liberals are wrong to think that Powell is their in-house advocate and conservatives are wrong to think that he is out of step with the President.[57] As a good soldier, he serves his President well. So, who had to influence whom? Could Powell's role in this affair be better seen as that of a facilitator, as one who first helped Bush's predilections prevail in the intra-Beltway debates and then presented them to the nation and the world with a more credible and more widely respected voice than the President's more hawkish aides could manage?

The President himself?

Though the evidence remains fragmentary, this account suggests that George W. Bush just might be his own foreign policy boss. As was often said during the election campaign, he is someone who is easily and perpetually underestimated. He prides himself on his capacity for judging and managing the people who work for him. His graduate training was in business administration, not politics or foreign policy. Clearly he does not know a great deal about the latter and has made serious errors along the way, particularly in failing to understand the interconnections among various international issues and how the reputation his administration has acquired on some could make it more difficult to get his way on others. His inner confidence not only has a way of coming off as arrogance, but it may well also cloud his judgment, causing him to underestimate opposition to his policies and the complications of implementing them on the ground, including in the complexities of postwar Iraq.

At the same time, his shortcomings in building an international coalition for the war effort do not mean that he has been equally inept at using the members of his team effectively or at knowing what he wants. Whether what he wants— to reconstruct Iraqi society and refashion the politics of the Middle East—is achievable, and at what cost, remains to be seen. But there is no doubt that he has shown real determination to get the job done and that he has consistently preferred to do this with partners, whenever possible with the U.N.'s blessing. Following the war, Bush displayed considerable skill and flexibility in negotiating the relative roles of the U.N. and the wartime coalition in Iraq's reconstruction. The Security Council passed Resolution 1483, which laid these out in some detail, without a negative vote or abstention.[58] While it would be stretching the evidence to call the President a closet internationalist, the common view that Secretary Powell is the only voice for international cooperation in the administration appears far too simplistic.

There is little indication that President Bush sympathizes with the more unilateralist instincts of the Cheney–Rumsfeld–Wolfowitz faction. He opposed their contention that the U.S. should strike Iraq, as well as Al Qaeda and the Taliban in Afghanistan, following the terrorist attacks of September 11, 2001.[59] If Bob Woodward's reconstruction is reasonably accurate, then it seems that those opposed in August 2002 to renewed U.N. inspections or the effort to craft a new Security Council resolution would only press their case at principals' meetings not attended by Bush. When the President was there, the differences on these questions among his chief aides seemed to be much more muted. It is also hard to imagine that the President would not have been consulted before the word was put out that the Vice-President's hard-line speech had not been cleared beforehand by the White House. Likewise, as persuasive as Powell can be, it seems unlikely that he could have overcome the determined opposition of Cheney and Rumsfeld, who were personally closer to Bush, and then top it off by convincing a reluctant president to go to the world organization.

If one does not assume that George W. Bush was little more than the object of others' persuasive powers, then a much more complex and subtle picture begins to emerge. For the President, Iraq represented a problem in political management as much as a foreign policy challenge. For important neo-conservative constituencies, which cut across both parties but are particularly prominent in the Republican ranks, Iraq represented something of a litmus test for assessing the gravity of a president's national security policies. Not only was it unfinished business from the first Bush presidency, it also had been regularly cited by Republican commentators as an example of the fecklessness of the Clinton administration, the U.N., and weak-kneed allies. For an inexperienced President Bush, it carried connotations not unlike those that Cuba posed in 1961 for President Kennedy.

After September 11, the real, potential, and projected links between Saddam Hussein, weapons of mass destruction, and terrorism added a powerful new dimension to the earlier symbolism, one that could attract a much broader domestic and international constituency. In other words, Bush had ample political reasons for not wanting to challenge Cheney and Rumsfeld directly on these matters, especially given how their constituencies tended to view the United Nations. Besides, there is no reason to assume that their differences extended beyond tactical questions, since they appeared to see eye to eye on the core objectives. Allowing the neo-conservatives' ire to be directed at Powell instead was most convenient. Again, it seems more than coincidental that the President did not attend those intra-administration sessions that were most stormy on these questions.

George W. Bush needed Colin Powell to carry a lot of political water on Iraq. The latter's well-established reputation for political independence made him an excellent messenger to a range of groups, at home and abroad, whose support would be essential to a successful campaign to overthrow Saddam Hussein, destroy his weapons of mass destruction, and restructure the Middle East, no less. As word would spread of Powell's valiant efforts to overcome the parochialism of the Cheney–Rumsfeld–Wolfowitz clique, his credentials for being a credible voice for the President's policies would be enhanced not only in Congress but also among moderates, Democrats, independents, the media, and, of course, potential coalition partners abroad. Powell presumably would be more committed to these advocacy roles once Bush allowed himself to be "persuaded" by Powell's arguments and then stood up for the Secretary of State in his intra-administration struggles. Much the same scenario might be conjectured for the Blair–Bush relationship as well.

If this intra-Beltway babble sounds too Machiavellian, to this observer it appears innocent compared to all of the cynical posing that passed for public diplomacy by the members of the Security Council in early 2003 prior to the commencement of the war in March. Though his critics like to caricature George W. Bush as something of a clumsy and dimwitted country bumpkin, he managed to frame the Iraq debate in the Security Council in quite clever and compelling terms. Not unlike the little boy and the emperor, he did not hesitate to shout out that the Council, at least on Iraq, had no more clothes to hide behind. On that, he was on target. During the Security Council's debates in early 2003, moreover, most of the other members did their best to prove him right. His warning that the U.N. was in danger of morphing back into the League of Nations was, of course, in part a commentary on the fact, noted earlier, that most member states are distinctly uncomfortable with those enforcement provisions of Chapter VII that were to have differentiated the U.N. from its defunct predecessor. Judging by their comments during the prewar debate, most member states would indeed prefer a weak League without U.S. dominance to a strong U.N. that would necessarily have to depend on U.S. assets for military enforcement in the tough cases.

On balance, President Bush probably was a net winner by taking his case to the U.N., despite his failure to obtain the Security Council's explicit authorization for the use of force in Iraq. Anti-American sentiments would probably have been higher if he had decided to use force without at least trying to test the waters at the world organization. If his ambitious postwar agenda goes well, then his gamble will look both prescient and courageous. Surely the decision to invade Iraq and to try to nurture the development of a more representative government there—with or without the world organization's support—represents the riskiest and highest-stakes venture of post-Cold War U.S. foreign policy so far. But, for this President and this administration, there were never any doubts, or internal debates, about what needed to be done. The role of the United Nations was only to be instrumental, as the preferred route to a predetermined destination. For the manager-President, the question of U.N. involvement has been a tactical and not a strategic matter, one about options and not fundamental principles. Of that, he needed no convincing.

Notes

1 How the President came to acquire his beliefs and perspectives on foreign affairs and who influenced his thinking along the way is a matter to be addressed by his biographers and is quite beyond the scope of this chapter.
2 Expressions of some of these concerns can be found in David M. Malone and Yuen Foong Khong, eds., *Unilateralism and U.S. Foreign Policy: International Perspectives* (Boulder: Lynne Rienner Publishers, 2003)
3 "Americans and Europeans Differ Widely on Foreign Policy Issues; Bush's Ratings Improve But He's Still Seen as Unilateralist," Pew Research Center multinational survey conducted with the *International Herald Tribune* and in association with the Council on Foreign Relations, April 20, 2002, http://people-press.org/reports/print.php3?ReportID=153; "Bush Unpopular in Europe, Seen as Unilateralist,"

same sponsors, August 15, 2001, http://people-press.org/reports/print.php3?Report ID=5; and Adam Clymer, "Surveys Find European Public Critical of Bush Politics," *New York Times*, August 16, 2001, p. A12.

4 Edward C. Luck, "The United States, counter-terrorism, and the prospects for a multilateral alternative," in Jane Boulden and Thomas G. Weiss, eds., *Terrorism and the U.N.: Before and After September 11* (Bloomington: Indiana University Press, 2004, forthcoming).

5 George Bush and Brent Scowcroft, *A World Transformed* (New York: Knopf, 1998), p. 356.

6 See, for example, David Cortright and George A. Lopez, *Sanctions and the Search for Security: Challenges to U.N. Action* (Boulder: Lynne Rienner Publishers, 2002).

7 An unusually candid and personal account of how these fissures appeared to the last head of the United Nations Special Commission, the pre-1999 inspections regime, can be found in Richard Butler, *The Greatest Threat: Iraq, Weapons of Mass Destruction, and the Growing Crisis of Global Security* (New York: Public Affairs, 2000). See also Jean Krasno and James Sutterlin, *The United Nations and Iraq: Defanging the Viper* (Westport, CT and London: Praeger, 2003).

8 See Edward C. Luck, "Making the World Safe for Hypocrisy," *New York Times*, March 22, 2003 and Michael J. Glennon, "Why the Security Council Failed," *Foreign Affairs* 82, no. 3 (May–June 2003), pp. 16–35. For three responses to Glennon's article, by Edward C. Luck, Anne-Marie Slaughter, and Ian Hurd respectively, see *Foreign Affairs* 82, no. 4 (July–August 2003), pp. 201–5.

9 The Roper Center for Public Opinion Research available through LexisNexis Academic. Beginning with December 2002, the respondents were given the choice of "strongly" or "somewhat" opposing or favoring the proposition, so these numbers aggregate the split results. In those months when the same question was asked in more than one survey by the same pollster, the numbers presented on this page and the next are an average of the multiple results for the month.

10 Ibid.

11 Ibid.

12 Gallup and Pew surveys found similar results over that period. See Pew Research Center for the People and the Press, Survey Reports, "Public More Internationalist than in the 1990s," December 12, 2002, http://people-press.org/reports/print.php3?ReportID=166.

13 More recent polls on Iraq confirmed this tendency. See "Reading the Polls on Iraq," *New York Times*, February 23, 2003, p. 5; Richard Morin and Claudia Deane, "Doubts Temper Support; Gender, Age and Politics Fuel Gaps in Opinion on Attacking Iraq," *Washington Post*, March 4, 2003, p. A17; and Pew Research Center and Council on Foreign Relations, "Post-Blix: Public Favors Force in Iraq, But U.S. Needs More International Backing," February 20, 2003.

14 Pew Research Center, "Post-Blix," p. 4.

15 These included a Fox News/Opinion Dynamics survey in February and one by the Chicago Council on Foreign Relations/German Marshall Fund in June. Both showed the traditional preference for U.N. support.

16 CBS *Face the Nation*, November 10, 2002.

17 Bob Woodward, *Bush at War* (New York: Simon and Schuster, 2002), pp. 332–6.

18 Pew Center, Survey Reports, "Support for Potential Military Actions Slips to 55%," October 30, 2002, p. 2, http://people-press.org/reports/print.php3?ReportID=163.

19 Pew Research Center, "Public More Internationalist," p. 4.

20 In a March 17, 2003 ABC News/*Washington Post* survey—two days before the bombing campaign was launched—75 percent of respondents disapproved "of the way the United Nations is handling the situation with Iraq and Saddam Hussein." The possibility of significant spillover effects was suggested by a Gallup poll taken a few days earlier. When the question was asked whether the U.N. "is doing a good

job or poor job in trying to solve the problems it has had to face," the "poor" responses outnumbered the "good" ones 58 to 37.

21 Dan Balz and Jim vande Hei, "Democratic Hopefuls Back Bush on Iraq; Gephardt, Lieberman, Edwards Support Launching Preemptive Strike," *Washington Post*, September 14, 2002, p. A04.

22 Alison Mitchell and Carl Hulse, "Threats and Responses: The Vote; Congress Authorizes Bush to Use Force Against Iraq, Creating a Broad Mandate," *New York Times*, October 11, 2002, p. A1.

23 Ibid.

24 Dana Milbank, "Democrats Question Iraq Timing; Talk of War Distracts from Election Issues," *Washington Post*, September 16, 2002, p. A01.

25 White House Press Release, "Excerpts from November 3, 2002 Presidential Remarks in South Dakota," http://www.whitehouse.gov/news/releases/2002/11/20021105.html.

26 Heather Hurlburt, "War Torn: Why Democrats Can't Think Straight About National Security," *Washington Monthly*, November 2002, pp. 29–30.

27 E.J. Dionne Jr., "The Herky-Jerky Approach," *Washington Post*, November 15, 2002, p. A33.

28 Richard C. Holbrooke, "Take It to the Security Council," *Washington Post*, August 27, 2002, p. A15.

29 Glenn Frankel, "Blair Assails Hussein, Backs Bush on Iraq; Pro-U.S. Stance Taken Despite Criticism at Home," *Washington Post*, September 4, 2002, p. A16. An early August survey published by London's *Daily Telegraph* found 28 percent calling a U.S. attack on Iraq justified and 58 percent unjustified. Dana Milbank, "White House Push for Iraqi Strike Is on Hold; Waiting to Make Case for Action Allows Invasion Opponents to Dominate Debate," *Washington Post*, August 18, 2002, p. A18. An earlier Channel 4 poll found a somewhat narrower margin, 52 to 34 percent, saying that British troops should not join a U.S. war with Iraq. Glenn Frankel, "Britons Grow Uneasy About War in Iraq," *Washington Post*, August 7, 2002, p. A14.

30 Graeme Wilson and Michael Clarke, "Bush and Blair Set for Council of War," *Daily Mail* (London), September 2, 2002.

31 See, for example, Patrick Wintom, "Threat of War; Camp David; Blair Will Urge Bush to Win U.N. Backing for Action; PM Argues Resolution Will Sway Doubters," *The Guardian* (London), September 5, 2002, p. 5; David Cracknell and Nicholas Rufford, "Blair and Bush Warn of Iraq Threat to UK," *Sunday Times* (London), September 8, 2002.

32 Woodward, *Bush at War*, p. 347.

33 Ibid., pp. 335–6.

34 "War in Iraq; How the Die Was Cast Before Transatlantic Diplomacy Failed; The Divided World; Part One," *Financial Times*, May 27, 2003.

35 David E. Sanger, "Blair, Meeting with Bush, Fully Endorses U.S. Plans for Ending Iraqi Threat," *New York Times*, September 8, 2002, p. 23.

36 Paul Waugh, "Blair: It Is Our Duty to Support US over Iraq," *The Independent* (London), September 4, 2002.

37 Jon Smith and John Deane, "Saddam Has to be Tackled One Way or Another— Tony Blair," *Sunday Tribune*, September 8, 2002.

38 Prime Minister's Speech to TUC Conference in Blackpool, September 10, 2002, Archive of the Prime Minister's Speeches, http://www.pm.gov.uk/output/Page1725. asp. Also see Tom Baldwin, "Blair Answers the Critics of War Against Iraq," *The Times* (London), September 11, 2002, http://www.timesonline.co.uk/article/0,,3463-411259,00.html.

39 David Cracknell and Nicholas Rufford, "Blair and Bush Warn of Iraq Threat to UK," *Sunday Times* (London), September 8, 2002.

40 Rumsfeld, Wolfowitz, and a number of other top Bush administration figures were

154 *Edward C. Luck*

associated with the Project for the New American Century's decidedly hawkish positions on Iraq. See, for example, letters from the Project to President Clinton and to Newt Gingrich and Trent Lott in 1998, http://www.newamericancentury.org/iraq-clintonletter.htm and http://www.newamericancentury.org/iraqletter1998.htm. Also see Paul Wolfowitz, "Rebuilding the Anti-Saddam Coalition," *Wall Street Journal*, November 18, 1997.

41 Glenn Kessler, "On Iraq, Powell is Front and Center; U.S. Moves Reflect His Belief in Getting International Support," *Washington Post*, September 12, 2002.

42 Ibid.

43 See, for example, James Dao, "Powell Charts Low-Key Path in Iraq Debate," *New York Times*, September 2, 2002, p. A1; and Glenn Kessler, "Powell Treads Carefully on Iraq Strategy; Weapons Inspections Urged Before Action," *Washington Post*, September 2, 2002, p. A01.

44 William Kristol, "The Axis of Appeasement," *Weekly Standard*, August 26–September 2, 2002.

45 William Kristol, "Bush v. Powell," *Washington Post*, September 25, 2001, p. A23.

46 Condoleezza Rice, "Promoting the National Interest," *Foreign Affairs* 79, no. 1 (January/February 2000), p. 60.

47 Woodward, *Bush at War*, pp. 332–4.

48 Ibid., pp. 335–6.

49 Ibid., p. 336.

50 Dana Milbank, "Cheney Says Iraqi Strike is Justified; Hussein Poses Threat, He Declares," *Washington Post*, August 27, 2002, p. A01.

51 Glenn Kessler, "Powell Treads Carefully on Iraq Strategy; Weapons Inspections Urged Before Action," *Washington Post*, September 2, 2002, p. A01.

52 Woodward, *Bush at War*, p. 345.

53 Julian Borger, "White House in Disarray Over Cheney Speech," *The Guardian* (London), September 2, 2002, p. 1.

54 Woodward, *Bush at War*, pp. 345–8.

55 Mike Allen, "War Cabinet Argues for Iraq Attack; Bush Advisers Cite U.S. Danger," *Washington Post*, September 9, 2002, p. A01.

56 E.J. Dionne Jr., "The Herky-Jerky Approach."

57 James Mann, "The Left and Right Have the Secretary All Wrong," *Washington Post*, September 1, 2002, p. B01.

58 Syria was absent for the vote, but later associated itself with the plan.

59 Woodward, *Bush at War*, pp. 49, 60–1, 83–5, 99, 107, and 137.

7 The war against Iraq

Normative and strategic implications

Mohammed Ayoob

In the twenty-first century, going to war entails not merely strategic calculations but normative ones as well. Norms of international society have changed sufficiently in the past few decades, and especially since the 1990s, to compel states and coalitions to justify decisions to go to war with reference to concerns such as peace, disarmament, justice, and, above all, international (as opposed to national) security. Simple *raisons d'état* calculations, even if the primary driving force behind such decisions, are no longer considered politically and morally sufficient.

This does not mean that the principal factors determining a decision to go to war have changed radically. At the broadest level, such decisions continue to be based on decision-makers' perceptions of how "national interest" will be advanced or retarded. While this is true in the abstract, it is widely acknowledged in the decision-making literature that in actual practice, and when the decision-making process is disaggregated, "national interest" boils down to the relative strengths of domestic coalitions for and against war, the level of engagement of important interest groups, the bureaucratic politics surrounding decisions of war and peace, and the top decision-makers' concern for their (and their state's) credibility in the eyes of friends and adversaries.

In the current context, however, when international norms require that war-making decisions be justified before international opinion, such essentially realist considerations usually have to be dressed up in moral garb in order to assuage skeptics, silence critics, and provide emotional comfort both to the governmental decision-makers and to the leaders of the community of states, who may have to endorse such decisions or at least live with their consequences. Normative justifications of decisions to go to war have, therefore, become routine since the end of the Cold War.

While one is tempted to dismiss this exercise as a charade, it goes beyond mere pretense. Normative justifications that go beyond *raisons d'état* calculations, when resorted to repeatedly, lead to the emergence and consolidation of a range of international expectations. In turn, they begin to change the normative framework within which states operate. This does not mean that strategic calculations become irrelevant. Wars are fought above all for strategic reasons. However, the normative and the strategic become closely intertwined. As a result, strategic decisions have to be explained in normative terms. The normative framework then begins to influence the way strategic decisions are made.

At the same time, normative considerations underpinning institutions and structures—both formal and informal—that set limits to the actions of states are augmented. As the literature on "international society" produced by the English school has asserted for decades, such structures and institutions are constructed on both normative and realist foundations.[1] It would not be wrong to assert that during the 1990s, states, and especially the major powers, have taken recourse repeatedly to normative justifications while addressing issues of war and peace. Many, if not most, military operations across international borders since 1990 have been undertaken in the name of humanitarian intervention, thus augmenting the perception that international normative concerns have become increasingly important in matters of war and peace. This belief has strengthened further the normative element underpinning these institutions and structures.[2]

The Bush administration's policies, particularly its decision to wage war against Iraq, however, have had adverse consequences for the normative and institutional structures of the post-Cold War world order. Rather than bolstering U.S. pre-eminence in the international system, the Bush administration has undermined the U.S.'s liberal hegemonic status.

The U.S. as liberal hegemon

For much of the 1990s, the United States used its power with some restraint, popularizing the notion that it was a "liberal hegemon" different from all previous hegemons. While the U.S. did demonstrate unilateral proclivities at times, the Clinton administration deliberately engaged in a rhetoric that represented such unilateralist moves as exceptions to the rule in terms of U.S. behavior and justified by special circumstances. In particular, the administration of Bill Clinton tried to keep relations with its major allies in the North Atlantic Treaty Organization (NATO) on an even keel even when intra-alliance differences arose, for example, over the Balkans. Washington deliberately allowed European countries to take the lead in managing issues of European order and stepped in forcefully only when it became clear that the European members of NATO were incapable of doing so. This apparent demonstration of "liberal hegemony," which was sensitive to institutional restraints and at least ostensibly committed to building international, especially intra-NATO, consensus, also succeeded in sending the message that normative considerations were almost as important as strategic ones for the management of international order.

The liberal hegemon, which the U.S. under Clinton attempted to approximate, voluntarily allows itself to be bound by restraints imposed by multilateral institutions as a *quid pro quo* for using these institutions to serve both its own purposes and those of the membership at large. Consequently, a symbiotic relationship develops between these multilateral institutions and the hegemon. In fact, in the ideal type it becomes very difficult, if not impossible, to distinguish the interests of the hegemon from those of such institutions and structures. The hegemon frequently sacrifices some of its immediate interests in order to promote the legitimacy and credibility of multilateral institutions. It recognizes that in the long run these institutions will promote and augment its preferred vision of international order, which in turn will guarantee the protection of its strategic interests.[3] In other words, it is necessary for a liberal hegemon to be committed to a strategy of multilateralism and consensus-building, especially since it espouses goals that are couched in normative terms. While it was widely recognized even during the Clinton era that reality continued to fall well short of the ideal, the expectation was that reality would approximate the ideal sufficiently to maintain the credibility of both the liberal order and the liberal hegemon.

Normative implications of the Iraq war

Several policies adopted by the George W. Bush administration, ranging from the nuclear to the environmental arenas, have seriously challenged the assumptions of liberal hegemony. None has challenged them more fundamentally than the decision to go to war against Iraq despite the opposition of both the majority of people in countries allied to the United States and a significant number of important states within NATO, the central security concert underpinning and legitimizing the U.S.'s liberal hegemony. Adding insult to the injury inflicted upon America's allies as well as the rest of the community of states was the Bush administration's rhetoric, which attempted to justify the decision to go to war on the basis of normative concerns relating to international security, peace, justice, and human rights. The United States not merely demonstrated a lack of concern for the views of its closest allies, it also set itself up unilaterally as the arbiter of the criteria by which such high-sounding goals are to be served and those who violate them punished.

This arrogation of moral authority and the right to make decisions about war and peace unilaterally on behalf of the society of states carries high potential costs. It undermines the normative consensus underpinning the post-Cold War international order, thereby beginning the process of its delegitimization. The French and German opposition to the U.S. attempt to get the Security Council to hold Iraq in "material breach" of its obligations was largely an expression of deep concern about the American proclivity for unilateralism and not of visceral anti-Americanism. It was, as Philip Gordon has pointed out, "a refusal to accept U.S. leadership simply because America is the great power," a sentiment shared by most members of the international community of states.[4] Zbigniew Brzezinski, former national security adviser to President Jimmy Carter, put it bluntly in an appearance on CNN when he declared that Washington was telling friends and foes alike to "line up" as if they were part of some "Warsaw Pact." He added that the United States has "never been so isolated globally—literally never—since 1945."[5]

American unilateralism on Iraq has clearly conveyed the message that the

United Nations, and particularly the Security Council, is useful as an instrument for imposing and managing international order only when it does Washington's bidding. When it resists U.S. designs, it is either berated or bypassed or both. This logic was foreshadowed by the rhetoric surrounding the U.S.-led NATO intervention in Kosovo in 1999 without the authorization of the Security Council. However, post-intervention U.S. actions had led many to believe that this was a one-time exception and that the U.S. had learned from Kosovo: while it could win wars without the U.N., it could not build peace without it.

However, the U.S. rhetoric surrounding the debate on invading Iraq, which amounted to demanding that the U.N. stand up and be counted or lose its relevance on issues of war and peace, made it very clear that unless the world organization agreed to act as an instrument of U.S. policy it would be consigned to the dustbin of history. Moreover, this time the emphasis was not on the special circumstances that forced the U.S. to act outside the U.N. but on America's moral right to make decisions about war and peace on behalf of the society of states, and that the rest must fall in line or be declared either knaves or fools or both.

It is this arrogance on the part of the world's leading producer and consumer of international order that bodes ill for the future of that order. It evokes the image of the United States as the "great irresponsible," to quote a term coined by the late Hedley Bull of Oxford University in 1980 to describe both of the superpowers who then seemed bent on undermining détente.[6] Consequently, it erodes the normative consensus underpinning that order and threatens to return the world to a more Hobbesian state where John Mearsheimer's "back to the future" scenario is likely to come true.[7] Unipolarity by itself does not inevitably create a "geopolitical backlash," as some neo-realists assume.[8] However, unilateralism when combined with unipolarity may do exactly that.

One should not conclude, however, that this U.S. policy will lead overnight to the emergence of a power or powers committed to balancing the unprecedented capabilities of the United States. It also does not mean that after the war its European opponents—principally France, Russia, and Germany—will not be willing to cooperate in the reconstruction effort in Iraq under U.S. leadership or will obstruct the U.N. from participating in reconstruction and humanitarian activities in Iraq. European countries are well aware of the disparity in power between the U.S. and themselves, of the interdependent nature of their economies, and of the U.S. capacity to shut out others from lucrative reconstruction and future oil contracts in Iraq. However, these calculations do not preclude that the lessons from the Iraq war may encourage some among the major transatlantic states, as well as others such as China, to rethink their basic assumptions about the post-Cold War order and consider building alternative structures of power capable of balancing the U.S. in the long run. As Ivo Daalder has remarked, "One crucial consequence of this transformation [in U.S.–European relations over Iraq] is the effective end of Atlanticism—American and European foreign policies no longer centre around the transatlantic alliance to the same overriding extent as in the past."[9]

The problem is not limited merely to geopolitical backlash and erosion of international consensus. Unilateralism begets selectivity and, therefore, the charge of hypocrisy, thus eroding the moral basis of international order.[10] The war in Iraq has highlighted the significance of this point in unprecedented fashion. At least a part of the case that was used to justify invasion and regime change was Saddam Hussein's sustained violation of the human rights of Iraqis. While none can deny that the Saddam regime was one of the most repressive in the region, many Arabs legitimately pose the question as to why Iraq should be singled out for forcible regime change when other repressive regimes, including those of Egypt and Saudi Arabia, are not threatened with the same consequences if they do not liberalize and democratize.[11]

The argument about Saddam Hussein's using chemical weapons against his own people does not make sense either with regional publics because it implies hypocrisy and double standards. The United States and the West in general were supportive of the Iraqi regime when it used these weapons against Iranian forces and the Kurds in the 1980s and deliberately turned a blind eye. In fact, there are credible reports that some Western countries, most prominently Britain, helped Saddam Hussein acquire the wherewithal to manufacture chemical weapons in the full knowledge that he was using them against Iranian troops during the Iran–Iraq war.[12] Then the West supported the Iraqi dictator with arms and money because he was engaged in a war against the Ayatollah Khomeini's Iran, which was considered the major threat to Western strategic interests in the region. The attempt to resurrect the chemical weapons issue to condemn Saddam appears self-serving to most people in the Arab world and the wider Middle East.

Finally, the issue of Iraq's weapons of mass destruction (WMD) and the threat they pose to its neighbors as a justification for war lacks credibility in the Arab world for two reasons. First, it is commonly recognized in the region that Saddam's WMD capability had either been wiped out during the 1990s or so degraded that it posed no real threat to its neighbors. This view, held across much of the Arab world, has been proven largely correct in the aftermath of the war and the U.S. failure to produce credible evidence of Iraqi WMD. In fact, the issue has become an embarrassment for the Bush administration and for its most ardent supporter, British Prime Minister Tony Blair. U.S. Defense Secretary Rumsfeld has been forced to admit that he does not know the answer to the question of whether Iraq was in possession of WMD at the beginning of the war.[13] This admission has led to harsh criticism by, among others, former British Foreign Secretary Robin Cook, according to whom Rumsfeld's statement "blows an enormous gaping hole through the case for war that was made on both sides of the Atlantic."[14]

A growing number of U.S. intelligence professionals have also criticized the way intelligence reports were distorted and used selectively by the Pentagon. A group of intelligence professionals wrote to President Bush on May 1, 2003, protesting against what it termed "a policy and intelligence fiasco of monumental proportions." It went on to state: "In intelligence there is one unpardonable sin—cooking intelligence to the recipe of high policy . . . There is ample indication this has been done in respect to Iraq."[15]

Second, most Arab states and their publics were far more exercised about Israel's universally acknowledged nuclear capability than they were about Iraq's chemical and biological weapons.[16] This concern has been heightened by a spate of recent reports that have indicated that Israel had readied its nuclear weapons for use during the October 1973 war.[17] Israel, because of its occupation and settlement of Palestinian lands, its increasingly bellicose posture under Ariel Sharon, and its demonstrated overwhelming military superiority over its Arab neighbors, is seen as a far greater threat to the Arab world, and even to Iran, than was post-1991 Iraq. As a result, most people in the Middle East conclude that the U.S. argument about Iraq's WMD threatening regional as well as international security was both a blatant use of double standards as well as a ruse to justify an invasion that was meant to serve other objectives.

The U.S. decision to go to war has, therefore, by and large been perceived around the region and more broadly as subversive of international order. The immediate impact of U.S. unilateralism will be felt most in transatlantic relations and in the immediate theater of operations, the Middle East, especially the Arab world. However, its long-term negative impact on the role of the U.N. and other multilateral institutions in the promotion of international order should not be underestimated. In particular, the U.N., while not quite the central player in the arena of international security, was in the process of becoming the main repository of international consensus on matters relating to conflict and order, war and peace. The legitimacy and credibility of the U.N. has suffered a severe blow and most states, following in the footsteps of the United States, are likely to treat it less seriously and defy its will more readily than they were inclined to do in the 1990s.

Global strategic implications

Given the disparity of power between the United States and its nearest competitors, the global reach of the U.S.'s military force, and currently its almost unbridgeable lead in high-tech weaponry, direct participation by its NATO allies was not essential to ensure U.S. victory in the war against Iraq.[18] Furthermore, given the current state of dependence of its European allies, Washington was correct in assuming that they—above all, Germany—would not deny America the air bases and other facilities needed to reinforce and supply U.S. forces in the theater of operations. Rumsfeld was reflecting the reality of this unequal distribution of power in the international system when he remarked that for the United States, "the mission determines the coalition and the coalition ought not determine the mission."[19] Clearly, permanent alliances were no longer necessary in order to undertake military missions. Indeed, they might turn out to be a hindrance to the achievement of the U.S.'s military and political goals.

To be fair, the current administration's unilateralism and pre-emptive stance are not unprecedented even in the post-Cold War era. They had surfaced immediately after the end of the Cold War among important circles in the first Bush administration, some of whom now form the core of the neo-conservative camp in the current administration. They were most clearly articulated during the writing of a new "Defense Planning Guidance" by the Pentagon in 1992. An early draft of the document, whose principal authorship is attributed to Paul Wolfowitz, then Under-Secretary for policy in the Defense Department and currently Deputy Secretary of Defense, proposed:

> that with the demise of the Soviet Union the U.S. doctrine should be to assure that no new superpower arose to rival America's benign domination of the globe. The United States would defend its unique status both by being militarily powerful beyond challenge and by being such a constructive force that no one would want to challenge us. We would participate in coalitions, but they would be "ad hoc." The U.S. would be "postured to act independently when collective action cannot be orchestrated." The guidance envisioned pre-emptive attacks against states bent on acquiring nuclear, biological or chemical weapons.[20]

Informed observers identify Wolfowitz as the intellectual powerhouse behind, and the most persistent advocate of, the war against Iraq.[21]

When one combines the unilateralist proclivities of Bush administration policy-makers with the increasing divergence in the world views of European and U.S. leaders and their publics, especially with regard to issues of war and peace, the two major pillars of the post-Cold War order seem to be drifting irreversibly apart.[22] The economic and military potential of the European Union (E.U.), possibly underestimated by Europeans themselves, and the increasing disjuncture in U.S. and European world views may, as Charles Kupchan, Associate Professor at Georgetown University, has argued, herald "the end of the West."[23] Kupchan, in fact, goes further to argue that decades of strategic partnership between the United States and Europe are about to give way to geopolitical competition.[24] While this may be overestimating the degree of political and strategic consensus within Europe, the U.S. decision to ride roughshod over popular European sentiment could heighten the sense of Europe's disillusionment with the United States and turn Kupchan's prognosis into a self-fulfilling prophecy. Although this is unlikely to happen in the short run, the Iraq war may have set in motion a process that could change the shape of international politics in the long run.

Regional strategic implications

The problem does not stop with a falling out between the United States and "old Europe." Above all, the impact of the war against Iraq on the Middle East, and especially its Arab component, is likely to be both considerable and long lasting. It was not without reason that Amr Moussa, Secretary-General of the Arab League and former Foreign Minister of Egypt, declared a few months before the fighting began that such a war "will open the gates of hell" in the Middle East.[25] The fallout could shake the existing regional order to its very foundations in the not too distant future. This may happen for a number of reasons, especially since the factors mentioned below have the potential to amplify each other and create a situation that could easily spin out of control.

The war is likely to add to the legitimacy deficit of pro-Western regimes in the Arab world. By all accounts, the chasm between Arab popular opinion and the stance adopted by several Arab governments on this war was so great that it made the disjuncture between European popular opinion and European governments supporting the United States pale by comparison.[26] While authoritarian Arab regimes have perfected the art of survival despite deep popular disenchantment, the U.S. venture against Iraq may be the one factor that could eventually bring suppressed resentments to the surface. This would be especially true of Egypt and Jordan, but Saudi Arabia and the Gulf sheikhdoms are also unlikely in the long run to escape the impact of popular anger. While one cannot predict with certainty the shape or form through which such resentment is likely to be expressed, it should not come as a surprise if some time during this decade the Arab world returns to a period of radicalism reminiscent of the 1956–8 period, when several pro-Western regimes either were toppled or barely survived.

Popular Arab anger this time is, if anything, greater for two reasons. First, as a result of the Al Jazeera television phenomenon, populations have been exposed to real-time coverage of regional and international events from an independent Arab perspective. Pictures of Iraqi civilian casualties, the destruction of Iraqi infrastructure, and the looting of Iraqi national treasures have added to the already deeply felt humiliation that Arabs and Muslims perceive is being heaped upon them by the West, including Israel. Unlike the case of the first Gulf war, this time the fighting, and especially its aftermath, has been viewed in the Arab world through Arab eyes and interpreted by Arab journalists.[27]

The Palestine connection

Furthermore, much of the Arab world is already seething with anger at the perceived injustices and humiliations heaped on the Palestinian people by their Israeli occupiers and what is perceived to be the near total lack of U.S. concern for their plight. President George W. Bush's characterization in April 2002, in the midst of the Israeli "reoccupation" of occupied territories, of Ariel Sharon as "a man of peace" rubbed a great deal of salt into Arab wounds.[28] It is the common perception in the Arab world that a major reason for the U.S. decision to invade Iraq is related to Washington's commitment to ensure Israel's hegemony in the region. In an interesting reversal of roles, the U.S. is now perceived by most Arabs as acting as Israel's proxy.[29]

In this context, the Road Map for Israeli–Palestinian peace that was made public by the Bush administration in May 2003 is perceived in the Arab world as another halfhearted attempt to assuage the concerns of pro-Western regimes that feel their legitimacy increasingly challenged. Israeli Prime Minister Ariel Sharon has accepted the "steps" envisaged in the Road Map, rather than the Road Map itself, with 14 reservations.[30] This appears to many in the Arab world to be a part of a well-calibrated strategy that would give the U.S. more credibility in Arab eyes while preserving all Israeli options. President Bush's and Secretary of State Powell's public assurances that they would do everything to protect Israeli security interests during the implementation of the Road Map also arouse suspicions in Arab minds. These views are not limited to Arabs alone. According to an article in a leading Israeli newspaper, "Israel's reservations on the Road Map plan that were attached to the government's decision, turn the document from a diplomatic initiative into an Israeli diktat of a Palestinian surrender agreement."[31]

In spite of the domestic controversy in Israel, when Sharon talks, as he has done recently, about ending "occupation," most Arabs believe that the bulk of the Palestinian people is liable to be affected and not all, or even most of, the territory occupied by Israel in 1967. The contours of the Israeli government's plan to end the occupation by cantonizing the Palestinian population have already emerged and were visible in the implementation of the Oslo process. This plan would create three Palestinian cantons divided from each other by Israeli-controlled roads, Israeli-built fences, and Israeli settlement blocks. Such an outcome will keep the Palestinians "caged" in their respective cantons and cut off from each other and from east Jerusalem.

According to reports in the Arab media, the Israeli plan would confine the overwhelming majority of the two million Palestinians in the West Bank within about 42 percent of the West Bank's territory, which would then be declared the "provisional Palestinian state" mentioned in the Road Map.[32] This Arab view is corroborated by what the Israeli government seems to be doing on the ground in terms of fencing off territories where the Palestinian population is concentrated and preventing Palestinians from traveling to other parts of the West Bank and to east Jerusalem. According to this view, these Palestinian cantons, whose civil administration will be transferred to the Palestinian Authority, will constitute the interim arrangement as envisaged in the Road Map. However, this "interim arrangement" may last indefinitely because Israel could scuttle the Road Map at that point in collusion with its U.S. supporters. The creation of such a "provisional Palestinian state" can be expected to take the international pressure off Israel and allow it to establish more settlements that could lead to the incorporation of more than half of the West Bank into Israel.[33] This view has gained credibility in the Arab world because of U.S. concessions to Israel on the implementation of the Road Map. It was brought home to the Arab publics once again when Prime Minister Sharon, during his visit to Washington in July 2003, rebuffed pressure from President Bush to halt the building of the security fence hemming in Palestinian populations.[34] Such episodes have strengthened the impression in the Arab world that Washington is either unwilling or unable to make Israel disgorge the occupied territories and that the "Road Map" is nothing but a charade.

The impression in the Arab world that the U.S. will not put meaningful pressure on Israel is immeasurably strengthened by what is considered the blatant use by the United States of double standards. This is seen to be the case particularly on two issues: the violation of Security Council resolutions and the possession of nuclear weapons by states in the Middle East. The latter has been analyzed earlier and does not need to be discussed again. However, the first issue deserves more examination. One cannot deny that the campaign launched against Iraq for its violation of Security Council resolutions stands in sharp contrast to the lenience shown toward Israeli defiance of the Security Council. No threats have been made by either the United States or the United Nations against Israel for its non-compliance with Security Council resolutions relating to Jewish settlements in the occupied territories, the status of Jerusalem, the treatment of Palestinians, and repeated violations of the Fourth Geneva Convention prohibiting demographic changes in occupied territory. In fact, had it not been for the use or threat of a U.S. veto, Israel would have been in violation of many more Security Council resolutions that were aborted due to U.S. opposition.

According to one estimate, Israel is currently in violation of, or non-compliance with, 32 Security Council resolutions passed since 1968. Iraq was estimated to be in violation of 16 resolutions before the invasion was launched. Interestingly, NATO member state Turkey comes second with 24 violations.[35] Additionally, according to the tabulation made by a pro-Israeli organization, the United States vetoed 35 draft resolutions condemning Israel that were brought before the Security Council between 1972 and 2002. According to this source, in each case the U.S. vote was the only one cast against the resolution.[36] This count does not include those draft resolutions that were never officially brought to the Security Council because it became clear during "unofficial" negotiations or "closed-door" discussions that Washington would veto them.

Some analysts have pointed out that Security Council resolutions condemning or criticizing Israel have been passed under Chapter VI of the U.N. Charter, which are different from the Chapter VII resolutions against Iraq.[37] However, for most Arabs such distinctions are without meaning. The unequivocal U.S. commitment to Israel, therefore, ruled out any attempt by other Council members to move a resolution condemning Israel under Chapter VII because such an act would have immediately invited a U.S. veto. To the politically conscious Arab public, providing Israel with such protection from resolutions under Chapter VII, while ensuring that Iraq was subjected to the same chapter, appears to be another case of the U.S. exercise of double standards.

That Israel is exempt from rules that apply to others because of its clout within the U.S. domestic political process has now become an article of faith among Arabs and Muslims. It is also assumed that Israel's special status has been taken to new heights by the Bush administration. The credibility of this assumption is augmented because some of the most influential members of the Pentagon, the State Department, and the National Security Council have had long-standing and close associations not only with Israel but also with its Likud establishment. According to a report in the *Washington Post*:

> Richard Perle, [now former] chairman of the Pentagon's Defense Policy Board, led a study group that proposed to Binyamin Netanyahu, a Likud prime minister of Israel from 1996 to 1999, that he abandon the Oslo peace accords negotiated in 1993 and reject the basis for them—the idea of trading "land for peace." Israel should insist on Arab recognition of its claim to the biblical land of Israel, the 1996 report suggested, and should "focus on removing Saddam Hussein from power in Iraq." Besides Perle, the study group included David Wurmser, now a special assistant to Under-Secretary of State John R. Bolton, and Douglas J. Feith, now undersecretary of defense for policy. Feith has written prolifically on Israeli–Arab issues for years, arguing that Israel has as legitimate a claim to the West Bank territories seized after the Six Day War as it has to the land that was part of the U.N.-mandated Israel created in 1948.[38]

The pro-Likud ranks swelled in December 2002, when President Bush appointed Elliot Abrams as director of Middle East affairs for the National Security Council. Abrams was a hard-line critic of the Middle East peace process and a controversial figure in Washington who had been indicted and convicted in the Iran–Contra scandal, but then had been pardoned by the first President Bush. According to one report, "Before joining the Bush administration, Abrams expressed skepticism about past U.S. peacemaking efforts in the region and praised Sharon for his 'strength' and 'firmness' toward the Palestinians in contrast to the 'weakness' displayed by his predecessor, Ehud Barak."[39] With people such as these in positions of decisive influence, it is widely assumed in the Arab world that it is unlikely that the Bush administration will be in a position to get tough with Israel if the situation demands such a posture.[40]

All recent U.S. administrations—Republican and Democratic—have been loath to put pressure on Israel because of the clout of the Israeli lobby. All administrations have had pro-Israel members in important positions who have been very influential in shaping U.S. policy toward the Middle East. The Clinton administration was no exception.[41] However, the difference was that in their public posture many of the influential pro-Israel members of earlier administrations supported a resolution of the Israeli–Palestinian conflict that would be seen to be responsive, however minimally, to the Palestinians' plight under Israeli occupation. Moreover, many of them genuinely believed that extremist zealotry of the Likud variety was likely to harm rather than promote Israel's long-term interests. They were pro-Israel in what appeared to be a "reasonable" sort of way.

In contrast, to quote a senior official, the current administration is staffed by "Likudniks."[42] Several of them, when out of office, have advocated that Israel repudiate the Oslo accord and keep control of the occupied territories.[43] This is what led former national security adviser Zbigniew Brzezinski to state that the fact that

> these admirers [of Sharon] are now occupying positions of influence in the administration is seen as the reason the United States is so eager to wage war against Iraq, so willing to accept the scuttling of the Oslo peace process . . . and so abrupt in rejecting European urgings for joint U.S.–European initiatives to promote peace between Israel and the Palestinians.[44]

The arguments of these pro-Israeli officials and advisers have been strengthened by the composition of the Israeli coalition government that came to power in March 2003. In the context of this coalition, it has become easier for the pro-Likud members of the administration to project Sharon as the Israeli "dove" on Palestinian issues. Consequently, President Bush is and will continue to be under pressure not to push Sharon very hard because it would be made out that the alternative would be infinitely worse.[45] True to script, the "doveish" Sharon, after a show of defiance and subsequent U.S. undertakings and concessions, has "persuaded" his divided cabinet to accept, of course with reservations, the "steps" laid out in President Bush's Road Map. It seems unlikely, however, that the Israeli government, confident of the protection provided to it by influential actors in Washington, will allow the Road Map to be implemented beyond the creation of a cantonized provisional Palestinian "state" which would admirably suit Israeli purposes. Sharon's track record suggests that this could be the most likely outcome of the current effort to implement the Road Map.[46] The resulting lack of movement on final status issues and the continuing settlement of Palestinian lands by Israeli Jews will lead to the evaporation of the two-state solution. As an astute Palestinian analyst of the conflict has pointed out, this will mean that the "essence of the Palestinian–Israeli conflict will change over the coming decade, from a struggle over the terms of partition of historical mandate Palestine into two separate states, to one over the national identity and political nature of a single modern-day Israel."[47] This change in the nature of the conflict can be reasonably expected to further inflame Arab and Muslim opinion against the U.S. since Washington will be blamed for not exercising its considerable influence over Israel to make the latter withdraw from the occupied territories.

Post-Saddam Iraq

A further reason for the negative regional fallout of the war in Iraq is related to post-Saddam Iraq. Washington has seemingly decided to set up a U.S. occupation regime for a relatively lengthy period because it does not have the confidence that squabbling Iraqi factions will be able to provide governance and stability to the country. Top U.S. officials in Iraq have signaled that the process of putting an interim Iraqi authority into office will take much longer than originally envisaged.[48] Given the divisions and antagonisms among the rival claimants to power and the fact that there is no nucleus for an alternative regime, as there was in Afghanistan in the shape of the Northern Alliance, the chances of installing a post-Saddam regime that is not dependent upon the Baathist structure appear close to nil.[49] Furthermore, the U.S. administration appears afraid of unleashing a democratic process that may lead to pro-Iranian Shi'a groups garnering the lion's share of the political spoils.[50] All this has made Washington wary of transferring power to Iraqi hands, even those handpicked by the U.S.

Paradoxically, if the U.S. leaves early it could lead to the disintegration of the Iraqi state into possibly two entities, which may end up being at war. Any possibility of Iraq's disintegration as a legal entity is likely to bring its neighbors, Turkey and Iran, into the fray. The fundamental fault line in Iraq lies between the Kurdish north and the rest of Iraq, which is Arab. The Sunni–Shi'a division among Iraqi Arabs is overdrawn. Both Sunni and Shi'a Arabs share Arab and Iraqi identities—the first is nonexistent among the Kurds and the second very weak. This means that Iraq, if it disintegrates, is likely to split into a Kurdish and an Arab state. This would make it all the more likely that Turkey would intervene to prevent the Kurdish state from being established, while Iran may come to exercise substantial, if not dominant, influence in the rump of Iraq where the Shi'a Arabs will constitute 75 percent of the population.

If even a part of this scenario unfolds, the United States will be caught in the unenviable position of being blamed by all sides. This could well be the case because the U.S. will try to prevent a Kurdish state from emerging in deference to the wishes of its Turkish ally, thus alienating its Kurdish friends. At the same time, the U.S. will attempt to checkmate Iran's involvement in Iraq, thus getting further sucked into the domestic political maneuverings in Iraq and maybe into another pre-emptive war, this time against Iran.

That a U.S.–Iran confrontation over Iraq could snowball into an all-out war could feed into other controversies bedeviling their relationship. These include Iranian support to the Lebanese Hezbollah, whom Washington considers to be terrorists, and U.S. allegations that Iran is building nuclear weapons and aiding Al Qaeda operatives responsible for a series of suicide bombings in Saudi Arabia.[51] President Bush seems to have already reached the decision that regime change in Iran is essential to protect U.S. and allied interests in the region. According to some reports, "President Bush has said U.S. policy toward Iran seeks regime change, but officials say he hasn't resolved how aggressively to pursue that [goal]."[52] The decision to launch a pre-emptive U.S. strike against Iran is likely to please the neo-conservatives and hard-line pro-Israel elements in the administration, who already have Iran on their agenda. However, it could lead to a major destabilization of the region and invite the near total antagonism of the Muslim world.

Finally, U.S. ambitions regarding Iraq are likely to escalate in the post-Saddam era, and long-term control of Iraqi oil resources can be expected to become the overriding goal of U.S. policy toward that country. Despite claims by some Iraqi technocrats that Iraq will control its oil, "The Security Council resolution is quite clear: Iraq is under occupation, and there is no government, no ministries . . . The Iraqi technocrats will manage on a day-to-day basis but the policy will be American, because there is no sovereign Iraq."[53] The longer this situation continues, the greater the temptation for Washington to use Iraqi oil for its own economic and political ends. Iraq's oil resources could pay for the war and keep Saudi Arabia and the other oil exporters from arbitrarily increasing oil prices and from pursuing oil policies that may hurt the United States.

Most people in the region already strongly suspect that this is one of the major U.S. goals and that the heavy U.S. military presence in the other oil-producing countries in the Gulf is a part of a long-established American objective of controlling the bulk of the world's exportable reserves concentrated in the Gulf.[54] However, any attempt to control Iraqi oil, even if temporarily, is bound to create its own backlash within Iraq and in the region and further complicate the problem for the United States in terms of both maintaining order within Iraq and extricating itself from the Iraqi quagmire.

Conclusion

Much of the credibility deficit from which the United States suffers in the region hinges on the question of why Iraq was targeted for regime change at this point in time. While the WMD threat argument, increasingly discredited by available evidence, is viewed as bogus by regional publics, the democratization argument hardly seems more genuine. In much of the Middle East the only plausible answer to this question is summed up in two words: oil and Israel. In other words, the common perception seems to be that the war against Iraq was planned in order to control its oil resources and to consolidate Israeli hegemony in the region by decimating the residual capabilities of the only Arab state with the potential to pose a challenge to Israel. It is widely believed in the region that the same logic now applies to U.S. policy toward Iran, which is the only Muslim country left in the Middle East with the potential to balance Israel in the long run in terms of both conventional and unconventional capabilities.[55]

The perception that the war against Iraq was fought at least in part to ensure Israeli hegemony in the region gains credibility from the fact that no matter what the long-term outcome of the war—whether the postwar situation is resolved cleanly or ends up in a quagmire—Israel stands to benefit. This conclusion hinges on the presumption, which appears to be quite logical when viewed through regional lenses, that if the United States were able to disarm Iraq and put a friendly regime in place without creating too much adverse fallout, it would assure Israeli hegemony for a long time to come in the guise of U.S. predominance. If the outcome turns out to be messy and ends up in civil and regional conflict that further inflames Arab and Muslim passions against the United States, it will still redound to Israel's benefit. It will do so by alienating almost all regional states from the United States, thereby making it much easier for Israel to argue that it is America's only viable ally and sole strategic partner in the region. If such alienation translates into the further rise of Islamic extremism, so much the better for Israel because it would demonstrate the validity of the clash-of-civilizations thesis by pitting "Islam" against the "Judeo-Christian West."[56] While the rise of Islamic extremism may spawn further terrorism against Israel, this is likely to be perceived by Israeli policy-makers and their American supporters as a short-term tactical cost for a major long-term strategic gain.

For the United States, the strategic and normative implications of the war can be expected to be long lasting. The Bush administration's decision to launch the war against Iraq is likely to lead to a high degree of Arab and Muslim alienation from the United States, thus putting America's regional interests at greater risk than they are already and also elevating the threat of terrorist attacks against U.S. targets both within the United States and abroad.[57] America's unilateral decision to go to war may well have caused major long-term harm to U.S.–European relations and to the normative consensus on which the post-Cold War order has been based.

In order to guarantee U.S. hegemony in the short run through unilateral measures, the Bush administration may well have ended up damaging the chances of prolonging the U.S.'s legitimate pre-eminence in the international system over a more extended period. This war could turn out to be a watershed dividing the post-Cold War era from what comes afterward. The U.S.'s alienation of major European states, as well as the deep sense of unease felt by Russia and China at Washington's unilateralism may well lead over the next two or three decades to the emergence of a new global balance of power, which could spell the end of American unipolar hegemony.

At the same time, many in the Middle East and the wider Muslim world trace the war against Iraq (and the earlier one against Afghanistan) to what one writer has termed "the roots of anti-Muslim rage" in the West in general and the United States in particular in the wake of the terrorist attacks of September 11, 2001.[58] Even before the war against Iraq, the view that the U.S. had launched a war against Islam had been gaining ground in the Arab and Muslim worlds.[59] The war against Iraq has confirmed this belief among many more Arabs and Muslims. If this becomes the conventional wisdom in the Muslim world, and it may well be on the way to becoming so, it could turn the clash-of-civilizations thesis into a self-fulfilling prophecy.

Notes

1 For the classic argument making this case, see Hedley Bull, *The Anarchical Society* (New York: Columbia University Press, 1977).

2 See, for example, the International Commission on Intervention and State Sovereignty, *The Responsibility to Protect* (Ottawa: ICISS, 2001); and the accompanying volume by Thomas G. Weiss and Don Hubert, *The Responsibility to Protect: Research, Bibliography, and Background* (Ottawa: ICISS, 2001).

3 This description of "liberal hegemony" is best explained and analyzed in John Ikenberry, *After Victory* (Princeton: Princeton University Press, 2000).

4 Philip Gordon, "The Crisis in the Alliance", *Brookings Iraq Memo* #11, February 24, 2003, http: //www.brook.edu/views/op-ed/gordon/20030224.htm.
5 Quoted in Patrick E. Tyler, "Can Bush Alter Course, or Is War Inevitable?" *New York Times*, March 4, 2003, p. A12.
6 Hedley Bull, "The Great Irresponsibles? The United States, the Soviet Union and World Order," *International Journal* 35, no. 3 (1980), pp. 437–47.
7 John J. Mearsheimer, "Why We Will soon Miss the Cold War," *The Atlantic* 266, no. 2 (August 1990), pp. 35–40.
8 Christopher Layne, "The Unipolar Illusion: Why New Great Powers Will Rise," *International Security* 17, no. 4 (Spring 1993), pp. 5–51.
9 Ivo H. Daalder, "The End of Atlanticism", *Survival* 45, no. 2 (Summer 2003), p. 147.
10 For details of this criticism, see Mohammed Ayoob, "Humanitarian Intervention and International Society", *Global Governance* 7, no. 3 (July–September, 2001), pp. 225–30.
11 For one example of such views expressed by leading Egyptian figures, see Steven Lee Myers, "Talk of Arab 'Democracy' is a Double-Edged Scimitar," *New York Times*, February 28, 2003, p. A11.
12 For example, see David Leigh and John Hooper, "Britain's Dirty Secret," *The Guardian*, March 6, 2003, p. 1.
13 Karen DeYoung and Walter Pincus, "U.S. Hedges on Finding Iraqi Weapons: Officials Cite the Possibility of Long or Fruitless Search for Banned Arms," *Washington Post*, May 29, 2003, p. A01.
14 Michael White and Nicholas Watt, "Blair Faces Revolt as US Admits Doubts," *The Guardian*, May 29, 2003, p. 1.
15 Jim Wolf, "U.S. Insiders Say Iraq Intel Deliberately Skewed," *Reuters*, May 30, 2003, http://dailynews.attbi.com/cgi-bin/news?e=pri&dt=030530&cat=news&st=newsiraqintelligencedc.
16 For an authoritative history of Israel's nuclear weapons program that concluded that Israel had crossed the nuclear weapons threshold on the eve of the 1967 Six-Day War, see Avner Cohen, *Israel and the Bomb* (New York: Columbia University Press, 1998).
17 For one such report, see Richard Sale, "Yom Kippur: Israel's 1973 Nuclear Alert," *Washington Times*, September 16, 2002.
18 For an overview of the disparity in power between the United States and other leading states, see Stephen G. Brooks and William C. Wohlforth, "American Primacy in Perspective," *Foreign Affairs* 81, no. 4 (July–August, 2002), pp. 20–33.
19 U.S. Secretary of Defense's press conference in Warsaw, Poland, September 25, 2002, http://www.defenselink.mil/news/Sep2002/to9252002_t925warsaw.html.
20 Bill Keller, "The Sunshine Warrior," *New York Times Magazine*, September 22, 2002, p. 48.
21 For example, see David Ignatius, "'Wolfowitz War': Not Over Yet," *Washington Post*, May 13, 2003, p. A19.
22 For a discussion of the divergent world views on the two sides of the Atlantic, see Robert Kagan, *Of Paradise and Power: America and Europe in the New World Order* (New York: Alfred A. Knopf, 2003). For an incisive analysis of the fundamental reason for the erosion of NATO's relevance, see Rajan Menon, "New Order: The End of Alliances," *Los Angeles Times*, March 2, 2003, available at http://www.cfr.org/publication.php?id=5639.
23 Charles A. Kupchan, "The End of the West," *The Atlantic* 290, no. 4 (November 2002), pp. 42–4.
24 Charles A. Kupchan, *The End of the American Era* (New York: Alfred A. Knopf, 2002).
25 Quoted in Jane Perlez, "Arabs, by Degrees, Oppose American Attack on Iraq," *New York Times*, September 6, 2002, p. A12.
26 For a penetrating analysis of Arab opinion, see Anthony Shadid, "Old Arab Friends Turn away from U.S.," *Washington Post*, February 26, 2003, p. A01.

27 Shibley Telhami has persuasively argued the point about the Al Jazeera phenomenon in his recent book *The Stakes: America and the Middle East* (Boulder: Westview, 2002), Chapter 3.

28 For President Bush's statement characterizing Ariel Sharon as a "man of peace," see Peter Slevin and Mike Allen, "Bush: Sharon a 'Man of Peace'," *Washington Post*, April 19, 2002, p. A01.

29 For a representative sample of Arab opinion on the issue, see Ayman El-Amir, "Israeli Roots of Anti-Americanism," *Al-Ahram Weekly On-Line*, September 12–18, 2002, http://weekly.ahram.org.eg/2002/603/sc191.htm.

30 James Bennett, "Sharon Gives Plan for Mideast Peace Qualified Support," *New York Times*, May 24, 2003, p. A1; and John Ward Anderson, "Peace Plan Backed by Israel with Conditions," *Washington Post*, May 26, 2003, p. A01. The 14 Israeli reservations can be found in "Israel's Road Map Reservations," *Ha'aretz* (English), May 27, 2003, http://www.haaretz.com/hasen/pages/ShArt.jhtml?itemNo=297230&contrassID=2&subContrassID=1&sbSubContrassID=0&listSrc=Y.

31 Akiva Eldar, "Analysis/A One-Way Street," *Ha'aretz* (English), May 27, 2003, http://www.haaretz.com/hasen/pages/ShArt.jhtml?itemNo=297222&contrassID=2&subContrassID=1&sbSubContrassID=0&listSrc=Y.

32 Azmi Bishara, "Sharon's Palestinian 'state'," *Al-Ahram Weekly On-Line*, July 24–30, 2003, http://weekly.ahram.org.eg/2003/648/op12.htm.

33 Graham Usher, "Israeli Diktat?" *Al-Ahram Weekly On-Line*, May 29–June 4, 2003, http://weekly.ahram.org.eg/2003/640/fr1.htm.

34 Richard W. Stevenson, "Sharon Tells Bush Israel Won't Halt Its Fence Project," *New York Times*, July 30, 2003, p. A1.

35 Stephen Zunes, "United Nations Security Council Resolutions Currently Being Violated by Countries Other than Iraq," *Foreign Policy in Focus*, October 2, 2002, http://www.fpif.org/commentary/2002/0210unres_body.html.

36 "U.S. Vetoes of U.N. Resolutions Critical of Israel (1972–2002)," *Jewish Virtual Library* (A Division of the American–Israeli Cooperative Enterprise), http://www.us-israel.org/jsource/U.N./usvetoes.html.

37 For example, see "Double Standards—Iraq, Israel and the U.N.," *The Economist*, October 12, 2002, pp. 22–4.

38 Robert G. Kaiser, "Bush and Sharon Nearly Identical on Mideast Policy," *Washington Post*, February 9, 2003, p. A01. The full text of the report prepared by the study group under Perle's leadership and titled "A Clean Break: A New Strategy for Securing the Realm" is available online at http://www.israeleconomy.org/pub.htm.

39 Michael Dobbs, "Back in Political Forefront: Iran–Contra Figure Plays Key Role on Middle East," *Washington Post*, May 27, 2003, p. A01. For Elliot Abrams's views on Sharon versus Barak see "Why Sharon?" published in Beliefnet.com on February 7, 2001, accessed online at http://www.eppc.org/publications/xq/ASP/pubsID.256/qx/pubs_viewdetail.htm on the website of the Ethics and Public Policy Center, Washington D.C. Before joining the NSC, Abrams served as the President of this think tank, which, according to its website, "was established in 1976 to clarify and reinforce the bond between the Judeo-Christian moral tradition and the public debate over domestic and foreign policy issues."

40 For two recent accounts of the clout of the Israeli lobby in the United States, see Joel Beinin, "Tel Aviv's Influence on American Institutions: The Pro-Sharon Think-tank," *Le Monde Diplomatique*, July 2003, http://mondediplo.com/2003/07/06beinin; and Serge Halimi, "Tel Aviv's Influence on American Institutions: A Pro-Israel System," *Le Monde Diplomatique*, July 2003.

41 To give just one example, Martin Indyk, NSC Senior Director for the Near East and South Asia, Assistant Secretary of State for the Near East, and twice ambassador to Israel during the Clinton administration, came into the ranks of the administration from his job as Deputy Director of Research at AIPAC, the Israeli lobby group in

Washington, with only one stop in between. This was at the then newly founded Washington Institute for Near East Policy. This organization, a pro-Israel think tank, was itself a spin-off of AIPAC, which provided it with office space for its first year in existence. Indyk became its founding Executive Director while Barbi Weinberg, herself an AIPAC Director, became its President. Incidentally, Dennis Ross, the Clinton administration's principal point person for the Middle East peace talks, is currently the Director of the very same Washington Institute for Near East Policy. This strengthens the conclusion that there is a revolving door policy in operation in relation to the Institute regardless of which party is in power in Washington. Details of Indyk's biography are taken from Grace Halsell, "Clinton's Indyk Appointment One of Many from Pro-Israel Think Tank" *Washington Report on Middle East Affairs*, March 1993, http://www.washington-report.org/backissues/0393/9303009.htm, and from the Brookings Institution webpage, http://www.brook.edu/dybdocroot/scholars/mindyk.htm. Indyk currently heads the Brookings Institution's Saban Center for Middle East Policy. Dennis Ross's biography can be found on the Washington Institute's webpage online at http://www.washingtoninstitute.org.

42 Quoted in Robert G. Kaiser, "Bush and Sharon Nearly Identical on Mideast Policy."

43 Douglas J. Feith has been the most prolific writer among those pushing these themes. For example, see the following articles by him: "Land for No Peace," *Commentary* 97, no. 6 (June 1994), pp. 32–6; "A Strategy for Israel," *Commentary* 104, no. 3 (September 1997), pp. 21–9; "Wye and the Road to War," *Commentary* 107, no. 1 (January 1999), pp. 43–7.

44 Zbigniew Brzezinski, "Why Unity is Essential," *Washington Post*, February 19, 2003, p. A29.

45 As one analyst has pointed out, in the new Israeli coalition government "Mr. Sharon has set himself up to function as the chief moderating voice on security matters in his cabinet. If Mr. Arafat is the Bush administration's dispensable man, Mr. Sharon in the short term may seem even more indispensable to the administration than he has been." James Bennet, "A Pivot Point for the Middle East," *New York Times*, March 2, 2003, p. 6.

46 According to David Shipler, a former Jerusalem bureau chief of the *New York Times*, "Mr. Sharon was once described to me as a man with 'no moral brakes.' His record suggests as much . . . He is known for deftly pretending not to be doing what he is doing, or pretending to be doing what he is not . . . That solution [the Road Map] requires the chief architect of those [Jewish] settlements to agree to their withdrawal may seem to guarantee failure." David K. Shipler, "Sharon Has a Map. Can He Redraw It?," *New York Times*, June 1, 2003, p. 1.

47 Yezid Sayigh, "The Palestinian Strategic Impasse," *Survival* 44, no. 4 (Winter 2002), pp. 7–21.

48 Patrick E. Tyler, "In Reversal, Plan for Iraq Self-Rule Has Been Put Off," *New York Times*, May 17, 2003, p. A1.

49 For a balanced analysis of the post-Saddam situation in Iraq, see Charles Tripp, "After Saddam," *Survival* 44, no. 4 (Winter 2002), pp. 23–37.

50 Glenn Kessler and Dana Priest, "U.S. Planners Surprised by Strength of Iraqi Shiites," *Washington Post*, April 23, 2003, p. A01.

51 For one report among many regarding U.S. allegations about Iran's Al Qaeda connections and nuclear weapons program and their likely impact on future U.S. policy, see Glenn Kessler, "U.S. Eyes Pressing Uprising in Iran: Officials Cite Al Qaeda Links, Nuclear Program," *Washington Post*, May 25, 2003, p. A01.

52 David S. Cloud, "U.S. Officials to Discuss Iran as Tensions Rise," *Wall Street Journal*, May 27, 2003. Also, see Tony Karon, "Is Iran Next?" *Time*, May 30, 2003, http://www.time.com/time/world/article/0,8599,455276,00.html.

53 Walid Khadduri, Editor-in-Chief of the well-respected *Middle East Economic Survey*

published from Cyprus, quoted in Neela Banerjee, "Iraq Will Control Its Oil, Iraqi Official Asserts," *New York Times*, May 26, 2003, p. A8.

54 For one of many reports on the subject, see Faisal Islam, "Bush's Gun Barrels Could End OPEC Stranglehold," *The Observer* (London), January 19, 2003, p. 9.

55 This conclusion is strengthened by Israeli commentaries, e.g. Aharon Levran, "The Real Threat is Iran," *Jerusalem Post*, May 16, 2003.

56 Samuel P. Huntington, *The Clash of Civilizations* (London: W.W. Norton and Company, 1996).

57 That American credibility has hit an all-time low in the Arab world is borne out by a survey commissioned by University of Maryland Professor Shibley Telhami in five Arab countries with regimes that are not unfriendly to the U.S.— Saudi Arabia, Egypt, Jordan, Morocco, and Lebanon—shortly before the beginning of the war against Iraq. The survey conducted between February 19 and March 11, 2003 found that of those surveyed only 4 percent in Saudi Arabia, 6 percent in Morocco and Jordan, 13 percent in Egypt, and 32 percent in Lebanon (which has a significant Christian minority) had a favorable opinion of the United States. An overwhelming percentage felt that U.S. policy toward Iraq is motivated mainly by oil and secondarily by U.S. support for Israel and very few believed that a war against Iraq would promote democracy in the Middle East. Furthermore, more than three-quarters of the respondents in every country believed that a war against Iraq would prompt more terrorism toward the U.S. An overview and summary of the findings can be accessed at http://www.bsos.umd.edu/SADAT/mesurvey.htm.

58 Omayma Abdel-Latif, "The Roots of Anti-Muslim Rage," *Al-Ahram Weekly On-line*, October 18–24, 2001, http://weekly.ahram.org.eg/2001/556/6war1.htm.

59 For an incisive firsthand report, see Fawaz A. Gerges, "A Time of Reckoning," *New York Times*, October 8, 2001, p. A17.

8 The future of U.S.–European relations

Chantal de Jonge Oudraat

Debates about the solidity of the transatlantic relationship have waxed and waned since the end of World War II. The fall of the Berlin Wall, developments after the September 2001 terrorist attacks, and the 2003 Iraqi war have led to much speculation about the future of transatlantic relations. Two main schools of thought can be distinguished—the establishment school and the estrangement school.

The establishment school of thought argues that there are no fundamental problems in U.S.–European relations.[1] Advocates of this view contend that the main pillars of that relationship are strong. They base this optimistic view on four main propositions. First, they maintain that the U.S. and Europe, despite the end of the Cold War, continue to face common threats. Second, they believe that governing elites on both sides of the Atlantic have a mutual appreciation of the transatlantic power relationship. Third, they argue that the U.S. and European governments have many common interests. Fourth, they insist that the North Atlantic Treaty Organization (NATO) is—and will continue to be—the centerpiece of U.S.–European relations.

The estrangement school of thought argues that the United States and Europe are drifting apart and are headed for divorce.[2] Proponents of this school of thought, the "estrangers," also have four main propositions. First, they contend that the strategic landscape has changed. With the end of the Cold War, the U.S. and Europe no longer face a shared threat to their survival. They therefore no longer need to be united on every issue. Second, they predict that America's unipolar moment will not last, and that it will lead to counterbalancing efforts by others—including the European Union (E.U.). Third, they argue that the U.S. and Europe have increasingly divergent interests and different ways of looking at the world, especially increasingly conflicting economic interests. Fourth, they believe that, with the disappearance of the Soviet threat, NATO has become irrelevant and will therefore disappear.

I argue that both schools of thought are off-target in important respects. First, the fundamentals of the transatlantic relationship are strong; in this regard, the establishment is right and the estrangers are wrong. Although the end of the Cold War brought about many structural changes in the international system, it did not change the fundamentals of the transatlantic relationship. The United

States and Europe still face many common threats. They also have a mutual appreciation of the existing transatlantic power relationship. In addition, they have many common interests. I contend that the transatlantic relationship will continue to be strong, and it will continue to be cooperative.

Second, both the establishment and the estrangers are wrong when it comes to understanding the form that the transatlantic security relationship will take in the years ahead. The establishment is convinced that NATO will remain the centerpiece of the strategic relationship. However, they ignore the fact that patterns of behavior and policy interactions are changing; NATO is no longer the focus of the transatlantic security relationship and over time it will become less important. The estrangers appreciate better that institutional frameworks are changing, but they are too fixated on what is happening to established institutions. Unlike the estrangers, I argue that the withering away of NATO does not mean that U.S.–European relations are headed for divorce. It only means that the *form* of the transatlantic security relationship is changing. The absence of any major security threat in Europe, and the fact that most threats to international security are now found outside of Europe, are diverse in nature, and are often ill-defined, are leading to the emergence of a different *type* of transatlantic security relationship. These extra-regional threats require flexible and multi-pronged responses. I contend that the institutional framework of the transatlantic security relationship is therefore transforming.

My third and final argument is that what is now emerging can best be described as a network—what I call the "transatlantic security network." The main actors of this network are states, and the core of this new transatlantic security network consists of bilateral relations between the U.S. and the leading European powers—France, Germany, and the U.K. Multilateral institutions—such as NATO, the U.N., the E.U., the Organization for Security and Cooperation in Europe (OSCE), and the Group of Eight (G-8)—are brought into policy deliberations by the leading powers only on an ad hoc basis. Ties in this network are fluid, dynamic, and issue-specific. They are shaped by the evolving transatlantic and global security agenda.

The fundamentals of the transatlantic relationship

The fundamentals of the U.S.–European relationship remain strong. The United States and Europe continue to face a range of common security threats, they continue to have common world views when it comes to these threats and the use of military force, and they continue to have many shared economic interests and social values.

The strategic landscape

It is indisputable that the end of the Cold War had far-reaching consequences for the international system and transatlantic relations. The estrangers believe that the disappearance of the Soviet threat removed the essential element that brought and kept the U.S. and Europe together for over 40 years—clear and present dangers to their common security. They argue that the disappearance of the Soviet threat has eliminated the rationale for U.S. engagement in Europe. They also foresee the emergence of an increasingly multipolar world, which will lead to more visible and significant conflicts of interest, if not major crises and war.[3] Many estrangers also believe that U.S. primacy will trigger counterbalancing behavior by European powers.[4]

However, none of this has happened, and it is not likely to happen any time soon. Conflict in the Balkans has perpetuated U.S. engagement in Europe. The U.S., albeit belatedly, has recognized that civil conflict in central and eastern Europe poses a threat to security in Europe and to U.S.–European relations.

Moreover, other security threats have brought the U.S. and Europe closer together. The proliferation of weapons of mass destruction (WMD) and terrorism top the list of security concerns on both sides of the Atlantic.[5] Although most of these threats have their origin outside of the West, modern, open societies are particularly vulnerable to these types of global threat. The U.S. and Europe thus have strong common interests to combat these dangers.

Finally, as William Wohlforth argues, unipolarity is likely to be both more durable and more peaceful than predicted by most estrangers.[6] The U.S.'s "decisive preponderance in all the underlying components of power: economic, military, technological and geopolitical" means that no other power is in a position to challenge the United States. Moreover, those who would be tempted to do so—China, France, Germany, Japan, and Russia—are likely to face counterbalancing efforts by other states in their respective regions.[7] Regional rivals pose a greater threat to those states than continuing U.S. preponderance.

The rift that developed in January 2003 in Europe over Iraq was in this regard illustrative. Indeed, the published letter of eight European leaders calling for Europe to stand united with the U.S. in its efforts to disarm Iraq was also motivated by fear and anger at Germany and France whose leaders presumed to have an exclusive right to speak on behalf of Europe.[8] Many countries—most notably the E.U. candidate countries—believed in the importance of keeping the United States engaged in Europe as the offshore balancer against a resurgent Russia and a too dominating Franco-German axis.

In sum, the end of the Cold War brought about important changes in the security landscape. It eliminated the Soviet threat in Europe, but it did not eliminate all security threats. The U.S. and Europe continue to have a strong, common interest in combating these threats jointly. Finally, the U.S. remains for many Europeans the ultimate guarantor of their security.

World views

For the estrangers, the drift in U.S.–European relations has its roots not only in the profound structural changes that took place in the international system toward the end of the twentieth century, but in fundamentally different—and diverging—world views. Robert Kagan, a conservative U.S. analyst, argues that

European strategic culture no longer supports realpolitik or balance-of-power politics. He contends that "Europe in the past half century has developed a genuinely different perspective on the role of power in international relations." Europe "has produced an aversion to force as a tool of international relations."[9]

Recent history does not support this conclusion. First, the huge disparity in power between Europe and the United States often limits European responses to international challenges, and excludes the use of force. Differences of opinion between the U.S. and Europe reside not so much in the definition of international security threats, but over the proper response to them. Europeans, because of their more limited capabilities and their different material interests in these issues, make different cost–benefit calculations than Americans. They do not have fundamentally different world views.[10]

Second, despite the fact that European states are advancing on the road of integration, national interests continue to define the position of all European countries. Europe was incapable of devising a unified and effective response to the wars in the Balkans. Similarly, it was unable to define a common stance on Iraq. In addition, E.U. countries remain deeply divided over issues ranging from agricultural policy to the building of a European defense capacity.

Third, Europe's aversion to the use of military force is difficult to square with overwhelming public support in Europe—around 75 percent—for the European Security and Defense Policy (ESDP).[11] Similarly, Europeans readily supported governmental requests to send combat troops to Afghanistan. Finally, several European governments provided assistance to the military operation in Iraq. Those who opposed the intervention—the French, in particular—did not do so because of a principled aversion to the use of force.

Europeans and Americans clearly do not see eye to eye on every issue. However, Europeans and Americans share many basic and fundamental values—democracy, free trade, market economies, and human rights. Power and the use of force are acceptable policy instruments for many European governments, even if the absence of adequate military capabilities limits European policy options in this regard.

Economic interests

The conflictual nature of U.S.–European trade relations and clashes over import restrictions on steel and on agricultural products like bananas, beef, and wine have received much publicity on both sides of the Atlantic. Competition policy and investment issues have also been the subject of many disagreements. Energy and environment issues as well as financial relations are also cited as "potential landmines." Renowned economic analysts argue that the United States and the E.U. "are on the brink of a major trade and economic conflict."[12]

Two issues need to be kept in mind when assessing these claims. First, Europe and the United States are not each other's main trading partners. Indeed, both have always been more heavily engaged with their regional trade agreement partners than with each other. Moreover, although the E.U. and the

U.S. account for 70 percent of world merchandise trade, their bilateral trade is less than 10 percent of world trade. E.U. merchandise exports to the U.S. amount to only 3.9 percent of the E.U.'s gross domestic product (GDP). U.S. exports to the E.U. amount to a mere 2.6 percent of the former's GDP. Services exports are around 1 percent of GDP for both regions.[13] Bilateral E.U.–U.S. trade is hence of comparatively little importance for either side.

Second, many E.U.–U.S. trade disputes are surmountable and, in fact, get resolved through negotiation or adjudication. If E.U.–U.S. trade disputes are disaggregated, it appears that most transatlantic conflicts concern market access—that is, limits on the import of certain goods and services. Gary Clyde Hufbauer, Senior Fellow at the Institute for International Economics, and Frederic Neumann at Johns Hopkins University have shown that these conflicts almost always get resolved through negotiation and World Trade Organization (WTO) adjudication mechanisms.[14]

If one looks at foreign direct investment (FDI) figures, one sees that close transatlantic economic relations and high levels of interdependence are in fact the rule.[15] It is notable that Europe is the main international investor in the United States. According to the U.S. Department of Commerce, European investment in the U.S. was almost $900 billion—64.8 percent of total U.S. inward stock and 25.8 percent of total E.U. outward stock. The U.S. has $650 billion of direct investments in Europe—46.1 percent of total U.S. outward stock and 24.1 percent of total E.U. inward stock.[16] Another issue raised in discussions about the state of E.U.–U.S. economic relations is the advent of the euro. Many U.S. analysts saw its introduction as an attempt to ensure a more significant geopolitical role for Europe in the world.[17] Some expect the euro to become a powerful rival to the dollar, and that it could eventually challenge the latter's position as an international reserve currency.[18] For the U.S. this would have consequences in terms of downward pressures on the dollar in currency markets, which in turn could make it costlier for the U.S. to borrow money abroad and might lead the Federal Reserve to raise interest rates.

While the introduction of the euro was a huge success in Europe, the euro has not yet attained similar international success and is far from dislodging the dollar. According to economist C. Fred Bergsten, for the euro to acquire its full international potential four things need to happen. First, Europe needs to integrate its money and capital markets. Second, Europe needs to speak with a single voice on macroeconomic and monetary issues. Third, Europe needs to improve its economic performance. Fourth, the United States has to stumble and engage in major economic mismanagement.[19] According to Bergsten, "inertia is so strong in financial affairs that it may be impossible to dislodge an incumbent unless that incumbent essentially abdicates."[20] This is unlikely to happen in the foreseeable future.

In sum, E.U.–U.S. economic disputes receive a great deal of publicity, but they do not contain the seeds of divorce and dissolution. On the contrary, strong E.U.–U.S. economic ties remain one of the pillars of the fundamentally cooperative E.U.–U.S. strategic relationship.

The changing institutional framework

During the Cold War, NATO was the embodiment of the strategic relationship between the U.S. and Europe. However, NATO, which admitted three former Warsaw Pact states in 1999 and extended invitations to seven more in November 2002, looks less and less like the military alliance it was during the Cold War. The ESDP formally came into being in December 2001, but a lack of strong political support and the absence of any real capabilities make it a Potemkin village and not a serious alternative to NATO.

The resultant institutional vacuum is filled by a U.S.-led network of bilateral relations. The ground rules of this network are being defined gradually. Many of the current tensions between the U.S. and Europeans, on the one hand, and amongst Europeans themselves, on the other hand, result from the uncertainties created by the changing institutional framework and the necessity of adapting to new security challenges.

NATO: much ado about nothing

The Atlantic alliance, established in 1949, was based on U.S. willingness to commit military forces to defend western Europe against a Soviet attack. Many transatlantic crises followed. Meg Greenfield, writing in 1980, concluded that last rites for the alliance were held approximately every 16 months.[21] Concerns about the health of the alliance have been particularly intense since the fall of the Berlin Wall in November 1989. The end of the Cold War eliminated one of the main rationales for NATO, and many—the estrangers, in particular—predicted its demise.

The leaders of NATO have argued that the alliance has adapted to these changing strategic circumstances and has reinvented itself. Starting in 1991, the alliance's leaders argued that it should become the vehicle for promoting and enforcing peace and stability throughout Europe. Peacekeeping in the Balkans and bringing stability to Eastern Europe through expansion of its membership were framed as justifications for NATO's continued existence.[22]

The NATO operations in Bosnia and Kosovo in the mid- and late 1990s were largely successful. At the same time, they sealed NATO's fate as a military organization because they revealed major shortcomings in European military capabilities. Subsequent efforts to improve European capabilities in precision engagement, strategic mobility, logistics, force protection, and communications have accomplished little. Kosovo, NATO's first combat mission, also revealed the shortcomings of NATO's integrated command structure. Soon after the war commenced, NATO had to abdicate its operational role to a U.S. task force once its initial plan—a short bombing campaign—failed to intimidate the Serbian leadership.[23]

U.S. leaders took away two main lessons from the war over Kosovo. First, it reinforced the U.S. idea that war by multilateral committee is a bad idea. The U.S. military also had more serious doubts about the reliability of its allies.

Second, Kosovo showed Washington that the U.S. could do it alone. Not surprisingly, when the U.S. launched its war against Al Qaeda and the Taliban it did not seek NATO's military assistance. The invocation of Article V by the North Atlantic Council on September 12, 2001 was not an American initiative and it was not followed by any significant NATO military action. It is clear now that Kosovo was a watershed: it signaled the end of NATO as a military combat organization. The February 2003 crisis, whereby France, Germany, and Belgium vetoed Turkey's request for assistance to defend itself in the case of war against Iraq, was another nail in NATO's coffin.[24]

NATO is still searching for a mission. The alliance, however, is ill equipped to deal with the two foremost security threats that face the U.S. and Europe—terrorism and the proliferation of weapons of mass destruction (WMD). First, these new threats are amorphous and their actors are often hard to identify. Military responses to these threats require highly mobile and flexible forces. However, most European countries have insignificant power-projection capabilities. Second, the pre-emptive missions that the current Bush administration is envisaging for these new threats require offensive capabilities and an offensive war-fighting doctrine. NATO does not have these types of capability and orientation. NATO Secretary-General Lord Robertson has repeatedly stated that NATO is a defense alliance and is not in the business of "looking for problems to solve."[25] This also explains why there was no role for NATO in the war in Iraq. Third, the war against terrorism requires good intelligence, but NATO lacks effective intelligence capabilities. In the Kosovo war the "U.S. met approximately 95 percent of NATO's intelligence requirements."[26] Intelligence sharing within NATO has also proved extremely difficult. This, in turn, impedes multilateral military action. Fourth, NATO's consultation and decision-making procedures are cumbersome and inflexible. NATO is not set up to make rapid decisions.

None of these problems is easily fixable. They reflect structural problems that plague all multilateral organizations. Organizing for undefined offensive operations that do not involve vital interests is extremely difficult, if not impossible, in such institutional settings. Intelligence sharing is also inherently problematic. In addition, making decisions quickly and without leaks—two essential requirements for pre-emptive operations—is virtually impossible in multilateral organizations.

Finally, today's security threats require more than just military responses. Indeed, the most effective responses are those that involve both military and law enforcement operations and those that can bring a variety of coercive and inducement instruments to bear. None of this bodes well for NATO.

ESDP: an irrelevant irritant

U.S. attitudes toward European defense initiatives have always been ambivalent. While supporting these initiatives, the U.S. has also always been very concerned about a loss of American predominance. This concern was rekindled in the 1990s when Europeans began to develop a European Security and Defense Policy (ESDP).

In 1991 E.U. member states asked the Western European Union (WEU) "to elaborate and implement decisions and actions of the Union which have defense implications." In June 1992 the WEU Council of Ministers adopted the so-called Petersburg tasks. These tasks included humanitarian and rescue missions, peacekeeping tasks, and combat tasks in crisis management, including peacemaking. However, E.U. efforts to establish an independent European military capability subsequently stalled. The wars in the Balkans showed Europe's inability to articulate an effective response through multilateral organizations such as the E.U. and the WEU. This pushed talk about a European defense capability to the background in the mid-1990s.

The idea of developing an autonomous European defense capability resurfaced in 1998 when British Prime Minister Tony Blair declared that Europe must have the capacity to carry out military operations without relying on the United States. To develop this initiative, Blair turned to the French. The 1998 Anglo-French declaration in St. Malo laid down the parameters of a European defense policy. Throughout 1999 the E.U. set out to create the appropriate structures and define the military arrangements for autonomous action. In December 1999 the Helsinki European Council decided that by 2003 E.U. member states must be able to deploy within 60 days and for one year a military force of up to 60,000 troops capable of carrying out all the Petersburg tasks. At the Laeken Summit in December 2001 the E.U.'s leaders declared the ESDP operational.

It is widely recognized that the E.U. will not be able to carry out "high-end" military operations by 2003. Two problems plague the ESDP.

First, the E.U.'s shortfalls in military capabilities are serious. It has been calculated that if the European Rapid Reaction Force (RRF) is to mobilize 60,000 troops it will need a pool of between 180,000 and 220,000 troops.[27] At present, only 100,000 have been committed. Moreover, many of these troops are not trained or equipped for the type of mission envisaged in the Petersburg tasks. The transformation of the defense postures of western European countries from homeland defense against a Soviet invasion to crisis management and "out-of-area" missions was initiated in the early 1990s, but progress has been slow. Unlike the U.S. military, European military forces were not, and still are not, organized for power projection. Most European states do not have the capabilities to mobilize troops quickly and efficiently. Combat support capabilities (particularly airlift, sealift, and air-to-air refueling), precision-guided munitions, command and control, interoperable secure communications, and intelligence are among the chronic deficiencies of European military organizations. Given the unlikelihood of significant increases in western European defense budgets, it is difficult to see how the capability problem can be solved in the near future.

Second, nobody really knows where and when the E.U.'s RRF would intervene. The E.U. lacks a strategic concept or even a general consensus on this critical issue.[28] France and Italy have a more expansive definition of "high-end" Petersburg tasks. They argue that they include Desert Storm and Kosovo-type operations. The United Kingdom and the Netherlands are more cautious, even though they recognize the need for the RRF to have real combat power. Germany and Sweden would prefer to focus on peacekeeping rather than full combat operations. In addition, little agreement exists as to whether terrorism should be part of the Petersburg tasks.

Unless strong political backing materializes for ESDP, this project will languish and may collapse. Significantly, the International Institute for Strategic Studies noted that throughout 2001 and 2002 "strong political guidance on ESDP was nowhere to be found."[29] ESDP's fundamental flaw, however, is that it is an ineffective instrument for addressing the security threats of the early twenty-first century. European governments should therefore acknowledge that ESDP has limited objectives. This would remove a prominent irritant in U.S.–European security relations.

The future of NATO and the ESDP

The estrangers are partially correct in predicting the withering away of NATO. The alliance's *raison d'être* was lost when the Cold War ended. The cessation of conflict in the Balkans put on hold its crisis management and European stabilization mission. Its remaining functions—the socialization of eastern European military organizations and training European militaries—will ensure its continued survival, but these are marginal activities. NATO has already lost its place as the main pillar of transatlantic security relations, and its position will continue to erode.

Many believe that the ESDP can fill the vacuum left by the decline of NATO. However, irrespective of Washington's attitudes toward the ESDP, European countries are deeply divided over the objectives of the ESDP. The lack of strong political support is most reflected in ESDP's striking lack of capabilities. ESDP is alive, but unlikely to thrive.

NATO and ESDP will play marginal roles in transatlantic security relations in the future because they are ill equipped to deal with the new security threats that the United States and Europe face—the proliferation of WMD and terrorism. These types of threat require innovative, adaptive, flexible responses.

The new transatlantic security network

The rigidities, limitations, and inefficiencies associated with established hierarchical security organizations in Europe are leading to the emergence of new forms of transatlantic security cooperation. The U.S., which sets the agenda in this regard, wants the help of many states when dealing with the new security threats. The campaign against Al Qaeda and other terrorists with "global reach" has seen the involvement of many states. Similarly, the United States sought international cooperation for the war against Iraq. However, much of this cooperation—including the transatlantic variety—is not channeled through such multilateral organizations as NATO or the United Nations, or through ad hoc coalitions, but through a web of fluid and mostly bilateral relations.

The transatlantic security relationship that is emerging can best be described as a network. The contours and parameters of the new transatlantic security network are being defined against the backdrop of the terrorist attacks of September 11 and the preventive war against Iraq. Not surprisingly, it gives rise to tensions on both sides of the Atlantic, and it will undoubtedly take several years before crystallizing. That said, five main characteristics of the network can be distinguished.

First, ties in this network are fluid, dynamic, and issue-specific; they are based on what social network specialists call "social capital" or "kinship." In the transatlantic security context, this refers to threats, power, and interests. The U.S. and Europe continue to face common threats. They also have a mutual appreciation of power disparities, and they share many interests. This is particularly true for the three leading European powers—France, Germany, and the U.K. However, the activation and operation of the network is issue-specific. Ties in the network are dynamic and fluid because they are determined by the evolving transatlantic and global security agenda. The network changes shape to deal with new security threats as they appear.

Second, the main actors of this network are states, and the heart of the network is the U.S., together with France, Germany, and the U.K. Bilateral relations between the U.S. and these three European powers form the core of the transatlantic security network.

Third, this core is supplemented by relations in and with existing international and multilateral organizations such as NATO, the E.U., the OSCE, the G-8, and the United Nations. These institutions are brought into policy deliberations on an ad hoc basis and for very specific purposes. During the Cold War, NATO was the centerpiece of the transatlantic security relationship but now has a secondary role; it has to compete with other institutions. For example, after the September 11 attacks against the World Trade Center and the Pentagon, the U.S. went first to the United Nations—not NATO—to gather support for retaliatory action. The General Assembly and the Security Council were mobilized to condemn the attacks in the strongest possible terms and to help track the financial movements of terrorist groups. Similarly, the U.N. became the focus for gathering support for a military attack on Iraq.

Smaller European powers will generally find themselves at the periphery of transatlantic security relations. In the new transatlantic security network those on the periphery have loose ties with the core. However, if a small country establishes a "niche" capability that makes it a valuable partner for the core, it can create a strong relationship with the core on specific issues. Role specialization is a particularly attractive option for smaller European countries.

Fourth, the transatlantic security network is relatively autonomous. Disputes in other areas, such as the economic arena, have little effect on relations in the security network. For example, U.S.–European trade disputes have not significantly influenced the transatlantic security dialogue. Similarly, disagreements related to environmental issues have not spilled over into the security arena.

Fifth, the ties in the new transatlantic security network are difficult to trace. Contacts and activities increasingly take place outside the public view. This is due to the nature of today's new security threats and the challenges of devising effective responses, as well as domestic politics. Terrorists and proliferators of WMD prepare in secret. Surprise rather than a public injunction is the more effective response to these types of enemy. Good intelligence is also a prerequisite for effectively countering their surreptitious actions. The data-gathering part of this activity is clandestine by nature. In addition, as policy responses become more varied and enter the arena of law enforcement, the judiciary, and the financial sphere, it becomes more difficult to keep track of government responses. Finally, domestic politics may obfuscate what is happening. Although Europe-bashing plays into politically expedient stereotypes in the U.S., so does playing the anti-American card in Europe. Moreover, governments generally are loath to be seen as "blindfolded" implementers of other governments' policies and decisions. For example, European governments have been very public in expressing their discontent about U.S. rejection of European offers of cooperation. They have been less public about their actual contributions to the war in Afghanistan, which have been more substantial than regularly acknowledged in the media.

Problems and prospects

As with any changes in security relations, there are potential problems that might become concrete. First, if the new transatlantic security network is to be sustained it must go beyond the purely bilateral "hub-and-spoke" model that the U.S. administration is currently championing. Each node of the network must be allowed some autonomy and the ability to create its own sub-networks—that is, build long-lasting coalitions of like-minded states. The United States should therefore relax its attitude toward the ESDP. It should also be careful to avoid fomenting division among European states. A divided Europe is not in the United States' long-term interests.

Second, European policy-makers must articulate a vision of a Europe that goes beyond the continent as a "civilian" power. If Europe wants to be a partner of the United States, it needs to indicate what international responsibilities it is willing to undertake—not to counterbalance the United States but to support it or to make it see reason when necessary. The draft strategic concept paper introduced by European High Representative Javier Solana in June 2003 is in this regard a step in the right direction.[30]

Third, for the transatlantic network to be effective and sustainable, the United States and Europe need to build an international consensus regarding the basic rules that govern the network. A key in this regard is the development of a common understanding on the use of force. How and when are pre-emptive and preventive attacks justified? The debate over Iraq shows that this will require patience and restraint but also, at times, boldness. The proliferation of WMD and the rise of terrorism require that everyone give this more serious attention.

Fourth, European policy-makers would do well not to emulate the domineering and brusque style of the Bush administration. For instance, French President Jacques Chirac's irritation with the letters by the eight and the Vilnius ten is understandable, but his public rebuke to "shut up" was reminiscent of Washington's rhetoric and inexcusable. Greater attention to the concerns of small and new partners has to be a guiding principle of European diplomacy.

Fifth, fluidity, nimbleness, and dynamism make networks effective, and overlapping capacities are not only inevitable but make them resilient. However, the activities of networks are hard to track because of the absence of a static physical infrastructure. This in turn impedes public accountability and may make investments in these networks difficult to justify to domestic constituencies.

Although tensions have heightened between the United States and some of its European allies over Iraq, the fundamentals of the transatlantic relationship remain strong. This is not to say that transatlantic tensions and grievances should not be taken seriously. However, many of the grievances are over style, process, and appropriate tactics in particular situations. They are not over core interests and policy objectives.

Unilateral and even pre-emptive actions are not in principle rejected by European powers. The debate between Europeans and Americans is not a debate over unilateralism versus multilateralism, but rather a debate over respecting differences.

The search for new forms of transatlantic cooperation is driven by the changing nature of the security challenges faced by the United States and Europe. The key challenge for policy-makers on both sides of the Atlantic is to create a system that allows for flexibility—yet remains accountable to the publics that the system serves.

Notes

1 Government and NATO representatives are typical spokespersons of this school of thought. See, for example, Ronald D. Asmus, "United We'll Stand," *Washington Post*, May 6, 2002; Debate, Ronald Asmus v. Charles Grant: "Can NATO Remain an Effective Military and Political Alliance if it Keeps Growing?" *NATO Review*, Spring 2002; Antony J. Blinken, "The False Crisis over the Atlantic," *Foreign Affairs* 80, no. 3 (May–June 2001), pp. 35–48; Wesley Clark, *Waging Modern War* (New York: Public Affairs, 2001); Wesley Clark, Chas Freeman Jr., Max Cleland, and Gordon Smith, *Permanent Alliance? NATO's Prague Summit and Beyond* (Washington D.C.: The Atlantic Council, Report of the Atlantic Council Working Group on the Future of the Atlantic Alliance, April 2001); Robert J. Lieber, "No Transatlantic Divorce in the Offing," *Orbis* 44, no. 4 (Fall 2000), pp. 571–84; Christian Tuschhoff, "The ties that bind: allied commitments and NATO before and after September 11," in Esther Brimmer, Benjamin Schreer, and Christian Tuschhoff, *Contemporary Perspectives on*

European Security (Washington D.C.: American Institute for Contemporary German Studies, The Johns Hopkins University, German Issues 27, 2002), pp. 71–95.

2   See, for example, Robert Kagan, "Power and Weakness," *Policy Review*, no. 113 (June–July 2002), pp. 3–28; Charles Kupchan, "After Pax Americana: Benign Power, Regional Integration and the Sources of a Stable Multipolarity," *International Security* 23, no. 2 (Fall 1998), pp. 40–79; Julian Lindley-French, *Terms of Engagement: The Paradox of American Power and the Transatlantic Dilemma Post-11 September* (Paris: Institute for Security Studies, May 2002, Chaillot Papers, no. 52); Jessica Matthews, "Estranged Partners," *Foreign Policy*, no. 127 (November–December 2001), pp. 48–53; John J. Mearsheimer, "Back to the Future: Instability in Europe After the Cold War," *International Security* 15, no. 1 (Summer 1990), pp. 5–56; John J. Mearsheimer, "The Future of the American Pacifier," *Foreign Affairs* 80, no. 5 (September–October 2001), pp. 46–61; John J. Mearsheimer, *The Tragedy of Great Power Politics* (New York: W.W. Norton and Company, 2001); Stephen M. Walt, "The Ties That Fray: Why Europe and America Are Drifting Apart," *The National Interest* 54 (Winter 1998–9), pp. 3–11.

3   See, for example, the writings of Mearsheimer and Walt.

4   See, for example, Kupchan, "After Pax Americana," and Peter W. Rodman, *Drifting Apart? Trends in U.S.–European Relations* (Washington, D.C.: The Nixon Center, 1999).

5   See, for example, the contours of an E.U. strategic concept in "A Secure Europe in a Better World," presented by Javier Solana, the E.U. High Representative for the Common Foreign and Security Policy at the European Council summit at Thessaloniki on June 20, 2003.

6   See William C. Wohlforth, "The Stability of a Unipolar World," *International Security* 24, no. 1 (Summer 1999), pp. 5–41.

7   Ibid. (quote from p. 7); and Stephen G. Brooks and William C. Wohlforth, "American Primacy in Perspective," *Foreign Affairs* 81, no. 4 (July–August 2002), pp. 20–33.

8   See the letter by the U.K., Spain, Italy, Portugal, Hungary, Poland, Denmark, and the Czech Republic published on January 31, 2003 in the *Wall Street Journal* and a number of European newspapers. It was followed shortly thereafter by a letter of the "Vilnius ten"—the ten NATO candidate countries, including five E.U. candidate countries. The letter provoked a strong public rebuke by French President Jacques Chirac telling E.U. candidate countries that they had better shut up.

9   See Kagan, "Power and Weakness," p. 12.

10 Even on policy questions, such as the war against terrorism and the Middle East, European and American policy positions are much closer than many think. See, for example, Marianne van Leeuwen, *E.U. and US Security Relations and the New Transatlantic Agenda: Two Case Studies* (The Hague: Clingendael, January 1999). See also Jim Hoagland, "Europe's Mideast Mellowing," *Washington Post*, July 14, 2002, p. B7. In terms of legal perspectives in the U.S. and Europe, I would argue that even in this area there is more of a coming together than a drifting apart. In 1997 Anne-Marie Slaughter wrote about how "judges are building a global community of law." She quoted U.S. Supreme Court Justice Sandra Day O'Connor who "predicted that she and her fellow justices would find themselves 'looking more frequently to the decisions of other constitutional courts'." See Anne-Marie Slaughter, "The Real New World Order," *Foreign Affairs* 76, no. 5 (July–August 1997), pp. 186–7. In June 2003 at the height of the "Atlantic rift" the U.S. Supreme Court did exactly that, when in the case *Lawrence v. Texas* it invoked a 1981 gay rights opinion by the European Court of Human Rights. See Linda Greenhouse, "In a Momentous Term, Justices Remake the Law, and the Court," *New York Times*, July 1, 2003.

11 See Frauke N. Bielka and Christan Tuschhoff, "Common Threats: Diverging Responses" (Washington, D.C.: AICGS-Paper, 2002) at http://www.aicgs.org. See also "Public Opinion and European Defence: Results of a European Opinion Survey" at http://europa.eu.int/comm/dg10/epo/eb/surveys.html.

12 See C. Fred Bergsten, "America's Two-Front Economic Conflict," *Foreign Affairs* 80, no. 2 (March–April 2001), p. 17.

13 See Joseph P. Quinlan, *Drifting Apart or Growing Together? The Primacy of the Transatlantic Economy* (Washington, D.C.: Center for Transatlantic Relations/SAIS, Johns Hopkins University, 2003). See also Andre Sapir, "Old and New Issues in E.C.–U.S. Trade Disputes," paper presented at the Conference on Transatlantic Perspectives on U.S.–E.U. Economic Relations: Convergence, Conflict, and Cooperation, John F. Kennedy School of Government, Harvard University, April 11–12, 2002. See also Wilhelm Kohler, "Issues of U.S.–E.U. Trade Policy," paper presented at the Conference on Transatlantic Perspectives on U.S.–E.U. Economic Relations: Convergence, Conflict and Cooperation, John F. Kennedy School of Government, Harvard University, April 11–12, 2002. Both papers can be found at http://www.ksg.harvard.edu/cbg/conferences.

14 See Gary Clyde Hufbauer and Frederic Neumann, "U.S.–E.U. Trade and Investment: An American Perspective," paper presented at the Conference on Transatlantic Perspectives on U.S.–E.U. Economic Relations: Convergence, Conflict and Cooperation, John F. Kennedy School of Government, Harvard University, April 11–12, 2002. This paper can be found at http://www.ksg.harvard.edu/cbg/conferences and at http://www.iie.com.

15 See Quinlan, *Drifting Apart or Growing Together?*

16 See T.R. Reid, "Buying American? Maybe Not. Many U.S. Brands European-Owned," *Washington Post*, May 18, 2002, p. E01.

17 See, for example, Rodman, *Drifting Apart?*, p. 13.

18 See C. Fred Bergsten, "The Euro versus the Dollar: Will there be a Struggle for Dominance?," paper presented to a Roundtable at the Annual Meeting of the American Economic Association, Atlanta, January 4, 2002, p. 7; and Rodman, *Drifting Apart?*, pp. 11–26.

19 See Bergsten, "The Euro versus the Dollar."

20 Ibid.

21 Quoted in "United in Disarray," *Washington Post*, May 29, 2002, p. A16.

22 In July 2003, NATO took over peacekeeping operations in Afghanistan and there was talk of a NATO peacekeeping role in Iraq. This globalized NATO's peacekeeping role and was put forward as a testimony to its relevance.

23 See James P. Thomas, *The Military Challenges of Transatlantic Coalitions* (Oxford: Oxford University Press 2000), Adelphi Paper no. 333, p. 47.

24 It must be noted that the United States did nothing to prevent this crisis from erupting. Aware of the positions of France and Germany, which argued that provision of such assistance would lock NATO "into a logic of war," the U.S. nonetheless pushed to have a formal decision by NATO.

25 Cited in Thomas E. Ricks and Vernon Loeb, "Bush Developing Military Policy of Striking First: New Doctrine Addresses Terrorism," *Washington Post*, June 10, 2002, p. A01.

26 See Thomas, *The Military Challenges*, p. 52.

27 See Jolyon Howorth, "The European Security Conundrum: Prospects for ESDP after September 11, 2001," Groupement d'Etudes et de Recherches, Notre Europe, Policy Paper, no. 1 (March 2002), p. 9.

28 The concept paper introduced by Solana at the E.U. Council's summit meeting in Thessaloniki was a step in that direction. See Solana, "A Secure Europe in A Better World."

29 International Institute for Strategic Studies, *Military Balance 2001–2002* (London: IISS, 2001), p. 29.

30 See Solana, "A Secure Europe in a Better World."

9   Legal unilateralism

José E. Alvarez[1]

In the wake of the United States' invasion of Iraq in March 2003, the future of transatlantic relations has become a hot topic. Some are predicting that the next "clash of civilizations" will be between Europe and the United States while others, more sanguinely, contend that the political and economic fundamentals of the transatlantic relationship remain strong.[2] I am content to leave these grander debates to non-lawyers capable of addressing them. The argument here is more focused on the emerging divergences in legal culture between Europe and the United States, particularly with respect to public international law and its institutions. My contention is that the perceived "unilateralism" of the U.S., which is the source of considerable transatlantic friction, has a legal dimension: European international lawyers take multilateralism more seriously than do many of their U.S. counterparts.

The clash of legalizations

History suggests that it is possible for countries that differ sharply with respect to legal traditions to share compatible or similar values. For decades, Europe and the United States have been staunch political allies despite distinct civil law and common law systems. Nations that have shared a fairly unified vision of what they were for (democratic values, human rights, ever-freer markets), as well as what they were against (totalitarian regimes, governmental violations of human dignity, economies driven by government directive), have long differed, for example, on how to define the nationality of their respective corporations or whether they would rely on juries to try criminal cases.

Transatlantic differences in national legal culture have sometimes had an impact on foreign affairs. The nations that regularly voted as a unit in global forums like the United Nations and united for common defense in NATO have nonetheless engaged in cordial but real competition when it comes to exporting their respective visions of the rule of law to newly decolonized states. Repeatedly, efforts to export law and legal institutions have floundered precisely because of real differences in legal culture between Europe and the United States reflected in the heritage of former colonies. John Kennedy's idealistic Alliance for Progress eventually found that its attempts to export U.S. law and

U.S.-style legal education did not find fertile ground in the civil law countries of Latin America, for example.[3] Nonetheless, at least when the rules governing foreign and national affairs occupied more or less separate domains, differences in national legal culture mattered relatively little at the level of inter-state relations. States that differed on the way the rule of law operated within national borders could still agree on distinct rules of the game with respect to foreign affairs.

Today, of course, the subject matter of international law can no longer be cabined easily within a defined realm of "foreign affairs." Thanks in part to the growth of the international law of human rights, there is scarcely a subject— from family law to criminal law—that is not now the subject of a multilateral or bilateral treaty or rule of international custom.[4] The abundant flows of capital, goods, people, and ideas across borders have increased efforts to harmonize the rules that govern formerly "domestic" affairs. They have also compelled states to address the interface between national and international law through the principal tools of public international law: treaties and custom, and the organizations that shape both. Despite evidence that the substantive rules of domestic law that govern societies in Europe and in the United States are becoming increasingly similar in a number of areas (particularly in economic areas such as trade and investment), it appears that Europe and the United States may be growing farther apart with respect to their attitudes toward the rules and institutions of public international law. While these differences in legal world views do not always explain differences in government policy on both sides of the Atlantic, they help to explain the way U.S. actions, in and out of the U.N., are perceived, particularly in leading European countries (such as France and Germany) and especially among legal elites in those countries and within their foreign ministries.[5]

The most visible recent manifestation of transatlantic legal cleavages among international lawyers emerged with the U.S. decision to wage war on Iraq in March 2003. Prominent international lawyers in Europe were virtually unanimous that such a war was either manifestly illegal or of dubious legality, and most believed that it was in any case unwise.[6] Their views reflected the widespread opposition to the war among Europeans generally. By contrast, while the majority of prominent international lawyers in the United States were probably of the same opinion, a number of them defended the recourse to the war, consistent with the prevailing views among the general public in the United States.[7]

While more salient during the current Bush administration, these cleavages, involving both academics and governmental elites, have not been limited to post-September 11 tensions. Over the past decade, Europe and the United States have been at odds over the U.S.'s refusal to become a party to a number of significant treaties, including the Anti-Ballistic Missile (ABM) Treaty, the Comprehensive Test Ban Treaty, the Biological and Toxin Weapons Convention Protocol, the Kyoto Protocol, the Statute of the International Criminal Court (ICC), the amended Convention on the Law of the Sea, the Convention on Biological Diversity, and the Landmines Convention. European and U.S. treaty negotiators have also clashed with respect to the negotiation of an accord on small-arms trafficking. European international lawyers have been highly critical of the United States' continued lack of ratification of a number of global conventions that most Europeans argue reflect universal human rights standards, including treaties adopted within the International Labor Organization (ILO), the Convention on the Elimination of Discrimination Against Women (CEDAW), the Convention on the Rights of the Child, the International Covenant on Economic, Social, and Cultural Rights, and Protocol One of the International Covenant on Civil and Political Rights.[8]

Disputes over global human rights standards, whether or not reflected in these treaties, have led to repeated refusals by European states and courts to extradite wanted criminals to the United States lest they face the death penalty and to international legal challenges over the U.S.'s refusal to comply with International Court of Justice (ICJ) orders to defer executions of those individuals whose rights under the Vienna Convention on Consular Relations may have been violated, in addition to well-known post-September 11 tensions over the U.S. handling of immigrants and those detained in Guantánamo.[9] Transatlantic relations have also been tested with respect to the U.S. tendency to resort to extraterritorial application of U.S. economic sanctions (most prominently with respect to Helms–Burton sanctions on Cuba, but also including unilateral sanctions against Libya and Iran); U.S. unilateral threats or efforts involving trade (pursuant to Section 301 of the U.S. Trade Act); and U.S. unilateral certifications of drug-producing and transit countries; as well as other recent U.S. unilateral deployments of force (e.g. Sudan, Libya, Afghanistan before 2002, and Iraq in 1998).[10]

Europeans generally, including their international lawyers, have been especially vocal critics of the Bush administration's announced intent to apply the doctrine of pre-emptive self-defense, whether with respect to terrorists, states that harbor terrorists, or those possessing weapons of mass destruction (WMD), as well as the administration's more immediate threats to act against the three members of its proclaimed "axis of evil."[11] Prominent European states have also clashed with both the Clinton and current Bush administrations with respect to initiatives within prominent international organizations—for example, World Trade Organization (WTO) remedies on bananas and beef hormones; U.N. peacekeeping in Bosnia-Herzegovina (1992–5); and Security Council sanctions on Iraq (1998–2001).[12]

Most recently, European–U.S. frictions have emerged with respect to continuing efforts by the Bush administration to undermine, and not merely refuse to participate in, the ICC. Transatlantic tempers continue to flare over Washington's efforts to have the Security Council exempt peacekeepers from the ICC's jurisdiction and U.S. attempts to negotiate bilateral agreements with state parties to the ICC under which these states would refuse to transfer to the Court any U.S. nationals.[13]

While some of these legal disputes have involved allegations that the United

States was breaching its international obligations, many involved disputes over the U.S.'s unwillingness to enter into international obligations. Some involved concerns that Washington was abusing the international negotiation process or established institutions in pursuit of a unilateralist agenda at odds with the broader interests of the international community of states. Undoubtedly, many of these conflicts reflect clashes of real or perceived national interests. Political scientists of the realist persuasion have managed to make a credible case that individually and collectively the smaller, weaker states of Europe have a correspondingly greater interest in the institutions of public international law than does the so-called hyperpower. Given their relatively weak trade leverage, European states would also naturally resist U.S. efforts to deploy its greater trade leverage—especially to promote policies inconsistent with the interests of European political elites or prominent European constituencies—and would generally prefer multilateral sanctioning efforts at the United Nations to U.S. unilateral economic sanctions. Europeans' affinity for certain arms-control measures and the multilateral use of force also might be seen as the necessary by-product of Europe's relative military weakness. States that refuse to devote, collectively or individually, a substantial percentage of their gross domestic products (GDPs) to military hardware and personnel might be naturally predisposed to accept arms-control agreements and more likely to resist the unilateral resort to force by others, particularly if such force might result in greater security threats to Europe itself. The relevance of perceived national interest is also clear to the extent that Europe itself is divided with respect to some of these issues; it would appear, for example, that at least some countries of eastern Europe, more immediately and vitally interested in U.S. foreign investment flows, have been more sympathetic to U.S. legal positions on some of these issues or at least less willing to take issue with them.

But these explanations of recent transatlantic international legal clashes do not wholly explain those that have a less obvious grounding in realpolitik, such as European affinity for human rights treaties or apparent greater sensitivity to the human rights impact of U.N. sanctions.[14] Nor is it obvious why Europeans, who ultimately rely on the U.S. military umbrella, would fail to endorse U.S. decisions that might enhance the ability of the U.S. to protect both itself and Europe (including actions that protect the U.S. privileged development or deployment of certain weapons or its use of landmines in the Korean peninsula), or why European governments as well as their lawyers would rail against U.S. unilateral actions directed at harms in third countries that both Europeans and Americans clearly abhor, such as drug-trafficking, trade protectionism, or human rights violations. It is also hard to explain why democratically governed welfare states on either side of the Atlantic would differ so sharply over whether individuals, including those living in their respective territories, should be subject to criminal accountability in the ICC when they commit grave international crimes. Surely neither the United States nor Germany wants to be perceived as a refuge for the world's perpetrators of genocide? Further, given undoubted common European–United States political and economic interests, including shared perceptions of national security threats, it is difficult to explain the depth of many of these clashes or the rancor with which many of them appear to be expressed.

Differences in national self-interest, at least if narrowly defined to exclude differences in legal culture, are not the full story. The realists do not tell us how states decide what their national interest is. They do not tell us why, for example, the states of "old Europe" appear disinclined to develop credible militaries. Constructivist political scientists, who have challenged or supplemented the work of their realist colleagues, have suggested that ideas, including legal ideas and the processes they set in motion, matter and help to determine what states perceive as their national interest.[15] The proposition advanced here is that most of these clashes can be attributed, at least in part, to the fact that a greater number of Europeans, including influential legal elites in and out of government, take a different approach to international law than do many of their U.S. counterparts. Those looking for an explanation for why Europeans appear to take multilaterialism much more seriously should consider, as part of their account, the fact that Europe's positivistic international lawyers take multilateralism more seriously.

European v. U.S. lawyers

The stark differences in legal philosophy between European and some prominent U.S. international lawyers were evident even before they became front-page news in the midst of U.N. debates over a second Iraqi war. At a European–U.S. conference on "unilateralism" in 2000, for example, Europeans identified the legal obligation to cooperate as the "basis for the whole postwar international legal order."[16] Across a range of issues, from trade sanctions to environmental actions, the Europeans asserted that the law of the U.N. Charter, as well as the rules in particular treaty regimes, accorded fundamental importance to the duty of states to respect the sovereign equality of states by neither unilaterally imposing their will on others nor substituting a "diktat for concerted action."[17] As a leading French public international lawyer, Pierre-Marie Dupuy, put it, states' right to act alone is "residual and conditioned."[18]

For Europeans at that conference, the "law of coexistence" meant that states could not resort to unilateral measures until they exhaust available means of international negotiation; that international law now requires states to "choose the path of compromise and negotiated settlement."[19] Unsurprisingly, Dupuy and the other Europeans found much in recent U.S. foreign policy that violated the principle of cooperation and treaties that incorporate it.[20] The Europeans were especially emphatic concerning the operative rules restricting unilateral recourse to force. Vera Gowlland-Debbas was critical of the now popular idea that member states might be implicitly authorized to take unilateral action in defense of collective goals pronounced by the Security Council when that body becomes paralyzed by the veto.[21] For her, the Charter's rules on the use of force, even in instances involving grave and ongoing human rights atrocities, were clear, emphatic, and subject to no exception: "resort to unilateral action in the absence of express Council authorization . . . remains an act of usurpation of Council powers and a resort to force which is prohibited under international law."[22]

The U.S. international lawyers participating at that conference were far more sanguine about unilateral action and far more dubious about the value of multilateral action, including by the U.N.[23] For the Americans, the starting point for assessing the legality of unilateral actions was neither normative principle nor treaty text, but the structure of the international legal system and its ability to effectuate laudable goals. Michael Reisman contended that while, in domestic legal orders characterized by effective institutions, unilateral acts by unauthorized participants were presumptively illegal, this was not the case in systems (such as the current international order) characterized by ineffective institutions, where unilateral acts may prove necessary to vindicate the fundamental, legitimate demands of its participants. For Reisman, the lawfulness of unilateral action (such as humanitarian intervention in Kosovo) should not be determined by the mechanical application of rules but by asking whether, in terms of the wider international legal process, the action "optimizes the many policies that may be expressed in rules."[24] Particularly when it comes to the vindication of human rights, where agreement of all the relevant members of the Security Council is unlikely, Reisman suggested that the present U.N. system fails to vindicate the interests of democratic governments that are under pressure to act in such cases and have the power to effectuate a unilateral remedy.[25]

Ruth Wedgwood was more blunt: the Security Council machinery has never worked quite as planned; the community of states has constantly had to adapt the Charter because of its blatant ineffectiveness; and the international community will need to allow more latitude for both regional and unilateral uses of force in defense of new realities such as WMD, undeterrable non-state terrorists, and a paralyzed Security Council unable to do the right thing.[26] Wedgwood disparaged the European tendency to rely on the governing text of international instruments: "The interpretative principles deployed in the application of a constitutive text may also depend," she argued, "on the nature of the values and interests at stake—the teleology of an instrument as much as its literal form."[27] When push comes to shove, she contended, we cannot wait for unanimity when important values are at stake. Given the need to take effective action to protect expanded notions of human security and human rights, Wedgwood called for a "morally driven" teleological reading of Chapter VII and the Charter generally and not one driven by originalist intention.[28] She concluded by defending the legality of not only NATO's Kosovo actions, but also the 1998 air raids on Iraq by the U.S. and U.K., as well as the U.S. air strikes on Sudan and Afghanistan in 1999.[29] Another U.S. international lawyer at that conference unapologetically asserted the right of powerful states to invoke political concerns to trump formal legal commitments—as the United States did when it refused to pay its U.N. dues. Another contended that the U.S. was justified in withholding its consent to the Landmines Convention because that suspect treaty was the product of fundamentally undemocratic modes of supranational law-making involving the participation of unaccountable, single-issue NGOs.[30]

Probing differences: three explanations

What accounts for these differences among people ostensibly committed to the rule of law in international affairs, trained in the same methods, and working with the same legal texts? One participant at the same conference (a Canadian international lawyer now in U.S. legal academia) suggested that one explanation might be differences in how international lawyers are trained on one side of the Atlantic compared to the other. According to this view, the blame or credit for the present state lies in the policy-oriented school of international law established by Professors Myres McDougal and Harold Lasswell at Yale Law School and their inordinate impact on the U.S. professorate. While defenders of the Yale School argue that it is ideally suited to adapting law to ever-changing circumstances, its critics contend that it provides little more than a rationalization for unilateral action by the powerful.[31] Others, while still focusing on differences in professional culture among international lawyers, cast their net wider. The problem or virtue of U.S. international lawyers, whether or not associated with the Yale School, is that they take an interdisciplinary approach. U.S. interdisciplinarity, whether associated with the political right (e.g. law and economics) or the political left (e.g. postmodern or critical approaches), leads to open-ended and sometimes critical perspectives on the law at odds with the more rule-oriented positivist training of European lawyers.[32] U.S. international lawyers, like other American lawyers, may also be affected by the peculiar kind of rule-skepticism associated with anti-formalism or the realist tradition in U.S. legal thought; they are trained to blur the boundary between law and "policy," which European positivists would describe as politics.[33]

A second explanation connects internationalist sensibilities to more general national legal traditions. In this view, the reactions of the U.S. international lawyers surveyed above are variations on a single national trait: a shared "civic religion" premised on the belief that all legitimate law, at the international and national levels, must be traced to acts of popular sovereignty as understood and mediated by the U.S. Constitution.[34] For many Americans, including some of its international lawyers, legitimate law is that which promotes or protects the particular form of democracy, human rights, and free markets that Americans enjoy under their constitution and legitimately seek to export.[35] As suggested by attempts to justify the failure to pay U.N. dues or complaints about the illegitimacy of the Landmines Treaty negotiations, it is inconceivable to many Americans that lawful political authority could be exercised outside of the U.S. Constitution. Even some cosmopolitan international lawyers believe in American exceptionalism. Some U.S. international lawyers apparently believe that theirs is the "City on the Hill" that others should emulate; that U.S. values, readily identified as global ones, are the values that international rules and institutions must advance, lest they be legitimately ignored or bypassed.[36]

In this view, the difference between European and some U.S. approaches to international law is not that the former approach to law is from a value-free perspective while the latter is not. On the contrary, Europeans may simply be prioritizing a different set of values or goals. They value "orderly decision, preceded by due deliberation and followed by authorized and inclusive application"[37]—undoubtedly from a belief that such procedures, anticipated in the U.N. Charter, are the best way to protect the sheer diversity of competing claims, benefit from the best advice, and emerge with the most well-considered options. At least some U.S. international lawyers have a more particularized agenda: using law to pursue benevolent goals such as the promotion of democracy, the promotion of human rights, or the eradication of ethnic cleansing.

To the extent that this is the case, the U.S.'s historical ambivalence toward multilateral institutions is just as likely to emerge from the left of the political spectrum as from the right. U.S. frustration with the U.N. has stemmed, for example, as much from its inability to confront genocide as it has from its foot-dragging on WMD. To the extent that European lawyers are on a comparable mission to save the world, their civic religion is multilateralism, a shared preference for the international over the national, integration and inter-state cooperation over sovereignty.[38]

There are soft and hard variations on such "cultural affinity" explanations for transatlantic differences. At the softer end are those that draw connections between international lawyers and certain national legal traditions. It might be argued that common-law lawyers, accustomed to activist judges who make law in the course of interpreting it, are more apt to stretch existing text to suit new situations, even in contexts which appear, to lawyers trained in civil law, as transparent rationalizations for flexing U.S. muscle. If common-law modes of thinking are generally more responsive to politics, this would provide another explanation for why the United States was able to find common cause with both Australia and the United Kingdom with respect to Iraq.[39] It might explain why international lawyers trained in common law, accustomed to teleological readings of their own laws, might be more amenable to those dynamic readings of the U.N. Charter that license unilateral action. It is also the case that some of the legal disputes surveyed above, including transatlantic differences with respect to U.S. behavior during and at the end of prominent treaty negotiations or concerning the propriety of unilateral remedies within certain regimes such as trade, may turn at least in part on substantive differences between civil and common law; they may also reflect diverging legal trends in particular areas of regulation.[40]

In its most extreme form, the cultural account may help to explain the views of John Bolton, presently the Under-Secretary for Arms Control and International Security in the Bush administration. Bolton argues that the absence of a credible tie between the rules of international law and politically accountable governmental action as provided by the U.S. Constitution means that international "law" does not exist; nations might be "politically" or "morally" bound to adhere to their treaties, but they cannot be said to be legally bound. In his view, it does a great deal of harm to extend the legitimacy of the term "law" to instruments as fundamentally different as the U.S. Constitution and the Statute of the ICC or the U.N. Charter. To Bolton, the U.S. battle against the ICC and other forms of supranational, "undemocratic" government is about nothing less than protecting U.S. sovereignty and Americans' right to accountable government.[41]

But Bolton also articulates what may be the firmest explanation for why European polities, and not merely their international lawyers, may have greater faith in multilateralism, namely the history of European integration. As Bolton points out, the "dissolving of nation-states into the European Union" reflects an express relinquishment of sovereignty, a divestment of authority in favor of a supranational institution that would be politically inconceivable to anybody in the United States.[42] Bolton criticizes this transformation of Europe as suggesting Europeans' lack of commitment to their own constitutional autonomy and as implying the existence of a global conspiracy to use supranational processes to subvert U.S. democracy. Others have looked to the legal forms of European integration, both within the European Union (E.U.) and within the European system for human rights, as models for correcting the flaws of international systems of governance, such as the U.N.[43]

Both critics and admirers of European integration agree, however, that decades of developments within the E.U.—including ever-growing attempts by individuals and national courts to use preliminary rulings by the Court in Luxembourg to overturn or reform national laws, the transformation of European law into directly applicable and hierarchically superior rules, the gradual empowerment of both international and national judges as de facto lawmakers accomplished through an international treaty teleologically interpreted, and the ever-expanding substantive reach of European law and its institutions—have had wider sociological effects. There are, in addition, the integrative effects prompted by the expansion and deepening of the European system for human rights, centered in Strasbourg.[44] The transformative processes set in motion by the Luxembourg and Strasbourg Courts provide a plausible basis for explaining why the multilateral commitments expressed by Europe's international lawyers resonate with ordinary Europeans.[45]

As a consequence of the relatively successful European schemes to govern their community as well as to resolve complaints relating to human rights violations within the continent, Europeans generally (and not just legal elites) see international commitments as part and parcel of domestic law. Europeans, including national judges and legislators in national capitals, have become accustomed to treating treaties and the legally binding decisions of international organizations as no less "law" than any edict issued by a domestic parliament or order by a domestic court. Years of judicial activism by international judges at Strasbourg and Luxembourg have gotten the average European citizen accustomed to the idea that sovereign prerogatives are not immutable and that international bureaucrats, including international judges, can overrule long-standing national laws in favor of new rules contained in an international treaty.

Europeans are more prepared to accept the idea that everything, even the most sensitive issues formerly regarded as within the essential core of sovereignty, such as the proclamation of a national emergency, is subject to international scrutiny and, ultimately, to the international rule of law. Ironically, the civil-law nations of Europe for which the notion of an activist lawmaking national judge was largely alien are now far more accustomed to judicial activism by their international brethren than are members of the U.S. polity.

European governments may or may not comply "better" or more often with their international obligations than does the United States government. As this author has argued elsewhere, European integrative processes respond to the unique agendas of the European continent and may not have a direct correlation with these states' receptiveness to global norms generated outside of Europe.[46] There is not a direct one-to-one correspondence between Europeans' deep and demonstrated commitments to comply with European law and their readiness to do the same with respect to rules promulgated by the U.N. or the WTO.[47]

The argument here is more modest. European integrative processes, accomplished via the tools of international law, have subtly altered Europeans' perceptions of themselves and of the nature of the nation state. Much more so than Americans, Europeans define sovereignty, as have Abram and Antonia Chayes, as "no longer consist[ing] in the freedom of states to act independently, in their perceived self-interest, but in membership in reasonably good standing in the regimes that make up the substance of international law."[48] Europeans are far more likely than Americans to give priority to status as a member of the international system, achieved through participation in the "various regimes that regulate and order the international system."[49] Relative to Americans, Europeans are more acclimated to the idea that sovereign rights can be traded away, that external intervention in the internal affairs of states by collective legal mechanisms is acceptable and often necessary, and that even matters dealing with national security are under a rule of law determined by a greater community of nations.

If Europeans have greater—some would say naïve—faith in the ability of international institutions to bring errant states into line, perhaps it is because they have seen it done with considerable success not just within the treaty structures of the European system for human rights and the European Union, but also through the Organization for Security and Cooperation in Europe (OSCE). Europeans are used to seeing treaties taken seriously, by both national and international judges and by both national and international civil servants. Since they have, for decades, seen some of their rights and duties as citizens, including in the so-called "private" sphere, affected by "public" international law rules, they are more amenable than Americans to the notion that the "social contract" extends beyond the nation state.

The differences between U.S. nationals and Europeans have become especially clear in the wake of September 11. Europeans are inured to international scrutiny even with respect to the war on terrorism—a war that they have waged for far longer than have Americans.

Since the first cases brought against the United Kingdom for its treatment of alleged Irish Republican Army (IRA) terrorists until today—when the Strasbourg Court is dealing with Turkey's treatment of political dissidents—Europeans have applied international law and international courts to claims of national self-preservation, necessity, and self-defense. European judges have repeatedly rejected the idea that the doctrine of self-preservation responds to no law, that the rule of law stops when terrorism begins, that states have the right to unrestricted powers when dealing with national security threats. In a series of judgments, the European Court of Human Rights has dared to suggest, for example, that the right-to-life provisions of a treaty require states to abstain from the lethal use of force when international judges determine that such force has exceeded what is reasonably required under the circumstances, and that the same right to life requires states to conduct effective investigations whenever they use lethal force, even as against alleged terrorists from Northern Ireland.[50]

By comparison, in the United States the very idea that anyone—particularly an international court—has the power to tell the Supreme Court or even Tom Ridge that he is out of line on the basis of international legal commitments is a non-starter. These attitudes are reflected in Washington's reluctance to acknowledge the application of international humanitarian law to those captured and its resort to lawless detention in Guantánamo—the legality of which, to date, is subject to no scrutiny except perhaps by U.S. courts.[51] We see the differences as well with respect to the well-known U.S. reluctance to commit to many forms of binding international dispute settlement, particularly with respect to human rights. Unlike our European allies whose national laws have had to undergo considerable modification in response to human rights rulings by international judges, the United States has generally avoided any effective judicial scrutiny when it comes to human rights. It has not opened itself to the individual complaints mechanisms of even those few human rights treaties it is party to, has renounced the compulsory jurisdiction of the World Court (in reaction to its rulings in the *Nicaragua* case), has refused to accept the jurisdiction of the Inter-American Court of Human Rights, and has refused to enforce provisional measures from the International Court of Justice (ICJ). For the United States, as opposed to Europe and even increasingly most governments in Latin America, international human rights are essentially for export.

While European lawyers today are engaged in adapting their laws (and even some of their constitutions) to a number of international regimes—whether the provisions of the Statute for the International Criminal Court or the requisites of a number of other global and regional treaty regimes—U.S. counterparts are spending their time dealing with the considerable political backlash generated by the relatively few somewhat intrusive international regimes that the U.S. is subject to, principally in the WTO and the North American Free Trade Agreement (NAFTA). While European international lawyers wrestle with balancing international constraints with local sensibilities through nuanced inquiries (as suggested by the European doctrines of "subsidiarity" and "margin of appreciation"),[52] U.S. lawyers at such nongovernmental organizations (NGOs) as Public

Citizen are waging highly public and often sophistic battles against the enforcement of international rules resulting from those relatively narrow economic regimes to which the U.S. is subject. While Europeans have handed over final judicial supervision of their national criminal trials to Strasbourg's international judges, members of the U.S. Congress are so frightened of the prospect that some U.S. citizens abroad might be subject to a different set of rules to guarantee their rights to fair trial that they have authorized the President of the United States to use "all means necessary" to extricate any U.S. national sought to be tried by the ICC in The Hague.[53] While even the European state that is culturally and politically closest to the United States, namely the United Kingdom, has effectively constitutionalized an international bill of rights, Bush administration lawyers, as well as prominent members of U.S. academia, are even now attempting to ensure that no federal court will find a cause of action based on customary international law generally or customary human rights norms in particular.[54]

My European students are amused at the high state of anxiety expressed in the United States over those few international regimes that might now have a potential impact on U.S. law. For them the idea that national environmental laws might be challenged as a violation of an international legal commitment—now possible under the WTO and the still fragmentary cases decided under the investment chapter of the NAFTA—is old news.[55] Europeans have been wrestling with the political backlash—or "democratic deficit"—generated by "unaccountable" supranational legal processes for a long time. While they have not solved these issues even at the European level, they are much farther along with respect to ameliorative remedies.[56] Europeans have repeatedly adjusted national constitutional norms in response to the needs of coexisting within a broader community of nations while the average U.S. citizen relies not only on the myth but the reality that the 200-year-old-plus U.S. Constitution is sacred, unalterable holy writ.[57] Bolton is probably right when he suggests that the typical American would be aghast at the notion of judges other than those authorized by the U.S. Constitution passing judgment on the rights and responsibilities of U.S. citizens. This would be regarded as "un-American" precisely because it has generally not happened, as compared to Europe where it happens every day.

These differences help to put in context why Europeans have taken such affront at many actions of the Bush administration, particularly after the tragic attacks of September 2001. For those who treat human rights provided in a treaty as binding national law, a nation that disregards these fundamental obligations, whether in Guantánamo or by pressing for inhumane economic sanctions, cannot be trusted to respect its other international obligations. This also explains why many Europeans view with considerable cynicism justifications of the latest U.S. invasion of Iraq grounded in the defense of human rights.[50] For such states, even instances not involving a formal breach of international law but merely a failure to engage speak volumes. The U.S. failure to negotiate in good faith in Kyoto, its sabotaging of other states' commitments to the ICC, and its undermining international commitments on landmines suggest a lack of respect for the reciprocal give-and-take which, to Europeans at least, is the essence of international law. While the failure of the Bush administration's U.N. initiative on Iraq has many causes—including opportunism by European states—we should not ignore the relevance of these differences of perspective, grounded in professional culture, legal tradition, and recent history.

Differences between Europeans and Americans emerge not only when the United States chooses to ignore multilateral institutions, but also over how the U.S. uses those institutions when it chooses to do so. It matters to Europeans how the U.S. uses the Security Council and not just whether it goes to it. The Iraqi debacle suggests that the problem that the United States faces, particularly vis-à-vis "old Europe," is not only its lack of engagement with multilateral processes. A nation that pays its full U.N. dues only after September 11 when it decides it needs the U.N. is not altogether trustworthy even when it resorts to the world organization. Europeans, as well as many others, judge good faith by how the United States has used the Security Council in the recent past. To many of them, the United States' post-Cold War use of the Council suggests a desire to use it as a multilateral fig leaf for what Dupuy would call "unilateral diktats," and not as a venue for good-faith multilateral civil discourse.

Europeans and others have now seen the U.S. pressure the Security Council (in Resolution 1422 of July 12, 2002) into carving out a legally dubious exception to the ICC's jurisdiction for U.N. peacekeepers that does no credit to either the Council or the Statute of the ICC. They have seen the U.S. use the Council (in Resolution 1373 of September 28, 2001) to enforce against all states selective provisions of the U.N. Convention on the Financing of Terrorism (a treaty then not yet in force), ignoring provisions in that treaty that recognize that the imposition of financial sanctions on individuals alleged to be terrorists or accused of providing material assistance to terrorists needs to conform to the standards of international human rights and international humanitarian law and may require some form of judicial review.[59] They have seen Washington's dominance on the Security Council repeatedly being used to pursue its own narrow geopolitical interests—such that the world organization is pressured to authorize force to prevent Haitian refugees from reaching the shores of Florida but not to prevent a horrific genocide in Rwanda. Due to the United States' undoubted power, the Security Council's selectivity on these and other issues is attributed, fairly or not, to U.S. lack of interest in using the Council to define or defend coherent international rules applicable to all.[60]

Explaining Iraq

The European reaction to Washington's attempt to use the Security Council to authorize renewed military action against Iraq needs to be put in this greater context. For European international lawyers, the legitimacy of Resolution 687, which imposed the terms of the peace on Iraq after the Gulf war, was conditioned on a continued commitment to multilateral cooperation. That "mother of all resolutions" was adopted when U.S. power in the Council was at its peak but also at a unique historical moment for the U.N., when hopes were high that the United Nations would finally work as intended without the veto. Particularly from the perspective of European positivist lawyers, a number of aspects of Resolution 687 were unprecedented and legally dubious, especially in hindsight.[61]

This resolution imposed by fiat duties on Iraq to destroy most of its weapons, including many not banned by any treaty to which Iraq was a party. It selectively imposed on only one country in the region requirements for a nuclear freeze, which the General Assembly had urged for the entire Middle East. It imposed, without benefit of due process or opportunity for Iraq to rebut, extensive financial liability for any and all consequences of the Gulf war, including liability far in excess under then existing international law (e.g. for environmental damage). It stipulated, again without benefit of judicial recourse or due process, boundary demarcations. Resolution 687 effectively put Iraqi sovereignty in receivership. A political body, namely the Security Council, rather than any court, determined that Iraq had breached the law, imposed a system of reparations, and suspended sovereign rights. The Council in Resolution 687 imposed a foreign presence on Iraqi territory, deprived it of a great deal of its oil revenues, authorized continued low-level economic war on its people, and arguably infringed Iraq's ability to engage in its own self-defense.

Resolution 687 criminalized the Iraqi regime no less than the war-guilt clause in the Treaty of Versailles branded Germany. Like a typical criminal sanction, Resolution 687 stigmatized Iraq as a rogue nation, deprived it of rights and immunities, and marked this change in status through the application of extensive sanctions and ongoing surveillance.[62] Resolution 687 is about criminalization— even though the community of states has repeatedly rejected the idea that they, as such, or their peoples as a collective, ought to be found guilty of committing international crimes. For many states, this was a controversial step. For the states of "old Europe," the relevant model for handling aggressors is not the highly punitive reparations of Versailles but the individual responsibility of Nuremberg. They reluctantly acceded to U.S. demands for Resolution 687 because the Nuremberg model of individual culpability was impossible to attain since the main culprit was out of reach and because, in the unique context of that post-Gulf war moment, they assumed that the Security Council and not any single state would be in charge of supervising Iraq's criminalization. They assumed that the international community of states, working through the Council, would suitably adjust the punishments as conditions warranted.[63]

This was the legal mind-set that the United States encountered when it sought, at the beginning of 2003, to transform Resolution 687 from a license to punish into a license to invade in order to impose "regime change." As shown by growing international opposition to Iraqi sanctions, the international community (and not merely the states of "old Europe") was already having second thoughts about the turn to the Versailles model before the Bush administration entered office. That administration offended many when it suggested, before eventually turning to the U.N., that there was no need for renewed Security Council authorization to use force. For members familiar with the reluctant deal struck in 1991, this was yet another demonstration of the United States' lack of good faith.

Neither in authorizing the Gulf war nor later in ending it, had any Council resolution authorized regime change in Baghdad. In neither case had the Security Council granted the United States carte blanche to wage war for an indefinite period.[64] In neither case had the Council given the United States unilateral, unrestricted authority to inflict punishments not spelled out in Resolution 678 or 687 or to set itself up as the Council's self-judging enforcer of Iraq's disarmament. U.S. arguments 12 years after the Gulf war suggesting that it had unilateral authority to topple Saddam Hussein based on that regime's failure to abide by the Council's orders suggested to many (and not merely Europeans) a contempt for the requirement to adhere in good faith to both the text and the intent of legal instruments. It appeared to be yet another instance in which the United States was treating law, determined by the collective and binding on all, as mere politics.

At bottom, the legal divide between the United States and Europe is not about perceptions of reality. European international lawyers would not disagree that the history of international law is replete with many instances in which might makes right. The difference lies in perceptions of what it is proper for lawyers to do. For European international lawyers, it is not the place of lawyers to relinquish their comparative expertise—their skill in deciphering legal texts—to have the ear of the Prince. They would contend that it is not the place of lawyers to encourage, applaud, or anticipate the breach of law by the powerful, even for ostensibly benevolent ends.

Notes

1 The author is grateful for comments received from colleagues George Bermann, Catherine MacKinnon, and Oscar Schachter.
2 Compare Charles A. Kupchan, "The End of the West," *Atlantic Monthly*, November 2002, p. 42 (suggesting a looming transatlantic "clash of civilizations") to Joseph P. Quinlan, *Drifting Apart or Growing Together? The Primacy of the Transatlantic Economy* (Washington: Center for Transatlantic Relations, 2003), http://sais-jhu.edu/trans atlantic/Quinlan%20Text.pdf (suggesting that economic ties are likely to remain the basis of a solid transatlantic alliance), as well as Chantal de Jonge Oudraat in this volume.
3 See, for example, José E. Alvarez, "Promoting the 'Rule of Law' in Latin America: Problems and Prospects," *George Washington Journal of International Law and Economics* 25, no. 2 (1991), p. 281.
4 Indeed, it is the perceived expansion of international law's realm, especially through the growth of international human rights, which causes some U.S. international lawyers to seek to limit the extent to which these rules can be treated as part of the law of the United States. See, for example, Curtis A. Bradley and Jack L. Goldsmith, "Customary International Law as Federal Common Law: A Critique of the Modern Position," *Harvard Law Review* 110, no. 4 (1997), p. 815.
5 As happens within the United States, governmental policies in Europe do not always reflect the views or the advice given by international lawyers. European states' foot-dragging on complying with WTO rulings on bananas and beef hormones, for

example, have drawn criticism from European international trade lawyers committed to the efficacy or legitimacy of the WTO. See, for example, "Speech by Pascal Lamy, European Commissioner for Trade at the Netherlands Confederation of Industry and Employers," *Rapid*, October 17, 2000.

6 See, for example, Letter to the Editor, *The Guardian*, March 7, 2003, http://www.guardian.couk/letters/story/0,3604,909275,00.html. In this open letter to 10 Downing Street, 16 prominent international law professors, including all but one of those presently teaching at the Universities of Oxford and Cambridge, the London School of Economics, and University College London, argued that the use of military force against Iraq in the absence of explicit Security Council authorization would violate international law, including the law of the U.N. Charter.

7 See, for example, Anne-Marie Slaughter, "Good Reasons for Going around the U.N.," *New York Times*, March 18, 2003, p. A33; W. Michael Reisman, "Assessing Claims to Revise the Laws of War," *American Journal of International Law* 97, no. 1 (2003), p. 82; Ruth Wedgwood, "Strike at Saddam Now," *National Law Journal*, October 28, 2002; Michael F. Glennon, "Why the Security Council Failed," *Foreign Affairs* 82, no. 3 (May–June 2003), p. 16. See also Paul Schott Steven, Andru E. Wall, and Ata Dinlenc, "The Just Demands of Peace and Security: International Law and the Case against Iraq" (The Federalist Society for Law and Public Policy Studies White Papers: 2003), http://www.fed-soc.org/War%20on%20Terror/iraqfinal—web.pdf. For a defense of the U.S. war on the Taliban against European skeptics, see Thomas M. Franck, "Terrorism and the Right of Self-Defense," *American Journal of International Law* 95, no. 4 (2001), p. 839. For reflection of the prevailing public sentiments in the U.S., see, "Iraq and International Law," *Washington Times*, March 14, 2003, p. A22.

8 For discussion of these disputes over U.S. treaty practices, see, for example, David M. Malone and Yuen Foong Khong, eds., *Unilateralism and U.S. Foreign Policy* (Boulder, CO and London: Lynne Rienner, 2003), particularly chapters by David M. Malone, Yuen Foong Khong, Nico Krisch, and Rosemary Foot.

9 See, for example, Douglass W. Cassel, "Ignoring the World Court," *Chicago Daily Law Bulletin*, 10 January 2002, p. 6; *Soering v. United Kingdom*, European Court of Human Rights, 161 Eur. Ct. H.R. (ser. A), 11 E.H.R.R. 439 (1989); European Parliament, "European Parliament Resolution on the Detainees in Guantánamo Bay," PE 313.865, www.europarl.eu.int/meetdocs/delegations/usam/20020219/004EN.pdf; Patrick Jarreau, "Les Etats-Unis confrontés aux demandes d'explications officielles d'une demi-douzaine de pays," *Le Monde*, May 21, 2003. U.S. actions in defiance of the World Court have led Europeans and others to renew their doubts concerning the United States' commitment to the peaceful settlement of disputes. Such doubts had been expressed a decade earlier in reaction to the United States' refusal to participate in the merits stage of the *Nicaragua* case before the ICJ and its subsequent termination of participation in that Court's Optional Clause. See, for example, General Assembly of the United Nations, "Judgment of the International Court of Justice of 27 June 1986 Concerning Military and Paramilitary Activities in and against Nicaragua: Need for Immediate Compliance," G.A. Res. A/Res/43/11, October 25, 1988.

10 See, for example, "European Union: Demarches Protesting the Cuban Liberty and Democratic Solidarity (Libertad) Act," reprinted in *International Legal Materials* 35, no. 2 (1996), p. 397; Monica Serrano, "Unilateralism, multilateralism, and U.S. drug diplomacy in Latin America," in Malone and Khong, eds., *Unilateralism and U.S. Foreign Policy*, p. 117; Pierre-Marie Dupuy, "The Place and Role of Unilateralism in Contemporary International Law," *European Journal of International Law* 11, no. 1 (2000), pp. 26–7; Vera Gowlland-Debbas, "The Limits of Unilateral Enforcement of Community Objectives in the Framework of U.N. Peace Maintenance," *European Journal of International Law* 11, no. 2 (2000), p. 361.

11 See, for example, "Russia, France, Germany say Iraq War Illegal," *Reuters*, March 20, 2003, http://www.gazeta.ru/2003/03/20/RussiaFrance.shtml. Joantha Freedland, "Patten Lays into Bush's America: Fury at President's 'Axis of Evil' Speech," *The Guardian*, February 9, 2002, Guardian homepages, p. 1; "French FM Renews Attack on U.S. Foreign Policy," *Agence France Presse*, March 1, 2002.

12 See, generally, David M. Malone, "A Decade of U.S. Unilateralism?" in Malone and Khong, eds., *Unilateralism and U.S. Foreign Policy*, p. 19; Per Magnus Wijkman, "U.S. Trade Policy: Alternative Tacks or Parallel Tracks?" in ibid., p. 251; Ramesh Thakur, "U.N. Peace Operations and U.S. Unilateralism and Multilateralism," in ibid., p. 153. See also Erika de Wet, "Human Rights Limitations to Economic Enforcement Measures Under Article 1 of the United Nations Charter and the Iraqi Sanctions Regime," *Leiden Journal of International Law* 14, no. 2 (2001), p. 277.

13 See, generally, documents available at http://www.iccnow.org/documents/other issues1422.html (over 30 statements submitted by representatives of various nations and the accompanying chart prepared by the NGO coalition for the ICC document the widespread opposition to relevant U.S. proposals at the Security Council: "Statements Made or Endorsed at the Open Meeting of the Security Council Discussion of the U.N. Mission in Bosnia and Herzegovina on July 10, 2002").

14 For an explanation of the deepening European commitment to enforcing international human rights within Europe that relies on "liberal" theory, see Andrew Moravcsik, "The Origins of Human Rights Regimes: Democratic Delegation in Postwar Europe," *International Organizations* 54, no. 2 (2000), p. 217.

15 See Robert O. Keohane, "International Relations and International Law: Two Optics," *Harvard International Law Journal* 38, no. 2 (1997), p. 487; Alexander Wendt, "Constructing International Politics," *International Security* 20, no. 1 (1995), p. 5.

16 See, for example, Dupuy, "The Place and Role," p. 22; Gowlland-Debbas, "The Limits of Unilateral Enforcement," p. 361; Philippe Sands, "'Unilateralism', Values, and International Law," *European Journal of International Law* 11, no. 2 (2000), p. 249. See also Bruno Simma, "From Bilateralism to Community Interest in International Law," *Recueil des Cours* 250, no. 6 (1994), p. 217.

17 Dupuy, "The Place and Role," p. 23.

18 Ibid., pp. 23–4 (citing as specific examples international rules such as those banning reprisals and unilateral denunciations of treaties). For Dupuy, international law requires states to seek in good faith to find through dialogue a solution compatible with the interests of all states concerned. "It obliges them . . . where cooperation and negotiation structures have been opened to them through treaties and the creation of international institutions, to have recourse to these norms and these institutions, on pain of incurring, if they are ignored, international liability vis-à-vis the states concerned" (p. 24).

19 Ibid., p. 25.

20 Ibid., pp. 26–9; Francesco Francioni, "Multilateralism à la Carte: The Limits to Unilateral Withholdings of Assessed Contributions to the U.N. Budget," *European Journal of International Law* 11, no. 1 (2000), p. 43; Sands, "Unilateralism," pp. 298–300.

21 Gowlland-Debbas, "The Limits of Unilateral Enforcement," pp. 327–77. While she acknowledged that the doctrine of implied powers has been used to justify General Assembly initiatives when the Security Council is paralyzed (through the Uniting for Peace Resolution), she argued that the *raison d'être* for that exception did not apply to individual state action. While the General Assembly could rely upon a teleological and evolutionary approach to Charter interpretation since this was needed to expand "the collective competence of the United Nations in the face of restrictive assertions of sovereignty by member states," the implied powers doctrine was "not intended to be used for a reactionary purpose, i.e., reversion to a sovereign unfettered right on the part of one or several states to usurp Council powers" (p. 374).

22 Ibid., p. 378.

23 See, generally, José E. Alvarez, "Multilateralism and Its Discontents," *European Journal of International Law* 11, no. 2 (2000), p. 393 (questioning the value, legitimacy or efficacy of a number of multilateral initiatives).
24 W. Michael Reisman, "Unilateral Action and the Transformations of the World Constitutive Process: The Special Problem of Humanitarian Intervention," *European Journal of International Law* 11, no. 1 (2000), p. 5, n. 2.
25 Ibid., pp. 14–15.
26 Ruth Wedgwood, "Unilateral Action in the U.N. System," *European Journal of International Law* 11, no. 2 (2000), pp. 352–9.
27 Ibid., p. 352.
28 Ibid., p. 356.
29 Ibid., pp. 357–9.
30 Allan Gerson, "Multilateralism à la Carte: The Consequences of Unilateral 'Pick and Pay' Approaches," *European Journal of International Law* 11, no. 1 (2000), p. 61; Kenneth Anderson, "The Ottawa Convention Banning Landmines, the Role of International Non-Governmental Organizations and the Idea of International Civil Society," *European Journal of International Law* 11, no. 1 (2000), p. 91. For completely different European reactions to these issues, see Francesco Francioni, "Multilateralism à la Carte: The Limits to Unilateral Withholdings," p. 43; Peter Malanczuk, "The International Criminal Court and Landmines: What Are the Consequences of Leaving the U.S. Behind?" *European Journal of International Law* 11, no. 1 (2000), p. 77.
31 James C. Hathaway, "America, Defender of Democratic Legitimacy?" *European Journal of International Law* 11, no. 1 (2000), pp. 127–31. Hathaway argues that the Yale School approach "is too readily exploited by powerful states anxious to disguise their particularistic agendas" (pp. 128–9). Note that while Hathaway is correct that the Yale School approach has had a singular importance in U.S. legal academia, many of those trained in its methods, such as Richard Falk and Oscar Schachter, have been anything but apologists for U.S. government policies. See also Gowlland-Debbas, "The Limits of Unilateral Enforcement," p. 380 (expressing a preference for the "pure theory of law" over more open-ended sociological exercises focused on ends not means).
32 See, generally, "Symposium on Method in International Law," *American Journal of International Law* 93, no. 2 (1999), p. 291 (surveying several of these interdisciplinary approaches). For an introduction to the predominant European "positivist" approach to international law, see Bruno Simma and Andreas L. Paulus, "The Responsibility of Individuals for Human Rights Abuses in Internal Conflicts: A Positivist View," *American Journal of International Law* 93, no. 2 (1999), p. 302.
33 See, for example, David Kennedy, "The Disciplines of International Law and Policy," *Leiden Journal of International Law* 12 (1999), pp. 9, 26.
34 See, for example, Paul W. Kahn, "Speaking Law to Power: Popular Sovereignty, Human Rights, and the New International Order," *Chicago Journal of International Law* 1, no. 1 (2000), p. 3.
35 See ibid., pp. 4, 18. The first and second explanations presented in the text may be complementary. It may not be an accident that the Yale School of International Law is premised on eight fundamental human values (power, enlightenment, wealth, well-being, skill, affection, respect, and rectitude) that coincide with the goals of both the U.S. Constitution and the international human rights program. See Siegfried Wiessner and Andrew R. Willard, "Policy-Oriented Jurisprudence and Human Rights Abuses in Internal Conflict: Toward a World Public Order of Human Dignity," *American Journal of International Law* 93, no. 2 (1999), pp. 318–19.
36 See Kahn, "Popular Sovereignty," p. 4.
37 See Reisman, "Unilateral Action in the U.N. System," p. 6.
38 See Alvarez, "Multilateralism and Its Discontents," p. 394. For a concrete example, see statement by Gowlland-Debbas, "The Limits of Unilateral Enforcement."

39 It would not, of course, explain other members of the "coalition of the willing," such as Spain.
40 Civil-law principles regarding the formation of contract may require those negotiating a contract to respect precontractual obligations, including an obligation to continue to negotiate in good faith. In civil-law countries, parties may be found liable for failure to conclude a contract. See Arthur von Mehren and James Russell Gordley, *The Civil Law System* (Boston: Little, Brown and Co., 1977), pp. 834–48. This may explain why European international lawyers see the duty to cooperate to conclude international contracts (namely treaties) as so fundamental. It may also explain their adverse reaction when the U.S. participates in an international negotiation, as it often does, yet fails to adhere to the treaty ultimately negotiated or WTO decisions such as Shrimp/Turtle which find U.S. unilateral measures unlawful in part because the United States failed to engage in international negotiations which might produce more mutually cooperative solutions. For a survey of divergent regulatory trends between Europe and the United States in a number of legal areas, see Daniel C. Esty and Damien Geradin, eds., *Regulatory Competition and Economic Integration* (Oxford: Oxford University Press: 2001).
41 John R. Bolton, "Is There Really 'Law' in International Affairs?" *Transnational Law and Contemporary Problems* 10, no. 1 (2000), p. 1.
42 Ibid., pp. 43–8. See also Bolton, "Unsign that Treaty," *Washington Post*, January 4, 2001, p. A21.
43 See, for example, Karen J. Alter, *Establishing the Supremacy of European Law* (New York: Oxford University Press, 2001); Ernst-Ulrich Petersmann, "Constitutionalism and International Adjudication: How to Constitutionalize the U.N. Dispute Settlement System?" *NYU Journal of International Law and Politics* 31, no. 4 (1999), p. 753.
44 See, generally, A.H. Robertson and J.G. Merrills, *Human Rights in Europe: A Study of the European Convention on Human Rights*, 4th edition (Manchester: Manchester University Press, 2001); J.G. Merrills, *The Development of International Law by the European Court of Human Rights*, 2nd edition (Manchester: Manchester University Press, 1993).
45 They would explain why the European Parliament, and not just European academics, has, for example, deplored U.S. bilateral agreements to get around the jurisdiction of the ICC or why that body has gone out of its way to affirm the application of international humanitarian law for prisoners held in Guantánamo.
46 See José E. Alvarez, "Do Liberal States Behave Better? A Critique of Slaughter's Liberal Theory," *European Journal of International Law* 12, no. 2 (2001), pp. 220–3.
47 See, for example, Jonathan Fenby, "Interpol Asked to Probe Chirac Dealings with Saddam Regime," *The Business*, May 4, 2003, p. 10 (suggesting France ignored aspects of the U.N. sanctions regime). And Europeans, like Americans, have not given direct effect to many of their international legal commitments outside of those undertaken within the European Union.
48 Abram Chayes and Antonia Chayes, *The New Sovereignty* (Boston, MA: Harvard University Press, 1995), p. 27.
49 Ibid.
50 See, for example, Oren Gross and Fionnuala Ni Aolain, "From Discretion to Scrutiny: Revisiting the Application of the Margin of Appreciation Doctrine in the Context of Article 15 of the European Convention on Human Rights," *Human Rights Quarterly* 23, no. 3 (2001), p. 625. See also Oren Gross and Fionnuala Ni Aolain, "Emergency, War and International Law—Another Perspective," *Nordic Journal of International Law* 70, no. 1 (2001), p. 29.
51 See *Al Odah v. United States*, 321 F.3d, p. 1134 (D.C. Cir. 2003) (finding that non-resident aliens held by the U.S. at Guantánamo Bay Naval Base had no Constitutional rights); "Response of the United States to Request for Precautionary Measures—Detainees in Guantánamo Bay, Cuba, April 15, 2002," reprinted in

International Legal Materials 41, no. 4 (2002), p. 1015 (contending that the Inter-American Commission on Human Rights lacked competence to examine U.S. actions in Guantánamo and also asserting that the Third Geneva Convention does not apply to its detainees there). But see Ruth Wedgwood, "Al Qaeda, Terrorism, and Military Commissions," *American Journal of International Law* 96, no. 2 (2002), p. 328 (defending the international legality of military commissions).

52   See, for example, Gross and Ni Aolain, "From Discretion to Scrutiny."

53   *American Servicemembers' Protection Act*, Public Law no. 107–206 sections 2001–15, 116 Statute 820 (2002), Section 2008a. As might be expected, concerns over this act (informally known as the "Hague Invasion Act"), including the implicit U.S. threat to invade the Netherlands, were expressed by that government as well as by the European Parliament.

54   *Human Rights Act of 1998*, U.K. Statute 1998, Chapter 42 (incorporating European Convention of Human Rights as domestic law). By comparison, note the efforts of Professors Curtis A. Bradley and Jack L. Goldsmith (see note 4) as well as the intervention by the U.S. Justice Department in a prominent human rights case before a federal court. See "Brief for the United States as Amicus Curiae," in *John Doe v. Unocal*, U.S. Court of Appeals for the Ninth Circuit, May 2003.

55   Compare the reaction of the U.S.-based NGO Public Citizen. See, for example, "NAFTA Chapter 11 Investor-to-State Cases: Bankrupting Democracy," *Public Citizen*, September 2001, http://www.citizen.org/documents/ACF186.pdf.

56   Thus, while Europeans are no strangers to the basic sovereignty concerns raised by John Bolton, their constitutional courts have carved out fundamental constitutional rights that are not subject to supranational negotiation. They have also built supranational institutions capable of providing some forms of democratic accountability, such as the European Parliament. See, generally, Eric Stein, "International Integration and Democracy: No Love at First Sight," *American Journal of International Law* 95, no. 3 (2001), p. 489. Indeed, it is precisely because Europeans have not fully solved their accountability and democracy complaints within the E.U.—because the E.U. has not yet jelled into a fully fledged single nation but remains a supranational structure with authority over sovereign states—that European integrative processes still hold lessons for general international law.

57   See, for example, Kahn, "Popular Sovereignty," p. 3.

58   It also generated European disdain for U.S. complaints during the Iraqi conflict that the Iraqis were not respecting the laws of war. See, for example, "Pas d'Interview," *Le Monde*, March 26, 2003, http://www.lemonde.fr.

59   See Erika de Wet and Andre Nollakemper, "Review of Security Council Decisions by National Courts," *German Yearbook of International Law* 45 (2002), p. 166 (discussing problems with the Council's counter-terrorism efforts).

60   Even when European governments, for their own reasons, acquiesce in these Council actions, they have an incentive to present these issues to their constituencies as actions taken or demanded by the hegemon, thereby enhancing widespread perceptions that the United States is a unilateralist bully.

61   See, generally, Martti Koskenniemi, "The Police in the Temple," *European Journal of International Law* 6, no. 3 (1995), p. 325.

62   See Gerry Simpson, *Unequal Sovereigns: Great Powers and Outlaw States in the International Legal Order* (London: Cambridge University Press, forthcoming January 2004).

63   See, generally, Jules Lobel and Michael Ratner, "Bypassing the Security Council: Ambiguous Authorizations to Use Force, Cease-fires and the Iraqi Inspection Regime," *American Journal of International Law* 93, no. 1 (1999), p. 124; de Wet and Nollakemper, "Review"; Philip Alston, "The Security Council and Human Rights: Lessons to be Learned from the Iraq–Kuwait Crisis and its Aftermath," *Australian Year Book of International Law* 13 (1992), p. 107.

64 See, for example, Lobel and Ratner, "Bypassing the Security Council," pp. 151–2 (discussing how U.S.–U.K. attempts to secure Council authorization to use force against Iraqi targets failed in late 1997 and early 1998 due to widespread opposition from other members of the Council, leading to U.S. arguments that specific Council authorization or a finding of "material breach" was unnecessary).

10 Tactical multilateralism

U.S. foreign policy and crisis management in the Middle East

Bruce D. Jones[1]

In the first decade of this century, the Middle East and neighboring regions emerged as a key battleground for what has become the central political war of the day: the use of U.S. power and its relationship with existing multilateral instruments. The collapse of the Middle East peace process, the September 11 terrorist attacks on the United States, and the wars in Afghanistan and Iraq have challenged both U.S. and international perceptions of threat, security, and order. In turn, the responses to these events have been influenced by the resulting debates.

U.S. actions in this arena have been attacked from a number of angles, but nowhere more sharply than on the question of unilateralism. These attacks built to a crescendo following the repudiation of the Kyoto treaty, the Comprehensive Test Ban Treaty, the Biological Weapons Convention review conference, and similar measures. As John Van Oudenaren has noted, "unilateralism has emerged as the most contentious issue in U.S.–European relations."[2]

More recently, Security Council deliberations over whether to authorize U.S.-led military action against Iraq, i.e. the debate over a putative "second resolution," became ideological and shrill, veering between competing exaggerations of the role of the U.N., and between competing idealistic accounts of the nature of U.S. power. In the face of American pundits who drew caricatures of U.N. negligence and appetite for appeasement that verged on black helicopter imagery, European politicians defended a U.N. whose role was so central and record so spotless that it was unrecognizable to anyone who had worked at the U.N. or studied its performance. While U.S. neo-conservatives described a role for American power that was both extraordinarily expansive and utterly benign, politicians, commentators, and populations from Europe, the Arab world, and elsewhere began to perceive U.S. actions as the greatest threat to world stability.

This battle between straw men and blind men obscured more than it has revealed about the sources of U.S. foreign policy in Iraq and the Middle East, or the role of the U.N. and multilateral action in that policy. The record reveals a more variegated picture of forms of engagement by the U.S. with multilateral institutions, allied powers, and regional actors in the implementation of its Middle East policy. In terms of decision-making, the evidence suggests that U.S. decisions concerning the use or avoidance of multilateral instruments for managing conflicts and crises in the Middle East stem neither from an ideological aversion to the U.N. or similar bodies nor from an ethical commitment to them. Rather, they are primarily tactical. Moreover, the evidence suggests that multilateral instruments work effectively only when they balance core principles with a constructive relationship with U.S. power.

Furthermore, the record reveals that the degree of multilateralism in any given U.S. policy is not a predictor of the degree of U.S. engagement, of the ethical content of that policy, or of real international support for the policy objective. Compared to the record of its immediate predecessor, the George W. Bush administration has in fact worked more with multilateral organizations and with key partners in managing crises in Israel–Palestine, Afghanistan, and Iraq. Yet there are a number of real problems in the administration's Middle East policy: the limitations on American engagement in the Israeli–Palestinian conflict; the administration's conception of the role of U.S. power in stimulating domestic and democratic reform in the Arab world, evidence for which is greater than the administration's opponents would concede but is less than portrayed; the confusing messages from Washington about the uses of U.S. power; and many elements of the Iraq policy. But the pros or the cons of the policy lie not in whether the approach is unilateral or multilateral, for the form of engagement does not particularly shape the nature of policy. Criticisms of the administration's unilateralism often elide the real problems of policy.

This chapter explores the multilateral component of U.S. foreign policy in the Middle East. To set the stage for discussion, it briefly reviews the concept of multilateralism as a tactical rather than ethical concept. It then focuses on the Israeli–Palestinian conflict, comparing and contrasting in more detail the approaches of the Clinton and current Bush administrations. It then looks briefly at the relationship between U.S. power and multilateral instruments, particularly the U.N., in the context of the war in Afghanistan and in the debate that preceded the start of war with Iraq.

This chapter concludes with an initial assessment of the impact of recent U.S. foreign policy decisions on the Middle East and on the multilateral instruments themselves. In some areas, Bush's Middle East policy has strengthened the hand of multilateral actors, in others weakened it. In between, the multilateral actors—the organizations themselves, and their key state backers—have inflicted some major wounds on themselves. The combination has clearly weakened the U.N., the North Atlantic Treaty Organization (NATO), and the European Union (E.U.), but probably less than has been claimed. Meanwhile, the impact of U.S. policy on the lives of citizens in the Middle East and the security of their states may be profound.

Multilateralism as a tactical concept

The period between the terrorist attacks on the United States on September 11, 2001 and the end of the U.S. war to overthrow Iraqi President Saddam Hussein saw an intense doctrinal debate in and around the U.S. administration about the nature and use of its power. The central questions are: to what extent should the U.S. use its overwhelming military power to project U.S. ideals and objectives overseas, especially democratic ideals (the so-called William Kristol/ Paul Wolfowitz doctrine)? Should the U.S. use its capacities to pre-empt potential attacks against its soil from rogue regimes, terrorist groups, or the potential nexus between them (the so-called Condoleezza Rice doctrine)? And should the U.S. military be deployed only in formations of overwhelming force (the so-called Colin Powell doctrine) or in more lean, more flexible—and therefore more readily and more frequently deployable—formations (the so-called Donald Rumsfeld doctrine)? A secondary debate is whether, or under what circumstances and to what extent, to work in coalitions of the willing or through multilateral institutions such as NATO and the U.N.

Outside the administration, and particularly in Europe, this secondary debate has been primary. The reason for the difference in relative order between U.S. approaches to the multilateral/unilateral mixture and the European/Russian approach is obvious: so long as the U.S. decides to work in a multilateral framework, rather than primarily in a unilateral one, Europeans and Russians (and others beyond) will have a voice in the "where," "when," and "how" of U.S. power projection. Thus winning the debate over process and form is critical to remaining part of the deeper discussion about U.S. power—the central ingredient, by common consent, in international order or disorder.

The European emphasis on multilateralism for its own sake has its corollary in a growing chorus of American voices (more outside the administration than in it) stressing the importance of unilateralism for its own sake. In this conception of U.S. power—voiced primarily by such figures as William Kristol and Richard Perle and principally associated with conservative think tanks like the American Enterprise Institute and the Hoover Institution and "do tanks" like the Lexington Institute—unilateralism has a value in its own right as a means of demonstrating the scale of U.S. power. Even if multilateral instruments such as the U.N. and NATO are disposed to assist the U.S. in achieving its foreign policy objectives, their assistance could be seen as detrimental. Only the unvarnished projection of U.S. power has the necessary potential demonstration effect to scare "rogue" actors into altering their behavior.

In U.S. foreign policy in the Middle East (and more broadly toward the Arab and Islamic worlds), neither the ethical multilateralism of the Europeans nor the ideological unilateralism of the American Enterprise Institute has been in evidence. Rather, the record suggests a "tactical multilateralism." With some exceptions, the record is one of use of multilateral instruments when they help achieve U.S. goals, tolerance for multilateral approaches where they do not impede U.S. objectives, and avoidance of multilateral institutions when they threaten to constrain U.S. policy. As Stewart Patrick, International Affairs Fellow of the Council on Foreign Relations, has put it: "The question of whether U.S. interests are best served by going it alone or with others has no general answer: it depends on the issue and the stakes, the policies of others, and the feasibility of collective action."[3]

Patrick's analysis of U.S. interests and multilateralism provides the conceptual framework for this chapter. In recent essays and through a two-volume edited collection of papers on multilateralism and unilateralism, he has articulated a conception of multilateralism grounded in an analysis of U.S. interests. He has reviewed the ethical and moral arguments made in favor of and against multilateralism and concluded that "discussion of these questions has been more polemical than analytical." As he notes, "Each side has claimed the moral high ground, bundling distinct normative assertions into rival prudential arguments while failing to acknowledge the principled nature of the opposition's arguments."[4] Moreover, he notes that both sides tend to associate the multilateral/unilateral debate with distinct conceptions of the content of alternative policies (in his discussion, Patrick uses "strategies" in the way that I use "tactics," as means to an end, as distinct from the end itself):

> Liberals tend to link multilateral strategies with internationalist or cosmopolitan aims, unilateral strategies with nationalist ones. Typically, they also accord multilateralism greater normative value, considering unilateralism prima facie morally suspect and bemoaning departures from collective action.
>
> In fact, the relationship between aims and strategies is not so straightforward. A state may act alone to advance cosmopolitan goals, for instance, just as it may exploit cooperation for narrow national objectives. Likewise, the ethical status of unilateralism cannot be judged without additional information about the nature of the foreign policy challenge, the aims being pursued, and the prospects for collective action.[5]

The multilateral/unilateral issue thus arises in U.S. foreign policy decision-making as a question of tactical options. For example, the administration did not go to the U.N. to deliberate whether or not disarmament of Iraq was among its goals, nor even as a means of deciding whether war, the threat of war, or some alternative like inspections was the appropriate strategy for disarming Iraq. Rather, the U.S. had essentially decided to go to war with Iraq prior to going to the U.N., and took a *tactical* decision that collective authorization would enhance legitimacy of U.S. actions and thus facilitate their implementation.

The Clinton era: engaged unilateralism

President William J. Clinton's deep engagement in the Middle East peace process had its roots in that of his predecessor, President George H.W. Bush, whose foreign policy team took advantage of the turbulence that followed the 1991 Gulf war to launch a new political initiative vis-à-vis Israel and its Arab neighbors. The Madrid process launched in 1992 officially had two co-sponsors, the U.S. and the Soviet Union, but in practice U.S. Secretary of State James Baker was its main facilitator.[6] The terms of reference for the Madrid summit stipulated that negotiations, though held in what amounted to a bilateral format, were to be based on a key multilateral agreement, namely Security Council Resolution 242. The U.N. itself was not a participant at the talks, the Secretary-General being invited only to observe the proceedings, along with the European Union. This exclusion of the U.N. was predicated on a specific agreement on the subject between Israel and the U.S.

The election of Bill Clinton in 1992 brought a hiatus to presidential peace-making activity in the Middle East. As the Brookings Institution scholar William Quandt has noted, a recurrent phenomenon that bedevils Middle East peace efforts is the tendency for incoming presidents to break with their predecessor's policy, and to take a pause before eventually being drawn into Arab–Israeli negotiations. But after a long initial hiatus, the Clinton era was characterized by a steady deepening of engagement up until 2000 when it became commonplace in Middle East policy circles to refer to President Clinton as the "Middle East desk officer."[7] The creation of a "peace team," led throughout the period by U.S. Special Middle East Coordinator Dennis Ross (who also had served under the first President Bush), to engage in virtually full-time Arab–Israeli negotiations, represented a significant commitment to reaching a breakthrough.

However, Clinton's policy was characterized also by a strong insistence on U.S. leadership, and at best a fluctuating engagement with allies and multilateral institutions. For the most part, U.S. policy in the period, actively supported by Israel, was to keep any third party actor other than the U.S. out of any negotiations. Of course, the first major political breakthrough of the era, the Oslo Accords, occurred under Norwegian sponsorship and with no U.S. involvement. So important was U.S. backing to those Accords, however, that the decision was taken by the Norwegian sponsors of the deal to ask the U.S. President to host the signing ceremony at the White House—a meeting that resulted in the now famous handshake between Israeli President Yitzhak Rabin and PLO Chairman Yasser Arafat.[8]

Notwithstanding the Norwegian role in Oslo, in the formal negotiating sessions that occurred during the 1990s, from Sharm el-Sheikh to the Hebron Agreements to Wye River to Camp David in July 2000, participation was strictly trilateral: U.S., Israeli, Palestinian. A variety of countries, including Canada and Sweden, hosted informal talks between Israelis and Palestinians but were never brought into formal negotiations. Formal negotiations during the Clinton period followed the Carter–Kissinger formula: U.S. leadership, advance consultations between the U.S. and Israel, and trilateral negotiations. At no stage of formal negotiations on final status issues did the U.S. deviate from this pattern.[9]

At times the U.N., the European Union (E.U.), and regional states (particularly Jordan and Egypt) played more active roles in coordination with U.S. efforts. Three episodes illustrate this: Israel's withdrawal from southern Lebanon, which was partially orchestrated, actively monitored, and formally certified by the U.N.; negotiations over the final status of the Temple Mount, after Camp David II, during which Israeli Prime Minister Barak requested

U.N. engagement and expressed a willingness to explore U.N. solutions to the Temple Mount question; and the Sharm el-Sheikh Summit in October 2000, a summit designed to secure a halt in violence (which broke out in late September 2000), which brought together President Clinton, President Hosni Mubarak of Egypt, King Hussein of Jordan, E.U. High Representative Javier Solana and Barak and Arafat, all at the initiative, and with the active participation, of the U.N. Secretary-General.

However, in the final status negotiations that followed the Sharm el-Sheikh episode, the Clinton administration once again returned to the trilateral format. Trilateral consultations were held in the period October–December 2000, and were used to prepare a series of peace proposals. Those proposals were then launched by President Clinton alone in December 2000. The mode was illustrative: Clinton called Barak and Arafat in sequence to Washington and in a closed setting read to them his proposals. No international consultations preceded or accompanied the launch of the proposals.

This chapter is not the appropriate place for a full account of the negotiations that surrounded the Clinton proposals.[10] However, it is worth mentioning an argument made at the time in Middle East peace process circles, and subsequently by members of the administration, that Clinton made a *tactical* error in not mobilizing a multilateral coalition, especially vis-à-vis Arafat.[11] Arafat's pattern of decision-making shows that he is more likely to act when confronted with a broad international coalition than when asked to make decisions solely with Americans. (This argument is developed below.) It is at least arguable that had Clinton mobilized President Mubarak, the Saudis, the E.U., the U.N. Secretary-General, and others to join him in a public, coordinated approach, Arafat's "wiggle room" would have been significantly reduced. This might have led to a firmer public acceptance of the Clinton proposals, establishing them as a basis for future negotiations. Whether this would have been a good outcome or a bad one depends on one's perspective on the various possibilities for final status arrangements. However, many international negotiators, including many current U.S. negotiators, believe that the Clinton parameters articulated the essential trade-offs and agreements that will ultimately guide a final status agreement between Israel and the Palestinians.[12]

The Bush policy: multilateral disengagement

If Clinton's policy thus was unilateral in its leadership style but inclusive in content, President George W. Bush's approach has been the opposite. Without question, the Bush administration's Middle East policy has been more multilateral in its form than his predecessor's. At the same time, major elements of his policy have not initially been accepted by other international actors. What is notable is that the adoption of a quasi-multilateral format (or at least, the willingness to engage in sustained consultations with key partners) has greatly muted public discord with the Bush policy, regardless of private disagreement— in sharp contrast to recent experience vis-à-vis Iraq.

The use of multilateral forums or consultative instruments by the Bush administration has two main dimensions: first, engagement with what has become known as "the Quartet," a consultative forum within which the U.S., the U.N., the E.U., and Russia have coordinated their policies on the Middle East peace process; and second, the decision to use the U.N. as a forum to announce a major policy shift, that of U.S. support for the establishment of a state of Palestine. These decisions appear to stem from two sources: an active decision to try to shift the center of Middle East gravity away from the Palestinian issue and toward Iraq; and the need, in the context of building support for a campaign against Saddam Hussein, to quell Arab dissatisfaction with that approach. It also constitutes a recognition, argued by Colin Powell but clearly accepted at least in part by others within the administration, that by using the Quartet and the U.N. the U.S. can both build support for its policy objectives and contain dissent against them.

The roots of the Quartet lie not with a U.S. decision, but rather with a series of collective demarches to Arafat comprising the U.N. special coordinator, the U.S. consul-general in Jerusalem, the E.U.'s special representative for the Middle East, and the Russian special envoy for the Middle East. Together, they met with Arafat and demanded that he take a series of steps to arrest persons involved in the assassination of Israeli cabinet minister Rehavem Ze'evi, outlaw the military wings of a series of organizations involved in terrorism, and declare a ceasefire and a renunciation of terrorism.[13] Following a series of consultations, the four issued a joint demarche stipulating these demands. Enough of them were implemented to create a perception of progress. The Israelis, while clearly seeing that Arafat had not made a strategic decision to renounce terror, did acknowledge that the collective pressure placed on Arafat by the Quartet had resulted in more action than he had previously taken under either Israeli or U.S. pressure.[14] While remaining deeply skeptical about the value of Arafat's promises and actions, the Israelis agreed to engage the Quartet, which subsequently issued a statement outlining requirements for Israel, and met with senior Israeli ministers and representatives of the Prime Minister. In subsequent months, the Quartet's activity expanded in scope, and grew to involve not only the four special envoys on the ground but also their principals, who met in New York, Madrid, and Washington to coordinate their overall approach to the crisis.[15]

The acceptance of the Quartet's role inside the Bush administration was mixed. The Quartet became associated with Powell. Opponents lobbied not only against the content of the Quartet's statements and actions but also against the existence of the body itself, arguing that it violated the central tenet of the doctrine of U.S.–Israeli coordination prior to the adoption of any negotiating position. Particularly in the context of the U.S.-led war on terrorism, any watering down of this doctrine was seen by some in Washington as injurious to U.S. interests in the region.[16]

Nonetheless, the Quartet expanded its scope, engaging in negotiations on final status issues, or at least on the method for reaching agreement on them—

developing a so-called "Road Map" for a restoration of dialogue, the conclusion of a final status agreement, and the establishment of a Palestinian state within three years. Though publication of this Road Map was repeatedly delayed by the President, in large part on the basis of Israeli concerns, in Aqaba in June 2003 Bush made a significant personal foray into the Middle East peace process. In orchestrating a meeting of Prime Minister Sharon and newly appointed Palestinian Prime Minister Mohamed Abbas (also known as Abu Mazen), Bush scripted and extracted important stated concessions from both leaders that were in line with both U.N. positions and Clinton's parameters (though neither were mentioned).

The consultative or multilateral dimension of the Bush policy was also present in the administration's decision to go to the U.N. to announce, in November 2001, a significant shift in its policy framework for the Middle East, namely acceptance of the goal of the establishment of a State of Palestine alongside the State of Israel as a central goal of U.S. policy in the Middle East.[17] This goal was subsequently enshrined in Security Council Resolution 1397, drafted and introduced by the U.S.[18] It is the implementation of these goals, albeit not quite in the sequence Bush suggested, that is the content of the Quartet's Road Map.

There have been disagreements between the U.S. and the other Quartet members, as well as with its key Arab partners (in this context the Egyptians, Jordanians, and Saudis). They disagreed on the sequence of steps to be taken in the Road Map, and about the *tactical* merits of publicly calling for Arafat's removal from power. This disagreement has been taken by some as constituting support among Quartet members for Arafat's continued role, but this is a misunderstanding. Rather, the concern among some European and Arab diplomats was that indigenous Palestinian reform efforts have been undermined, not reinforced, by U.S. calls for Arafat's ouster. Evidence for this argument can be seen in the shift in Arab rhetoric before and after the June 24, 2002 Midde East speech given by Bush, which called for Arafat's ouster. Prior to Bush's speech, key Arab leaders such as Mubarak were speaking openly about their disappointment in Arafat and their belief that he was an obstacle to progress. Afterwards, there has been virtual silence on the subject, even from those leaders who most virulently oppose his continuing role. At least one effect in the Middle East of strong U.S. positions taken in a unilateral format is actually to undermine public support for those very policy goals, by compelling Arab leaders to appear to be acting in support of U.S., rather than Arab, interests. However, recent progress on the reform agenda, in particular the creation of a post of prime minister and the appointment to that post of Abu Mazen, can be seen as an important instance of reconciliation of these differences: the diplomacy pushing Arafat to accept the prime minister position was led by the Quartet, while the U.S.—at least in principle—accepted that this appointment constitutes a de facto lessening of Arafat's power sufficient to constitute fulfillment of the objectives set out in Bush's June speech.

Thus it is fair to say that the Bush administration has far more actively engaged both partners and multilateral institutions, particularly the U.N. and the E.U., than did the Clinton administration. In the period prior to the Aqaba summit, the lack of Bush's engagement contributed to the inability of diplomatic activity to displace the continuing terrorism and violence. But again, there is an important separation between the content of U.S. foreign policy in the Middle East and the tactical question of its form—unilateral, multilateral, or a varying mix of the two, depending on objectives.

Of course, Bush's acceptance of a Quartet role in shaping negotiations, his consultations with allies, his close cooperation with Arab regional actors, and his speeches at the U.N. do not constitute a formal multilateralism of the kind sometimes advocated by critics of U.S. policy. In the Middle East peacemaking process, the U.N. is a junior if active partner, rather than the main forum or the principal actor. But then, it rarely has been. In the 1940s, 1960s, and again in the 1970s the U.N. Secretary-General appointed political mediators to the Arab–Israeli theatre, with Security Council backing. But in the wake of the U.S.–Israel–Egypt peace deal brokered by Jimmy Carter at Camp David, and Arab reaction to that peace (including blocking an agreed U.N. peacekeeping force to monitor the settlement), the U.N.'s role in peacemaking in the Middle East faltered.[19] Only recently has the U.N. Secretary-General regained a substantive role in negotiations.

Moreover, the Quartet as a multilateral format is significant. The participation of the E.U.'s High Representative for Common Foreign and Security Policy means that, at least in principle, the entire European Union is engaged. The Quartet's consultations with Jordan, Egypt, and Saudi Arabia (three of the states nominated by the Arab League to follow up on the Saudi peace plan promulgated in April 2001) mean that through it the U.S. is consulting not just bilaterally with Arab partners but with a grouping of Arab states that represent a common Arab position. And the participation of the Secretary-General is significant not only for his personal contribution but also for the symbolic presence of the United Nations and a connection and commitment to the core Security Council resolutions on the Middle East. He routinely briefs the Council on Quartet activities, and the Council has repeatedly endorsed both his role and the Quartet's existence and activity. Thus, if not a formal multilateral instrument per se, it nevertheless represents a significant effort in consultation with European and Arab states, and to a certain extent with the Council and the broader U.N. community. The Bush administration's multilateralism on Middle East issues may be tactical rather than formal, but it is nevertheless extensive.

Multilateral action and reaction: wars in Afghanistan and Iraq

A tactical use of multilateral instruments is also in evidence in U.S. diplomacy leading up to the war in Afghanistan, and during that war, and in the lead-up to the war in Iraq. In the case of the war with Afghanistan, it is abundantly clear that U.S. policy objectives—namely the surrender of the Al Qaeda leadership to the U.S. by the Taliban regime or the simultaneous destruction of that regime and the Al Qaeda operation in Afghanistan—were set by Washington, alone, in the immediate aftermath of the September 2001 attacks on Washington and New York. That those goals attracted broad international support in the context of the terrorist attacks, underscored by the rapid passage of Security Council Resolution 1337, and NATO's decision to invoke Article 5 of its charter, meant that there was a welcoming international framework within which the U.S. could work to achieve its objectives.

U.S. action inside Afghanistan, moreover, followed a growing pattern in the 1990s of managing peace enforcement missions, that of U.N. authorization for multinational coalitions of the willing rather than direct U.N. operations. Similar methods had been used in Haiti, eastern Zaire, and East Timor. The U.N.'s main direct involvement came in the form of U.N. Special Envoy Lakdhar Brahimi's role, in very close coordination with U.S. Ambassador Richard Haass and U.S. Special Envoy Zalmay Khalizad, in orchestrating the Bonn Agreements and subsequently in mounting the U.N. Assistance Mission in Afghanistan (UNAMA) in support of the Afghan Transitional Authority (ATA).

There is no space in this chapter to examine U.S. policy in Afghanistan. But in terms of the broad argument, two points are important. First, the roles played by the U.N.—in authorizing U.S. action, in the person of Brahimi, and in mounting UNAMA—were actively supported by the U.S. as in its interests and were conducted in close coordination with U.S. policy-makers. Second, the fact that U.S. policy objectives received broad international support meant that this first exercise in the projection of U.S. power in the "war on terrorism" did not directly, or at first glance, challenge international order and the multilateral mechanisms designed to secure it. But the fact that the U.S. opted to go through the U.N. en route to Kabul in no way suggests that U.N. decision-making shaped the U.S. response. As a senior U.S. congressman put it at a meeting organized by the Lexington Institute, "if the U.N. had resisted the U.S. war in Afghanistan, there would have been 100 votes in the Senate to abrogate the San Francisco Treaty."[20]

Strikingly, the Iraq question has elicited not only the current Bush administration's deepest engagement of the world organization and of allies, but also the most troubling policies. When President Bush went to the United Nations in October 2002 to seek a new resolution on the disarmament of Iraq, he used the occasion to stress the U.S. commitment to the U.N. His mission, he argued, was to ensure that Security Council resolutions were enforced, and his desire, he claimed, was to see a strong and effective world organization. His approach was thus couched not in instrumental or tactical but in ethical terms. When the U.S. indicated that it might abandon efforts to secure a second resolution on Iraq in March 2003, the response by Russia and the key European governments was also couched in ethical and legal terms. Only the U.N., it was stressed, has the ethical or legal right to sanction war. U.S. action outside of the U.N. would be illegal, and would not enjoy the support of the French and German governments in particular.

Between October and March, the November Security Council Resolution

1441 constituted both a significant diplomatic victory for the U.S., and a significant development in terms of international law and norms with relation to weapons of mass destruction (WMD). This resolution marked the first time that an individual state, regardless of its membership status in relevant U.N. conventions and treaty bodies, has been barred under international law from possession of certain categories of weapons and weapons systems. The deployment of the United Nations Monitoring, Verification and Inspection Commission (UNMOVIC) may also be seen as an important development in institutional capacity to deal with disarmament.

Both the U.S. and the European presentations of position, however, were exaggerated. While Bush may have stated that he was committed to seeing strong U.N. action in Iraq, his policy objectives were neither set in a context of U.N. deliberations nor based on U.N. norms and law. Rather, they were set unilaterally on the basis of U.S. interests. The decision to go to the U.N. was apparently based on an assessment by Powell and others that it would be possible to get a strong resolution in support of U.S. policy objectives, which would enhance their legitimacy in the Arab and Muslim worlds where potentially allied governments such as Jordan, Saudi Arabia, and Turkey would have an easier time with their domestic constituents. In other words, the U.S. made a tactical move at the international level to help potential allies in their internal tactics. The broad declarations of ethical support for the U.N. were hardly credible, given that they had been preceded by months of public rhetoric about a probable U.S. war on Iraq and the irrelevance of U.N. authorization.

But scarcely more credible were Russian and European objections to the U.S. approach, which should be viewed in the context of their own tactical approach to the U.N. In the 1990s France on several occasions deployed forces in Africa without seeking the authorization of the U.N., though in some cases—such as in eastern Zaire—the Security Council acted as French troops were in motion to "authorize" those deployments.[21] Moreover, France has been instrumental in keeping Algeria, a major human rights crisis, off the U.N.'s agenda throughout the 1990s, preferring to maintain its own, unilateral role in handling that crisis. Russia has not only insisted on keeping the Chechnya question off the Security Council's agenda, and has in its response to Chechnya clearly violated U.N. human rights law and international humanitarian law, but has also in past instances deployed forces without U.N. authorization. Germany's objection to the deployment of force outside the context of U.N. authorization is consistent with its Constitution, but its objections to the Iraq policy would have been more compelling had they not been forged with clear electoral objectives in mind. Moreover, Germany has on important occasions acted unilaterally, though not necessarily illegally, in support of its own interests and against those of the multilateral forums it claims to support—for example in unilaterally recognizing Croatia, in defiance of the European Union. Outside the Security Council, the objections of such countries as Turkey were equally suspect, given that government's (if not the full parliament's) willingness to support U.S. action in exchange for financial and political incentives. In short, all those countries that critiqued Bush's unilateralism have also displayed, on issues that raise key national interests, precisely the same tactical relationship to the United Nations. Moreover, their vote to endorse the U.S. occupation, after a war they opposed, was seen by many in the U.N. as firm evidence of their hypocritical relationship to the world body.

Implications of U.S. policy on the Middle East and multilateral institutions

This chapter has probed U.S. foreign policy since September 11, but it has done so in a longer historical and comparative context. Two key questions now can be answered. Has this false debate over Iraq policy damaged the U.N. or the broader multilateral order? Has U.S. policy in the Middle East and, in particular, the absence of U.N. authorization for military action in Iraq increased or decreased potential stability in the region or otherwise affected the Middle East?

Effect on the Middle East

It is of course far too early to say what the medium- and long-term effects will be on the lives of the citizens of the Middle East, on their governments, and perhaps particularly on the relationships between the two. Indeed, in each aspect of U.S. policy, there is an equally strong case for sharply divergent judgments about its impact.

This is true of what must be seen as a core interest of U.S. policy in the region, namely Israeli security.[22] Factors potentially increasing Israeli security in the region include the removal of the Saddam Hussein regime in Iraq. Even if postwar Iraq is unstable and becomes a source of internal conflict, perhaps even drawing in regional actors, there is no prima facie reason to believe that this decreases Israeli security. Arguably, the opposite case could be made because regional competition over control of Iraq and its resources could develop in unpredictable ways, some of which are consistent with long-term Israeli security. Yet there are at least two factors potentially undermining Israeli security. First, the rise in anti-U.S. sentiment in the Middle East, connected as it is through the U.S.–Israeli relationship to anti-Israeli sentiment, is potentially damaging. A second factor is the potential for a weakening of Israel-friendly Arab regimes (particularly Jordan) as a result of the growing divergence between public attitudes to the Iraqi and Palestinian issues and those governments' stances. A third factor—according to some Israeli security analysts, the most important[23]—is a possible beginning of an erosion of the public basis for a long-standing, and vital, Israel–Turkey strategic alliance. The gulf between Turkey's military, its government, and its population on the Iraq issue may have the effect over the medium or long term of narrowing popular tolerance or support for Turkey's continued strategic alliance with Israel. U.S. actions in Iraq also create simultaneously a growing risk of further confrontations with Syria and Iran, as well as the possibility that those states will perceive that risk and seek to avoid direct confrontation either with the U.S. or with Israel. For example, fears that Iran would use the conflict in Iraq to activate the Iranian-backed segments of Hezbollah inside Lebanon have so far proved overstated, though tensions between the U.S. and Iran have been rising since the end of the war and exchanges of fire between Israel and Hezbollah along the Israel–Lebanon boundary resumed in August 2003 after a hiatus of almost a year.[24]

A second problematic area is the potential for a peace agreement between Israelis and Palestinians. On the one hand, U.S. actions in Iraq can be taken as a significant policy victory for those voices within the administration (military hawks, Middle East hawks, and the pro-Likud faction of the Israel lobby) that sought to de-emphasize the Palestinian question and focus U.S. attention on Iraq and Iran. Against those who argued that U.S. actions in Iraq were likely to lead to renewed U.S. engagement on the Israeli–Palestinian front, some U.S. administration officials stressed that there was no basis for this assumption.[25] However, President Bush's personal engagement in bringing Sharon and Abu Mazen together in Aqaba, and his repeated statements about his personal commitment to sustained involvement, seemed to herald a new level of U.S. commitment to managing the Israeli–Palestinian conflict. Part of the conception among those supporting a new push on the Palestinian issue after the Iraq war is that the toppling of Saddam Hussein's regime has enhanced Israel's security, both by removing a direct enemy and by installing a pro-U.S. regime in the country in the neighborhood of a potential State of Palestine, but also through the "demonstration effect" of the untrammeled and potent use of U.S. power on potential challengers to the United States. However, the durability of Bush's commitment remains to be demonstrated.

A third policy issue concerns the greater promotion of Arab democracy. Within the Palestinian context, the arena in which the policy of promoting democracy in Arab countries has had a short period to play out, the evidence is decidedly mixed. Recent conversations with Fatah activists and Palestinian Authority/Palestine Liberation Organization officials suggest that there is some reason to believe that the U.S. insistence on freezing the peace process until Arafat is removed from power has had the effect of increasing the space available to reformists. Simultaneously, the perceived strong bias in Bush's statements about Sharon ("a man of peace") versus Arafat have constrained those same actors by creating a too-close association in public attitudes between U.S. rhetoric and anti-Arafat sentiment, which remains widespread in Palestinian factions and communities. Further, it seems clear that a side effect of the policy has been to strengthen Hamas's bid to lay claim to leadership in the Palestinian national movement. Freezing the peace process made the more moderate tactics of alternative movements, such as the moderate wing of Fatah, seem futile, easing Hamas's path in mobilization and recruitment. More recently, the strong U.S.–Quartet push for Abu Mazen's premiership and for regional support for his peacemaking efforts did not produce internal support for Abu Mazen, whose poll numbers hovered in single digits. The fact that he was publicly identified by the U.S. as an acceptable counterpart actually tarnished his perception among the Palestinian population. At the same time, while not supporting Abu Mazen many Palestinians saw him as useful precisely because Israel and the U.S. approved of him, meaning that Sharon might have been more willing to deliver. Thus U.S. support for Abu Mazen might have been helpful in peace process terms, but was unlikely to contribute significantly to the greater democratization of Palestinian public life.

A fourth area is that of U.S.–Arab/Muslim relations. Here, the initial impact seems unequivocal: the combination of one-sided public rhetoric on the Israeli–Palestinian issue, a hands-off attitude toward the Palestinian crisis, and U.S. policy toward Iraq, against a backdrop of long-standing U.S. support for unpopular regimes in the Middle East (particularly Egypt and Saudi Arabia), has been fueling anti-U.S. sentiment in the region and strengthening the hands of extremist Islamic forces. The mishandling of postwar Iraq has added still more fuel to these simmering fires. Bush's engagement on the Palestinian question, if sustained, may help; some Arab newspapers (particularly those that are government-owned or -influenced) have begun making more positive comments about the United States, following Bush's personal commitments made in Aqaba.[26] While the endorsement of a few, government-edited newspapers is not likely to significantly reshape Arab public opinion, a sustained engagement on the Palestinian question would certainly remove from critics one of the most important arguments against U.S. foreign policy.

Indeed, shifts in U.S. policy are likely to be far more significant in altering Arab popular perceptions than public relations. On this issue, current U.S. policy is arguably operating on a fundamental misconception—namely the "public diplomacy" argument that opposition to the U.S. can be challenged by more information about U.S. policy. This approach seems to elide the fact that Arab newspapers and television stations (whether government-owned or privately operated) provide extensive coverage of U.S. policy statements and actions. Sometimes this is accompanied by critical commentary. But Arab newspapers routinely print the full statements of President Bush and Secretary of State Powell (along with those of European leaders and the U.N. Secretary-General) for their readers, and these statements are often broadcast in full on the main satellite channels. U.S. policy is so out of sync with general Arab attitudes that these statements need no critical commentary to provoke negative reactions in the general public.

Furthermore, it is important to understand the distinction between Arab public opinion about the United States and Arab opinion about U.S. *policy*. Historically, both anecdotal evidence and polling data suggest a wide variation in attitudes between Middle Eastern countries such as Egypt and Jordan (as well as among Palestinians), where attitudes have tended to be positive about U.S. society and negative about U.S. foreign policy, and Muslim countries outside the region like Pakistan where there is a more negative perception of U.S. society as a whole.[27] But this may be changing in the aftermath of the Iraq war. There were, for example, frequent reports during the war of Jordanian youths castigating their parents for using U.S. products—whereas prior to the war U.S. products were very popular among Jordanian youths, even though U.S. policy toward the Palestinians and Iraqis was abhorred. An important first step in devising a sounder long-term policy will be to generate more precise knowledge about the nature of opinion among various Arab and Muslim populations about the U.S., its policies, and in particular the relationship between the U.S. and their own governments.[28]

Over the longer term, it is questionable whether U.S. policy-making, as currently structured, is capable of addressing these issues in a sustained way. The U.S. does have some significant assets, namely a highly competent diplomatic service in the Middle East, which is greatly respected in Arab capitals; a significant Arab-American community which potentially can serve as a bridge between communities; and significant financial resources both to put into its policy and communication efforts and, more importantly, to channel into the economic development of Arab states. Foreign policy, however, is shaped far more by inter-agency interactions in Washington, and by relations between Congress and the administration, than it is by reports from U.S. ambassadors or the advice of public relations officials.

In any case, in the longer term Washington will have to pay increasing attention to the challenge of its relationship with the Arab and Muslim worlds—both the relevant governments, and their populations. Though it is too early to discern the long-term impacts of recent U.S. actions, it is possible to speculate about how to tackle some of the most salient issues.

The backdrop is the identification in U.S. defense policy circles of a so-called "arc of instability" that encompasses the Middle East, the former Soviet republics in the Caucasus, and the predominantly Islamic republics of Central Asia, and stretches across to encompass the Islamic parts of southeast Asia, particularly Indonesia.[29] The National Defense University identified this "arc of instability" as the source of most, if not all, of the major threats. This grand strategy conception of the region may be limited to the analytical community, and may not wholly shape the conceptualization among U.S. decision-makers— who, like all political decision-makers, tend to approach issues more on a crisis-by-crisis basis than in terms of grand strategy. But it suggests a mind-set in parts of Washington, which over the long haul may influence U.S. policy and behavior.

In one sense, the Middle East is like all other parts of the world in that since the end of the Cold War, and in particular since September 11, the pole of gravity around which all foreign policies revolve—and, increasingly, even domestic policies—is the relationship with the United States. (During the long, uncertain period of vote recounting during the 2000 U.S. presidential election, an Arab foreign minister actually asked a U.N. official whether he had any inside information about who would win the recount: "We're tired of waiting to see who will rule us."[30]) In particular, foreign policies are increasingly shaped by the perceived costs of being on the wrong side of U.S. policy as it relates to the "war on terrorism" and the perceived benefits of being an ally. However, many of these same states' domestic policies are caught by precisely the opposite dynamic: the public perception that governments that support U.S. policies are "lap-dogs" or are selling out their own publics. This contradiction was very much in evidence during the build-up to the war in Iraq, and particularly squeezed the moderate Arab governments—who, for foreign policy reasons, tended to want to ally themselves with the U.S., albeit discreetly, but were under major domestic pressure to resist.

In short, the scale and nature of U.S. power is such that—particularly, but not exclusively, in the Middle East—the U.S. is generating its own opposition. Public opposition to the U.S. is squeezing governments, including those with which the U.S. might work toward a democratic transformation. What this suggests is that there will be a growing problem for the U.S. about how it projects its power and its policy. Here, multilateral institutions may over time play a useful role. The nature of political debate in the Middle East is such that even if Arab governments have little choice but to concede to most U.S. demands, the act of concession to those demands is one that diminishes the legitimacy of governments in the eyes of their populations, and generates resistance against both the demand in question and its source. Thus U.S. pressure for greater liberalization or democratic reform in any given Arab country may be resisted by precisely those groups seeking to move forward on a democratic agenda (as witnessed during June 2003 in the case of Iran). At the same time, domestic reaction to the same message transmitted by a multilateral organization, particularly the U.N., will be far more positive and progressive—as occurred in the case of the release of the U.N. Development Program's far-sighted *Arab Human Development Report*.[31] Thus multilateral institutions may be better placed, in the Middle East context, to advance agendas shared by the larger community of states and the U.S. than Washington acting alone.

Effect on multilateral institutions

This raises the question of the relationship between the U.S. and the multilateral instruments for managing world order, and the question of whether the U.N. in particular has been damaged by U.S. policy in the Middle East—as frequently claimed in the aftermath of the launch of the U.S. war in Iraq. It is again too early to say, but some speculation here may also be undertaken.

On the central question of the impact on the United Nations, I would speculate that damage to the Security Council from U.S. actions and attitudes is probably significantly less than has been stated, for five reasons. First, the U.N. has been bypassed by the U.S. before, notably in Kosovo, without causing grievous damage. Second, in the aftermath of the war the members of the Security Council moved rapidly to return to consensus—through the unanimous vote in favor of the U.S. and U.K. resolution on the oil-for-food program in March 2003, and in the 14–0 vote (with Syria absent, but later supporting) in favor of Resolution 1438 which endorsed the U.S. and U.K. occupation forces as the legal, interim authority in Iraq. Third, it is worth paying attention to a noticeable shift in Bush's rhetoric about the U.N., from his early references to the League of Nations and irrelevance should the U.N. not choose to endorse his policy on Iraq, to his Azores speech reference to an effort, after the Iraq war, to reform the U.N. and enhance its effectiveness. This shift suggests that Bush's policy and that of the administration will not be to scrap the U.N. but rather to engage in reform; there is ongoing debate within the administration about what form that reform should take.[32] Fourth, while the U.S. has expressed its deepest anger against the U.N. and against particular states in the Security Council, it has been working precisely with those states on the North Korea issue.[33]

Fifth, I suspect, however, that the question of pre-emption will not really be tested by the Iraq conflict. Although the Bush administration and the Tony Blair administration have both made frequent public statements about the future threat posed by Saddam Hussein, and used this in domestic contexts as a justification for war, in the Security Council and in authorizing documents they have been more careful to cast their actions in terms of enforcing several previous resolutions. In other words, while both cases could be made, there will probably be enough evidence and enough law to cover the war in Iraq within existing Security Council parameters.

The damage to the U.N. must also be viewed in historical context. Damage to the U.N. from the Iraq episode is probably less than claimed because the standard by which it is being judged is absurd. To say that because of Iraq the U.N. will "no longer be central to the management of international security" is to propose that it was; but it has not been. Marginal and largely inactive on security issues during the Cold War, the U.N. in the post-Cold War period has been extremely active on security issues but largely in marginal conflicts. Even during the 1990s, a decade of significant U.N. evolution in terms of peacemaking and peacekeeping policy and roles, the U.S. on at least three occasions authorized unilateral military action with neither reference to nor authorization from the U.N.: in Panama, in Afghanistan, and in the Sudan. U.S. military forces worked outside the framework of U.N. policy and sanctions vis-à-vis Croatia (though using private rather than governmental actors to train and equip the Croatian forces), and managed the North Korea nuclear crisis in 1994 outside the framework of the Non-Proliferation Treaty. The U.S. took NATO into out-of-area operations for the first time, launching military action against Yugoslav forces in Kosovo, without U.N. authorization. Nor was it alone—as noted above, several other actors including Russia, France, and Germany took unilateral actions on key international foreign policy and security issues, as did sub-regional actors such as Nigeria. The ethical merits or broad popularity of some (though far from all) of these actions may create an important political difference between these actions and the war against Iraq, but they do not support a conception of the U.N. as once central to international security.

This chapter was being finalized just after a terrorist attack against U.N. headquarters in Baghdad killed at least 23 U.N. staff members—grievous damage indeed. The attack quickly led for calls for a wider U.N. role in Iraq.

Inside the U.N. itself, however, there was a degree of skepticism, as some believed that the organization had exposed itself to risk by seeking a major political role when there was neither a political nor a principled basis for it to play one.

In short, there is some merit in the skepticism shown by the current Bush administration (and its predecessors) toward the U.N. as a tool for managing the central challenges of international security. While the constantly shifting basis of U.S. policy toward Iraq leaves more than enough room for skepticism about both the motivations and the future agenda of the Bush administration, there is also room for a great deal of skepticism about whether the U.N., as currently configured, can realistically be expected to play a credible role in managing key contemporary threats to international security. Can the U.N. be a credible instrument for managing the proliferation of weapons of mass destruction (WMD)? Can it prevent wars with the potential for use of nuclear weapons in south Asia, on the Korean peninsula, and perhaps beyond? Can it generate real progress on Arab–Israeli conflicts? Can it combat terrorism? Can it protect civilians and the human rights of oppressed communities? If the answer is "yes" to any of these questions, then it must surely be on the basis of a deep and sustained reform at least an order of magnitude greater than anything that occurred in the 1990s.[34]

Under current international political realities, the only possible source for a deep reform is a U.S. government acting on the basis of a credible policy, in collaboration with allies.[35] Recent statements by European and other leaders that the U.N. must exist as a universal instrument for challenging U.S. power can only be described as romantic and injurious to the survival of the U.N. The idea that a single superpower would continue to support either politically or financially a body whose central function would be to limit its power has no basis in either history or theory.

The key question becomes, is there an agenda for real reform of the U.N. and related multilateral security instruments that meets both key U.S. security interests and a broad enough conception of legitimacy to sustain international engagement and commitments? This remains to be seen as does the content of Bush's intention to help the U.N. "get its legs, legs of responsibility, back."[36] But the basis for real reform must have two elements. First, a more realistic stance on the limits of the U.N. on the part of those allies and the pro-U.N. community, and a willingness in that community to make real commitments to credible, enforceable multilateral regimes for containing and preventing the spread and use of WMD and of terrorism, as well as commitments to managing other security threats. Second, a more consistent stance by the Bush administration will be necessary on the key question of the basis on which U.S. power and force will be used, and a willingness to work with key allies to develop a legal and institutional framework on that issue. Realism on both fronts will be necessary; straw men and blind men have nothing to add.

Notes

1 During the period 2000–2, the author served as Chief of Staff to the U.N. Special Coordinator for the Middle East Peace Process. However, the views expressed in this paper are those of the author alone and do not necessarily reflect U.N. attitudes or policy.

2 John Van Oudenaren, "What is 'Multilateral'?" *Policy Review* no. 117 (February–March 2003), pp. 33–47 at p. 33.

3 Stewart Patrick, "Beyond Coalitions of the Willing: Assessing U.S. Multilateralism," *Ethics and International Affairs* 17, no. 1 (2003), pp. 37–54 at p. 37; and Stewart Patrick and Shepard Forman, eds., *Multilateralism and U.S. Foreign Policy: Ambivalent Engagement* (Boulder, CO: Lynne Rienner, 2002), pp. 27–44. See also David M. Malone and Yuen Foong Khong, *Unilateralism and U.S. Foreign Policy: International Perspectives* (Boulder, CO: Lynne Rienner, 2003).

4 Patrick, "Beyond Coalitions," p. 38.

5 Ibid., p. 40.

6 A comprehensive history is found in William B. Quandt, *Peace Process: U.S. Diplomacy and the Arab–Israeli Conflict since 1967*, revised edition (Washington: Brookings Institution Press, 2001).

7 Author's notes, Gaza/Jerusalem, November 2000.

8 Interview with Norwegian officials; author's notes, Gaza/Jerusalem November 2000.

9 On Kissinger's thinking about the U.S.–Israeli relationship and its role in U.S.–Arab relations, see Quandt, *Peace Process*, pp. 183–8.

10 For a recent critique of the Taba talks and their success or failure, see David Makovsky, "Taba Mythchief," *The National Interest*, no. 71 (Spring 2003), pp. 119–29.

11 See Hussein Agha and Rob Malley, "Camp David: The Tragedy of Errors," *New York Review of Books*, August 9, 2001, pp. 59–65. Also see Denny Morris interview with Ehud Barak, *New York Review of Books*, June 13, 2002, http://www.nybooks.com/articles/15501; and Agha and Malley's response, *New York Review of Books*, June 13, 2002, http://www.nybooks.com/articles/14380.

12 For a contrasting view, see Makovsky, "Taba Mythchief," pp. 119–29.

13 Author's notes, Gaza/Tel Aviv/Ramallah/Jerusalem, October–November 2001.

14 Author's notes, Tel Aviv, October 2001.

15 Statements by the Quartet from these meetings are available at http://www.state.gov/p/nea.

16 For a recent article expressing strong concern about the Quartet's role and its Road Map, see Mort Zuckerman, "A Road Map to Nowhere," *U.S. News and World Report*, March 17, 2003, pp. 55–6.

17 http://www.whitehouse.gov/news/releases/2001/11/20011110-3.html.

18 http://ods-dds-ny.un.org/doc/UNDOC/GEN/N02/283/59/PDF/N0228359.pdf.

19 For an account of U.N.–Israel relations prior to the 1990s, see Brian Urquhart, "The United Nations in the Middle East: A 50-Year Retrospective," *Middle East Journal* 49, no. 4 (Autumn 1995), pp. 572–81.

20 Author notes, U.S. Army/Lexington Institute conference on U.S. National Security Objectives for the Twenty-First Century, Washington, D.C., November 2002.

21 Some U.N. officials are in fact concerned about the implications of France's "inside/outside" role vis-à-vis U.N. peacekeeping, whereby French troops have with increasing frequency been deployed to African contexts (most recently Côte d'Ivoire) in ways that reinforce U.N. objectives, but outside the framework of U.N. authorization. Correspondence, U.N. officials, June 2003.

22 This section is based in part on author interviews with Israeli security analysts, all of them current or former senior officials of the Israeli Defense Forces.

23 Author interview, former Israeli officials of the Prime Minister's office and the IDF planning services, New York and Washington, D.C., November 2002.

24 See Roula Khalaf and Guy Dinmore, "U.N. Nuclear Body Raises Iran Concern," *Financial Times*, June 6, 2003.
25 Author's conversations with U.S. officials, State Department and National Security Council, March 2003. Also statements by senior U.S. officials in closed sessions, Washington, March 2003.
26 Susan Sachs, "Bush's Commitment to Mideast Peace Plan Gives Rise to Optimism in the Arab World," *New York Times*, June 8, 2003, p. 8.
27 For an account of public opinion in various Arab countries, see in particular "What Arabs Think: Values, Beliefs and Concerns—Landmark Study of Arab Values and Political Concerns. The Views of 3,800 Arab Adults Polled by Zogby International," http://www.zogby.com, October 4, 2002.
28 Among the more important are the programs on U.S.–Arab relations at Brookings Institution's Saban Center, and the Council on Foreign Relations' program on U.S. relations with women in the Islamic world.
29 Author notes, U.S. Army/Lexington Institute conference.
30 Author's field notes, January 2001.
31 United Nations Development Program, *Arab Human Development Report* (New York: UNDP, 2002).
32 For an account of more radical views among intellectuals close to (but not in) the administration, see James Traub, "The Next Resolution," *New York Times Magazine*, April 13, 2003, p. 50.
33 There is a certain irony in that the U.S. official tasked with threatening North Korea—to use his word—with U.N. Security Council action is none other than Assistant Secretary of State for Arms Control John Bolton, infamous for having walked away from the Biological Weapons Convention review conference.
34 A clear statement of this position to date can be found in Edward Luck, "Making the World Safe for Hypocrisy," *New York Times*, March 22, 2003, p. A11.
35 Here, Poland's recent initiative to assess the appetite among member states for a revision to the U.N. Charter takes on a more interesting light in view of its role as part of the military force currently deployed in Iraq.
36 The full sentence quotation reads: "And we hope tomorrow the U.N. will do its job. If not, all of us need to step back and try to figure out how to make the U.N. work better as we head into the twenty-first century. Perhaps one way will be, if we use military force, in the post-Saddam Iraq the U.N. will definitely need to have a role. And that way it can begin to get its legs, legs of responsibility back." President Bush, Azores, March 16, 2003, http://www.whitehouse.gov/news/releases.

Conclusion

Whither human rights, unilateralism, and U.S. foreign policy?

Thomas G. Weiss, Margaret E. Crahan, and John Goering

For more than three centuries, the concept of state sovereignty has been continuously refined, debated, and redefined from its origins in the Westphalian era. The Congress of Vienna, the League of Nations and the creation of the United Nations in 1945 each marked critical, yet partial and imperfect, turning points in the re-conceptualization of the sovereign authority and obligations of states.[1] This uneven, even fitful, evolution continues into the present. From the perspective of this volume, constrained sovereignty is an outcome of the human rights "revolution"—symbolically begun with the signing of the Universal Declaration of Human Rights in 1948.[2] Although Stephen Krasner argues that it has always been "organized hypocrisy,"[3] most U.N. member states and their governmental representatives accept, with varying degrees of institutionalized commitment, contemporary definitions of and limits to their own state's sovereignty on behalf of a rights regime negotiated on numerous occasions under United Nations auspices. Hence a significant change over the life of the world organization has been that an increasing number of its 191 member states agree that state sovereignty can be legitimately circumscribed in order both to ensure international peace and security and to help eliminate gross violations of human rights. In short, as the authors in this collection attest, there has been a gradual ascendancy in the importance of human rights as a factor in world politics.

This evolution was prompted in large measure by the shattering historical traumas of the Thirty Years' War and the Napoleonic wars together with the twentieth century's equivalents in World Wars I and II. With the increasing incidence of civil, as opposed to inter-state, war in the contemporary era, there have been major developments in terms of humanitarian intervention that have increasingly reinforced the principle that state sovereignty encompasses and requires the protection of the basic rights of individuals as defined by the U.N. Charter and other declarations, conventions, and treaties.[4] With each redefinition of the most effective means to concomitantly ensure state sovereignty and the rights of peoples within a country's borders, issues of balance have prominently and even contentiously emerged. The issue of necessary balance includes questions regarding the legal and moral criteria for effective responses by the U.N. or others to gross human rights violations. The role of the United Nations, as the ultimate multilateral ombudsman, has grown with the codification of the re-balancing between rights and state sovereignty. As recent events have shown, however, the world organization's role and even future are not fully guaranteed.

Advances in human rights promotion as well as multilateral cooperation accelerated with the end of the Cold War. Temporarily, at least, we heard numerous euphoric soundings about a "new world order" including from former President George H.W. Bush, ironically on September 11, 1990.[5] Such optimism about the growing role of international law and organizations was dealt a sizeable blow, however, barely a decade later. The severity, meaning, and effects of that "blow" from terrorists constitute the focus of most of the chapters within this collection.

The events of September 11, 2001 focused the attention of the public, policy-makers, and experts on determining, under tragically altered circumstances, the political and policy meaning of the U.N. Charter's affirmation in Article 2 (1), which specifies the "sovereign equality of its Members." This was particularly true given that the attacks were at that point directed at the world's only superpower, whose visceral response was to bring to bear its military, as well as its economic and diplomatic, powers, and to officially commit itself to a permanent war against such terrorism. Indeed, several of the contributors to this book suggest the accuracy of former French Foreign Minister Hubert Védrine's characterization of the United States as the *hyperpuissance*.[6]

Unsurprisingly, the early inclination of the United States—including the bulk of its citizens—was to respond directly and without expending time on extensive multilateral consultations. Nevertheless, the community of states at the United Nations voiced support for self-defense measures in the Security Council and General Assembly in September 2001. And once the authors of the attack were identified, the U.S. worked largely through multilateral channels in pursuing Al Qaeda in their redoubts in Afghanistan, and the Taliban government that harbored them. Since the toppling of the latter, policy-makers have been searching for logical next steps in the war on terrorism.

It is at this juncture that issues of legitimate response to September 11 become more complex. The war on Iraq seemingly became part of the war on terrorism by default, and U.S. action assumed center stage in the debate about the use and relevance of multilateral instruments, including the U.N. The ensuing debate over sovereignty, human rights, and war at times seemed to overlook the progress of the prior five decades.

The chapters in this book were selected to probe the gnarly issues that seemingly transcend the traditional frontiers of international borders, law, politics, ethnicities, religions, and cultures. They involve the interplay of foreign policy and domestic politics, including the tension within recent U.S. administrations between moderate multilateralists and conservative unilateralists. The complexity of these issues is well reflected in the range of opinions included within this volume and echoes the more general public policy debate within the U.S. and internationally.

This concluding chapter aims not to break new ground, but rather to raise questions that, we hope, can inform national and international public policy debates in the "post-September 11 era"—the current inadequate label that substitutes for the term "post-post-Cold War era." As our introduction to this collection, and the first half of the book, deal extensively with the repercussions of Washington's current policies for the enjoyment of human rights domestically and internationally, we will not retrace those arguments here. Nonetheless, it is worth reiterating how criticisms of the Bush administration for jeopardizing fundamental rights in the pursuit of the war on terrorism have become commonplace. As the Lawyers Committee for Human Rights, in paraphrasing Senator John McCain, cautioned: "secrecy can breed increased distrust of governmental institutions."[7]

This chapter thus mainly grapples with the implications of unilateralism for international peace and security, as well as the legitimacy of U.S. leadership throughout the world. While the impact of the wars on terrorism and Iraq on human rights has been largely negative in the views of contributors, the impact on multilateral cooperation has been far more ambiguous. The U.S., despite its intentions and raw power, seems impelled to restore and utilize multilateral instruments in order to achieve its goals in Iraq and elsewhere.

A key question at the heart of this collection is how best to defend a state's sovereignty and the rights of its citizens in the face of terrorism in the context of a heavily interdependent and globalized world. The U.N. Charter's recognition of the need to move away from an absolutist interpretation of state sovereignty toward greater multilateral cooperation in order to better ensure international peace and security was the product of its drafters' experience of the realities of two world wars, economic depression, and genocide. These hard-bitten individuals were inclined more toward realpolitik than toward idealism in international relations.[8] The question arises, then, to what degree does their reasoned judgment about the value of multilateralism via international law and organizations continue to provide the most effective response to current terrorist threats?[9] Is contemporary terrorism so fundamentally different from the violence of the past, including the state terrorism visited upon the world by fascism and despotism, that the mechanisms developed since the early 1940s should be materially revamped or even abandoned? There is virtually no support among the analysts in this volume for ending the multilateral bonds and institutions that serve so many vital functions, and ultimately U.S. interests.

An additional concern is whether unilateral pre-emptive responses are more effective in the long term and less socially, politically, and even fiscally costly than multilateral ones.[10] In short, what are the underlying prerequisites for effective policies to respond to the present challenges to national and international security? And, as ever, how do we best protect the fundamental fabric of civil liberties within a new system of commitments to security, when fear typically trumps other concerns?

The current Bush administration's response to terror, as detailed in its September 2002 "National Security Strategy of the United States of America,"[11] has been characterized by Yale University historian John Lewis Gaddis as proactive in its promotion of both democracy and market economics. Furthermore, he believes, it also reflects a concern for how the U.S. will respond given that there is no apparent necessary contradiction between the exercise of great power and respect for universal principles. With respect to Iraq, he suggests that behind U.S. security policy lies "an incontestable moral claim: that in some situations preemption is preferable to doing nothing. Who would not have preempted Hitler or Milošević or Mohammed Atta, if given the chance?" For such a policy to work, the U.S. must not stand "defiantly alone."[12] A prerequisite for the success of such policy is consistency in pursuing support from other countries on critical matters, most notably in crises. How multilateral pre-emption might work through such instruments as the Security Council remains, of course, unclear.

The core of Gaddis's observation is echoed by former Secretary of State Madeleine K. Albright. She holds that President George W. Bush's national security strategy for dealing with the sponsors of the September 2001 and subsequent attacks would be more effective if there were an emphasis on the belief that terrorism is always wrong:

> The lesson for us now is that the longer the illusion of evil as somehow justified lasts—whether buttressed by propaganda, ignorance, convenience, or fear—the harder it is to dispel. That is why we must take nothing for granted. We must be relentless in shaping a global consensus that terrorism is fully, fundamentally, and always wrong. No exceptions, no excuses.[13]

As a pragmatic practitioner of statecraft, Albright recommends building consensus around basic indisputable principles from which agreed actions would flow. A new doctrine of multilateral pre-emption against terrorism would be established, underpinned by widespread support that would make for easier and less costly implementation. That successful national security policy requires multilateral support to ensure its success is a view powerfully presented in virtually every contribution to this volume.

There is, of course, nothing neat and readily formulaic about any transition to more effective international forms to combat terrorism. Mary Robinson, former United Nations Commissioner for Human Rights, for example, recently acknowledged that "it is both in the national interest of the United States and in our collective interest to defend, strengthen, and yes, reform, the multilateral system in which we have invested so much so that it can meet the challenges of the twenty-first century."[14] U.N. Secretary-General Kofi Annan opened the September 2003 General Assembly with his support for the view that "only 'radical' revisions in the institution are likely to preserve it."[15]

The possibility of reform of the current system for loosely enforced security principles and human rights is among the underlying motivations behind this collection. Is it possible, at this early stage in the fight against terrorism, to construct new policies for a world more frightened than hopeful? What are the most effective links between international peace and security and human rights within a reorganized United Nations? Indeed, is a reformed U.N. even a remote possibility? It certainly will be a difficult sell in the United States.

The case for and complexity of multilateralism is reinforced when one considers the transnational nature of terrorist networks and the possibility that they may gain access to nuclear weapons. Terrorist networks, comprising both non-state and state actors with strong financial and criminal connections, can be found around the globe in countries ranging from the highly industrialized to the least developed.[16] Indeed, many aspects of controlling terrorism—from intelligence gathering to halting money laundering—require enhancing multi-lateral cooperation, not reducing it. A case could be made for increasing efforts to agree upon U.N. conventions and treaties that bind signatories to common actions in pursuit of shared objectives, especially with respect to monitoring and control of the production of weapons of mass destruction (WMD).

However, given that the United States is the world's only remaining super-power, a question arises as to the degree to which, and for what tactical objectives, multilateralism is politically realistic. It is a truism that "great powers do not make great multilateralists."[17] Indeed, some key voices within the Bush administration appear to believe that unilateral leadership is not only viable in today's multilateral world, but also widely acceptable to many other countries. Such a position was clearly laid out by the President in his June 1, 2002 speech at West Point in which he suggested that other powers willingly accept U.S. leadership given its benign nature rooted in shared values and universal princi-ples. The U.S.'s political–military capacity—spending in 2003 more on its armed forces than all other countries combined—makes the United States the leader of the community of "willing" states. Moreover, the U.S. formal commit-ment to democracy and human rights is reason enough, according to Bush, for countries to accept actions that appear to violate the prohibition in inter-national law against the utilization of military intervention to achieve regime change.[18] It is difficult at this early stage in the evolution of this new doctrine to identify its costs as well as its benefits. Political polling data in late summer and early fall 2003 suggest, however, one possible cost of the Bush administration's strategy: its popularity both domestically and internationally.

Whatever one's judgment about the plausibility or desirability of U.S leader-ship at the dawn of the twenty-first century, clearly the administration's thinking and actions have generated concern among both U.S. friends and foes, which reached a new apex in March 2003 when Washington and London went to war against Iraq without the consent of the Security Council but after beginning negotiations to seek formal approval. This situation exacerbated tensions that went far beyond the long-standing desire on the part of many countries, includ-ing U.S. allies, to "reform" the Security Council in order to address the fundamental power imbalance between those states with veto power and those without.[19] Indeed, as several of the contributions in this volume suggest, there is increasingly widespread international concern that U.S. security doctrine is undercutting the widely accepted legal principles according to which inter-national organizations, most notably the U.N., function.[20]

The question thus arises: when does superpower status outstrip the willingness of other countries to accept actions that can undercut basic principles of international behavior regarded as essential for long-term international peace and stability? Indeed, as U.N. Under-Secretary-General for Communications and Public Information Shashi Tharoor told some of our authors and recently reminded readers of *Foreign Affairs*:

> The U.N. was meant to help create a world in which its member states would overcome their vulnerabilities by embedding themselves in international institutions, where the use of force would be subjected to the constraints of international law. Power politics would not disappear from the face of the earth but would be practiced with due regard for universally upheld rules and norms. Such a system also offered the United States—then, as now, the world's unchallenged superpower—the assurance that other countries would not feel the need to develop coalitions to balance its power. Instead, the U.N. provided a framework for them to work in partnership with the United States.[21]

Evidence of erosion of international acceptance of U.S. leadership was apparent in Washington's failure to secure a follow-up resolution to Security Council Resolution 1441 prior to the onset of the war in Iraq. In May 2003 Security Council Resolution 1483 begrudgingly acknowledged the Iraqi Coalition Provisional Authority, but it was inadequate to secure widespread international military and financial support for the ongoing occupation of the country. It is too early to determine the impact of various options on the Security Council's negotiating table for next steps in Iraq. However, it would appear possible that other countries may increasingly opt to operate as blocs in dealing with major powers including the United States rather than through international organizations such as the United Nations. The strong opposition to U.S. and European trade proposals at the World Trade Organization's September 2003 meeting in Cancún illustrates the potential for new coalitions of states to emerge within or outside the U.N. framework that will recalibrate options for comprehensive multilateralism on any issue.

The main reason for the creation of the U.N., "to save succeeding generations from the scourge of war" according to the opening sentence in the Preamble to the Charter, involved institutionalizing criteria to authorize international action, in order to separate legitimate from illegal use of force. Over time, an international consensus has emerged that the criteria for legitimate intervention include that the action be multilateral (this thereby reduces the likelihood that action be taken that benefits a single country or small group of countries), that it be agreed upon by a relevant international organization (usually the Security Council), that the intervention itself cause less harm than allowing the existing situation to continue, that it be in response to a long-term threat to international peace and security or to human rights, that it be limited in time and scope, and that it not be intended to effect regime change.[22]

The case of Iraq raises the question of whether some of these international norms are more legitimate than others, and whether some actors are more important than others. Can international law long sustain double standards in which the United States imposes its judgments? With respect to Iraq the shifting, and increasingly contested, justifications offered for military intervention by the Bush administration have caused the issue of legitimacy to permeate domestic as well as international political, diplomatic, and scholarly debate. While no definitive answer is at hand, the presumed moral legitimacy of armed, unilateral pre-emption appears to have begun a healthy debate over the legitimacy of such action by the U.S. and the U.K.

We are all familiar with the reasons adduced for the war in Iraq, especially in view of the public debate over the presence or absence of WMD in Iraq and whether violation of U.N. resolutions justified military intervention. As emphasis on this issue receded when the proverbial "smoking gun" was not found, the focus changed to democracy promotion and defense of the rights of the Iraqi people. Skepticism concerning U.S. intentions resulted. Many observers saw this as a convenient but unpersuasive argument because it was made *ex post facto*, seemingly as an afterthought.

Experience suggests, moreover, that democracy does not necessarily follow military intervention even when previously established democracies are restored. Indeed, democracy promotion under the best of circumstances has been repeatedly shown in recent years to be arduous and extremely costly even in countries where democracy formerly reigned (e.g. Uruguay and Argentina). Given the history of Iraq, the task is particularly difficult although, according to European Union Commissioner for External Relations Chris Patten, not impossible. His prescription is "free trade, generous aid, a willingness to link that aid to good behavior, and a little consistency."[23] Furthermore, short-term objectives, he warns sensibly, should not overwhelm human rights promotion.

Currently it appears that the task on the ground will require more resources, expertise, and time than the U.S. is able and seemingly willing to commit. As we write this in October 2003, the unsettled situation in Iraq has already revealed thorny problems, including the resistance of sectors of the population to U.S. military occupation and even to Western concepts of democracy. It is possible that democracy promotion mechanisms, such as elections, could bring to power antidemocratic elements with agendas that would severely disadvantage sectors of the population including ethnic and religious minorities, as well as women. In short, if there is a greater degree of political participation in Iraq, can there be guarantees that democracy will result in respect for the human rights of all? Does U.S. promotion of democracy in states such as Iraq ensure state commitment to rights, and, if not, what is the remedy once such an electorally legitimate government has been "grown"? Who decides what democracy and rights really mean in Iraq?

The presumption that a stronger civil society necessarily results in greater democracy has been challenged by studies of Weimar Germany and more recently in countries as varied as Nigeria and Argentina.[24] In a country such as

Iraq without a strong history of democratic political participation, entrenched rule of law, regular alteration of governments freely chosen, and widespread recognition of the full spectrum of human rights, the prospect that a stable democratic regime will emerge out of military intervention is doubtful. If the U.S. is willing to devote extraordinary sums of money, time, and expertise to the enterprise—all of which are in short supply—would that ensure the desired outcome?

Growing budgetary constraints and fiscal worries in the U.S. are a necessary part of the run-up to the November 2004 elections that make it improbable that the financial resources will be readily available. Furthermore, there is increasing popular, as well as state and local, pressure on Congress to appropriate more monies for domestic security, which experts agree is woefully underfunded.[25] To increase significantly the budgetary allotments for Iraqi physical and civil society reconstruction which is a prerequisite for greater enjoyment of socioeconomic rights in that country appears beyond U.S. will or capacity, much less so the long-term programs necessary for democracy promotion. It is nonetheless uncertain whether the escalating federal deficit will serve as a brake on any major increases. Finally, the recent U.S. census has confirmed that the number of poor people in thiss country rose by 1.3 million in 2002.[26] This may augment pressures for more appropriations for domestic programs, particularly in an election year.

Other factors complicating any simple world view include increasing distrust both domestically and internationally of U.S. intelligence services given the inadequacy of Iraqi threat assessments adduced as justification for the war. The legitimacy of coercive disarmament, via military means, is also being widely questioned, particularly whether it tends to inflame rather than squelch potentially explosive situations. In addition, U.S. disregard for the existing arms control regime, which monitors and inhibits the spread of WMD, has essentially weakened proven defenses against the proliferation and misuse of WMD. While the record of U.N. weapons inspections and the International Atomic Energy Agency are not perfect, history suggests that they have made a positive contribution to arms control. Indeed, the growing and potential international support for building U.N. capacity for arms inspections is another ironic victim of the war in Iraq.[27]

Beyond this, some commentators have concluded that President Bush has lowered the threshold for the use of nuclear weapons. Former Secretary of State Albright, for one, has argued that the President erred by emphasizing, in his State of the Union address and subsequent statements, not the value of building an antiterror coalition, but rather his unilateral intention to maintain U.S. "military strength beyond challenge, thereby making the destabilizing arms races of other eras pointless." He then asked Congress for the authority to explore new uses for nuclear weapons, creating the perception overseas that he was lowering the threshold for nuclear strikes—despite the United States' vast conventional military superiority and the risks posed to U.S. security by the proliferation of WMD.[28]

This emphasis has led to considerable concern among some experts that such a policy will encourage the development and acquisition of such weapons by other countries. This is particularly worrisome if, as Harvard Professor Michael Ignatieff asserts, "The administration, purposely or not, routinely conflates terrorism and the nuclear threat from rogue nations."[29] Since the United States has already specifically identified some states with nuclear capability such as North Korea as "rogues," and hence enemies in its war on terrorism, the question arises as to whether or not this might actually further stimulate their pursuit of WMD. The case of North Korea is particularly illustrative of the problems inherent in Washington's conflation in that the former's interest in developing its nuclear capabilities appears to be more of an attempt to assert national sovereignty in the face of eroding domestic support and tense relations with its neighbors than any strategy based on terrorism. This is precisely the type of potentially threatening situation for which the United Nations and other international organizations were created. The irony of the current situation is becoming apparent to many observers. Georgetown University's John Ikenberry, for instance, has argued that: "The worst unilateral impulses coming out of the Bush administration are so harshly criticized around the world because so many countries have accepted the multilateral vision of international order that the United States has articulated over most of the twentieth century."[30]

Given the real and potential threats to the U.S., as well as international security, emanating from the possessors of nuclear weapons in the Middle East and Asia, a strong international monitoring system would seem to be in the U.S.'s national interest, however broadly or narrowly defined. On this issue, it would appear natural that Washington assume a leadership role that incorporates other powers as well as the full spectrum of interested parties. The threat of war utilizing WMD is perhaps as strong today as it was when the United Nations and its monitoring system were first devised.

What if the United States does not assume a leadership role in this realm that is capable of mobilizing broad-based support? How effective will the tried and true mechanisms for avoiding such catastrophes be under such conditions? Indeed, pessimism could be even more justifiable if as former U.N. High Commissioner for Human Rights Mary Robinson reminds us in the Foreword to this book, the historical standard-bearer on this and other issues relevant to international peace and security and human rights fails to hold the standard high.

Clearly the threats facing the world today require strategies that are multilateral in both their ends and their means.[31] That, as the conventional idiom would state, is the bottom line of this book. While there are no immediate and fully satisfying answers about how to re-establish traditional U.S. leadership in both human rights and multilateral engagements, the process of critical analysis as exemplified in this volume is a step in the right direction.

Notes

1 On the origins and evolution of the concepts of the state and sovereignty see Bernard Guernée, *States and Rulers in Later Medieval Europe*, trans. Juliet Vale (New York: Blackwell, 1985); Andrew Vincent, *Theories of the State* (London: Blackwell, 1987); Julian H. Franklin, *John Locke and the Theory of Sovereignty* (Cambridge: Cambridge University Press, 1978); W. Ross Johnston, *Sovereignty and Protection: A Study of British Jurisdictional Imperialism in the Late Nineteenth Century* (Durham, N.C.: Duke University Press, 1973).

2 See, for example, Thomas Risse, Stephen C. Ropp, and Kathryn Sikkink, eds., *The Power of Human Rights: International Norms and Domestic Change* (Cambridge: Cambridge University Press, 1999); and Jack Donnelly, *Universal Human Rights in Theory and Practice*, 2nd edition (Ithaca, N.Y.: Cornell University Press, 2003).

3 Stephen Krasner, *Sovereignty: Organized Hypocrisy* (Princeton: Princeton University Press, 1999).

4 International Commission on Intervention and State Sovereignty, *The Responsibility to Protect* (Ottawa: ICISS, 2001). For the background research, see Thomas G. Weiss and Don Hubert, *The Responsibility to Protect: Research, Bibliography, and Background* (Ottawa: ICISS, 2001).

5 See "Address Before a Joint Session of the Congress on the Persian Gulf Crisis and the Federal Budget Deficit," September 11, 1990, http://bushlibrary.tamu.edu/papers/1990/90091101.html.

6 The implications for international law and organization are explored in Michael Byers and Georg Nolte, eds., *United States Hegemony and the Foundations of International Law* (Cambridge: Cambridge University Press, 2003); and Rosemary Foot, S. Neil MacFarlane, and Michael Mastanduno, eds., *U.S. Hegemony and International Organizations* (Oxford: Oxford University Press, 2003). For contemporary political snapshots, see Niall Ferguson, "Hegemony or Empire?" *Foreign Affairs*, 82 no. 5 (September–October 2003), pp. 154–61; and Joseph S. Nye Jr., "The Velvet Hegemon," *Foreign Policy*, no. 136 (May–June 2003), pp. 74–5.

7 Lawyers Committee for Human Rights, *Assessing the New Normal: Liberty and Security for the Post-September 11 United States* (New York: Lawyers Committee for Human Rights, September 2003).

8 See Stephen C. Schlesinger, *Act of Creation: The Founding of the United Nations* (Boulder, CO: Westview, 2003).

9 For the international legal framework for responding to terrorism see Inter-American Commission on Human Rights, Organization of American States, *Report on Terrorism and Human Rights* (Washington, D.C.: Organization of American States, 2002), pp. 33–68.

10 For alternative scenarios, see Council on Foreign Relations, *A New National Security Strategy in an Age of Terrorists, Tyrants, and Weapons of Mass Destruction* (New York: Council on Foreign Relations, 2003).

11 "National Security Strategy of the United States of America, September 2002," http://usinfo.state.gov/topical/pol/terror/secstrat/htm.

12 John Lewis Gaddis, "A Grand Strategy," *Foreign Policy*, no. 133 (November–December 2002), pp. 54, 56.

13 Madeleine K. Albright, "Bridges, Bombs, or Bluster?", *Foreign Affairs* 82, no. 5 (September–October 2003), p. 11.

14 Mary Robinson, "Shaping Globalization: The Role of Human Rights," Fifth Annual Grotius lecture, American Society of International Law, April, Washington, D.C., 2003.

15 See "Adoption of Policy of Pre-emption Could Result in Proliferation of Unilateral Lawless Use of Force, Secretary-General Tells General Assembly," SG/SM 8891

GA/10157, September 23, 2003, http://www.un.org/News/Press/docs/2003/sgsm
8891.doc.htm.

16 See Mónica Serrano, "The political economy of terrorism," and Rama Mani, "The
root causes of terrorism and conflict prevention," in Jane Boulden and Thomas
G. Weiss, eds., *Terrorism and the U.N.: Before and After September 11* (Bloomington, IN:
Indiana University Press, 2004), Chapters 9 and 10.

17 Steven Holloway, "U.S. Unilateralism at the U.N.: Why Great Powers Do Not
Make Great Multilateralists," *Global Governance* 6, no. 3 (July–September 2000),
pp. 361–81.

18 Gaddis, "A Grand Strategy," pp. 52–4.

19 See Thomas G. Weiss, "The Illusion of U.N. Security Council Reform," *Washington
Quarterly* 26, no. 4 (Autumn 2003), pp. 147–61.

20 James P. Rubin, "Stumbling into War," *Foreign Affairs* 82, no. 5 (September–October
2003), pp. 48–9.

21 Shashi Tharoor, "Why America Still Needs the United Nations," *Foreign Affairs* 82,
no. 5 (September–October 2003), p. 79.

22 Margaret E. Crahan, "A conceptual, legal, and political framework for human
rights," in United States Southern Command, *The Role of the Armed Forces in the Protection of Human Rights* (Miami, FL: United States Southern Command, 1996).

23 Chris Patten, "Democracy Doesn't Flow from the Barrel of a Gun," *Foreign Policy*,
no. 138 (September–October 2003), p. 43.

24 Sheri Berman, "Civil Society and the Collapse of the Weimar Republic," *World Poli-
tics* 49, no. 3 (April 1997), pp. 401–29; Naomi Chazan, "Engaging the state:
associational life in sub-Saharan Africa," in Joel S. Migdal, Atul Kohli, and Vivi-
enne Shue, eds., *State Power and Social Forces: Domination and Transformation in the Third
World* (New York: Cambridge University Press, 1994), pp. 255–89; Stephen
N. Ndegwa, *The Two Faces of Civil Society: NGOs and Politics in Africa* (West Hartford,
CT: Kumarian Press, 1996); Ariel Armony, *The Dubious Link: Civic Engagement and
Democratization* (Stanford: Stanford University Press, 2004).

25 Council on Foreign Relations, *Emergency Responders: Drastically Underfunded, Dangerously
Unprepared* (New York: Council on Foreign Relations, 2003).

26 "Census Shows Ranks of Poor Rose in 2002 by 1.3 Million," *New York Times*, September 3, 2003.

27 For an overview, see Jean E. Krasno and James S. Sutterlin, *The United Nations and
Iraq: Defanging the Viper* (Westport, CT: Praeger, 2003).

28 Albright, "Bridges, Bombs, or Bluster?," p. 4.

29 Michael Ignatieff, "Why Are We in Iraq (and Liberia? and Afghanistan?)," *New York
Times Magazine*, September 7, 2003, p. 42.

30 G. John Ikenberry, "Is American Multilateralism in Decline?" *Perspectives on Politics* 1,
no. 3 (September 2003), p. 545.

31 See Thomas G. Weiss, David P. Forsythe, and Roger A. Coate, *The United Nations and
Changing World Politics*, 4th edition (Boulder, CO: Westview, 2004).

Index

Routledge essential reading

The Dictionary of Terrorism
2nd edition
Richard Thackrah
Freelance writer on Security Issues, UK
hbk: 0–415–29820–2
pbk: 0–415–29821–0

Global Terrorism
James and Brenda Lutz
Indiana University, USA
hbk: 0–415–70050–7
pbk: 0–415–70051–5

The Terrorism Reader
David Whittaker
Formerly of University of Teesside, UK
hbk: 0–415–30101–7
pbk: 0–415–30102–5

Global Responses to Terrorism
9/11, Afghanistan and Beyond
Mary Buckley and Rick Fawn
MB: Royal Holloway, UK RF: University of St Andrews, UK
hbk: 0–415–31429–1
pbk: 0–415–31430–5

War without End
The Rise of Islamist Terrorism and Global Response
Dilip Hiro
Freelance journalist
hbk: 0–415–28801–0
pbk: 0–415–28802–9

Information and ordering details:
For price availability and ordering visit our website **www.tandf.co.uk**
Subject web address : www.politicsarena.com
Alternatively our books are available from all good bookshops